S0-ERP-947

LRC - Batavia HS
Batavia, IL 60510

AMERICAN HEROES

MAGILL'S CHOICE

AMERICAN HEROES

Volume 3

Jack Nicklaus — Babe Zaharias
Indexes
719-1078

from
The Editors of Salem Press

SALEM PRESS, INC.
Pasadena, California   Hackensack, New Jersey

Cover image: © Joseph Helfenberger/Dreamstime.com

Copyright © 2009, by SALEM PRESS, INC.
All rights in this book are reserved. No part of this work may be used or reproduced in any manner whatsoever or transmitted in any form or by any means, electronic or mechanical, including photocopy, recording, or any information storage and retrieval system, without written permission from the copyright owner except in the case of brief quotations embodied in critical articles and reviews. For information address the publisher, Salem Press, Inc., P.O. Box 50062, Pasadena, California 91115.

∞ The paper used in these volumes conforms to the American National Standard for Permanence of Paper for Printed Library Materials, Z39.48-1992 (R1997)

Some of the essays in this work originally appeared in the following Salem Press sets: *Great Lives from History: The 18th Century* (2006), *The 19th Century* (2006), and *The Twentieth Century* (2008), updated through 2008. New material has been added.

Library of Congress Cataloging-in-Publication Data
American heroes / from the editors of Salem Press.
    p. cm. — (Magill's choice)
    Includes bibliographical references and index.
    ISBN 978-1-58765-457-2 (set : alk. paper) — ISBN 978-1-58765-458-9 (v. 1 : alk. paper) — ISBN 978-1-58765-459-6 (v. 2 : alk. paper) — ISBN 978-1-58765-460-2 (v. 3 : alk. paper) 1. Heroes—United States—Biography. 2. Celebrities—United States—Biography. I. Salem Press.
    CT105.A47 2008
    920.02—dc22
                                                                            2008017124

First Printing

PRINTED IN CANADA

Contents

Complete List of Contents xlix
Key to Pronunciation lv

Jack Nicklaus 719
Chester W. Nimitz 723

Barack Obama 728
Sandra Day O'Connor 733
Osceola 739
Jesse Owens 742

Thomas Paine 747
Rosa Parks 752
George S. Patton 758
Alice Paul 763
Robert Edwin Peary 768
John J. Pershing 774
Colin Powell 779

A. Philip Randolph 785
Jeannette Rankin 793
Ronald Reagan 798
Red Cloud 805
Walter Reed 809
Paul Revere 814
Sally Ride 819
Paul Robeson 824
Jackie Robinson 832
John D. Rockefeller 838
Knute Rockne 844
Eleanor Roosevelt 847
Franklin D. Roosevelt 852
Theodore Roosevelt 859
John Ross 864
Bill Russell 868
Babe Ruth 874

Sacagawea 880
Jonas Salk 885
Pete Sampras 889

Margaret Sanger	893
Junípero Serra	898
Alan Shepard	902
William Tecumseh Sherman	907
Sitting Bull	913
Margaret Chase Smith	917
Elizabeth Cady Stanton	922
Adlai E. Stevenson	928
James Stewart	934
Anne Sullivan	938
Ida Tarbell	942
Zachary Taylor	947
Tecumseh	952
Norman Thomas	956
Jim Thorpe	963
Harry S. Truman	968
Sojourner Truth	974
Harriet Tubman	979
Nat Turner	984
Earl Warren	988
Booker T. Washington	994
George Washington	1000
John Wayne	1005
Ida B. Wells-Barnett	1009
Elie Wiesel	1013
Hazel Wightman	1019
Oprah Winfrey	1023
Tiger Woods	1029
Orville and Wilbur Wright	1034
Chuck Yeager	1040
Babe Didrikson Zaharias	1044
Subjects by Category	1051
Ethnicity Index	1057
Subject and Personages Index	1061

Complete List of Contents

Volume 1

Publisher's Note vii
List of Contributors ix
Complete List of Contents xvii
Key to Pronunciation xxiii

Hank Aaron 1
Ralph Abernathy 4
Abigail Adams 9
John Adams 14
Samuel Adams 19
Jane Addams 26
Muhammad Ali 31
Maya Angelou 38
Susan B. Anthony 43
Neil Armstrong 48

Robert D. Ballard 55
Benjamin Banneker 60
Clara Barton 64
Alexander Graham Bell 70
Mary McLeod Bethune 75
Black Hawk 80
Daniel Boone 84
Omar Nelson Bradley 89
Louis D. Brandeis 94
Joseph Brant 100
William J. Brennan 105
John Brown 109
Olympia Brown 115
Ralph Bunche 119
Richard Byrd 124

Frances Xavier Cabrini 129
Rachel Carson 133
Jimmy Carter 138
George Washington Carver 144

Mary Ann Shadd Cary 149
Carrie Chapman Catt 152
Wilt Chamberlain 158
César Chávez 161
Shirley Chisholm 164
Hillary Rodham Clinton 171
Ty Cobb 175
Bessie Coleman 179
Bill Cosby 183
Crazy Horse 187
David Crockett 194
Walter Cronkite 198

Clarence Darrow 201
Dorothy Day 207
Eugene V. Debs 212
Stephen Decatur 217
Jack Dempsey 221
Joe DiMaggio 227
Walt Disney 231
Dorothea Dix 238
Jimmy Doolittle 243
Helen Gahagan Douglas 247
William O. Douglas 251
Frederick Douglass 254
W. E. B. Du Bois 259

Amelia Earhart 265
Mary Baker Eddy 270
Marian Wright Edelman 277
Thomas Alva Edison 281
Albert Einstein 287
Dwight D. Eisenhower 292
Chris Evert 297

Louis Farrakhan 302
Betty Ford 305
Benjamin Franklin 309
John C. Frémont 315
Betty Friedan 322

William Lloyd Garrison 327
Marcus Garvey 333

Complete List of Contents

Bill Gates 337
Lou Gehrig. 341
Geronimo 346

Volume 2

Complete List of Contents xxxiii
Key to Pronunciation xxxix

Althea Gibson 351
John Glenn. 356
Emma Goldman 361
Al Gore 367
William Crawford Gorgas 371
Billy Graham 376
Nathanael Greene 380
Wayne Gretzky 387

Mary A. Hallaren 390
William F. Halsey 393
Fannie Lou Hamer 398
Alexander Hamilton 402
Learned Hand 408
Barbara Harris 413
Ernest Hemingway 417
Patrick Henry 422
Katharine Hepburn 426
Aileen Clarke Hernandez 432
Wild Bill Hickok 437
Oveta Culp Hobby 441
Bob Hope 446
Grace Murray Hopper 450
Sam Houston 455
Samuel Gridley Howe 460
Dolores Huerta 465
Charles Evans Hughes 471
Cordell Hull 478

Andrew Jackson 483
Jesse Jackson 488
Stonewall Jackson 494
Thomas Jefferson 498
Steve Jobs 503

Bobby Jones	507
John Paul Jones	513
Mother Jones	519
Barbara Jordan	524
Michael Jordan	529
Chief Joseph	533
Kamehameha I	538
Helen Keller	542
John F. Kennedy	546
Robert F. Kennedy	551
Billie Jean King	557
Martin Luther King, Jr.	562
Robert M. La Follette	569
Robert E. Lee	574
John L. Lewis	579
Meriwether Lewis and William Clark	584
Liliuokalani	589
Abraham Lincoln	594
Charles A. Lindbergh	600
Belva A. Lockwood	606
Henry Cabot Lodge	610
Huey Long	616
Joe Louis	621
Juliette Gordon Low	627
Shannon W. Lucid	632
Douglas MacArthur	635
Dolley Madison	642
James Madison	646
Malcolm X	650
Wilma Mankiller	655
Rocky Marciano	660
George C. Marshall	664
John Marshall	669
Thurgood Marshall	675
Golda Meir	680
Thomas Merton	686
John R. Mott	690
John Muir	696
Edward R. Murrow	700

Complete List of Contents

Ralph Nader 705
Carry Nation 709
Martina Navratilova 714

Volume 3

Complete List of Contents xlix
Key to Pronunciation lv

Jack Nicklaus 719
Chester W. Nimitz 723

Barack Obama 728
Sandra Day O'Connor 733
Osceola 739
Jesse Owens 742

Thomas Paine 747
Rosa Parks 752
George S. Patton 758
Alice Paul 763
Robert Edwin Peary 768
John J. Pershing 774
Colin Powell 779

A. Philip Randolph 785
Jeannette Rankin 793
Ronald Reagan 798
Red Cloud 805
Walter Reed 809
Paul Revere 814
Sally Ride 819
Paul Robeson 824
Jackie Robinson 832
John D. Rockefeller 838
Knute Rockne 844
Eleanor Roosevelt 847
Franklin D. Roosevelt 852
Theodore Roosevelt 859
John Ross 864
Bill Russell 868
Babe Ruth 874

Sacagawea	880
Jonas Salk	885
Pete Sampras	889
Margaret Sanger	893
Junípero Serra	898
Alan Shepard	902
William Tecumseh Sherman	907
Sitting Bull	913
Margaret Chase Smith	917
Elizabeth Cady Stanton	922
Adlai E. Stevenson	928
James Stewart	934
Anne Sullivan	938
Ida Tarbell	942
Zachary Taylor	947
Tecumseh	952
Norman Thomas	956
Jim Thorpe	963
Harry S. Truman	968
Sojourner Truth	974
Harriet Tubman	979
Nat Turner	984
Earl Warren	988
Booker T. Washington	994
George Washington	1000
John Wayne	1005
Ida B. Wells-Barnett	1009
Elie Wiesel	1013
Hazel Wightman	1019
Oprah Winfrey	1023
Tiger Woods	1029
Orville and Wilbur Wright	1034
Chuck Yeager	1040
Babe Didrikson Zaharias	1044
Subjects by Category	1051
Ethnicity Index	1057
Subject and Personages Index	1061

Key to Pronunciation

Vowel Sounds

Symbol	Spelled (Pronounced)
a	answer (AN-suhr), laugh (laf), sample (SAM-puhl), that (that)
ah	father (FAH-thur), hospital (HAHS-pih-tuhl)
aw	awful (AW-fuhl), caught (kawt)
ay	blaze (blayz), fade (fayd), waiter (WAYT-ur), weigh (way)
eh	bed (behd), head (hehd), said (sehd)
ee	believe (bee-LEEV), cedar (SEE-dur), leader (LEED-ur), liter (LEE-tur)
ew	boot (bewt), lose (lewz)
i	buy (bi), height (hit), lie (li), surprise (sur-PRIZ)
ih	bitter (BIH-tur), pill (pihl)
o	cotton (KO-tuhn), hot (hot)
oh	below (bee-LOH), coat (koht), note (noht), wholesome (HOHL-suhm)
oo	good (good), look (look)
ow	couch (kowch), how (how)
oy	boy (boy), coin (koyn)
uh	about (uh-BOWT), butter (BUH-tuhr), enough (ee-NUHF), other (UH-thur)

Consonant Sounds

Symbol	Spelled (Pronounced)
ch	beach (beech), chimp (chihmp)
g	beg (behg), disguise (dihs-GIZ), get (geht)
j	digit (DIH-juht), edge (ehj), jet (jeht)
k	cat (kat), kitten (KIH-tuhn), hex (hehks)
s	cellar (SEHL-ur), save (sayv), scent (sehnt)
sh	champagne (sham-PAYN), issue (IH-shew), shop (shop)
ur	birth (burth), disturb (dihs-TURB), earth (urth), letter (LEH-tur)
y	useful (YEWS-fuhl), young (yuhng)
z	business (BIHZ-nehs), zest (zehst)
zh	vision (VIH-zhuhn)

AMERICAN HEROES

JACK NICKLAUS

❝ *Focus on remedies, not faults.* **❞**

Golfer

One of the greatest golfers in the history of the sport, Nicklaus ended his remarkable career after seventy-three Professional Golf Association (PGA) victories, which included a record eighteen wins in major championships. He was named Golfer of the Century by the PGA in 1988 and received the Presidential Medal of Honor in 2005. Additionally, he designed hundreds of golf courses and clubs around the world.

Born: January 21, 1940; Columbus, Ohio
Also known as: Jack William Nicklaus (full name); Golden Bear
Area of achievement: Sports

EARLY LIFE

Jack Nicklaus (NIHK-luhs) and his younger sister, Marilyn, were the only children of Charlie and Nellie Nicklaus, growing up in the Columbus suburb of Upper Arlington. His father was a pharmacist who established a string of Columbus-area stores named Nicklaus Drugs.

Nicklaus would develop his father's passion for all sports, but it took a doctor's advice to his father, who had broken his ankle, to walk for exercise that landed Nicklaus and his father on a golf course. Golfing would become a regular event for the two. At the age of nine, Nicklaus began playing locally at Scioto Country Club, and he was encouraged by Scioto Club professional Jack Grout to join the club's junior program. Under the tutelage of Grout, who Nicklaus credits with teaching him how to play golf, Nicklaus won the Scioto Club juvenile trophy at the ages of ten and eleven. He went on to win a series of state junior championships in his early teens and was considered the best junior golfer in Ohio in the 1950's.

Even though Nicklaus excelled at other sports in high school and had aspirations of one day playing with Ohio State University's football team, virtually all his free time was devoted to golf. From an early age, Nicklaus played golf with his father's friends, and in tournaments he defeated older boys regularly. After winning the Ohio Open at the age of sixteen, Nicklaus knew that golf had become his sport.

After graduating from Upper Arlington High School in 1957, Nicklaus enrolled at Ohio State to pursue a degree in pharmacy. During his freshman year he met Barbara Bash. They were married on July 23, 1960. His golf success led him to decide to leave Ohio State before graduating.

LIFE'S WORK

Nicklaus's success as a golfer spanned six decades. At Ohio State, he helped the Buckeyes win the Big Ten golf championship in 1961 as the individual medalist. That same year, he was the individual medalist at the National Collegiate Athletic Association (NCAA) championships. Even more important to his career was winning the U.S. Amateur championship in 1959 and 1961; he was a member of the U.S. Walker Cup

Jack Nicklaus. (Ralph W. Miller Golf Library)

team that played at Muirfield in Scotland in 1959, and he led the United States to victory in 1960 at the World Amateur championship.

Nicklaus's decision to turn professional was not an easy one, in part because Nicklaus's hero, Bobby Jones, remained an amateur golfer his entire career and because Nicklaus's father had always envisioned his son as Jones's heir apparent. Contributing to Nicklaus's decision to turn pro was the birth of the Nicklaus's first child, Jack William Nicklaus II, on September 23, 1961, and the need to practice and play full-time rather than part-time while selling insurance. On November 8 he officially became a professional golfer. To be the best golfer possible and to support his family, Nicklaus needed to become a member of the PGA tour.

Before Nicklaus made his professional debut on the tour in 1962, he signed a management agreement with Mark McCormack, who was already the agent for Arnold Palmer and Gary Player. McCormack and his agency, International Management Group (IMG), were instrumental in Nicklaus's achievements off the golf course. Endorsements and speaking engagements became the norm for Nicklaus as a result of his association with IMG in the 1960's.

While his pro career began uneventfully, it was Nicklaus's eleventh tournament, the 1962 U.S. Open at Oakmont Country Club in western Pennsylvania that changed everything for him. Paired with Palmer, Nicklaus, who was ten years younger, defeated the King of Golf forty miles from Palmer's hometown of Latrobe. Later, nicknamed Golden Bear for his build and prodigious drives off the tee, Nicklaus would win thirty-eight tournaments, including seven majors during his first eight years on the tour.

Always a colorful dresser on the links, Nicklaus enhanced his image and popularity by shedding extra pounds during the year following his father's death from cancer in 1970. His most memorable stretch of the 1970's was when he won the PGA championship in 1971 and the Masters and the U.S. Open in 1972; he lost the British Open in 1972 to Lee Trevino by one stroke. Nicklaus considered this loss the most devastating of his career. Of the thirty-seven tournaments he won in this decade, eight were majors.

Entering his third decade on the PGA tour, Nicklaus won the U.S. Open and the PGA championship again in 1980. His eighteenth and final victory in a major was the Masters in 1986. He was forty-six years old, the oldest golfer to win a major. Nicklaus continued to play on the PGA tour after joining the PGA senior tour in 1990. His final appearance in a major was the British Open at the Old Course at St. Andrews, Scotland, in 2005. Complementing his individual accomplishments was his participation as a member of the U.S. Ryder Cup teams that competed against golfers from Europe. He served as team captain in 1987.

A significant challenge for Nicklaus beyond the tour was fulfilling his dream of building a golf course in his home state. Increasingly interested in designing golf courses and inspired by Augusta National, the home of the Masters tournament in Georgia, Nicklaus spent time and money on developing the Country Club of Muirfield Village and Muirfield Village Golf Club, home to the annual Memorial Tournament in Dublin, Ohio, a suburb of Columbus where the Nicklaus family maintains a home. The Muirfield courses opened in 1974, and the first Memorial Tournament was held there in 1976. He also decided to break from McCormack and IMG and established his own business, Golden Bear, near his Florida home in Palm Beach.

Equally important for Nicklaus was the continuous support of his wife, Barbara, and their five children. Beginning with the 1982 U.S. Open, sons Jackie and Gary often caddied for their famous father, and the Nicklaus family received the Golf Family of the Year Award from the National Golf Foundation in 1985. In 1999 he was named Male Sportsman of the Century by *Sports Illustrated* magazine.

SIGNIFICANCE

Although he earned a total of $5.7 million as a player, less than the amount of the average single-tournament purse for most PGA events today, Nicklaus took professional golf to a new level. A worldwide ambassador of the game, he epitomized the sportsmanship and etiquette of golf's rich history. His style of play and golf swing have been emulated and written about extensively, and his relationship with other players, fans, and the media remained positive throughout his career. As a young player in the 1960's, Nicklaus was befriended by the great golfer Jones; like Jones, Nicklaus, too, befriended another young golfing great, Tiger Woods.

Nicklaus's interest in golf-course architecture and his ability to design quality courses made him a major part of the development of more than 250 courses around the world. The success of his company, now called Golden Bear International, enabled

Nicklaus to continue marketing his own line of equipment and apparel and to offer golf academies for budding golfers from around the country. Nicklaus's legacy continues into the twenty-first century.

—*Kevin Eyster*

FURTHER READING

Andrisani, John. *The Nicklaus Way: An Analysis of the Unique Techniques and Strategies of Golf's Leading Major Championship Winner.* New York: HarperCollins, 2003. Details Nicklaus's golf game and makes its intricacies accessible for the average golfer. Includes illustrations.

Jacobs, Timothy, ed. *Golf Courses of Jack Nicklaus.* New York: Gallery Books, 1989. Highlights twenty-nine courses designed by Nicklaus. Includes photographs and illustrations of each course.

Nicklaus, Jack. *Jack Nicklaus: My Story.* New York: Simon & Schuster, 1997. Nicklaus's second of two autobiographies, this book includes twenty chapters and is dedicated to his wife and children. Includes several photographs and an appendix of Nicklaus's tournament record.

Nicklaus, Jack, with Ken Bowden. *Jack Nicklaus: My Most Memorable Shots in the Majors.* Trumbull, Conn.: Golf Digest, 1988. Examines fifty-four of Nicklaus's shots between the years 1959 and 1986. Includes detailed illustrations of each hole by Jim McQueen. Foreword by Barbara Nicklaus.

Nicklaus, Jack, with David Shedloski. *Jack Nicklaus: Memories and Mementos from Golf's Golden Bear.* New York: Stewart, Tabori, and Chang, 2007. Nicklaus reflects on the most important events in his life. Photographs throughout.

Nicklaus, Jack, with Herbert Warren Wind. *The Greatest Game of All: My Life in Golf.* New York: Simon & Schuster, 1969. Nicklaus's first of two autobiographies includes five sections and is dedicated to his father and to his wife, Barbara. Includes many photographs. Foreword by Robert Tyre Jones, Jr.

Shaw, Mark. *Jack Nicklaus: Golf's Greatest Champion.* New York: Sports Publishing, 2002. Shaw details Nicklaus's accomplishments in 1972, which the writer considers the golfing great's best year on the tour. The epilogue compares Nicklaus's game with such contemporaries as Palmer, Player, and Tom Watson, as well as with Woods.

Sounes, Howard. *The Wicked Game: Arnold Palmer, Jack Nicklaus, Tiger Woods, and the Story of Modern Golf.* New York: HarperCollins, 2004. Based on more than 150 personal interviews and extensive research, Sounes explores the lives of Palmer, Nicklaus, and Woods, with emphasis on their contributions to the game. Includes several photographs of each golfer.

CHESTER W. NIMITZ

❝ *God grant me the courage not to give up what I think is right even though I think it is hopeless.* ❞

Military leader

Nimitz commanded American forces in the Pacific during World War II and played a crucial role in winning the important and difficult Battle of Midway. After the war, he became chief of Naval Operations.

Born: February 24, 1885; Fredericksburg, Texas
Died: February 20, 1966; Yerba Buena Island, San Francisco, California
Also known as: Chester William Nimitz (full name)
Area of achievement: Military

EARLY LIFE

Chester William Nimitz (NIH-mihts) was the son of Chester B. Nimitz and Anna Henke Nimitz. Although his father had died before he was born and the family was never well-off financially, he enjoyed a happy childhood with his cherished and hardworking mother and his not-so-hardworking but happy-go-lucky stepfather (who was also his uncle), William Nimitz. Perhaps the most important male influence on the boy, however, was that of his grandfather, Charles Henry Nimitz, who filled his mind with tales of nautical adventure. Despite such talk of the sea, Nimitz's ambition as a teenager was to become a soldier, so impressed was he by officers from the Army post at Fort Sam Houston. There were no vacancies at West Point, however, so he attended the United States Naval Academy instead, and was graduated on January 30, 1905, seventh in a class of 114.

Blond and handsome, kindly and humorous, above all capable of laughing at himself when the need arose, young Nimitz was prime material for a happy marriage; yet nuptials did not occur until April 9, 1913, when he wed Catherine B. Freeman of Wollaston, Massachusetts. They had four children: Catherine, Chester, Anna, and Mary.

LIFE'S WORK

Nimitz's early interests were in engineering and submarines. During World War I, he served on an oiler and also with the submarines, ending the war as a lieutenant commander. In the postwar period, he had the usual kinds of assignments that rising officers enjoyed: attendance at the Naval War College, teaching in ROTC, service with battleships, and command of a cruiser. He never became an aviator, a fact that might have caused problems for a lesser man during World War II, when he was called on to command an aircraft carrier-oriented fleet. Nimitz became an admiral in 1938 and in 1939 took charge of the Bureau of Navigation, the office that controlled personnel assignments.

This latter post gave him access to President Franklin D. Roosevelt, who, along with almost everyone else, took a liking to the new admiral. In early 1941, Roosevelt offered Nimitz command of the Pacific Fleet, but he declined because of lack of seniority—a lucky move: Had he accepted the offer, he, instead of Admiral Husband E. Kimmel, might have had to take the blame for the disaster at Pearl Harbor later that same year.

After the invasion at Pearl Harbor, Kimmel was dismissed and Nimitz was named to replace him as Commander in Chief Pacific (CINCPAC), as of December 31, 1941. From his desk in Pearl Harbor, Nimitz would lead all the American forces, Army as well as Navy and Marines, in the North, Central, and South Pacific areas; he also was in direct command of all naval units in those areas by virtue of wearing a different hat. Thus, in a sense, he was his own boss, being both theater commander and theater naval chieftain. This arrangement worked well but did not eliminate all command problems in the war against Japan.

One of Nimitz's difficulties was with General Douglas MacArthur, commander of the Southwest Pacific Area (SWPA). MacArthur wanted his theater to be the scene of the principal thrust against Japan, even if that meant reducing Nimitz's activity to nothing. Probably MacArthur would have been happiest if Nimitz and his theater had been put under SWPA command. The Navy Department would never have allowed either the lesser or the greater of MacArthur's ambitions to come true, but Nimitz had to operate throughout the war with the knowledge that the Army in general, and MacArthur in particular, wanted a greater share of material and command.

Nimitz also had to contend with his own boss, Admiral Ernest J. King, chief of Naval Operations and commander in chief of all American warships around the world. King was a ferocious man, just as harsh as Nimitz was kindly, and he worried about CINCPAC's aggressiveness. King thought that Nimitz might not be willing to dismiss those who fell short of perfection; he also wondered at first about Nimitz's willingness to take enormous risks in fighting the Japanese. Perhaps the real problem was that King could not resist the temptation to become personally involved in running the Pacific war. Another thing that bothered King about Nimitz was the latter's reluctance to do battle against MacArthur. King was responsible for upholding the Navy's prerogatives in the face of demands from his equals in the highest councils of war—the British, the Army, and the Army Air Forces; therefore, he could not afford to be affable, or so he seems to have reckoned. Nimitz, on the other hand, outranked all the generals and admirals in his own theater and was not in a position to thwart MacArthur's plans directly; he, therefore, could approach the war in a more genial frame of mind. For all that, King and Nimitz made a good team, each compensating for the other's rare moments of bad judgment.

Since Nimitz was tied for the most part to his desk, the battles in his theater were conducted either by commanders at sea or on the invaded islands: Admirals Frank Jack Fletcher, William F. Halsey, and Raymond A. Spruance, and Marine generals A. Archer Vandegrift and Holland M. Smith, among others. Nevertheless, as commander in chief, Nimitz bore the ultimate responsibility for their campaigns, except insofar as King himself sometimes determined the overall strategy—and except for the times when Halsey's services were lent to MacArthur.

Undoubtedly, the most important battle in which Nimitz's role was most personal and crucial was that fought near the island of Midway in 1942. The Pacific Fleet was much inferior to that of Japan, and so it was vital for the Americans, if they were to hold

Midway, to know what the Japanese intended to do. Fortunately, Nimitz could tap the resources of a brilliant cryptologist, Lieutenant Commander Joseph J. Rochefort, Jr., who had recently broken the Japanese naval code and thereby was able to predict the enemy's plan. It was Nimitz himself, however, who had to decide whether to believe Rochefort's evidence, and it was also Nimitz who next had to convince a headstrong King that Rochefort was right. Even after that, there were plans to be made and risks to be taken. It was Nimitz who decided not to use the United States' elderly battleships in the coming fight because they would only get in the way; a nonaviator, he nevertheless put his faith in his aircraft carriers. It was Nimitz who decided on the deployment of those carriers, although Fletcher and Spruance were in command afloat. The result of all these plans and decisions, along with the skill and luck of those on the scene, was an overwhelming American victory, one of the great turning points of the war.

Nimitz was farther removed from the controls during the battles on and around Guadalcanal in August and November, 1942. These were King's pet projects and conducted on the scene by the South Pacific commanders, who reported to Nimitz. Though close victories, they served to confirm the verdict of Midway: From then on, it was not a question of whether the United States would win the war against Japan but of how soon and at what cost. If Nimitz took too long or spent too much American blood, the public might demand that MacArthur be given the lion's share of men, material, and tasks. Nimitz was responsible more than any other person for his forces moving

Chester W. Nimitz (left). (NARA)

Nimitz, Chester W.

ahead rapidly and, for the most part, with no more bloodshed than necessary. His campaigns in the Gilberts, the Marshalls, the Marianas, Iwo Jima (Iwo To), and Okinawa were all successful. During the reconquest of the Philippines, however, Nimitz was in general an onlooker: Halsey still reported to him but was operating according to MacArthur's plan. Thus, there was no unity of command during the Battle of Leyte Gulf (October 23-26, 1944); the only common commander of all American forces at Leyte was President Roosevelt himself. Nimitz did intervene once to correct an unfortunate move by Halsey.

World War II ended with Nimitz and MacArthur accepting Japan's surrender, both of them now wearing the five stars of the new American ranks, respectively fleet admiral and general of the Army; this was an honor shared by only five other officers as of V-J Day.

On December 15, 1945, Nimitz succeeded King as chief of Naval Operations. It was a time of demobilization, but the biggest issue facing the new chief was that of unification of the services. Although CINCPAC's joint command had worked well, and although command disunity had bedeviled the Leyte Gulf campaign, Nimitz nevertheless agreed with most Navy men in objecting to unification on the national level. Sailors feared that the new Air Force might try to take over the Navy's aerial component, while the Army, having lost its airplanes, might attempt to seize control of the Marine Corps as compensation. However, when Congress "unified" the services in 1947, the Navy Department retained its airplanes and the Marines. Nimitz deserves some of the credit for his department's victory: He had made himself welcome at the White House of President Harry S. Truman, a man who, unlike Roosevelt, had originally favored the Army.

Although five-star officers do not retire in the usual sense, Nimitz nevertheless went off active duty in December, 1947. In 1949, however, Truman offered to reappoint him as chief of Naval Operations in the wake of the so-called Admirals' Revolt against the Defense Department, an incident touched off by Navy-Air Force rivalry. What Truman wanted was a conciliator, but Nimitz declined the offer. Instead, he spent his retirement as regent of the University of California, as United Nations plebiscite administrator for Kashmir (1949-1950), and as roving ambassador for the United Nations (1950-1952). In the late 1950's, he helped E. B. Potter edit an important textbook of naval history, *Sea Power: A Naval History* (1960).

By 1965, Nimitz was suffering from osteoarthritis and pneumonia; the latter had bothered him off and on for many years despite his generally robust condition. Strokes and heart failure followed, and he died in San Francisco on February 20, 1966.

Significance

Despite King's occasional misgivings, Nimitz's career proves that nice guys do not necessarily finish last. He fully deserved his elevation to five-star rank for his all-important role in the Battle of Midway and his more distant but still vital part in subsequent American Pacific victories. His postwar services also justified the honor. Although he disliked controversy, and therefore did not subsequently write his memoirs or even allow a biography in his lifetime, he nevertheless was able to carry out the duties of a great commander without inordinate displays of ego or temper. Whether such a pleasant man could have held off the War Department and the British in Washington during World War II is another question, but perhaps the American Joint Chiefs of Staff and the Anglo-American Combined Chiefs of Staff would have benefited from his reasonable and amiable presence. He was too quiet a man to make good "copy" for the press, as was the case with some other famous World War II commanders, but he achieved as much greatness or more.

—*Karl G. Larew*

FURTHER READING

Buell, Thomas B. *Master of Sea Power: A Biography of Fleet Admiral Ernest J. King.* Boston: Little, Brown, 1980. This book does not rank with E. B. Potter's biography of Nimitz, but it is quite worthwhile and helps the reader to see Nimitz from the point of view of Washington and London.

Dull, Paul S. *The Imperial Japanese Navy, 1941-1945.* Annapolis, Md.: Naval Institute Press, 1978. This is a highly successful attempt to see the war in the Pacific from the Japanese navy's viewpoint.

Hoyt, Edwin P. *How They Won the War in the Pacific: Nimitz and His Admirals.* New York: Lyons Press, 2000. Examines how the top admirals worked together during World War II, concentrating on Nimitz. Describes Nimitz's strategy for winning the war in the Pacific and how his wisdom, strength, and ability to remain calm during times of great stress made him a great admiral.

James, Dorris Clayton. *The Years of MacArthur: Volume II, 1941-1945.* Boston: Houghton Mifflin, 1975. A gigantic, brilliant biography. James accomplishes the nearly impossible: He provides a balanced, fair treatment of one of America's most controversial leaders.

Morison, Samuel E. *The Two-Ocean War: A Short History of the United States Navy in the Second World War.* Boston: Little, Brown, 1963. Admiral Morison, himself a professional historian, oversaw the production of the Navy's multivolume official history of World War II; this is a one-volume distillation of that effort.

Potter, E. B. *Nimitz.* Annapolis, Md.: Naval Institute Press, 1976. This is a long but well-written, authoritative, and masterful biography by an eminent naval historian. It is by far the most important source for any sketch of Nimitz's life.

Potter, E. B., and Chester W. Nimitz, eds. *Sea Power: A Naval History.* Englewood Cliffs, N.J.: Prentice-Hall, 1960. A useful textbook covering all the history of naval warfare.

Prange, Gordon W., Donald M. Goldstein, and Katherine V. Dillon. *Miracle at Midway.* New York: McGraw-Hill, 1982. One of Prange's posthumous books, perhaps a bit flawed because it was put together after his death; nevertheless, it provides interesting and dramatically told insights concerning Nimitz's most famous battle.

Spector, Ronald H. *Eagle Against the Sun.* New York: Free Press, 1985. A well-balanced, well-written, and up-to-date account of the Pacific war by a highly respected, rising young historian.

Obama, Barack

BARACK OBAMA

> *" In the face of impossible odds, people who love their country can change it. "*

U.S. senator and presidential candidate

Obama, a community organizer, legal scholar, and politician in Illinois, rose to national prominence when he was asked to give the keynote address at the 2004 Democratic National Convention. He was elected to the U.S. Senate later that year, and in June, 2008, he became his party's presumptive nominee for the office of president of the United States.

Born: August 4, 1961; Honolulu, Hawaii
Also known as: Barack Hussein Obama (full name)
Area of achievement: Government and politics

EARLY LIFE

Barack Obama, the son of a white American woman and a black Kenyan man, was born in the multicultural and racially diverse state of Hawaii in 1961. For most of his childhood, he was raised in a middle-class American family. Between the ages of six and ten, however, he lived in Jakarta, Indonesia, with his mother, Ann Dunham, and his Indonesian stepfather, Lolo Soetoro. In Indonesia, he witnessed firsthand the extreme poverty of developing nations. He was also educated for most of his time in Indonesia at a Catholic school while living in a neighborhood populated by devout Muslims. He returned to Hawaii before entering fifth grade, to live with his maternal grandparents and attend the Punahou School, an elite college preparatory academy. Thus, by the time he reached adolescence, Obama had a far broader range of cultural experience than the average American teen.

While attending the Punahou School, Obama sometimes experienced his complex background and experience as a burden. Despite the diversity of Hawaii's populace, which includes Caucasians, Asians, and Pacific Islanders, the state is home to relatively few African Americans. In Obama's memoir, *Dreams from My Father* (1995), he describes being teased about his name and heritage on his first day in school. His feelings of isolation eventually led him to drink alcohol and use drugs, as he drifted onto a dangerous path. After graduating from high school, he attended first Occidental College in Los Angeles and then Columbia University in New York City. While at Columbia, Obama reapplied himself to his studies, developing intellectually and eschewing the partying lifestyle he had enjoyed in Los Angeles. He earned a bachelor's degree in political science and took a job with Business International Corporation.

After a year, Obama found that he was increasingly dissatisfied in the business world. He quit his professional job and began looking for work that would enable him to empower impoverished people to improve their lives. He answered an advertisement from a Chicago community organizing group seeking to recruit an organizer to work with African Americans on the city's South Side. The largely white group, desperate for an African American organizer who could relate to their target population, was happy to find Obama and hired him, providing him a salary of $13,000 per year.

Obama, Barack

Barack Obama. (AP/Wide World Photos)

Life's Work

Obama moved to Chicago in 1985 to begin his career in public service. That career got off to a slow start. The young community organizer had spent the previous three years living a solitary, secular, intellectual life in New York. To make a difference in Chicago's poorest neighborhoods, he first had to learn to temper his idealism with a certain amount of realist cynicism, and he had to learn to listen to people and understand the actual needs of a community before acting on its behalf. He also confronted the difficulty of relating to fundamentally religious communities as a nonreligious person. This difficulty led him to seek a church in which he could feel comfortable; he found Trinity Church of Christ, a church with a strong history of working for social justice to which he could relate. With the help of Trinity's pastor, the Reverend Jeremiah Wright, Obama began to see how faith could nurture the sort of community activism he sought to encourage. He found his own faith in the process.

Obama helped organize the residents of a housing project on Chicago's South Side, with modest success. He determined, however, that to be effective in fighting bureaucracy, he would need to gain a law degree. In 1988, he enrolled at Harvard Law School. Obama was elected the first African American president of the *Harvard Law Review*, a position he won by building a coalition of liberal and conservative law students, convincing the liberals that he would represent their point of view and the conservatives that he would treat them fairly and take seriously their concerns.

Obama, Barack

Upon completing his J.D., Obama returned to Chicago. There, in 1992, he led a massive voter-registration drive that resulted in more than 150,000 African Americans in Chicago registering to vote. For the first time in the city's history, African American voters outnumbered white voters. The drive helped Carol Moseley Braun become the United States' first female African American senator, and it announced Obama's arrival as an important player in electoral politics—one who used the methods and tactics of community organizing.

In 1993, Obama joined the law firm of Miner, Barnhill, and Galland and began representing community organizers, as well as working on voting rights and antidiscrimination cases. That same year, he became a lecturer in constitutional law at the University of Chicago Law School. He continued to work for the firm until 2003, and he remained on the faculty of the law school until 2004.

Obama's tenure teaching constitutional law is telling, and not only because of the importance of that branch of the law for civil and voting rights. At its base, constitutional law involves weighing and adjudicating legitimate conflicting interests. Its practitioners must thus be able to understand the validity of both sides in a dispute, to respect two opposing viewpoints but ultimately come down on one side or the other if a compromise proves infeasible. Obama's experience as a constitutional scholar thus augmented his exposure to and respect for widely varied points of view, providing him with a philosophical context from which to appreciate the diversity of interests making up the American political landscape.

Obama became an Illinois state senator in 1996, representing an economically diverse district that included inner-city slums and upper-middle-class dwellings. He worked across party lines to pass ethics reform, establish a state-funded program to screen patients for prostate cancer, investigate nursing home abuses, and reform the state's laws regarding capital punishment. One of his signature accomplishments was the passage of a law requiring the police to videotape interrogations of homicide suspects. The bill met with initial resistance from Chicago's police force, but Obama won over his opponents, convincing them that such monitoring was in the best interests of law enforcement. The measure ultimately passed with broad support.

Obama was reelected to the Illinois state senate in 1998, 2000, and 2002. In 2002, on the eve of the U.S. invasion of Iraq, Obama gave a speech opposing the coming war at a time when such opposition was considered extremely risky politically. His description of an open-ended and costly conflict with no clear mission and unforeseeable consequences would later seem quite prescient. In 2000, he attempted to jump to the U.S. Congress, but he was defeated in the Democratic primary by incumbent representative and former Black Panther Bobby Rush. In 2004, he ran for an even higher office, that of U.S. senator.

In the summer of 2004, Obama was selected to deliver the keynote address at the Democratic National Convention. This speech would serve as his introduction to the national stage. The theme of the speech was unity in diversity: Whereas pundits divided the nation into "red" conservative states and "blue" liberal states, Obama said, there were religiously devout people living in the blue states and defenders of civil liberties living in the red states. Each supposedly monolithic state was diverse, but the diversity of all the states contributed to the identity of the whole, to the United States of America.

Obama, Barack

The speech was an unqualified success, partly because it was so palpably moving to so many people and partly because the party's presidential candidate, John Kerry, was not himself as accomplished a speaker as Obama. It seemed immediately apparent that Obama—who had yet to be elected to the U.S. Senate—would one day run for president, although at the time it was assumed that he would not be ready for such a campaign until 2012 or 2016.

Obama returned home to Illinois after the July convention a political celebrity who was running unopposed in the senatorial race. His Republican opponent had withdrawn from the race a month earlier in the wake of scandals engendered by a messy divorce. The Republican Party scrambled to find someone to run against Obama, until in August the conservative African American politician and diplomat Alan Keyes of Maryland agreed to move to Illinois to enter the race. Predictably, Obama easily defeated Keyes, who had less than three months to acquaint himself with Illinois politics and to convince Illinois voters that he had their interests at heart.

As a freshman senator, Obama surrounded himself with a high-powered staff and sought advice from party elders. His most significant legislation in his first year was cosponsored with Republicans: Obama worked with Dick Lugar of Indiana to expand an existing program for eliminating stockpiled weapons of mass destruction: The Lugar-Obama initiative included conventional as well as nonconventional weapons. With Tom Coburn of Oklahoma, Obama cosponsored the Coburn-Obama Transparency Act, which created a Web site, USAspending.gov, that makes available to the public a searchable database of all recipients of awards and contracts from the federal government. At the beginning of 2007, with a newly elected Democratic majority in both the House and the Senate, Obama cosponsored with Democrat Russ Feingold of Wisconsin a major ethics reform law that increased the transparency of bundled campaign contributions and decreased Congress members' ability to accept gifts from lobbyists.

In February of 2007, Senator Obama announced his candidacy for the office of president of the United States. At the time, he was known largely for his 2004 keynote address, and most Americans knew little else about the candidate. His two major opponents for the nomination were more familiar: Hillary Rodham Clinton had been First Lady for eight years, and John Edwards had been his party's vice presidential candidate in 2004. Obama spent much of 2007 introducing himself to the electorate. He declared his intention to bring "a new kind of politics" to Washington, D.C., and he promised to take no campaign contributions from federally registered lobbyists or political action committees (PACs). In addition to courting wealthy individuals, Obama began to solicit small contributions through his Web site. He was able to raise unprecedented amounts of money from small donors in this fashion, and by April of 2008, more than 1.5 million individuals had given money to his campaign.

The Democratic primaries began in Iowa in January of 2008. Obama won the Iowa caucuses decisively, establishing himself as a serious candidate. Clinton won the New Hampshire primary, and she won the popular vote in the Nevada caucuses, although Obama won more delegates in the contest. Obama then won South Carolina's primary. By this time, it was clear that Obama and Clinton were the only two serious contenders for the Democratic nomination. After more than twenty states voted on February 5, both were still in the race. It became clear that neither candidate would be able to achieve an early victory, and the contest between them was to last until the final primary contest on June 3. At the end of the closely fought race, Senator Obama had earned enough combined pledged and unpledged delegates to clinch the nomination, and Senator Clinton acknowledged him as the party's nominee, effectively ending the primary contest.

SIGNIFICANCE

Barack Obama's campaign for president was a watershed event in American political history. As the first African American presidential nominee of a major political party, he established that an African American could plausibly seek the highest elective office in the country. Thus, win or lose, his campaign was in itself taken to be transformative of the American cultural and political landscape. For much of the primary campaign, he positioned himself as a candidate who transcended race. After a scandal arose involving his pastor, however, he was forced to address issues of race in America directly. The Reverend Jeremiah Wright had made statements that, especially when divorced from their context in brief media snippets, seemed to many to be anti-white. Obama responded with a speech on the persisting anger between African American and white communities that was hailed as among the nation's most important public statements on the issue. Speaking as a multiracial man, he emphasized the legitimacy of points of view on both sides of the racial divide, and he called for Americans to recognize the reality of racial anger and to confront it constructively, rather than simply condemning its expression.

Equally important, Obama demonstrated that it was possible to mount a serious campaign for the presidency based on community organizing and grassroots activism. Indeed, in many ways, he was an organizer masquerading as a politician, and his campaign was designed from the start as a vehicle to empower communities rather than simply as a tool to get him elected. Conventional wisdom held that field campaigns—that is, campaigns based on legwork in the field, including canvassing door-to-door and phone banking—could only succeed in small states. Large states would be won or lost by the television advertising and other media exposure that were necessary to reach their vast populations. Alongside such advertising, however, Obama launched field operations involving thousands of volunteers in almost every state, including states such as California that had never witnessed such campaigns before. Obama lost the primary elections in most of the largest states, but he managed to narrow Senator Clinton's margin of victory in all of them. He thus demonstrated that it was possible for fieldwork to be effective, as he was able to win enough delegates in each of the large states to stay competitive, while his grassroots campaigns in the smaller states resulted in lopsided victories, causing him to win more delegates overall than did Clinton. He thereby succeeded in returning a measure of power to grassroots communities, making them genuine players in national electoral politics.

In the general election, Obama's strategy was to continue to change the balance of power in electoral politics by registering as many new voters as possible, recalling his first important political campaign in 1992. By 2008, the political map of the United States was considered almost immutable. Most states would always give their electoral college votes to the same party, regardless of that party's candidate, so the presidential race was decided in a limited number of "battleground states." Obama's candidacy questioned this conventional wisdom, as several once-reliably Republican states were considered "in play." Thus, his campaign set out to "redraw the political map," fundamentally altering the nature of the presidential race. Obama also continued his drive to reform the electoral process while running for office. Under his leadership, the Democratic National Committee embraced the values of its candidate, announcing that it too would no longer accept contributions from federal lobbyists.

FURTHER READING

Dupuis, Martin, and Keith Boeckelman. *Barack Obama: The New Face of American Politics*. Westport, Conn.: Praeger, 2008. Academic biography of Obama, charting his political career, by two professors of political science.

Lizza, Ryan. "Barack Obama's Unlikely Political Education." *The New Republic*, March 19, 2007. Detailed account of Obama's experience as a community organizer, emphasizing the role of organizer Saul Alinsky's theories in Obama's training and activism.

Mendell, David. *Obama: From Promise to Power*. New York: Amistad, 2007. Biography of Obama by a Chicago journalist who covered him from the beginning of his political career. The work benefits equally from Mendell's high level of access to his subject and his insight into the worlds of local and national politics.

Obama, Barack. *Dreams from My Father*. Rev. ed. New York: Three Rivers Press, 2004. Obama's memoir, initially published in 1995 before he ran for national office, is a much more candid autobiography than the average work by a politician.

—Andy Perry

SANDRA DAY O'CONNOR

> *Society as a whole benefits immeasurably from a climate in which all persons, regardless of race or gender, may have the opportunity to earn respect, responsibility, advancement and remuneration based on ability.*

U.S. Supreme Court justice (1981-2006)

O'Connor served as an Arizona state legislator and judge before becoming the first female justice on the Supreme Court of the United States in 1981.

Born: March 26, 1930; El Paso, Texas
Also known as: Sandra Day (birth name)
Area of achievement: Law and jurisprudence

EARLY LIFE

Sandra Day O'Connor (oh-KAW-nur) was born Sandra Day in El Paso, Texas, and brought up on a rustic cattle ranch in southeastern Arizona, the oldest of three children. Her early life was marked by hard work and academic excellence: She was reading by age four, and by age ten she was riding horses, repairing fences, and driving tractors. She also developed studious habits as a youngster, reading the many magazines and

O'Connor, Sandra Day

books provided by her parents. Encouraged to value education by her college-educated mother, Ada Mae Wilkey Day, Sandra was sent to live with her maternal grandmother to attend a private girls' school in El Paso. Between the ages of six and fifteen, Sandra typically spent summers with her parents on the ranch and school months away from home. Hardworking and self-reliant, she graduated from public high school in El Paso, Texas, at the relatively young age of sixteen.

Sandra Day went immediately on to college, entering Stanford University in California, where she completed both her undergraduate and law degrees by the time she was twenty-two. She attained magna cum laude status for her B.A. degree in economics, and she ranked in the top 10 percent in her law school's graduating class. One of the few women in the law school, she was chosen to be a member of the Society of the Coif, an exclusive honor society for superior students. She also served on the editorial staff of the highly regarded *Stanford Law Review*, and while there she met two fellow students who would play important roles in her life: John O'Connor III, whom she would marry, and William H. Rehnquist, with whom she would serve on the U.S. Supreme Court for twenty-five years.

LIFE'S WORK

After completing law school, Sandra Day O'Connor planned to practice law and interviewed with several of the traditionally all-male private law firms in California. De-

Sandra Day O'Connor.
(Library of Congress)

spite her strong academic credentials, the only offer she received was to serve as a legal secretary. She turned that offer down and began what was to become an extraordinary career in public service. She served briefly as deputy attorney for San Mateo County, California, before moving to West Germany because of her husband's Army assignment. On returning to the United States, she proceeded to have and rear three sons while maintaining a busy schedule of volunteer activities in Phoenix, Arizona. Still unable to secure a law-firm position, she started a small private practice in Phoenix and became active in Republican Party politics in her county. Devoted to public service, she became one of Arizona's assistant attorney generals in 1965 and then a state senator in 1969. At age forty-two, O'Connor became the first woman to hold the majority leader position in a state senate.

Although she enjoyed the respect of her senate colleagues and the support of her constituents, O'Connor opted for the intellectual challenge of the judiciary over the political demands of the legislature. She successfully sought election in 1974 as a state trial judge, and four years later she was appointed by Governor Bruce Babbitt to the Arizona Court of Appeals. As both a state legislator and a judge, she developed a reputation as an extremely diligent, intelligent, and fair-minded public servant. Influenced in her youth by her father, Harry Day, who had an intense dislike for Franklin D. Roosevelt and the policies of the Democratic Party, O'Connor became a loyal Republican Party activist, serving on the Arizona committee to reelect President Richard M. Nixon in 1972 and working for Ronald Reagan's presidential nomination in 1976. Her judicial temperament, fidelity to the Republican Party, impressive academic credentials, and impeccable moral character made her a prime candidate for a federal court appointment.

No woman had served on the Supreme Court of the United States for the nearly two hundred years since its opening session in 1789. In fulfillment of a campaign pledge to appoint a qualified woman to the U.S. Supreme Court, President Ronald Reagan nominated Sandra Day O'Connor on July 7, 1981, to become the 106th justice in the Court's history. This historic decision by President Reagan followed a three-month-long search headed by Attorney General William French Smith, who, ironically, had been a partner in one of the California law firms that had refused to hire O'Connor years before. Despite some questions that were raised about her relatively brief experience as an appellate court judge, and some concern about her views on abortion rights, her nomination was enthusiastically supported by both conservatives and liberals. O'Connor impressed members of the Senate Judiciary Committee with her careful and prudent approach to controversial legal issues, asserting her strong conservative belief that judges ought to restrain themselves from injecting personal values into their judicial decisions. Her merit on full display, she was confirmed by the U.S. Senate by a vote of 99 to 0 in September of 1981. O'Connor's womanhood, for so long an obstacle to career advancement, now provided the occasion for her rise to the pinnacle of the legal profession.

O'Connor served for twenty-five years as a distinguished and highly respected associate justice of the Supreme Court. As a new member of the Court in 1981, she immediately impressed colleagues with her disciplined work habits and dignified yet congenial manner. Shortly after arriving, she initiated an aerobics class in the Supreme Court gymnasium for all women employees, which she attended faithfully for many years. Although slowed by a bout with breast cancer in 1988, O'Connor maintained one of the most grueling work schedules of any justice throughout her career on the Court. Exceedingly well prepared for each case, she was noted for asking incisive questions during the Court's oral argument and for producing written opinions expeditiously. She also was active off the Court, regularly attending Washington, D.C., social events with her husband, arranging family skiing trips, and lecturing widely on legal topics.

On the Supreme Court, O'Connor had a significant influence on many of the most controversial social and political issues of her time. She developed a reputation as a pragmatic justice who wrote moderately conservative judicial opinions. On the nine-member Court, she often cast the deciding vote, repeatedly discovering some reasonable middle-ground position between her more ideological liberal and conservative brethren. As a result, for much of her tenure, O'Connor was characterized as perhaps the most powerful woman in America, one whose vote would shape public policy in the areas of abortion rights, religious liberty, affirmative action, federalism, and women's rights.

In one of her most important rulings, O'Connor defined the standard for state abortion regulations. Rejecting both the arguments of conservatives that the Constitution does not prevent states from prohibiting early-term abortions and the arguments of liberal feminists that states could place no constitutional restrictions on a woman's right to choose an abortion, she ruled in *Planned Parenthood of Southeastern Pennsylvania v. Casey* (1992) that states could regulate abortion up to the point that these restrictions become an undue burden on the woman seeking the abortion. O'Connor's deciding vote in this case maintained early-term abortion as a constitutional right even while allowing states to impose some conditions. In *Stenberg v. Carhart* (2000), she again cast a deciding vote in striking down a state law that banned a controversial ("partial birth") late-term abortion procedure as insufficiently protective of the mother's health. However, to underscore O'Connor's importance in casting pivotal votes, in 2007, with O'Connor retired and replaced with a more conservative justice, the Supreme Court upheld a similar federal ban on "partial birth" abortion.

In the controversial area of religion, O'Connor was typically a voice of moderation. Against liberals who advocate a virtually total separation of religion from state activities and against conservatives who argue that the Constitution allows more active government support of religion, O'Connor articulated the position that a government policy violates the Constitution only if it intends, or appears, to endorse religion. In a case from 2002 involving public vouchers given to parents who used the money to send their children to parochial schools, O'Connor cast the decisive fifth vote ruling that vouchers did not violate the Constitution so long as the parents, and not the parochial schools, were the primary recipients of the government money.

O'Connor actively participated in moving the Court to a more conservative stance on affirmative action even while defending such programs against more conservative justices who would abolish them in all circumstances. In a case that displayed her sensitivity to discrimination against women as well as her support for some types of affirmative action programs, she argued in *Johnson v. Transportation Agency of Santa Clara County* (1987) against the complaint of a white man who was passed over for a skilled job in favor of a woman who, though well qualified, scored slightly lower on an interview score. At the time, none of the 237 skilled positions in the agency was held by a woman. For O'Connor, this was sufficient evidence that the county had discriminated against women. In subsequent cases, she sought to limit government affirmative action programs to those circumstances in which they serve a compelling interest. In 2003 O'Connor cast the deciding vote in *Grutter v. Bollinger*, ruling that state universities may use race-conscious affirmative action programs when admitting students to achieve the compelling interest of a "diverse" student body.

O'Connor was the only one of her colleagues on the Court to have been an elected state legislator. This fact, combined with her fundamentally conservative values, made O'Connor a strong advocate of limits on the power of the federal government over the states. Her conservative views on federalism emerged in such important decisions as *Gregory v. Ashcroft* (1991), in which, writing for the majority of the Court, O'Connor ruled that Missouri's constitutional requirement of mandatory retirement for judges did not violate the federal Age Discrimination in Employment Act. Similarly, in *New York v. U.S.* (1992), O'Connor's majority opinion declared that the federal government could not order state governments to assume ownership of nuclear waste if they failed to create adequate disposal sites as required by federal law. She also believed in restraining the power of the federal government even where women's rights may be compromised. In 2000 she joined a ruling to strike down the Violence Against Women Act, a federal law that would have allowed victims of sexual violence to bring civil suits against their attackers in federal court. Her views on federalism also shaped her rulings on capital punishment. Her rulings generally sided with the states in limiting death row appeals, though she did rule in *Atkins v. Virginia* (2002) that states may not execute the mentally retarded.

O'Connor's long-standing commitments to judicial impartiality and restraint and to state sovereignty came into question when she cast a deciding vote in the controversy surrounding the presidential election of 2000. The Supreme Court, splitting five to four in *Bush v. Gore*, ordered Florida to stop a recount of disputed ballots, resulting in the election of the Republican candidate, George W. Bush, and the defeat of the Democratic candidate, Al Gore. O'Connor rejected the Florida Supreme Court's order for a recount, a vote that some critics viewed to be inconsistent with her abiding belief in state sovereignty. She, along with four of her Republican colleagues on the Court, withstood public criticism for participating in what many saw as an unprecedented, and partisan, intrusion of the Supreme Court into the election of a president.

On women's rights, O'Connor stood forcefully for the principle that the Constitution mandates gender equality and that civil rights laws should be interpreted to protect women against discrimination in education and employment. As a state senator, she supported the Equal Rights Amendment. In 1993, Justice O'Connor wrote an opinion for a unanimous court in *Harris v. Forklift Systems* that made sexual harassment in the workplace easier to prove, and in 1999, in *Davis v. Monroe County Board of Education*, she cast the decisive fifth vote holding school officials liable for preventing student-on-student sexual harassment. Although O'Connor was not a liberal feminist, her efforts to preserve a woman's constitutional right to choose abortion, her votes on the Court to end discrimination against pregnant workers, and her opposition to the exclusion of women from men's private clubs demonstrated her commitment to gender equality.

In one of her last cases, *Hamdi v. Rumsfeld* (2004), O'Connor confronted the problem of individual rights in wartime and the scope of the president's powers in war.

O'Connor, Sandra Day

Writing for a divided court, in an opinion she later called one of her most important, she ruled that "a state of war is not a blank check for the President when it comes to the rights of the Nation's citizens."

In her last years on the Supreme Court, O'Connor managed to write three books, including a memoir of her formative years on the Arizona ranch. She announced her retirement from the Supreme Court on July 1, 2005, at the age of seventy-five, and she continued to serve until her replacement, Samuel Alito, was sworn in on January 31, 2006. After leaving the Court, she continued her public service as a member of the Iraq Study Group in 2006, as chancellor of the College of William and Mary, and as a leading advocate for an independent judiciary at national and international conferences.

Significance

O'Connor's pathbreaking rise to the Supreme Court was a significant moment in the greater transformation of women's lives in American society during the last half of the twentieth century. Her celebrated nomination to the Court, applauded by people of all political views, reflected the growing consensus that women were deserving of high governmental office and that they had been unjustly excluded from these positions for far too long. Her appointment to the Court also coincided with the increase in popularity of conservative political ideas in the 1980's, a trend to which she contributed.

O'Connor's accomplishments go beyond the circumstances of her appointment. On the Court, she influenced many important areas of American law, often casting pivotal votes in highly controversial cases. Scholars have proposed that O'Connor lent a uniquely feminine perspective to cases heard by the Court, marked in part by her consistent ability to see both sides of complex issues and her tendency to forge a reasonable compromise that is consistent with her basic conservative values. Other scholars argued that several of the justices became noticeably more receptive to arguments in favor of gender equality after O'Connor's arrival on the Court. O'Connor was joined by a second woman justice after President Bill Clinton nominated Ruth Bader Ginsburg to fill a vacancy on the Supreme Court in 1993.

Although women continue to be underrepresented in political office, O'Connor retained a unique public profile as one of the most popular and easily recognized Supreme Court justices ever. Her determination to succeed in the predominantly male world of law and politics and her ability to combine motherhood and family with a career dedicated to public service made her a positive role model for many young women.

—*Philip R. Zampini*

Further Reading

Biskupic, Joan. *Sandra Day O'Connor*. New York: HarperPerennial, 2005. The best full-length biography, covering her personal life and professional career. Very well-researched by a skilled journalist and written in an engaging style.

Greenburg, Jan Crawford. *Supreme Conflict*. New York: Penguin Press, 2007. A journalist's account of the political battles over the direction of the Supreme Court during the George W. Bush administration. The book offers a behind-the-scenes look at the politics of judicial appointments, with much to say about O'Connor's importance, the drama surrounding her retirement, and the search for her replacement.

Maveety, Nancy. "Justice Sandra O'Connor: Accommodationism and Conservatism." In *Rehnquist Justice: Understanding the Court Dynamic*, edited by Earl Maltz. Lawrence: University Press of Kansas, 2003. A scholarly analysis of O'Connor's jurisprudence and critical role on the Supreme Court.

O'Connor, Sandra Day. *The Majesty of the Law*. New York: Random House, 2003. A collection of the justice's reflections on the Supreme Court, legal history, individual justices, the role of women in law, and the legal profession.

O'Connor, Sandra Day, and H. Alan Day. *Lazy B*. New York: Random House, 2002. A memoir, coauthored with her brother, of her formative years on the cattle ranch in Arizona during the 1930's. Reveals some of the pleasures and pains of Depression-era ranch life that would shape O'Connor's worldview.

Tushnet, Mark. *A Court Divided*. New York: W. W. Norton, 2005. An analysis of the Supreme Court during the tenure of Chief Justice William H. Rehnquist. The author, a professor of law, focuses on the internal divisions among the justices and illustrates O'Connor's pivotal role in many policy areas.

OSCEOLA

" Let our last sleep be in the graves of our native land! "

Native American leader

Allegedly a participant in the First Seminole War, Osceola became a leader of the Seminoles, who refused to be moved west of the Mississippi; he initiated the Second Seminole War.

Born: c. 1804; Tallassee on the Tallapoosa River near present-day Tuskegee, Alabama
Died: January 30, 1838; Fort Moultrie, Charleston, South Carolina
Area of achievement: Native American affairs

EARLY LIFE

Osceola (ah-skee-OH-lah) insisted, and some historians maintain, that both his father (whose name is now longer known) and mother (Polly Copinger) were Creeks and that his mother later married an Englishman, William Powell. However, a study by Patricia R. Wickman provides impressive evidence that Powell was indeed Osceola's father, that Copinger's grandfather (James McQueen) and father were white, and that the boy also had black ancestors, as did many children who were born in the Upper Creek town of Tallassee. Nevertheless, Osceola was considered to be an Upper Creek, like his mother.

Osceola's mother's uncle, Peter McQueen, was chief of the village where Osceola was born and became a leader of the Red Sticks during the Creek War of 1813-1814. As that conflict escalated, many Creeks fled from Alabama into Florida. Among the refugees were Osceola and his mother, who followed McQueen and became separated

Osceola

from Powell during the migration. The young Osceola was captured by Andrew Jackson's troops during his 1818 campaign in Florida, but he was released because of his age. Allegedly he fought against Jackson in the First Seminole War.

LIFE'S WORK
Osceola settled in central Florida after Jackson's campaign and, like many dislocated Creeks, became known as a Seminole. He was never a hereditary chief, nor was he apparently ever elected to such a post; however, in the controversy surrounding the signing of the treaties of Payne's Landing in 1832 and of Fort Gibson in 1833, both of which provided for the relocation of the Seminoles to the West, he emerged as a leader of those who opposed removal.

A heated clash with Wiley Thompson, the federal Indian agent for central Florida, made Osceola an outlaw. Abolitionists later wrote that Thompson aided two slave catchers to capture one of Osceola's wives, who was a mulatto, but there is no evidence for this tale. Instead, the conflict apparently originated when Thompson called a council at Fort King to confirm the earlier treaties. Most of the Seminoles who were present silently refused to sign the documents placed before them, but Osceola allegedly plunged a knife through the agreement. Again, no contemporary account supports this story.

Other confrontations in the summer of 1835 led Thompson to have Osceola imprisoned in shackles, but Osceola was released when he agreed to support removal. Rather than abide by his agreement with Thompson, Osceola organized Seminole resistance and killed Charley Emathla, a chief who had supported emigration. Osceola and his followers then attacked a baggage train during December, 1835. Later that same month, he killed Thompson, while allies ambushed a force of more than one hundred regulars and killed all but three of them. On New Year's Eve, 1835, a large party led by Osceola attacked another detachment of regulars and punished them severely in the First Battle of the Withlacoochee, where Osceola was wounded slightly in the hand or arm but escaped capture.

This began the Second Seminole War, which would last until 1842. Until his capture in 1837, Osceola was the primary target of army operations because the U.S. military recognized his importance as a leader in the resistance. Participants in the campaigns against him noted that many of his followers were black. They would have supported him instead of the hereditary chiefs, and his desire to protect them may have been part of his motivation for continuing to fight long after his health began to fail. His evasion of army columns and bold attacks made him something of a folk hero in the United States, but it also earned him the hatred of military leaders, especially after he liberated more than seven hundred Indians held in a detention camp in June, 1837.

In October, 1837, General Thomas S. Jesup, frustrated by Osceola, treacherously accepted his request for a parley under a flag of truce. The Seminole leader, who was then suffering from malaria, and more than eighty of his followers were captured at their camp near Fort Peyton in a flagrant violation of the truce. Despite the public outcry, he was taken to Fort Mellon at St. Augustine, where two of his wives and two children, as well as his half sister and others, joined him. These two wives may have been the two sisters he had married in accordance with Creek custom, though there appear to have been others.

Osceola

After several other Seminoles escaped, Osceola and his group were transferred on New Year's Eve, 1837, to Fort Moultrie at Charleston, South Carolina. There his health declined rapidly, and he died on January 30, 1838. Allegations vary as to the cause of his death, but most agree that his depression contributed to his rapid demise. Wickman says that quinsy, or tonsillitis complicated by an abscess, was the immediate cause of Osceola's death, and both malaria and recurring fevers were contributing factors in his declining health.

Significance

Osceola was buried outside Fort Moultrie on Sullivan Island with military honors, but before interment his head was removed by Frederick Weedon, the physician who had attended him during his fatal illness. It was displayed in a medical museum maintained by Valentine Mott of the Medical College of New York until the building was allegedly destroyed by fire in 1866.

The betrayal of Osceola destroyed any realistic hope of unity among the Seminoles. The war continued sporadically until 1842, when most of the surviving Seminoles moved West, as his family had after his death. Only a few remained in the swamps. The circumstances of Osceola's fight, capture, and death, which were often misrepresented, made him a folk hero to many. No fewer than twenty towns in the United States now bear his name, as do three counties, two townships, one borough, two lakes, two mountains, a state park, and a national forest.

—*Richard B. McCaslin*

Further Reading

Boyd, Mark F. "Asi-Yaholo, or Osceola." *Florida Historical Quarterly* 23 (January-April, 1955): 249-305. This is an overview of Osceola and the events of his life.

Covington, James W. *The Seminoles of Florida*. Gainesville: University Press of Florida, 1993. Covington covers the history of the Seminole Indians, their relations with the U.S. government, and the social conditions under which they lived during various periods.

Hartley, William, and Ellen Hartley. *Osceola: The Unconquered Indian*. New York: Hawthorn Books, 1973. This illustrated biography of Osceola includes bibliographic references.

Mahon, John K. *History of the Second Seminole War, 1835-1842*. Rev. ed. Gainesville: University of Florida Press, 1992. Mahon's detailed study of the Second Seminole War includes illustrations, maps, and a bibliography.

Missall, John, and Mary Lou Missall. *The Seminole Wars: America's Longest Indian Conflict*. Gainesville: University Press of Florida, 2004. A history of the three Seminole wars, examining their causes and significance in American history.

Wickman, Patricia R. *Osceola's Legacy*. Tuscaloosa: University of Alabama Press, 1991. Wickman interweaves a biography of Osceola with the history of the Seminoles and considers the implications of the events of his lifetime for later interactions between Native Americans and the U.S. government. The book contains a bibliography and an index.

JESSE OWENS

> *" Awards become corroded; friends gather no dust. "*

Olympic athlete

The winner of four gold medals at the Berlin Olympics in 1936, Owens served as an inspirational model of success for African Americans and later became a symbol and eloquent spokesperson for the United States as a land of opportunity for all.

Born: September 12, 1913; Oakville, Alabama
Died: March 31, 1980; Tucson, Arizona
Also known as: James Cleveland Owens (full name); J. C. Owens
Area of achievement: Sports

EARLY LIFE

Jesse Owens (OH-ehnz) was born to Henry Cleveland Owens and Mary Emma (née Fitzgerald) Owens, both sharecroppers and descendants of slaves. James Cleveland, the last of nine children who survived infancy, was called J. C. When he was eight or nine years old, the family moved to Cleveland, Ohio, for better work and educational opportunities. On his first day of school, he introduced himself as "J. C.," but his teacher misunderstood him to say "Jesse." The young Owens bashfully accepted the mistake, thus taking on the name by which he would become famous.

At Fairmount Junior High School, his exceptional athletic ability caught the eye of a physical education teacher, Charles Riley. A white man, Riley became Owens's coach, his moral monitor, and his surrogate father, teaching him citizenship as well as athletic techniques. Riley worked long hours with his pupil and continued to do so through high school. While on his high school track team, Jesse set several interscholastic records. In 1932, he failed to win a place on the United States Olympic squad, but by the time he had finished high school, in 1933, he had won much acclaim as a track athlete of extraordinary promise.

Owens wished to attend the University of Michigan. No track scholarships were available in that day, however, and Jesse's parents could not afford tuition. He therefore matriculated at Ohio State University, athletic boosters having arranged for him to work at part-time jobs to pay his expenses. He waited on tables in the dining hall, operated an elevator in the State House, and served as a page for the Ohio legislature.

Poorly prepared for college work and distracted by athletics, he was never a good student. After his first term he was constantly on academic probation; once, he had to sit out the indoor track season because of bad grades. All the while he excelled in sports, setting numerous Big Ten and national track records. His finest day was May 25, 1935, at the Big Ten championships in Ann Arbor. Within a single hour he set new world records in the 220-yard sprint, the 220-yard hurdles, and the long jump and tied the world record in the 100-yard dash. Well over a year before the Berlin Games of 1936, Owens emerged as a young man destined for Olympic fame.

His physique, style, and personality made him a sportswriter's dream. He carried about 165 pounds on a compact frame of five feet, ten inches. A model of graceful form, he ran so smoothly that each performance seemed effortless. Whether on or off the track, he frequently flashed a warm, spontaneous smile. Never did he refuse an interview or autograph. In the face of racial insults and discrimination, he kept a mild, pleasant demeanor. Like most blacks of his generation, Owens survived by turning the other cheek, by presenting himself as a modest individual who did not openly retaliate against the bigotry of his day.

At the Olympic trials in the summer of 1936, he finished first in all three of the events he had entered. Several weeks later, he took the Berlin Olympics by storm. First, he won the 100-meter dash in 10.3 seconds, equaling the world record. Next he took the gold medal in the long jump with a new Olympic distance of 8.06 meters. Then he won the gold in the 200-meter race with a new Olympic mark of 20.7 seconds. Toward the end of the week, he was unexpectedly placed on the American team for the 400-meter relays. He ran the opening leg in yet another gold-medal, record-making effort.

By the end of that fabulous week in Berlin, an attractive yarn attached itself to the name of Jesse Owens. Supposedly, he was "snubbed" by Adolf Hitler, who reportedly refused to congratulate him publicly after his victories. Actually, the story was concocted by American sportswriters, who were all too willing to read the worst of motives into Hitler's behavior and to assume innocent excellence from America's newest hero. Although it had no basis in fact, the story of "Hitler's snub" was repeated so often

Jesse Owens. (AP/Wide World Photos)

that people took it as truth. It remains one of the great anecdotes of American popular culture.

LIFE'S WORK

For several years after the Berlin Olympics, life did not go smoothly for Owens. American officials had planned a barnstorming tour for the track team immediately after the Berlin Games. At first, Owens cooperated, running exhibitions in Germany, Czechoslovakia, and England. Having received numerous offers from the United States to capitalize on his Olympic fame, he balked when the team departed from London for a series of exhibitions in Scandinavia. The Amateur Athletic Union suspended him from any further amateur competition.

Accompanied by his Ohio State coach, Larry Snyder, Owens returned to the United States only to find that all the "offers" were phony publicity stunts by unscrupulous entrepreneurs. They never seriously intended to give a young black man—not even an Olympic hero—a steady job at decent pay. Instead, Owens found a lucrative assignment in the presidential campaign of Alf Landon, who paid him to stump for black votes. That turned out to be a futile effort but no more futile than a subsequent string of unsatisfactory jobs. For a time, Owens directed a band for Bill "Bojangles" Robinson on the black nightclub circuit. Tiring of that, he organized traveling basketball and softball teams, raced against horses at baseball games and county fairs, served for a summer as a playground director in Cleveland, and briefly worked as a clothes salesman. He suffered his biggest failure in a dry-cleaning venture that went bankrupt within six months.

Now married with three young daughters, Owens at twenty-seven years of age returned to Ohio State to finish his baccalaureate degree. However, he could not bring his grade average up sufficiently to earn his degree. At the outbreak of World War II, he took a government appointment as director of a physical fitness program for blacks. Two years later, he took a job with Ford Motor Company in Detroit, in charge of Ford's black labor force. Dismissed from that position at the end of the war, by 1946 Owens no doubt winced when he looked back on the ten years since his Olympic victories. During that decade he had held about ten jobs, all confined to the segregated black community.

Finally, in the 1950's, Owens broke out of that ghetto existence. When, after the onset of the Cold War, America needed a successful black to display to the world as an exemplar of the cherished American ideal of equal opportunity, Jesse Owens fit the bill. Having moved to Chicago in 1949, he worked with the Southside Boys Club and gave addresses to both black and white audiences in the greater Chicago area. Soon, he was in great demand throughout the United States as a spokesperson for American patriotism and the American Dream. In 1951, he returned to Berlin with that message. In 1955, he toured India, Malaya, and the Philippines under the sponsorship of the United States Department of State, and the following year he attended the Melbourne, Australia, Olympic Games as a personal representative of President Dwight D. Eisenhower. Never again would Owens be shunted aside as a black man in a white man's world. For the last two decades of his life, he gave more than one hundred speeches a year in praise of athletics, religion, and the flag.

Becoming politically more conservative as he got older, Owens refused to join the Civil Rights movement. His moderate position put him out of touch with the younger, angrier generation of blacks. He was rejected as an "Uncle Tom" in the 1960's. After Tommie Smith and John Carlos gave their world-famous black-power salutes at the Olympic Games held in Mexico City in 1968, Owens demanded apologies, but to no avail.

He received numerous honors during his final years. In 1974, the National Collegiate Athletic Association presented him its highest recognition, the Theodore Roosevelt Award for distinguished achievement. Two years later, President Gerald R. Ford bestowed on him the Medal of Freedom Award for his "inspirational" life, and, in 1979, Democratic president Jimmy Carter honored him with the Living Legends Award for his "dedicated but modest" example of greatness. Less than a year later, on March 31, 1980, Jesse Owens died of lung cancer. Ironically, America's greatest track-and-field athlete fell victim to a twenty-year habit of cigarette smoking.

Significance

When Owens achieved stardom in the Berlin Olympics of 1936, rigid racial segregation pervaded baseball, football, and basketball in the United States. Owens and Joe Louis stood virtually alone as black athletes who had excelled against whites. African Americans viewed them as examples of success, inspirational models of black ability, symbols of racial pride and dignity.

Although he was America's first Olympic superstar, Owens did not become a widely acclaimed hero until after World War II. As Americans transposed their hatred of Hitler and the Nazis to Stalin and the communists, Owens's rags-to-riches story confirmed American values as superior to communist claims to a better way of life. "In America, anybody can become somebody," Owens often said, and American politicians, the media, and the public at large loved him for it. Especially to people in the nonaligned developing world, he was an effective spokesman for American democracy.

Four years after Owens's death, the 1984 Los Angeles Olympics demonstrated his perennial popularity. In Los Angeles, Carl Lewis won gold medals in the same four events Owens had dominated half a century earlier, with much better statistical results. However, Owens's fame remained undiminished. Each time Lewis won a race, he was compared to Owens. Old film clips from the Berlin Games were aired repeatedly on television, showing the graceful Owens in action. Numerous interviews with family and friends kept his memory alive. Arguably, Owens was the posthumous star of the Los Angeles Olympics.

Owens's life illustrates the principle that an athlete becomes a national hero only when his or her achievements, personality, and image coincide with momentous events to fulfill a cultural need beyond the athletic arena. As long as people struggle against the odds of racial prejudice and economic deprivation, the story of Owens will be told. He overcame the odds.

—*William J. Baker*

Owens, Jesse

FURTHER READING

Baker, William J. *Jesse Owens: An American Life*. New York: Free Press, 1986. The only complete, critical biography available. Based on archival research, the black press, interviews with family and friends, and FBI files on Owens, all fully documented. A candid appraisal of Owens's limitations and vices as well as his achievements and virtues, set against the background of American society.

———. *Sports in the Western World*. Totowa, N.J.: Rowman and Littlefield, 1982. Places Owens in the larger context of sport history, briefly focusing on his Olympic victories in the face of Hitler's ambitions in 1936. A survey, undocumented but with a good critical bibliography of sport history.

Edwards, Harry. *The Revolt of the Black Athlete*. New York: Free Press, 1970. A first-hand account of the movement for black athletes' rights in the 1960's by the leader of the revolt that culminated in Mexico City. Depicts Owens as a lamentable representative of an older generation's acquiescence to racial abuse. A fiery, argumentative treatise.

Mandell, Richard D. *The Nazi Olympics*. New York: Macmillan, 1971. The best treatment of the Berlin Games of 1936. Strong on Nazi ideology and technical efficiency behind the games, also on daily events and profiles of athletes. Well documented from German as well as English sources, a gem of cultural history.

Owens, Jesse, with Paul Neimark. *Blackthink: My Life as Black Man and White Man*. New York: William Morrow, 1970. A tirade against black-power advocates, especially against black athletes who openly protested American racism. Mostly autobiographical, with Owens illustrating his own acquaintance with bigotry, concluding that patience and moral character rather than angry rebellion would produce social change. Evoked hostile response from black readers, prompting Owens to collaborate once again with Paul Neimark to produce *I Have Changed* (New York: William Morrow, 1972), another collection of stories from his life to explain his point of view.

———. *Jesse: A Spiritual Autobiography*. Plainfield, N.J.: Logos International, 1978. An indulgent use of anecdotes in the service of homilies. As always, Owens's recollections cannot be taken at face value. Some are outright fabrications; most are romantically embellished.

———. *The Jesse Owens Story*. New York: G. P. Putnam's Sons, 1970. A lightweight, ghost-written autobiography directed toward a teenage readership. More inspirational than factually accurate; anecdotal, not analytical. Undocumented and untrustworthy, the Jesse Owens story as Owens himself wanted it told.

Quercetani, Roberto L. *A World History of Track and Field Athletics, 1864-1964*. London: Oxford University Press, 1964. Useful reference for Owens's achievements in comparison with other athletes before and since his day. Covers his intercollegiate as well as his Olympic victories.

Schaap, Jeremy. *Triumph: The Untold Story of Jesse Owens and Hitler's Olympics*. Boston: Houghton Mifflin, 2007. Based on extensive research and access to Owens's family, this book recounts Owens's performance at the Olympics in a dramatic and entertaining style.

THOMAS PAINE

" *Government, even in its best state, is but a necessary evil; in its worst state, an intolerable one.* **"**

Political philosopher

Paine was a participant in both the American and French Revolutions, and, through his writings, he attempted to foment revolution in England as well. He was interested in the new scientific ideas of his age, spent considerable energy on the design of an iron-arch bridge, and tried to resolve the age-old conflicts between science and religion by espousing Deism.

Born: January 29, 1737; Thetford, Norfolk, England
Died: June 8, 1809; New York, New York
Also known as: Thomas Pain (birth name)
Areas of achievement: Government and politics; philosophy

EARLY LIFE

Thomas Paine's father, Joseph Pain (Thomas later added an "e" to his name), was a Quaker stay maker. Working as a craftsman, he provided whalebone corsets for local women. Paine's mother, Frances Cocke, the daughter of a local attorney, was an Anglican who was older than her husband and of difficult disposition. Because a daughter died in infancy, the Pains then concentrated all of their efforts on their son.

Thomas was taught by a local schoolmaster from the age of seven to thirteen and then apprenticed to his father to learn the trade of a stay maker. This was clearly not entirely to his liking, as he managed at one point to run away and spend some time at sea. Upon his return, he practiced his craft in various places in England. In 1759, Paine married Mary Lambert, but his wife died a year later. Dissatisfied with his occupation, he tried others, including a brief stint at schoolteaching and perhaps also preaching. Still seeking his niche in the world, Paine returned home for a time to study for the competitive examination to become an excise collector. He passed the exam and obtained positions collecting customs revenues from 1764 to 1765 and from 1768 to 1774. He was twice dismissed from his posts for what higher authorities saw as laxity in the performance of his duties. The second dismissal came after Paine participated in efforts to obtain higher wages for excisemen, during the course of which he wrote a pamphlet, *The Case of the Officers of the Excise* (1772).

The time he spent on these endeavors, as well as his arguments, contributed to the loss of his position. Paine was married to Elizabeth Ollive in 1767, and, while continuing as an exciseman, he also helped her widowed mother and siblings run the family store. By 1774, the business was in bankruptcy, Paine and his wife had separated, and he was without a government position, with little prospect of regaining one. It was at this point in his life that Paine, so far a failure at everything he had tried to do, obtained a letter of introduction from Benjamin Franklin and moved to America.

Paine, Thomas

LIFE'S WORK

Thomas Paine arrived in the colonies at an auspicious moment. A dispute over "taxation without representation," simmering between England and its colonists since the passage of the Stamp Act in 1765, had led to the Boston Tea Party and then to the passage of the Coercive (or Intolerable) Acts (1774). Paine obtained a position as editor for the new *Pennsylvania Magazine*, published in Philadelphia. Meanwhile, American feelings had boiled over, and the Revolutionary War had begun. As an author, Paine had finally found where his true talents lay. In January of 1776, he wrote *Common Sense*, a pamphlet attacking the king, advocating independence, and outlining the form of government that should be adopted. The work was a tremendous success, a consequence of its timely arguments as well as its clear, forceful language. Reprinted in numerous editions, passed from hand to hand, it reached an audience of unprecedented size. At age thirty-nine, Paine had at last achieved a measure of success. He went on to become the leading propagandist of the American Revolution.

During the war, Paine served as secretary to a commission on American Indian affairs and as secretary to the Committee for Foreign Affairs of the Second Continental Congress. He resigned under pressure from the second position during a bitter political debate over the actions of Silas Deane. He later served as a clerk for the Pennsylvania Assembly and participated in a diplomatic venture to France, seeking additional help for the fledgling nation. He is best known, however, for his continued efforts to promote the American cause. By 1783, he had written a total of sixteen *Crisis* papers as well as other pamphlets. In the *Crisis* papers, with ringing language meant to stir the soul and bolster the war effort, he appealed to patriotic Americans to rally to the cause.

As the war came to a conclusion, Paine turned his efforts to providing some measure of financial security for himself. He appealed to the national Congress and a number of state legislatures for compensation for his previous literary efforts on behalf of the American cause. He was ultimately granted a small pension by Congress, land by the New York legislature, and money by the Pennsylvania government. The Virginia legislature refused to come to his aid after he wrote a pamphlet, *The Public Good* (1780), arguing that all the states should cede their western land claims to the national government. In this work and others, Paine's talents were utilized by those who wanted to bolster the powers of the central government. In 1786, he wrote a pamphlet, *Dissertations on Government, the Affairs of the Bank, and Paper Money*, in which he defended the Bank of America, chartered by Congress and the state of Pennsylvania as an instrument to raise money for the government and to aid commerce. In the course of this work, he condemned paper money, maintaining that anything but gold or silver was a dangerous fraud.

Always interested in science and new technology, he also busied himself with designing an iron-arch bridge that would be able to span greater distances than was possible with existing methods. Unable to obtain sufficient money or interest for his project in the United States, he left for France in 1787 and from there made several trips to England, primarily to raise support for a workable model.

Paine arrived in France just as the French Revolution began to unfold, although this drama did not at first engage his attention. With the publication of Edmund Burke's *Reflections on the Revolution in France* (1790), Paine again took up his pen for a radical cause, producing, in two parts, *The Rights of Man* (1791, 1792). Whereas the conservative Burke emphasized the value of traditions and claimed that all change should come about gradually, Paine argued for government based on consent, defended revolution as a corrective remedy for unjust government, suggested ways to bring revolution to England, and proposed an early form of social welfare. The second part of *The Rights of Man* led to his being tried and convicted in absentia in England for seditious libel. Paine barely escaped arrest by the English authorities and took passage to France, where he became intimately involved in the course of the French Revolution.

When Paine returned to France in 1792, it was as an elected delegate to the French assembly. There he was caught up, and ultimately overcome, by the tide of the revolution. Paine associated with the political representatives of the middle and upper classes, with literary figures, and with those who spoke English, never having mastered French sufficiently to converse without a translator. Despite his attacks on monarchy in his previous writings, the depths of French radicalism, the swiftness of change, and the quick trial and execution of the king all went beyond what he could support.

Associated with the Girondist faction of French politics and an object of increasing antiforeign sentiment, Paine was arrested after the Jacobins achieved power; he subsequently spent ten agonizing months in jail while prisoners around him were carted off to the guillotine. Once the virulence of the revolution ran its course, Paine seemed less of a threat to those in power. As a result, a new American minister to France, James Monroe, was able to appeal for his release from prison, arguing that Paine was an American, rather than English, citizen.

While in prison, Paine began the last work for which he achieved fame or, in this case, infamy: *The Age of Reason* (1794). The first part of this book was an attack on religion and a defense of Deism, while the second part was specifically aimed at Christianity and included numerous pointed refutations of biblical passages. It was a work that sparked in rebuttal many pamphlets in England and the United States and was also the source of much of the hostility directed against Paine in later years.

Paine's spell in prison had undermined his health and warped his judgment, although he had never been astute in practical politics. Remaining in France, even though after 1795 he was no longer a member of the French assembly, he wrote a pamphlet attacking George Washington and meddled in American foreign policy. In 1802, after an absence of fifteen years, he returned to the United States, taking up residence in, among other places, Washington, D.C., and New York City. He wrote letters and a few pamphlets, but he was anathema to the Federalists and a political liability to the Republicans. He died on June 8, 1809, in New York City, and his body was taken to the farm in New Rochelle, which the New York government had given him years before, and buried. Some time after his death, his bones were clandestinely dug up by an Englishman who took them off to England hoping to exhibit them; they ultimately disappeared.

Paine, Thomas

Significance

Thomas Paine said that his country was the world, and his life illustrates the truth of this statement. His numerous pamphlets and books zeroed in on the main issues of his time, while the clarity and strength of his language have given his works an enduring appeal. He wrote in support of freedom from arbitrary government and against what he saw as outdated religious superstitions. In addition, he was an active participant in two major revolutions, as well as a friend and acquaintance of major figures in three countries. He was also the center of some controversy, at times difficult to tolerate, exhibiting a disinclination to bathe, a lack of care about his apparel, a propensity to drink, and a tendency to impose on the hospitality of friends for months, and even years, at a time. He was a complex and interesting individual who sparked debate in England, America, and elsewhere among his contemporaries—debate that has continued among historians since his death.

Paine's interest for Americans, though, stems primarily from his authorship of *Common Sense* and the *Crisis* papers. He has frequently been described as the right person in the right place at the right time. The first pamphlet sold 120,000 copies in three months and went through twenty-five editions in 1776 alone. It met the needs of the moment and substantially helped push Americans toward independence. In it, Paine attacked monarchy as being "ridiculous" and George III for being the "Royal Brute of Great Britain." He thought it absurd for England, an island, to continue to rule America, a continent. Paine maintained not only that it was "time to part" but also that it was America's obligation to prepare a refuge for liberty, "an asylum for mankind." After independence was declared, Paine, in the first of his numerous *Crisis* papers, noted that in "times that try men's souls," the "summer soldier" or the "sunshine patriot" might "shrink from the service of his country," but the true patriot will stand firm, conquer tyranny, and obtain the precious prize of freedom.

These stirring words, more than anything else he did or wrote in his long and controversial life, assured Paine's place in history. Simply put, he was the most important propagandist of the American Revolution. As such, his later sojourns in England, France, and ultimately back in the United States constitute merely an interesting postscript to his real contribution to American history.

—*Maxine N. Lurie*

Further Reading

Aldridge, Alfred Owen. *Man of Reason: The Life of Thomas Paine*. Philadelphia: J. B. Lippincott, 1959. This scholarly work, based on research in England and France, attempts to give a fair assessment of a complex man. Although the book at times is laudatory, Aldridge basically sees Paine's life as a tragedy.

Conway, Moncure Daniel. *The Life of Thomas Paine*. 2 vols. New York: G. P. Putnam's Sons, 1892. The best nineteenth century biography, written by the first scholar to do extensive research on Paine. This is still a useful work. Conway also published a collection of Paine's writings.

Dorfman, Joseph. "The Economic Philosophy of Thomas Paine." *Political Science Quarterly* 53 (September, 1938): 372-386. Examines the economic ideas expressed in Paine's major pamphlets and his other ideas that had economic implications, downplaying their radicalism.

Edwards, Samuel. *Rebel! A Biography of Tom Paine.* New York: Praeger, 1974. This is a popular biography that covers all of Paine's life. It defends the achievements of Paine's early years, emphasizing his radicalism, but is more critical of the older Paine, noting his eccentric behavior. Edwards accepts as fact some scandalous stories about Paine.

Foner, Eric. *Tom Paine and Revolutionary America.* 1976. Rev. ed. New York: Oxford University Press, 2005. This scholarly biography of Paine concentrates on his American years and on his radicalism. Foner analyzes Paine's political and economic thought and emphasizes the degree to which he was consistent throughout his life.

Fruchtman, Jack, Jr. *Thomas Paine: Apostle of Freedom.* New York: Four Walls Eight Windows, 1994. An insightful biography. Fruchtman maintains that Paine was a pantheist who saw God's handiwork in nature and in humanity's struggles to improve the common good.

Hawke, David Freeman. *Paine.* New York: Harper & Row, 1974. One of the most complete biographies of Paine. Hawke downplays Paine's radicalism, noting that he frequently was only reflecting the ideas of his times, and emphasizes the degree to which he wrote pamphlets for pay. This is a scholarly work that portrays Paine with all of his faults.

Jordan, Wintrop D. "Familial Politics: Thomas Paine and the Killing of the King, 1776." *Journal of American History* 60 (1973): 294-308. This article discusses the appeal of *Common Sense* and its significance in preparing the way for a republic by attacking the idea of monarchy in general and the "brute" King George III in particular.

Keane, John. *Tom Paine: A Political Life.* London: Bloomsbury, 1995. A comprehensive biography of Paine, who is depicted as a generous, farsighted enemy of hypocrisy and injustice, who also could be conceited and dogmatic.

Paine, Thomas. *The Complete Writings of Thomas Paine.* Edited by Philip S. Foner. New York: Citadel Press, 1945. An accessible and well-prepared edition of Paine's works. Foner also edited a paperback edition of Paine's major pieces.

Rosa Parks

> *I have learned over the years that when one's mind is made up, this diminishes fear; knowing what must be done does away with fear.*

Civil rights activist

Parks, best known for refusing to relinquish her seat to a white passenger on a bus in Montgomery, Alabama, in 1955, was a civil rights advocate before her historic and heroic act. The bus boycott that followed marked the first major civil rights action for Martin Luther King, Jr., and brought him and his message to the national stage.

Born: February 4, 1913; Tuskegee, Alabama
Died: October 24, 2005; Detroit, Michigan
Also known as: Rosa Lee McCauley (birth name); Rosa Louise Lee McCauley Parks (full name)
Area of achievement: Civil rights

Early Life

The older of two children, Rosa Parks (ROH-zah parks) was born to Leona Edwards McCauley and James McCauley. Her mother was an educator and her father was a carpenter. The influences in young Rosa's life included her mother and her grandparents. According to Parks, half of her life was spent in a segregated South that "allowed white people to treat black people without any respect." Her parents were separated a great deal of the time. James's occupation in carpentry and construction took him away from home often. Leona resented being left alone.

By the time Parks's brother was born, her parents had separated formally. She did not see her father again until she was five years old. Parks, her mother, and her brother moved in with her maternal grandparents. They lived in Pine Level, Alabama, where Parks was to spend her formative years. Her brother Sylvester, who was two years and seven months younger, doted on Parks's every word and action. She became his protector and primary caretaker while their mother worked.

Parks was small for her age. Her health was poor and her growth appeared to be stunted. She also suffered from chronic tonsillitis. Although these problems kept her out of school for a year, Parks still observed many differences between the white and black schools. Blacks not only had to heat their own schools but also had to build them, whereas white schools were funded by the town, county, or state. There were no buses to transport blacks, and black children attended school for five months, while white students went for nine. Such a discrepancy existed because the majority of black parents were sharecroppers, and their children were needed in the spring and fall to plow, plant, and harvest.

Parks's great-grandfather (her grandmother's father) was a Scots-Irishman who migrated to the United States in the nineteenth century. He was an indentured servant who married an African slave. He and Mary Jane Nobles married and had two daughters and one son before slavery was abolished in 1865. After emancipation, six other children were born to the couple. Parks grew up in a home where family history was important. She listened to stories about slavery, segregation, and the Ku Klux Klan.

As a young girl, Parks worked as a field hand, tended to household chores, and cared for her ill grandparents. Her mother spent much of her time teaching. Soon, her mother decided that Parks should go to a nine-month school. This could only be done if Parks moved away from Pine Level. Consequently, Parks was sent to Montgomery, Alabama, to live with her maternal aunt, and she attended a private girls' school. While enrolled in the Montgomery Industrial School for Girls, which was staffed by white northerners, Parks was responsible for doing household chores and domestic work outside the home.

By the time Parks was eleven years old, her childhood seemed far behind. She cleaned two classrooms at her school in exchange for free tuition. After graduation, she enrolled in Booker T. Washington High School. After her mother became ill, she dropped out of school to care for her. Parks's outlook on discrimination and segregation was influenced by family stories, her time at the Montgomery Industrial School for Girls, and her experiences as a child. She detested the plight of blacks and the advantages that whites possessed, often at the expense of African Americans. As a teen, she sewed, read, and attended the local African Methodist Episcopal (AME) church. Her love for singing and praying continued throughout her life. Active in the Allen Christian Endeavor League, Parks kept busy as a member of the AME church.

In her nineteenth year, Parks met Raymond Parks through a mutual friend. Both had been previously unlucky in love, and they did not pursue a romantic relationship immediately. Raymond was a barber and an active participant in the Civil Rights movement. Parks resisted his advances, but his persistence wore her down. Their common interest in civil rights tended to bond them. During their many conversations, she discovered that their interests and backgrounds were often the same. Both were born in February in the segregated South, were committed to the advancement of blacks, and were of mixed racial heritage. Like herself, Raymond cared for an ill mother and grandmother. They both shared a love of God, and, like Parks, Raymond was an active participant in his church.

In December of 1932, Rosa and Raymond were married in her mother's house. In 1933, she obtained her high school diploma at the age of twenty. The couple settled in Montgomery. Parks engaged in a variety of occupations in an effort to augment her spouse's income. She worked as a seamstress, a domestic, and an office clerk. She became the secretary of the Montgomery chapter of the National Association for the Advancement of Colored People (NAACP) in 1943. She was also an adviser to youth organizations. She joined the Montgomery Voters League and began to encourage blacks to become politically empowered.

Also, Parks had a never-ending thirst for education. She attended seminars and workshops whose topics dealt with the civil rights struggle. She waged her own personal battle against segregation. Instead of riding on segregated buses, she often opted to walk home. She went out of her way to avoid drinking from segregated water fountains. At the age of forty, Parks was a well-known civil rights activist in her community. In an era when discriminatory laws made it difficult for African

Parks, Rosa

Rosa Parks is fingerprinted after her arrest for refusing to give up her seat on a bus. (Library of Congress)

Americans to register to vote, Parks succeeded, on her third try.

Toward the end of World War II, Parks worked briefly at Maxwell Air Force Base, near Montgomery. Discrimination among the races was not permitted there, and that experience, Parks later told an interviewer, was a revelation to her. She also received support from some white people, in particular Clifford and Virginia Durr, for whom she sometimes worked. They sponsored her attendance at the Highlander Folk School in Monteagle, Tennessee, in the summer of 1955. It was a educational center that supported equality among social classes and races.

Life's Work

"The only tired I was, was tired of giving in." These were the words Parks spoke on Thursday, December 1, 1955. She had been returning home from her job as a seamstress. She boarded the segregated bus in the manner usual to Montgomery. Blacks would enter the front, pay, get off, and reenter to take their seats through the back door. The first four rows of seats in the bus were reserved for whites, while African Americans could occupy only those behind the reserved seats. On this particular day, however, the front of the bus quickly filled up. The area where blacks were designated to sit would have to be vacated if more whites boarded. As it happened, a white person did board, and he required a seat.

What happened next is forever part of American history. The blacks in the front of the black section were told by the driver, James F. Blake, to relinquish their seats. All complied except for Parks. She was dealing with the same driver who had evicted her more than a decade earlier from his bus. Parks remained adamant on this occasion. This particular request was not to be taken lightly. Blake threatened to call for the police if she did not do as he asked, but Parks still refused to stand up. She had been arrested that evening for refusing to relinquish her seat to a white patron, thereby violating the segregation laws of Montgomery. Clifford Durr was hired to take her case. She was released on a $100 bond.

Traditionally, the majority of the riders on the Montgomery bus system had been black. They believed that they were within their rights in requesting better treatment in exchange for their consistent patronage. Following Parks's action, black passengers around the community began to defy the requests of bus drivers to move for white passengers. Rumblings of boycotts and demonstrations ensued, but there was no mass organized effort.

The African American community did eventually mobilize, however. An organization called the Women's Political Council passed out thousands of pamphlets, asking for a one-day bus boycott. A community meeting was held on December 5 in the Holt Street Baptist Church. The Montgomery Improvement Association was created, and a young, charismatic minister, the Reverend Martin Luther King, Jr., was elected its president. Parks agreed to allow her case to serve as the focus of the civil rights struggle. The one-day bus boycott was considered a success. By the time Parks was tried and found guilty, the boycott was in its second month. The cooperation of the black ridership was 100 percent. Parks was fined ten dollars and told to pay an additional four dollars in court fees. She refused to pay and appealed.

Because 75 percent of Montgomery's ridership was black, the bus company was quickly sliding into bankruptcy. Parks and her husband lost their jobs. They were harassed with phone calls, letters, verbal threats, and intimidation. The 381 days of boycotting led to the banning of segregation on municipal buses. On December 21, 1956, Parks sat in the front of the newly integrated city buses in Montgomery. However, this victory cost her, and the black community, much. As a result of her part in the boycott, Parks and her husband were unemployable. Moreover, segregationists retaliated by attacking black churches and black leaders' homes with bombs and fire.

Because she was unable to find work, and with Raymond suffering from ill health, Parks, her mother, and Raymond moved north. They settled in Detroit, Michigan, where Parks's brother Sylvester resided. After spending a year there, Parks opted to take a job at the Hampton Institute in Virginia as a host at the Holly Tree Inn. The inn was a residence and guest house on the historically black college campus. Thinking that her husband and mother would find positions in Virginia, Parks took the job, but the job market in Virginia was not as favorable as she had hoped. Raymond and Leona remained in Detroit for the year Parks was in Virginia. She returned to Detroit in 1959 and took a position as a seamstress. She continued her work in the African American community, joining another civil rights group, the Southern Christian Leadership Conference (SCLC).

On March 1, 1965, Parks was hired as a staff assistant to U.S. Representative John

Conyers. She worked for him for twenty-three years. During her tenure with Conyers, Parks lost her brother, spouse, and mother. Raymond died in 1977 after a five-year struggle with cancer. Three months later, Sylvester met the same fate. In 1979, her mother, Leona, also died of cancer. Having had no children, Parks was left alone, except for distant relatives. Despite personal tragedy and failing health, she continued to work tirelessly for the rights of all people. In 1980 she joined her voice to those calling for an end to apartheid in South Africa and in 1988 opened the Rosa and Raymond Parks Institute for Self-Development, a career counseling center. In 1992 she published her autobiography, *Rosa Parks: My Story*, which was written for young readers as a history of the conditions that led to the Civil Rights movement and of her part in the movement.

In August of 1994, Parks was briefly hospitalized for injuries she sustained after a thief broke into her Detroit home, robbed her of $50, and assaulted her even though he recognized her. Community outrage over her assault led to the quick arrest of her assailant.

Beginning in the late 1990's, Parks took action against entertainers who questioned or sought to capitalize on her legacy. In 1998 the hip-hop singer OutKast used Parks's name for a song title without permission. Arguing that part of the song was disrespectful, she sued OutKast and LaFace Records one year later. A U.S. District Court upheld OutKast's right to use her name. A second lawsuit ended in a compromise in 2005; OutKast admitted no wrongdoing, but the record company paid Parks a cash settlement and agreed to sponsor education programs about her life. In 2002, African American activists Jesse Jackson and Al Sharpton called for a boycott on her behalf against the film *Barbershop*, in which a character claims that Parks did not deserve her fame because African Americans before her also had refused to make room for whites on buses.

Parks humbly accepted her status as a national treasure and symbol. Her many awards included the Spingarn Medal (1979), the Martin Luther King, Jr., Nonviolent Peace Prize (1980), and the Eleanor Roosevelt Women of Courage Award (1984). She possessed more than ten honorary degrees. On February 28, 1991, the Smithsonian Institution unveiled a bust of her. She continued to raise funds for the NAACP and was an active member of her church and of the SCLC. The SCLC sponsored the annual Rosa Parks Freedom Award.

City streets in Detroit and Montgomery were named for Parks. The African American Museum in Detroit unveiled her portrait in January of 1988, in time for her seventy-fifth birthday. She was honored in 1990 at the Kennedy Center in Washington, D.C., and in 1996, President Bill Clinton awarded her the Presidential Medal of Freedom. She received the Congressional Gold Medal in 1998 and was inducted into the International Women's Hall of Fame. In 2000, Alabama presented the first Governor's Medal of Honor for Extraordinary Courage and named her to the Alabama Academy of Honor, and the Rosa Parks Library and Museum opened at Troy State University in Montgomery.

Parks died on October 24, 2005, in her Detroit home after suffering from progressive dementia. Three days later, the cities of Detroit and Montgomery both cordoned off the front seats in their municipal buses with black ribbons, reserving them in her honor until her funeral. The AME church in Montgomery held a memorial service on

Parks, Rosa

October 30, while the nation's flags flew at half staff by order of President George W. Bush. Among the speakers was U.S. Secretary of State Condoleezza Rice, who credited Parks with making it possible for African Americans to rise to the highest levels of government service.

Parks's coffin was taken to the Capitol Rotunda in Washington, D.C., to lie in state. She was the first woman to be so honored. She was buried in Woodlawn Cemetery in Detroit on November 2.

Significance

Parks's legacy includes being hailed as the mother of the Civil Rights movement by the U.S. Congress. She received innumerable awards but maintained that she was unaccustomed to being a public person. By her own admission, she possessed more awards than she was able to count, yet she continued to accept all invitations to speak, lecture, or simply be honored until late in her life.

Parks remained a dignified individual who continued to influence society. She symbolized many things to many people. For those in the 1950's and 1960's, she ignited a movement that was long dormant, and for future generations her name, along with that of Martin Luther King, Jr., especially, became synonymous with the Civil Rights movement in the United States.

—*Annette Marks-Ellis*

Further Reading

Axelrod, Alan. *Profiles in Audacity: Great Decisions and How They Were Made*. New York: Sterling, 2006. Axelrod's purpose in this collection of biographical sketches is to investigate why and how people made history-altering decisions, and his short chapter on Parks discusses her act of conscience and how it turned into a cause célèbre for the Civil Rights movement in the United States.

Brinkley, Douglas. *Rosa Parks*. New York: Viking Books, 2000. Examines Parks's civil rights activism in the context of the turbulent times of the late 1950's and 1960's in a concise biography written for general readers. He emphasizes her quiet courage and humor.

Kohl, Herbert. *She Would Not Be Moved: How We Tell the Story of Rosa Parks and the Montgomery Bus Boycott*. New York: New Press, 2005. This spare, readable book argues that children's versions of the Rosa Parks story are often distorted; in particular, Kohl seeks to dispel myths that she was uneducated and poor. Also, he demonstrates the extent of careful planning and reflection on the part of both Parks and the African American community in their resistance to segregation.

Parks, Rosa. *The Autobiography of Rosa Parks*. New York: Dial Books, 1990. This autobiography is an insightful look into the life, times, and experiences of Parks. Through her own words, Parks reminisces about her childhood, family influences, marriage, and civil rights activism.

Robinson, Jo Ann Gibson. *The Montgomery Bus Boycott and the Women Who Started It*. Edited by David J. Garrow. Knoxville: University of Tennessee Press, 1987. This text focuses on the historic 381-day bus boycott. Discusses in great detail Parks's role in the action.

Patton, George S.

Williams, Donnie, with Wayne Greenhaw. *The Thunder of Angels: The Montgomery Bus Boycott and the People Who Broke the Back of Jim Crow*. Chicago: Lawrence Hill Books, 2006. Focuses on the courage and commitment of the average African American participating in the boycott and the importance of the figures who have been eclipsed in history by Parks and King.

GEORGE S. PATTON

" *Courage is fear holding on a minute longer.* "

Military leader

Though never a theoretician, Patton was a masterful military tactician who demonstrated the advantages of mobility and aggressive offensive action as essential elements of modern warfare.

Born: November 11, 1885; San Gabriel, California
Died: December 21, 1945; Heidelberg, Germany
Also known as: George Smith Patton (full name); Old Blood and Guts
Area of achievement: Military

EARLY LIFE

George S. Patton (PA-tuhn) was born to George Smith Patton, the descendant of a well-established Virginia family rooted in the culture of genteel southern aristocracy and steeped in the military tradition one commonly associates with that class, and Ruth Wilson, the daughter of B. D. Wilson, a California businessman who made a sizable fortune in the winery business. Owing to the affluence of his family, Patton's childhood was happy and largely carefree. He did suffer from dyslexia, and as a result his parents decided to enroll him in a private school just prior to his twelfth birthday. His classmates represented some of the wealthiest families in Southern California, but it was with the tradition of his paternal forebears that Patton's affinities lay.

The year 1902 proved to be critically important in Patton's early life. He had decided to pursue a career in the military and thus sought appointment to the United States Military Academy at West Point, New York. He also met Beatrice Banning Ayer, the daughter of Frederick Ayer, a wealthy industrialist from Massachusetts. She would later become his wife—and her marriage to him would on more than one occasion prove beneficial to Patton's career. There were no senatorial or congressional vacancies available at West Point in 1902, so Patton enrolled for one year at Virginia Military Institute, his father's alma mater. During that year, Patton's father worked untiringly to ensure his son's appointment to West Point, and his efforts were rewarded the following year.

At nineteen, Patton was tall—slightly over six feet—very athletic, and quite handsome. An arm injury prevented his playing varsity football, but he took up the broadsword, excelled in the high hurdles, and became a skilled horseman. In fact, three years

Patton, George S.

after graduating from West Point, he competed in the Modern Pentathlon event in the 1912 Stockholm Summer Olympics and finished fifth. Patton had two physical traits, however, which were of great concern to him—a high-pitched, almost squeaky voice, and a very fair and placid facial expression. To correct the latter he practiced in front of a mirror to develop what he called "my war face." There was little that could be done about his voice, but his frequent use of profanity may well have been designed to compensate for what he considered to be a flaw.

LIFE'S WORK

Patton was graduated from West Point in June, 1909. He married Beatrice in May of the following year, and in March, 1911, their first daughter, Beatrice, was born. Following his initial assignment at Fort Sheridan, near Chicago, Patton utilized family influence to secure a tour of duty at Fort Myer in Washington, D.C. Knowing that advancement in the peacetime army would be painfully slow, Patton actively sought to make contact with the "right people." His personal wealth and family connections certainly facilitated his efforts—a fact well illustrated in 1915, when he secured an assignment to a cavalry regiment at Fort Bliss, Texas, while the rest of his outfit went to the Philippines. It proved to be a particularly fortuitous assignment for Patton, who met and served as aide to General John J. Pershing when the latter was ordered into Mexico in 1916. Patton, who served with distinction in Mexico, regarded Pershing as a model soldier and continued to serve as his aide when the latter was chosen to head the American Expeditionary Force to France in 1917.

Once in France, Patton relinquished his staff position for a combat command. He was particularly interested in the tank, which promised to be the cavalry arm of the modern army. His dream of leading a tank unit in combat became a reality during the St. Mihiel campaign. During one engagement he was wounded, but he continued to direct his tanks to their targets by runners. When the newspapers ran the story of the "Hero of the Tanks" who directed his men while lying wounded in a shell hole, Patton became an instant hero. His actions won for him the Distinguished Service Cross and the Distinguished Service Medal. Later, he would admit to his father that he had always feared that he was a coward but had now begun to doubt it.

The peacetime army was a difficult place for Patton. He tried desperately to gain appointment as commandant to West Point and even sent a personal letter to Pershing in which he poignantly argued that he could transmit his ideal of "blood and gutts [*sic*]" to the cadets under his command. The argument failed, but the sobriquet remained for all time.

Denied West Point, Patton pursued the course one might expect of an ambitious young officer on the rise. In 1923, he attended the Command and General Staff College at Fort Leavenworth, Kansas, and in 1931 he entered the Army War College. During the intervening years, he served tours of duty in Hawaii and in Washington, D.C. His commanding officer in Hawaii described him as "invaluable in war . . . but a disturbing element in time of peace," a prescient evaluation, indeed. Patton lost his father in 1927 and his mother the following year. He consoled himself with the knowledge that he had not been a failure in their eyes and had achieved more, perhaps, than they had dreamed for him. Now he was free to fulfill his own destiny.

Patton, George S.

George S. Patton.
(Library of Congress)

In 1938, Patton was ordered back to Fort Myer to replace General Jonathan Wainwright. He was fifty-three years old at the time, and although the war clouds were gathering in Europe and Asia, it seemed likely that age alone might preclude his being considered for a possible combat command. Following the outbreak of war in Europe, however, two decisions by Army Chief of Staff George Marshall changed all that. The German Blitzkrieg convinced Marshall that the U.S. Army needed an armored force. He ordered the creation of two armored divisions and chose Patton to command the Second Armored Division—destined to win fame as "Hell on Wheels." Patton, obviously elated, wrote to his friend and army colleague, Terry Allen, "Now all we need is a juicy war."

Patton got his war and saw his first action in North Africa when, as part of Operation "Torch," his forces landed on the beaches of Morocco. Following the debacle at Kasserine Pass in Tunisia, he was ordered to assume command of the United States Second Corps. He chose Omar N. Bradley as his deputy and initiated a program of rigid training and discipline designed to redeem the valor of American arms. His subsequent victory over the Germans at Al-Guettar was therefore a source of great satisfaction to him. As initially planned, Patton gave up the Second Corps to Bradley to assume command of the Seventh Army that was to participate in the invasion of Sicily.

The Sicilian campaign was one of triumph and tragedy for Patton. Convinced that American forces had been assigned a subordinate role in the operation, he nevertheless managed to turn adversity into advantage by taking the historic town of Palermo and then beating General Bernard Law Montgomery and the vaunted British Eighth Army to Messina. Unfortunately, his shining victories were soon tarnished by the revelation of the famous slapping incident—actually two of them—wherein he struck two enlisted men who had been hospitalized for "battle fatigue." Patton's violent temper and his susceptibility to radical shifts in mood were well known. Some of his biographers have suggested that he may have suffered from what is known as subdural hematoma, the result of head injuries sustained in falls from and kicks by some of his horses. Whatever the cause, the results were devastating.

Bradley was chosen to command American ground forces preparing for the Normandy invasion, and it was not until the summer of 1944 that Patton was given command of the newly activated Third Army. Patton was determined to redeem himself, and his accomplishments as commander of the Third Army were truly remarkable. His forces liberated almost all of France north of the Loire River and were responsible for relieving the besieged 101st Airborne Division at Bastogne during the Ardennes Offensive. Patton considered the latter to be the Third Army's most brilliant operation and "the most outstanding achievement of this war."

As the war began to wind down, Patton expressed his fear of the "horrors of peace." His intemperate remarks expressing hatred of the Russians and contempt for the Jews were most embarrassing to the American High Command. Consequently, when the press subsequently reported that he had compared the Nazi Party to the Democratic and Republican parties, Dwight D. Eisenhower, Supreme Allied Commander in Europe, had little choice but to relieve him of command. On December 9, 1945, the day before he was to leave to return to the United States, the car in which he was riding slammed into a truck. Patton suffered severe lacerations, a broken nose, and two fractured vertebrae. At best it was feared that he would be a semi-invalid, but that was not to be. He died on December 21, 1945, and was buried in Hamm, Luxembourg.

Significance

The name Patton is and perhaps always will be synonymous with war—particularly World War II. No doubt Patton would have relished that association. He regarded war as the greatest of human endeavors and the battlefield as a place of honor. Patton idolized the great military leaders of the past—Hannibal, Caesar, and Napoleon—and spent much of his life preparing himself to be a worthy follower of the tradition they represented. Like them, he would one day lead great numbers of men into battle. It was his destiny.

Patton achieved his destiny, though he did so late in life. World War II was his stage, and though he occupied it for only a brief period of time and never in more than a supporting role, he created a legend. He played to an appreciative audience as a tenacious, innovative, and daring battlefield commander. Had he lived, years of peace might have dimmed the luster of his star. Death intervened to prevent that, and before the applause faded, Patton was born into immortality.

Patton, George S.

His death prompted a flood of praise, most of which paid tribute to his skills as a great fighting general. Perhaps the accolade he would have appreciated most, however, came from a former adversary, Field Marshal Gerd von Rundstedt, who, in a postwar interview with American military personnel, said simply, "Patton was your best."

—*Kirk Ford, Jr.*

FURTHER READING

Axelrod, Alan. *Patton: A Biography*. New York: Palgrave Macmillan, 2006. Brief but solid biography focusing on the contradictions in Patton's personality.

Blumenson, Martin. *Patton: The Man Behind the Legend, 1885-1945*. New York: William Morrow, 1985. Blumenson's skills as a writer and military historian are evident in this biography. The author reminds his readers that the Patton legend was molded from human clay.

————, ed. *The Patton Papers: 1885-1940*. 2 vols. Boston: Houghton Mifflin, 1972. Blumenson's judicious selection from the voluminous Patton Papers allows the reader to see Patton as he saw himself and to know his fears, failures, strengths, and weaknesses.

Farago, Ladislas. *The Last Days of Patton*. New York: McGraw-Hill, 1981. Focusing on the events surrounding Patton's tragic death in December, 1945, Farago attempts a more detailed investigation of the incident than was conducted at the time.

————. *Patton: Ordeal and Triumph*. New York: I. Obolensky, 1963. Considered by many to be the definitive biography of George Patton, this impressive work was the basis for the critically acclaimed film *Patton*, released in 1970.

Hirshson, Stanley P. *General Patton: A Soldier's Life*. New York: HarperCollins, 2002. Exceptionally good biography based on extensive research and offering a balanced account of Patton's life, career, and personality from every conceivable angle.

Patton, George S. *War as I Knew It*. New York: Houghton Mifflin, 1947. This work is best when viewed as a critique of the role of the battlefield general and the problems associated with high command. As military history it suffers from too much detail.

Reynolds, Michael. *Monty and Patton: Two Paths to Victory*. Staplehurt, England: Spellmount, 2005. Compares and contrasts the personalities, lives, and military careers of Patton and British general Bernard Law Montgomery.

Royle, Trevor. *Patton: Old Blood and Guts*. London: Weidenfeld and Nicholson, 2005. Biography tracing Patton's life and military career.

Showalter, Dennis. *Patton and Rommel: Men of War in the Twentieth Century*. New York: Berkley Caliber, 2005. Showalter, a distinguished historian of World War II, provides a thoroughly researched and well-written dual biography of Patton and Erwin Rommel.

ALICE PAUL

❝ *There will never be a new world order until women are a part of it.* **❞**

Suffragist

The leader of the radical wing of the woman suffrage movement that helped pass the Nineteenth Amendment, Paul also introduced the Equal Rights Amendment.

Born: January 11, 1885; Moorestown, New Jersey
Died: July 9, 1977; Moorestown, New Jersey
Areas of achievement: Women's rights; civil rights

EARLY LIFE

Born to a wealthy Quaker (Society of Friends) family, Alice Paul entered the women's movement at a very early age. Her father, William Paul, served as president of the Burlington County Trust Company, and her mother, Tacie Parry Paul, was clerk of the Moorestown Friends' Meeting. Both strongly encouraged young Alice's interest in equal rights.

Alice's early life focused almost entirely on her Quaker heritage. The Friends created a humane, optimistic religion during the seventeenth century, and they were one of the few sects that preached equality between the sexes. The fact that the Quakers allowed women to become missionaries and ministers created a unique religious environment. Although not much is known about Alice Paul's childhood, many scholars agree that it was the egalitarian, flexible, and tolerant nature of Quaker society that allowed her to develop as perhaps America's greatest radical feminist.

Although both of Alice's parents encouraged her independent attitudes, her mother served as her chief mentor. Alice's father died before she reached adulthood. Tacie Paul was one of many Quaker women (such as Lucretia Mott) who was involved in the nineteenth century American woman suffrage movement.

Alice followed in her mother's footsteps, enrolling in the Moorestown Quaker school and later graduating from another Friends' institution, Swarthmore College. During these formative years, Alice also used Lucretia Mott as her role model. Mott, one of the founding mothers of the American woman suffrage movement, helped organize the first women's rights convention in 1848 at Seneca Falls, New York, where she and Elizabeth Cady Stanton wrote the Declaration of Sentiments. Alice began her great crusade for equal rights as a graduate student at England's Woodbridge Quaker College and the London School of Economics, where she joined Emmeline, Christabel, and Sylvia Pankhurst, the radical British feminists who taught her the aggressive tactics that later produced American congressional support for the Nineteenth Amendment.

During Paul's years in Britain, she formed a close, lifelong friendship with another American suffragist, Lucy Burns, who also belonged to the Pankhursts' Women's Social and Political Union. Nearing the end of this political apprenticeship, Paul resolved to bring confrontational feminism to the United States.

Paul, Alice

LIFE'S WORK
When Paul returned to the United States in 1910, she found Susan B. Anthony's bill granting women the right to vote still stalled in a congressional committee. Even though Anthony had submitted her bill in 1896, American women still lacked "The Franchise." Paul concluded that the situation in America called for drastic measures.

Paul persuaded the National American Woman Suffrage Association (NAWSA) to allow her to coordinate its lobbying effects in Congress and promptly organized a huge march on the White House backed by a suffrage army estimated at 500,000 people. Her dramatic entrance into Washington politics duly impressed the new president, Woodrow Wilson, whose inauguration occurred the next day. Immediately after the opening of the new Congress, Paul employed her aggressive tactics on the returning politicians to secure the Anthony Bill's release from committee to the floor of the House of Representatives. It would have been an overwhelming task for any lobbyist. Given Paul's extreme shyness, introverted Quaker personality, and lack of rhetorical skills, the bill that Congress passed, the president signed, and the states ratified became a signal triumph for her organizational genius.

During World War I, Paul quickly became the radical leader of the feminist movement. First, she changed NAWSA's lobbying focus from the states to the national legislature. She became a public relations expert at a time in history when such experts were rare. Paul's training in British circles enabled her to overcome opposition from the Washington, D.C., police, who wanted her marchers to parade on Sixteenth Street in front of the foreign embassies (instead of picketing the White House). She stood her ground, insisting that the ladies must be seen by the president and First Lady. She won the debate—the first of many such victories resulting in the ratification of the Nineteenth Amendment to the Constitution.

In 1917, when the United States declared war on Germany and President Wilson declared that the "world must be made safe for democracy," Paul decided that the time was right for another parade and picketing of the White House. "Why should American women support the war to make the world safe for democracy," her pickets emphatically asked, "when they have no democracy since they cannot vote?" When the White House called the police, Paul and her loyal "soldiers," facing arrest and imprisonment, followed tactics learned in England and refused to eat. Force-fed by law enforcement officials afraid of the possible public outcry produced by the hospitalization or death of a suffragist, Paul turned that tactic as well to the advantage of her cause.

Not everyone in the suffrage movement approved of Paul's tactics. More radical than the mainstream NAWSA's moderate leadership, she organized the National Woman's Party in 1913. The Quaker activist incorporated the party on September 20, 1918, but kept it largely inactive until the passage of the Nineteenth Amendment became a certainty.

After the Congress and the states approved woman suffrage, Paul reactivated the National Woman's Party in 1921. Although most women perhaps believed that equal rights would result automatically from the ratification of the Nineteenth Amendment, Paul and her colleagues remained unconvinced.

The principal philosophical ideas Paul wrote into the National Woman's Party platform reflected her skepticism that voting rights would lead to equal rights. Women, she argued, would no longer constitute the "governed half" of the American people. In the future, they would participate equally in all aspects of life.

The National Woman's Party organized most of the serious agitation—such as jail-ins, marches, fasts, and picketing—that occurred before the ratification of the Nineteenth Amendment. When ratification occurred, the more moderate NAWSA transformed itself into the League of Women Voters. Paul, however, believed that the battle would not be over until equal rights had been achieved for all Americans, regardless of sex.

For Paul, true freedom extended far beyond the simple attainment of suffrage. She single-mindedly pursued the goal of removing all legal obstacles for women throughout the United States. After careful consideration and examination of the tactics and strategies that won the battle for woman suffrage, she concluded that the only means to legal equality was the passage of a federal Equal Rights Amendment (ERA). This was an extremely radical idea when Paul introduced it in 1923 at Seneca Falls, New York, where the first women's rights convention had been held in 1848. The central point she

Alice Paul.
(Library of Congress)

expressed focused on the philosophy that women would never be subjugated again "in law or in custom, but shall in every way be on an equal plane in rights." In this way, her Woman's Party gave birth to the Equal Rights Amendment.

Paul's proposed amendment split the women's movement. Some women believed that voting rights naturally would produce equality, making a second amendment unnecessary. Since the ERA radically redefined power relationships between men and women, even stronger opposition than originally existed to the Nineteenth Amendment developed within the male establishment.

Critics dismissed Paul as either a harmless but misguided "bleeding heart liberal" or a dangerously deranged radical. Democrats and Republicans alike warned the public against being receptive to her ideas. As the nation turned more conservative during the 1920's, with the election of President Warren Harding and the widespread repudiation of progressivism, the popularity of Paul and her party declined, and she did not resurface as a significant force until the reintroduction of the ERA in 1972.

Following Paul's creation of the National Woman's Party and the introduction of the Equal Rights Amendment, the popularity of women's rights declined in the United States during the Depression of the 1930's. As the fight for jobs excluded more and more American women, Paul took her campaign to Europe, where she founded the World's Woman's Party. Since Paul always expressed strong opposition to the League of Nations' failure to allow female political participation, she continued her lobbying efforts on behalf of women until the organization collapsed during World War II. When the League gave way to the United Nations, Paul played a key role in introducing an equal rights provision in the preamble to the U.N. charter.

Following Paul's European experiment, she returned to the United States, where she resumed her efforts to pass the new, revamped Equal Rights Amendment. During the late 1960's, Paul campaigned against the Vietnam War while working for the ERA. Still marching and fighting for equal rights at the age of eighty-five, she finally surrendered to old age and moved to a Quaker nursing home in her native Moorestown, New Jersey, where America's great radical feminist died on July 9, 1977, at the age of ninety-two. She never lived to see the passage of the amendment to which she had devoted her entire life.

Significance

Few leaders in the politics of women's liberation were more significant than Alice Paul. Her longevity and radical proclivities outdistanced others who garnered more press and historical notice. For sixty-five years, from 1912 until her death in 1977, Paul stood ready to give her best to the cause of equal rights.

Despite her reputation for radical measures, Paul was not an abrasive personality. Although some thought her insensitive, perhaps what they perceived was the absentmindedness of an intellectual who received her Ph.D. in sociology in 1912, before she launched her suffrage career. She understood both the politics and the economics of equal rights. The real struggle, she once argued, would not be won in state or even national legislatures. Women would have to win economically before they could win politically. Political forms would crystallize, she hypothesized, only when women had gained economic power. More important, she emphasized that having money was not enough. Knowing how to use money to attain political ends was the key.

Paul was not as well known as other feminists—Susan B. Anthony, Lucretia Mott, and Elizabeth Cady Stanton. Her strategies and tactics, however, have since been considered to have been paramount in obtaining the Nineteenth Amendment to the Constitution. Although she died without realizing victory in her struggle to institute the Equal Rights Amendment, many of the goals she sought came to pass nevertheless, partly because of the half-century of supreme effort she exerted to realize her great dream.

—*J. Christopher Schnell*

FURTHER READING

Barker-Benfield, G. J., and Catherine Clinton, eds. *Portraits of American Women: From Settlement to the Present.* New York: St. Martin's Press, 1991. A collection of scholarly articles on significant American women from Pocahontas to Betty Friedan. The article on Alice Paul by Christine A. Lunardini presents a particularly effective analysis.

Becker, Susan D. *The Origins of the Equal Rights Amendment: American Feminism Between the Wars.* Westport, Conn.: Greenwood Press, 1981. An analysis of Paul's postsuffrage role in reorganizing the women's movement along the international lines of the World's Woman's Party.

Butler, Amy E. *Two Paths to Equality: Alice Paul and Ethel M. Smith in the ERA Debate, 1921-1929.* Albany: State University of New York Press, 2002. Paul and Smith were proponents of equal rights for women, but they had different views about the best way to attain those rights. This book explains their differences and its impact on the cause of women's rights.

Flexner, Eleanor. *Century of Struggle: The Woman's Rights Movement in the United States.* Rev. ed. Cambridge, Mass.: The Belknap Press of Harvard University Press, 1975. A classic history of the women's movement (highlighting Alice Paul's role) by one of the great feminist historians.

Gallagher, Robert S. "I Was Arrested, of Course . . ." *American Heritage* 25, no. 2 (February, 1974): 16-24, 92-94. A fascinating and penetrating interview conducted with Paul three years before her death.

Irwin, Inez Haynes. *The Story of Alice Paul and the National Woman's Party.* Fairfax, Va.: Denlinger's, 1977. This is the primary history of the National Woman's Party.

Morgan, David. *Suffragists and Democrats: The Politics of Woman Suffrage in America.* East Lansing: Michigan State University Press, 1972. This is a narrow British interpretation of the politics of the American woman suffrage movement.

Stevens, Doris. *Jailed for Freedom.* New York: Boni & Liveright, 1920. Reprint. Freeport, N.Y.: Books for Libraries Press, 1971. This primary source focuses on the militant feminists who campaigned for the vote between 1913 and 1919. The work includes a valuable chapter on "General Alice Paul."

ROBERT EDWIN PEARY

> " *I knew immediately when I had reached the North Pole, because in one step the north wind became a south wind.* "

Explorer

After several unsuccessful attempts, Peary became the first white person, along with explorer Matthew A. Henson, an African American, to reach the geographic North Pole.

Born: May 6, 1856; Cresson, Pennsylvania
Died: February 20, 1920; Washington, D.C.
Area of achievement: Exploration

EARLY LIFE

Robert Edwin Peary (PEER-ree) was born in Cresson, Pennsylvania, a backwoods farm community. His New England forebears were Frenchmen (Peary is an American modification of the Gallic Pierre) who had made barrel staves for their livelihood. His father died when he was three, and his mother, Mary Peary, was forced to raise her only child on meager resources.

Peary's mother was extremely possessive and forced her son to dress in girlish clothes. He was nicknamed Bertie and was regarded as a sissy by his peers. He would spend the remainder of his life attempting to compensate for his tortured early years.

Peary studied civil engineering at Bowdoin College in Brunswick, Maine, and resolved to outdo his rivals. He became active in sports, drama, and debate. Symbolically, he dressed up as Sir Lancelot at his college fraternity masquerade party. For graduation exercises, he composed an epic poem in which he imagined himself to be Sir Roland.

LIFE'S WORK

Peary received a degree in civil engineering in 1877 from Bowdoin College. After his graduation, he served as a draftsman for the United States Coast and Geodetic Survey. While in that position, he applied for and received a commission in the Civil Engineer Corps of the U.S. Navy in 1881.

In 1886, Peary borrowed five hundred dollars from his mother, took a summer leave of absence from the Navy, gathered a crew, and embarked on what would be the first of eight expeditions to the Arctic. Peary, along with a Danish skiing companion, made a one-hundred-mile journey over the inland ice from the southwest coast of Greenland. The purpose of his first expedition was to acquire some fame by discovering what existed on north Greenland's ice cap: Was Greenland an island continent, or did it, as some geographers believed, thrust its ice cap right up to the North Pole? This expedition accomplished little. However, Peary quickly learned what he needed to do in the future, and when his leave of absence expired, he returned to duty in Nicaragua with an obsession to return to the Arctic and to continue his quest for fame.

Peary's second expedition was delayed until 1891. In 1888, he returned to his Navy job on the Nicaraguan canal route for what would be a two-year tour. That same year, Peary married Josephine Diebitsch, the daughter of a professor at the Smithsonian Institution. She was a tall, spirited woman whose appearance closely resembled his mother's. Peary's mother moved in with the newlyweds. This uncomfortable arrangement lasted a year. Josephine soon realized that her husband was really married to his Arctic adventures; to solve her dilemma, she accompanied him on his second expedition. By this point, Peary had become skillful in getting what he needed to continue his explorations. He pulled strings and used his gifted oratorical skills and enormous self-confidence to obtain ten thousand dollars from financial backers and an eighteen-month leave of absence from the Navy.

The stern, blue-eyed Peary sported a reddish-blond mustache; despite his serious nature, his overall appearance resembled that of the walrus-like Ben Turpin, the silent-screen comedian. His face was already wrinkled from his time in Nicaragua and from exposure to Arctic blizzards and sun. His six-foot, sturdy physique with broad shoulders and narrow hips, his finely tuned body, which had already passed its thirty-fifth birthday, was ready for the mental and physical challenges ahead.

For his second trip to the Arctic, which began in 1891, his strategy was to take with him a party of six "campaigners," including Frederick Cook (a doctor), and a seventh person, his wife, Josephine. Josephine attracted much attention from the newspapers: She would be the first white woman to winter at such a high altitude in Greenland. Once in position, Peary planned to conduct a "white march" over the great ice of northeast Greenland and to claim for the United States a highway to the North.

On June 6, 1891, the *Kite* sailed from Brooklyn, destined for the northwest coast of Greenland. Cook, nicknamed the Sigmund Freud of the Arctic, proved to be a helpful passenger; his obsession to reach the North Pole went back to his own deprived childhood, during which he won prizes in geography and worked in his free time to help support his poor family. To pay for medical school, he had worked nights as a door-to-door milkman.

The *Kite* was in the process of ramming its way through the ice of Baffin Bay when Peary broke his lower right leg by striking it against the iron tiller. Cook quickly set the leg in splints, and Josephine relieved Peary's pain with morphine and whiskey. Peary would later praise Cook as a helpful and tireless worker who was patient and cool under pressure.

On July 30, 1891, the party landed on the foot of the cliffs in Inglefield Gulf, immediately north of Thule, the Greenland military base of the United States. With his right leg strapped to a plank, Peary continued to demonstrate leadership as he carried a tent ashore and supervised the construction of a prefabricated, two-room cabin named Red Cliff House. As the party settled in for the long polar night, the Etah Eskimos flocked from hundreds of miles away to see the first white woman to come to their country.

Peary soon began to recover from his broken leg. Josephine recorded in her journal that, within three months, he had discarded his crutches and had begun running footraces with Cook to build up his leg. The Eskimos watched as Peary took snow baths in subzero temperatures. To demonstrate his endurance to the Eskimos, he wore a hooded parka and caribou socks and slept in the open all night without a sleeping bag.

Peary realized that, to endure in the Arctic, he would have to adopt the survival techniques of the Eskimos. He learned from the Eskimos that expeditions required dog teams, sleighs, fatty meat for nourishment, and light fur garments. However, he treated the Eskimos, who would continually come to his aid, as subhumans. He rejected the hospitality of their igloos and refused to learn their language, in contrast to Cook and Matthew A. Henson (1866-1955), his exploring partner and, some claim, the first nonindigenous person to reach the North Pole just before Peary in 1909.

During May of 1892, Peary set out eastward, on his white march across the ice cap of north Greenland. Initially, the Eskimos and Cook accompanied him. Cook had gone ahead as a forward scout. When the two men rendezvoused, Peary ordered Cook to return to look after Josephine. The Eskimos feared that the evil spirit Tormarsuk presided in the interior, and they departed with Cook.

Peary and Eivind Astrup, a Norwegian ski champion, proceeded. In sixty-five days, the two men completed the unbelievable distance of six hundred miles over unknown terrain. On July 4, Peary named an easterly inlet Independence Bay, planted two U.S. flags, and held a small celebration with the Norwegian skier. After they had rested, they turned around to retrace the six hundred miles back.

The trip would bring Peary fame, yet he had made costly cartographic errors that would eventually cause the death of a Danish scientist who attempted to confirm Peary's discoveries. From Navy Cliff, Peary had believed that he had seen the Arctic Ocean, but he had actually been one hundred miles from the coast. Independence Bay had not been a bay but rather a deep fjord, and his conclusion that Peary Channel marked the northern boundary of the Greenland mainland was erroneous. In 1915, the U.S. government withdrew Peary's maps of Greenland, and Peary's reckless, unscientific behavior became legend.

After the journey, Peary raised twenty thousand dollars on the lecture circuit. Cook resigned from Peary's organization when Peary refused to allow him to publish ethnological findings on the Eskimos. No one in the group was allowed to publish anything, except in a book bearing Peary's name as author.

Peary's next expedition included a pregnant Josephine, a nurse, an artist, eight burros, and a flock of carrier pigeons. On September 12, 1893, Josephine gave birth to the first white child to be born at that latitude. The Pearys' nine-pound daughter was named Marie Ahnighito. Her middle name came from the Eskimo woman who had chewed bird skins to make diapers for the blue-eyed child, nicknamed the Snow Baby.

The birth of the child was the only happy event of this expedition, as discontent broke out among the crew. Peary's drive and relentless nature began to cause problems. Astrup had a nervous breakdown and committed suicide on a glacier. Most of the remainder of the crew could no longer tolerate Peary, and they took the next supply ship back to the United States, as did Josephine, her child, and her nurse.

On future expeditions, Eskimos would lose their lives for Peary; Peary himself lost eight of his toes to frostbite. Now nearly completely disabled, he simply stuffed his boots with tin-can lids to protect his stumps. Nothing short of death itself would stop Peary's single-minded quest.

Peary's first serious attempt to reach the North Pole began during the four-year expedition starting in 1898. Henson, who was African American, had mastered the skills of Arctic exploration and was the only member from the original crew. The 1898-1902

Robert Edwin Peary.
(Library of Congress)

mission failed to get to the North Pole, but Peary was able in 1902 to travel to eighty-four degrees, seventeen minutes north. On his seventh mission, in 1905-1906, Peary reached eighty-seven degrees, six minutes north, only 174 nautical miles from the North Pole, before having to retreat.

In 1908, Peary, though disabled, aging, and weatherbeaten, knew that he had the physical and mental resources for one final attempt to reach the North Pole. It would be his eighth and final trip. Several millionaires in the Peary Arctic Club pledged $350,000 for the final outing, and *The New York Times* paid $4,000 in advance for the exclusive story. The National Geographic Society of Washington and the American Museum of Natural History in New York bestowed their prestige on him. The Navy once again released him with pay after President Theodore Roosevelt personally intervened.

In 1905, at a cost of $100,000, Peary had built, according to his own design, a schooner-rigged steamship named the *Roosevelt*. He took six men with him, the most loyal being Henson, who had nursed Peary and had saved his life on numerous occasions. A remarkable man, he had mastered everything for the mission, including the language of the Eskimos, who worshiped him as the Maktok Kabloonna (black white man). Both Peary and Cook, who was involved in a rival expedition, believed that the best companion for such an outing was a nonwhite person, since whites, ultimately, could not seem to get along.

The flag-decorated *Roosevelt* got under way from New York Harbor on the steamy afternoon of July 6, 1908. At Oyster Bay, Long Island, President Roosevelt came aboard and shook hands with every member of the crew. At Sydney, Nova Scotia, Peary's wife Josephine, fourteen-year-old Marie, and five-year-old Robert, Jr., once again bade farewell to Peary. At Anoatok, on the northwest coast of Greenland, the Eskimos reported to Peary that Cook had already passed westward on his march to the Big Nail.

Peary ordered Captain Bob Bartlett to begin ramming the *Roosevelt* through the ice packs and to head toward Cape Sheridan, the proposed wintering berth, which was 350 miles away. On September 5, the *Roosevelt* had reached its goal of eighty-two degrees, thirty minutes latitude—a record north for a ship under its own steam.

Cape Sheridan became home base. Ninety miles northwest lay Cape Columbia, which Peary decided would be the ideal jumping-off spot. Four hundred and thirteen miles of Arctic Ocean ice separated Cape Columbia from Peary's goal, the North Pole, the Big Nail, ninety degrees north latitude.

Peary was ready for the final chance to realize the greatest dream of his life. On the appointed Sunday morning, twenty-four men, 133 dogs, and nineteen sleighs departed. The expedition was broken up into five detachments: Each one would break trail, build igloos, and deposit supplies in rotation. Peary would follow the group from the rear as each exhausted team rotated back toward land.

On April 1, Bartlett took a navigational fix and determined a reading of eighty-seven degrees, forty-seven minutes north latitude. He took no longitudinal reading, which made his determination dubious, but Peary was convinced that he was 133 nautical miles on a direct beeline to the North Pole. Peary then surprised and disappointed Bartlett and ordered him home. The only qualified nautically trained witness who might verify the North Pole sighting finally departed.

Peary continued on with Henson, four Eskimos, five sleighs, and forty dogs. On April 6, 1909, at ten in the morning, after a labor of twenty years, Peary became the first white man to reach the North Pole. (Henson also reached the Pole, possibly before Peary.) Once there, Peary draped himself in the American flag. Henson later recalled in his memoirs that his fifty-three-year-old commander was a deadweight "cripple," a mere shadow of the civil engineer in Nicaragua. One of the Eskimos remarked, "There is nothing here. Just ice!"

SIGNIFICANCE

En route from his last mission to the Arctic, Peary learned that Cook had claimed to reach the Pole on April 21, 1908, nearly a year before Peary. Later, Cook was so hounded by the press and others that he took to wearing disguises and left the country for a year. When he returned, he spoke in his defense on the lecture circuit. Ultimately, his claims were disregarded, but the controversy was kept alive by the press because the dispute made a good story. Peary's claims were not scientifically documented. The National Geographic Society did a hasty, perfunctory examination of Peary's trunk of instruments in the middle of the night in a railway baggage station and agreed that Peary had discovered the North Pole.

Peary, Robert Edwin

In the 1930's, Gordon Hayes, an English geographer, scrupulously and fairly examined Cook's and Peary's claims. He concluded that neither one had got within one hundred miles of the North Pole. Nevertheless, Peary is credited with reaching the North Pole, attaining the fame he so desperately desired. After much lobbying and a congressional hearing, Peary was promoted to rear admiral. He served for a year as chair of the National Committee on Coast Defense by Air during World War I. He retired and received a pension of sixty-five hundred dollars a year. He had achieved his goal, and the United States and the world recognized him for the twenty years of supreme sacrifices he had made.

Shortly after his return from the Arctic, Peary began suffering from anemia. On February 20, 1920, he died from that affliction at the age of sixty-four. He was buried with full honors at Arlington National Cemetery in Washington, D.C. His casket was draped with the remnants of the American flag with which he had covered himself as he stood atop the world on the North Pole. The National Geographic Society constructed a huge globe of white granite, representing the Earth and inscribed with Peary's motto, "I shall find a way or make one," and a legend proclaiming him "discoverer of the North Pole."

—*John Harty*

FURTHER READING

Brendle, Anna. "Profile: African-American North Pole Explorer Matthew Henson." *National Geographic News*, January 15, 2003. A brief article on Henson's career and accomplishments as an Arctic explorer. Announces Henson's posthumous receipt of the Hubbard Medal, the National Geographic Society's highest honor, in 2000.

Cook, Frederick A. *My Attainment of the Pole*. New York: Polar, 1911. Cook's own descriptions of his expedition. Some claim that it was a hoax, and others state that he only got to within one hundred miles of the North Pole.

Diebitsch-Peary, Josephine. *My Arctic Journal: A Year Among Ice-Fields and Eskimos*. New York: Contemporary, 1893. Peary's wife gives her account. Includes "The Great White Journey."

Henderson, Bruce. *True North: Peary, Cook, and the Race to the Pole*. New York: W. W. Norton, 2005. Recounts the rivalry between Peary and Frederick Cook, who both claimed they were the first to reach the North Pole. Peary is portrayed as an obsessive fame seeker who committed underhanded acts to undermine Cook's claim.

Henson, Matthew A. *A Black Explorer at the North Pole*. Foreword by Robert E. Peary. Introduction by Booker T. Washington. 1912. Reprint. New introduction by Susan A. Kaplan. Lincoln: University of Nebraska Press, 1989. Henson's account of the journey. Henson began his life in poverty, attained fame, and worked as a civil servant, retiring on a pension. He was an active and distinguished member of the New York Explorers Club.

Hunt, William R. *To Stand at the Pole: The Dr. Cook-Admiral Peary North Pole Controversy*. New York: Stein and Day, 1982. Contains a detailed account of the controversy over which person (Cook or Peary) got to the North Pole first. The mystery is not answered. Contains an excellent bibliography.

Pershing, John J.

Peary, Robert E. *The North Pole: Its Discovery in 1909 Under the Auspices of the Peary Arctic Club.* 1910. New ed. New York: Cooper Square Press, 2001. Peary wrote three books—the others are *Nearest the Pole* (1907) and *Northward over the "Great Ice"* (1898). *The North Pole* is Peary's own account of reaching the Pole. Exciting as an account but criticized by others. Includes a foreword by President Theodore Roosevelt.

Rasky, Frank. *Explorers of the North: The North Pole or Bust.* New York: McGraw-Hill Ryerson, 1977. Chapters 10 and 11 are devoted to Peary. A human account of the explorer, faults and all. Short, readable, extremely detailed report of the important events. Good starting point.

Rawlins, Dennis. *Peary at the North Pole: Fact or Fiction?* New York: Luce, 1973. Argues that Peary never made it to the North Pole.

JOHN J. PERSHING

" A competent leader can get efficient service from poor troops ... an incapable leader can demoralize the best of troops. "

Military leader

A career soldier, Pershing was ready when called on to lead the American Expeditionary Force to Europe in World War I, helping preserve democracy in the first global conflict.

Born: January 13, 1860; Laclede, Missouri
Died: July 15, 1948; Washington, D.C.
Also known as: John Joseph Pershing (full name); Black Jack
Area of achievement: Military

EARLY LIFE

The oldest of John Pershing and Elizabeth Pershing's nine children, John Joseph Pershing (PUR-shing) was born in the year preceding the outbreak of the Civil War. Tensions ran high in this midwestern state, and Pershing's father suffered for his staunch support of the Union, which he served as a sutler. Pershing early aspired to a career in law, and initially his goal appeared attainable. A brief period of postwar prosperity, however, soon gave way to virtual bankruptcy for the family, and when Pershing's father gave up storekeeping to work as a traveling salesperson, John took to farming and odd jobs. One of them, as janitor for the nearby black school in Prairie Mound, led to a permanent position as a teacher there. In 1882, he attended the Normal School in Kirksville, obtaining a bachelor's degree in elementary didactics. That same year, he took the test for appointment to the United States Military Academy and received a nomination. To meet the age limitation for entrants, he changed his birth month from January to September.

Pershing, John J.

After a month in a Highland Falls, New York, preparatory school, Pershing enrolled with 129 other young men at West Point. Somewhat older than his classmates, he commanded their respect, holding his five foot ten inch frame ramrod-straight and casting a stern glance at the world from steel-gray eyes; the mustache and silvered hair would come later. Pershing proved an adequate student and a first-rate leader, whom schoolmates elected class president each year. In each of his four years, he held the top position for cadets, culminating in his selection as first captain of the Corps of Cadets in his final year. In 1886, he was graduated and commissioned a second lieutenant of cavalry.

LIFE'S WORK
A career as a soldier did not hold great promise in the late nineteenth century. Pershing spent his first years with the Sixth Cavalry, fighting in the last of the Indian Wars. Later, he commanded a troop in the Tenth Cavalry, an all-black unit with whom Pershing gained unusually good rapport. His service on the frontier was broken by a tour at the University of Nebraska, where he transformed a slovenly cadet corps into one of the country's finest detachments of college trainees. During his off-duty time, he earned a law degree and gave serious thought to resigning. In 1898, he returned to his alma mater as a tactical officer, instructing West Point cadets in the fundamentals of soldiering. In that year, troubles with Spain over Cuba erupted into a war, and Pershing sought duty with the force being organized to invade the Caribbean island.

Unable to go to Cuba as a cavalryman, Pershing obtained a temporary assignment as a quartermaster. In that position, he gained important insight into the follies of the army's system for providing supplies to its line units. That lesson was stored away for future use in Europe during the first global conflict of the twentieth century.

Pershing was promoted to captain in 1901, fifteen years after he was commissioned. Because promotions were based on seniority, he expected little further advancement. The early years of the new century saw him in the Philippines, leading American soldiers in a pacification effort against nationals who resisted the United States government's efforts to bring Western-style democracy to the islands. Pershing earned a reputation as a successful negotiator with Philippine leaders, and his remarkable march around Lake Lanao was noted not only in the Philippines but also in Washington, D.C.

A tour on the newly formed general staff gave Pershing the opportunity to meet the woman he would eventually wed: Frances Warren, daughter of Wyoming senator Francis E. Warren, a Republican and member of the Senate's military committee. Pershing and Frances were married in January, 1905, and left almost immediately for Japan, where Pershing was to serve as a military observer during the Russo-Japanese War.

Then, in 1906, Pershing's efforts on behalf of his country were generously rewarded. In an unusual move, President Theodore Roosevelt nominated the captain for promotion to brigadier general, allowing him to jump over almost one thousand officers senior to him and bypass the field grade ranks (major, lieutenant colonel, and colonel). The new general spent much of the next decade in the Philippines, returning to the United States for assignment at the Presidio, San Francisco, in 1914. Almost im-

Pershing, John J.

John J. Pershing.
(Library of Congress)

mediately, Pershing left for El Paso, Texas, to organize a force that would invade Mexico to capture the bandit Pancho Villa.

While Pershing was in Texas, his family, which now included three girls and a boy, remained in California. On August 26, 1915, tragedy struck the Pershings. Coals ignited wax on the ground floor of their wood-frame quarters, and Frances and the three girls perished in the ensuing fire; only Pershing's son, Warren, was saved. With stoic courage, Pershing made his way to California, accompanied the bodies to Wyoming for burial, then returned to his troops on the Mexican border.

The Punitive Expedition that Pershing commanded from 1915 to 1917 was ostensibly organized in retaliation for raids conducted by Villa within the U.S. city of Columbus, New Mexico. Pershing's force of twenty thousand men traversed the Mexican desert for months, while political negotiations continued between President Woodrow Wilson and the various factions trying to seize permanent control of the government in Mexico. The force withdrew in 1917, when the war in Europe forced Wilson to shift his attention to that region of the world.

Pershing, John J.

In May, 1917, Pershing was notified that he had been selected to organize an American force for duty with the Allied forces in Europe. Hastily assembling a small staff, he traveled to England and then to France, where he spent a year shaping a force that would ultimately consist of more than one million Americans. Handpicked subordinates wrestled with problems of obtaining supplies, coordinating troop movements, quartering the divisions and separate units, feeding and clothing the newly arrived recruits, and training men to survive as individuals and fight as units. Pershing's time was occupied in constant inspections and in wrangling with Allied commanders, especially marshals Philippe Pétain of France and Douglas Haig of England, both of whom wanted to detail small American units for duty with French and British units already employed on line against the Germans. Convinced that Americans should fight in American units, commanded by American officers, Pershing held out against their constant requests. Only reluctantly did he finally commit some battalions of the First Infantry Division for duty with the French. His strategy paid off in the late summer of 1918, when the American First Army achieved smashing victories against the Germans along the Saint-Mihiel salient and then in the Meuse-Argonne area of France.

The entrance of American forces into the war helped deal the final death blow to Germany's hopes for conquest. In November, 1918, the Germans agreed to the terms of surrender, and Pershing was faced with the problems of dismantling the huge military machine he had worked so hard to assemble. For the better part of the next two years, he was engaged in returning troops to America and drafting detailed reports of the actions of his army during the war. In 1920, Congress passed a law designating Pershing general of the armies, allowing him to keep the four-star rank that had been bestowed on him temporarily while he was in command of the American Expeditionary Force (AEF). There was some talk of Pershing running for president, and he allowed his name to appear on the ballot in the Nebraska primary as a favorite son candidate; a poor showing convinced him, however, to abandon that campaign.

In July, 1921, President Warren G. Harding and Secretary of War John Weeks named Pershing chief of staff of the Army. In that position, the hero of World War I fought a three-year battle against the Congress and a large contingent of American people who wanted to return the American military to its prewar position: small and poorly funded. Pershing argued (in vain) for larger permanent forces and an active program to train men for future service through the National Guard and Army Reserve. Despite his pleas, the size of the Army shrunk, its budget dwindled, and its capability to mobilize evaporated. In September, 1924, Pershing retired.

The following years were far from quiet ones, though, since duty with various government commissions kept the general busy. In 1924, he served with the delegation trying to resolve the Tacna-Arica boundary dispute between Peru and Chile. He later served with the American Battle Monuments commission and continued to provide sage advice to his successors in the office of the chief of staff. In 1936, Pershing became seriously ill, but he recovered and once again offered his services to the country when America became embroiled in World War II. President Franklin D. Roosevelt sought his advice, and in fact Pershing helped convince the president to keep General George C. Marshall in Washington, D.C., rather than let him assume field command in

Pershing, John J.

Europe. Marshall, a protégé of Pershing who had been a key staff officer in the AEF, often consulted his mentor during World War II.

Pershing received special honors when the Congress ordered a medal struck in his honor in 1946. He died on July 15, 1948. In accordance with his wishes, he was buried at Arlington National Cemetery, under a simple headstone, among the soldiers whom he had led in "the Great War."

Significance

Pershing's lifelong career of service to his country has secured for him a place among American military heroes. The epitome of the American soldier-leader, he was purposely self-effacing when placed in political circles, remaining true to the principle of military subordination to civilian control with great conviction. His efforts as a stern disciplinarian, a brilliant organizer of large forces, and a staunch believer in the capabilities of the American soldier were a vital element in the Allied success in World War I. In addition, his consistent support for the citizen-soldier helped set the model for future generations of planners and shaped the future of American military organization for the remainder of the century. Finally, his sagacious tutelage of subordinates such as George C. Marshall and George S. Patton provided America the military leadership it needed to rise to the challenge posed by Adolf Hitler and his confederates in World War II.

—*Laurence W. Mazzeno*

Further Reading

American Military History. Washington, D.C.: Office of the Chief of Military History, 1969. Official history of American military involvement at home and abroad; includes accounts of the Indian Wars, the Punitive Expedition in Mexico, and World War I, providing excellent background and highlighting Pershing's contributions when in command.

Goldhurst, Richard. *Pipe, Clay and Drill: John J. Pershing—The Classic American Soldier*. New York: Reader's Digest Press, 1977. A solid biography that places Pershing's actions within the larger context of American political enterprises. Detailed chapters on the Punitive Expedition.

Grotelueschen, Mark Ethan. *The AEF Way of War: The American Army and Combat in World War I*. New York: Cambridge University Press, 2007. Examines the American Expeditionary Force's doctrine and methods of fighting, including Pershing's command of the force.

Liddell-Hart, Basil Henry. *Reputations Ten Years After*. Boston: Little, Brown, 1930. Hart's chapter on Pershing provides an antidote to hagiographic portraits that were popular immediately after the war and points out Pershing's difficulties in dealing with high-ranking officials of Allied forces.

O'Connor, Richard. *Black Jack Pershing*. Garden City, N.Y.: Doubleday, 1961. An objective biography, highly readable and informative, of modest length.

Smythe, Donald. *Guerrilla Warrior: The Early Life of John J. Pershing*. New York: Charles Scribner's Sons, 1973. A detailed, scholarly account of the early years of Pershing's life through his participation in the Punitive Expedition.

_____. *Pershing: General of the Armies.* Bloomington: Indiana University Press, 1986. Smythe's definitive biography focuses on Pershing's role as commander in chief of the American Expeditionary Force in World War I and his tenure as chief of staff of the Army.

Vandiver, Frank. *Black Jack: The Life and Times of John J. Pershing.* 2 vols. College Station: Texas A&M University Press, 1977. A comprehensive biography, based largely on records in the Library of Congress, National Archives, and other collections. Places Pershing's actions in the context of America's coming of age as a world power.

Weigley, Russell A. *A History of the United States Army.* New York: Macmillan, 1967. A scholarly yet highly readable account of the growth of the American military establishment; chapter on World War I provides excellent summary of Pershing's actions and an assessment of his accomplishments as commander of the American Expeditionary Force.

Welcome, Eileen. *The General and the Jaguar: Pershing's Hunt for Pancho Villa, a True Story of Revolution and Revenge.* New York: Little, Brown, 2006. Recounts Pancho Villa's attack on Columbus, New Mexico, in 1916, and General Pershing's subsequent search for Villa.

COLIN POWELL

" *Don't be afraid to challenge the pros, even in their own backyard.* **"**

U.S. secretary of state (2000-2005)

The first African American to achieve the highest-ranking position in the U.S. armed forces, Powell successfully organized and supervised U.S. military operations in the Gulf War of 1991 and served as secretary of state in the early stages of the invasions of Afghanistan and Iraq. He was forced to resign as secretary of state following intense criticism by previously supportive conservatives over bureaucratic infighting concerning the future course of the Iraq War.

Born: April 5, 1937; New York, New York
Also known as: Colin Luther Powell (full name)
Areas of achievement: Military; diplomacy; government and politics

EARLY LIFE

Colin Powell (KOH-lihn POW-ehl) was born in New York City to Luther Powell and Maud McKoy, who were immigrants from Jamaica who came to the United States in the 1920's. Both worked in Manhattan's garment district. Their first child, a daughter, was born in 1931. Five-and-a-half years later Powell was born. The Powells moved from Manhattan to the Bronx in 1940 and settled in Hunt's Point, an ethnically mixed working-class section of the city. Powell's boyhood friendships reflected that ethnic mixture, which may have contributed to his attitudes toward race.

Powell attended neighborhood public schools. The New York City school system was then among the strongest in the country, and although Powell did not stand out scholastically, he benefited from the high quality of his teachers. In high school he took the college preparatory program and as a senior applied for admission to New York University and to the City College of New York (CCNY). Admitted to both, he elected to attend CCNY, at that time the only free public university in the United States.

City College was a remarkable school. It attracted first- and second-generation students from every immigrant group arriving in New York. Its alumni flocked to graduate and professional schools in greater numbers than from any other undergraduate institution. Powell began as an engineering student but switched to geology when, as he put it, he could not "visualize a plane intersecting a cone in space." The highlight of Powell's university career was his service in the Reserve Officers' Training Corps. There Powell found himself in his element. He enjoyed every aspect of his military training and became a member of the Pershing Rifles, an elite military fraternity. He graduated in June of 1958, his degree in geology less important to him than his commission as a second lieutenant in the U.S. Army.

Life's Work

A few days after graduation, Powell traveled to Fort Benning, Georgia, for five more months of military training, including attendance at the Infantry Officer Basic Course. He volunteered for and successfully completed Ranger School and Airborne (parachute) training. His first full-duty assignment was in Germany as a platoon leader in the Second Armored Rifle Battalion of the Forty-eighth Infantry. As all of Powell's later fitness reports confirmed, he was an able and adaptable officer from the beginning of his military career. His record was typical of officers on the fast track, that is, officers who earn early promotion because they have been identified as more talented than their contemporaries.

On his return from Germany, Powell was assigned to the Fifth Infantry Division at Fort Devens, Massachusetts. While there, he met Alma Johnson, a young woman who worked as an audiologist with the Boston Guild for the Hard of Hearing. Johnson and Powell began dating and were married shortly before he received orders for Vietnam.

Powell served two tours of duty in Vietnam. During the first, 1962-1963, he worked as adviser to a South Vietnamese army battalion in the A Shau Valley, one of the most dangerous and active areas of the war. His unit saw a great deal of action, and Powell was wounded by a Viet Cong booby trap. During his second Vietnam tour (1968-1969), Powell already was a major, senior enough in rank to be a battalion executive officer in the Americal Division. However, when the division's commander, Major General Charles Gettys, learned that Powell had been the second-ranking graduate of the Army's Command and General Staff College at Fort Leavenworth, Kansas, he assigned Powell to be the staff G3 operations officer for the entire division. Powell was successful in this position, but his tour ended when he suffered a broken ankle in a helicopter crash. His two tours in Vietnam persuaded him that war must have clear political and military objectives and a definable end. This belief was to shape his later service in positions far more senior than divisional G3.

Powell, Colin

After Vietnam, Powell served in a variety of military and political positions. His crucial introduction to the civilian side of senior leadership occurred when he was awarded a White House Fellowship in 1972. These fellowships are awarded on a competitive basis to a select group of young professionals. Powell's assignment as a White House Fellow was to the Office of Management and Budget (OMB) under Caspar Weinberger, later to be secretary of defense. Weinberger's deputy, Frank Carlucci, would also later become secretary of defense. Powell learned about budgeting, the importance of press relations, and, more generally, how to handle himself in the senior political world. The White House Fellowship marked Powell, both in the Army and in the government, as a rising young officer. The contacts he made at OMB were also to serve him well in later years.

After his fellowship year, Powell received assignments of increasing responsibility. He commanded a brigade of the 101st Airborne Division in 1976-1977. He was military assistant to the deputy secretary of defense from 1979 to 1981 and the secretary of defense from 1983 to 1986. Later in 1986 he was given overall command of V Corps in Europe. From 1987 to 1989 he was President Ronald Reagan's national security adviser, working on the most delicate and secret issues of national security policy. Among these were nuclear disarmament and the issue of the American position on the dissolution of the Soviet Union. During his service as national security adviser,

Colin Powell.
(U.S. Air Force)

Powell, Colin

Powell continued to impress those with whom he was working, among them Vice President George H. W. Bush.

Bush became president in January, 1989. Powell refused several jobs in the new administration, including director of the Central Intelligence Agency. Preferring to remain in the Army, he was promoted to general and put in charge of the Army Forces Command. Ten months later, when Admiral William Crowe retired as chair of the Joint Chiefs of Staff, Powell was the obvious choice for the position. Although he was the most junior of the fifteen existing four-star generals, he had a unique combination of civilian and military service, a record of success in every job he had undertaken, and excellent personal and professional relations with other senior members of the defense and foreign policy establishment. After brief consideration, President Bush nominated him for the position. Powell was quickly confirmed by the U.S. Senate.

Powell's new job did not involve the direct command of troops. Troops are controlled by what are called unified and specified commanders. The Joint Chiefs chair is the head of the Joint Chiefs of Staff and the principal military adviser to the president and secretary of defense. The chair is given immense power and influence. Powell determined to use this influence to prevent unwise military entanglements—the lesson of Vietnam—and to promote his conception of the size and organization of the U.S. military establishment in the wake of the collapse of the Soviet Union.

Powell had hardly settled in to his new office when a crisis emerged in Panama. The United States had been awaiting an opportunity to depose or help depose the Panamanian president, General Manuel Noriega, who was engaged in the business of illegal drugs. On Powell's second day in office, reports were circulating of an imminent anti-Noriega coup. Should the United States enter the fray? Powell and his senior colleagues decided that the reports were too fragmentary and the probability of success too remote. In the end the reports were proved right, for the coup collapsed after only a few hours.

Two months later, after the Panamanian Defense Forces (PDF) shot and killed a U.S. service member, beat up another, and brutalized the latter's wife, the United States acted. American forces invaded Panama, routed the PDF, and captured Noriega within a few days. This operation was conducted consistently with Powell's insistence that there be attainable military objectives and a way out of the commitment after the objectives were achieved.

Powell's greatest achievement as chair of the Joint Chiefs was the successful organization and implementation of the Persian Gulf War of 1991. On August 2, 1990, Saddam Hussein's Iraqi forces invaded Kuwait and threatened the security of neighboring Saudi Arabia, a U.S. ally. For a variety of reasons, President Bush determined that the United States could not tolerate these extensions of Iraqi power. Operation Desert Shield began almost immediately. Desert Shield forces were sent to Saudi Arabia to protect the Saudis from an Iraqi attack. Within a few months the American commitment of forces to Desert Shield amounted to nearly 250,000 troops. Simultaneous economic and diplomatic pressures were applied to Iraq to persuade Hussein to withdraw from Kuwait. When it became clear that these pressures were not succeeding, Bush ordered preparations for the start of Operation Desert Storm—the forcible expulsion of Iraq from Kuwait. Overall responsibility for these operations was with Powell.

Powell, Colin

The buildup continued, eventually reaching 500,000-plus detachments sent by many of America's allies and by many Arab countries.

Powell was instrumental in insisting to his superiors that the military and political objectives be clearly defined. Moreover, he worked closely with General H. Norman Schwarzkopf, the operation's field commander, to ensure that the strategy of attack did not involve costly frontal assaults on fortified positions. In January, 1991, air attacks began against Iraq and Iraqi forces. A ground assault was launched in February. Four days of fighting were sufficient to clear Kuwait of the invaders and destroy most of Iraq's heavy armored divisions. Bush, Secretary of Defense Dick Cheney, and Powell halted the war immediately thereafter to prevent further slaughter of Iraqi forces.

Powell's term as chair lasted into the Clinton administration, and when it expired he retired from the Army. In 1995 and 1996 there was intense speculation as to whether Powell would accept a vice presidential nomination on the Republican Party ticket, but he declined the offer. Alma Powell was very much opposed to any run for elective office for her husband, and Powell himself has stated that he has little taste for electoral politics. He spent the next few years writing, lecturing, and promoting youth programs through an organization called America's Promise. His autobiography, *My American Journey*, which was published in 1995, was very successful. More than one million copies were sold, and the royalties made Powell wealthy.

In 1999, Powell again was pressed to seek elective office. Many members of the liberal wing of the Republican Party were hoping that he would get the party's nomination for the presidency in 2000. After much consideration, and after additional discussion with Alma, Powell again declined to run. The 2000 election did bring George W. Bush to the presidency after a bitter and divisive struggle over contested electoral votes in Florida. Bush, essentially inexperienced and ignorant of foreign affairs, needed a person of stature to become secretary of state. He turned to Powell, who accepted Bush's offer. Powell's new job was announced in December of 2000.

As secretary of state, Powell found that the Defense Department (DOD), under Donald Rumsfeld, and the president's more immediate foreign policy staff under National Security Adviser Condoleezza Rice, did not agree with his approach to foreign and defense policy. Powell's underlying policy in the wake of the Soviet collapse was to expand alliances and trade, especially with Russia and China. He believed that economic growth and security would foster peaceful solutions to international disputes and rivalries. The White House and the DOD, however, favored more aggressive extensions of American power. Powell prevailed in the first nine months of his tenure because in the absence of war the DOD had a relatively small role in the making of foreign policy.

American foreign policy changed, however, with the terrorist attacks on the World Trade Center and the Pentagon on September 11, 2001. The United States immediately began its invasion of Afghanistan to destroy the Taliban and al-Qaeda and to find Osama Bin Laden, al-Qaeda's leader. Also, many in the Bush administration wanted to depose Hussein, the Iraqi dictator, who was said to be preparing weapons of mass destruction for use in the already unstable Middle East or for delivery to terrorists to use against the United States. Although Powell warned Bush privately against this

Powell, Colin

new foreign policy, he publicly supported it. Some of his biographers believe that his penchant for obeying orders accounts for the apparent contradiction. Whatever the reason, his great prestige in the United States and around the world would, in the end, help Bush develop support for the invasions of Afghanistan in the fall of 2001 and of Iraq in March, 2003.

As secretary of state, Powell's major role in the Iraqi invasion was to promote the development of an international coalition, first to support American military action in the invasion and subsequently to assist in the rebuilding of Iraq after the defeat of its forces. Powell's warnings to Bush had been correct, however. As the Iraqi operation bogged down, its supporters in the White House and the DOD became increasingly hostile to Powell. The public saw intense bureaucratic infighting, and Powell was asked to resign by the president's chief of staff, Andrew Card, at the end of Bush's first term (2005).

After his second retirement, Powell continued to lecture, write, and promote moderate Republican policy. He remained influential in the foreign policy sphere, most notably in successfully opposing Senate confirmation of John R. Bolton as ambassador to the United Nations.

Significance

Powell's career was marked by four major achievements and one significant failure. First, he achieved the highest military rank of any African American before him. To have an African American at the very top of the military chain of command was considered a good thing for the armed services considering that the ranks of the U.S. armed forces are disproportionately black. Second, he was the first black American to be secretary of state. Powell's success could be read, as many have argued, as a sign that racism was on the decline, at least in the military and at the federal level of government. Third, Powell's tenure also led to a restoration of public confidence and pride in the U.S. armed forces and to increased confidence among military members themselves. The defeat and bitterness of Vietnam were lessened in the celebration of the Persian Gulf War victory. For this, some of the credit belongs to Powell. His policy on force reductions was appropriate, given the collapse of the Soviet Union, and was a step toward a more realistic and affordable military policy for the United States. Finally, Powell's insistence that military objectives be defined and attainable made national foreign policy more realistic.

Powell's great failure, however, was his inability to persuade the neoconservatives of the Bush administration to alter their approach to the war in Iraq. His early public support for the Iraq war—which, after several years had proved unpopular to the majority of Americans—and his later ambivalence about the invasion and occupation will likely remain his legacy as secretary of state.

—*Robert Jacobs*

Further Reading

DeYoung, Karen. *Soldier: The Life of Colin Powell.* New York: Alfred A. Knopf, 2006. A definitive biography of Powell's life and career, meticulously researched and clearly written. Sealed archives on the Persian Gulf War, set to open in the mid-

twenty-first century, should reveal more about his role in that war.
Powell, Colin L., with Joseph E. Persico. *My American Journey*. New York: Random House, 1995. Powell's own summation of his life. Especially strong on the details of his military career. Although Powell was assisted in writing this book by Joseph Persico, enough of his character and personality comes through to make this book worthwhile beyond the fundamental factual details.
Roth, David. *Sacred Honor: A Biography of Colin Powell*. San Francisco, Calif.: HarperCollins, 1993. Roth, one of Powell's public affairs officers after the Gulf War, has prepared this admiring biography of the former general. His discussions of Powell's character and religious views are not found in other works about him.
Schwarzkopf, H. Norman. *It Doesn't Take a Hero*. New York: Bantam Doubleday Dell, 1993. General Schwarzkopf's autobiography is strong on the relation between the field commander, Schwarzkopf, and Powell in the planning and execution of the Gulf War, although Schwarzkopf naturally focuses on his own activities.
Steins, Richard. *Colin Powell: A Biography*. Westport, Conn.: Greenwood Press, 2003. This is a good short biography of Powell that, unfortunately, does not include coverage of the start of the invasion of Iraq in 2003.
Woodward, Bob. *The Commanders*. New York: Simon & Schuster, 1991. Woodward's book focuses on the war and peace decision-making process in Washington, especially regarding the Panamanian and Iraqi operations during Powell's tenure as Joint Chiefs chair. Much of the material comes from anonymous sources.

A. Philip Randolph

> **" *A community is democratic only when the humblest and weakest person can enjoy the highest civil, economic, and social rights.* . . . "**

Labor leader

Having a passionate desire for economic justice and an unwavering advocacy for social and political equality among all persons, Randolph significantly improved the status of African American labor and greatly advanced the civil rights of minority people throughout the United States.

Born: April 15, 1889; Crescent City, Florida
Died: May 16, 1979; New York, New York
Also known as: Asa Philip Randolph (full name)
Areas of achievement: Labor movement; civil rights

Early Life
Asa Philip Randolph (A-sah PHI-lihp RAN-dolf) was born to Elizabeth Randolph from Baldwin, Florida, and the youngest of four daughters born to James and Mary Robinson, and James William Randolph, a descendant of slaves who worked for the

Randolph, A. Philip

Virginia planter John Randolph. A devoted member of the African Methodist Episcopal (AME) church, Elizabeth was an intelligent and proud woman who deeply resented bigotry and segregation, and her father, James Robinson, independent and resourceful, supported his family by running a small lumber business that supplied pine logs, cross ties, pulpwood, and other materials for the railroads and paper mills in northern Florida. Philip's father was born in 1864 and acquired a rudimentary education from northern missionaries who came South after the Civil War. He became an accomplished tailor and AME minister, serving several poor congregations in Jefferson County, Florida. Outraged by the failure of Reconstruction to secure full racial equality for black people, the itinerant preacher militantly fought to defend his community's newly acquired political rights. James was also strongly influenced by Henry McNeal Turner, the AME bishop and Georgia legislator who sought better wages and living conditions for black workers. Elizabeth and James were married in 1885. They were to have two sons, James William, Jr. (1887), and later A. Philip. In 1891, the Randolphs moved to Jacksonville, Florida, where the family lived frugally in a modest home enriched with purpose, respect, and love.

A. Philip Randolph.
(Schomburg Center, The
New York Public Library)

Randolph, A. Philip

Several influences shaped Philip's formative years. He greatly admired his brother, a brilliant student, whom Philip readily acknowledged he "loved very much." As youngsters, they often played roles championing the rights of blacks. They remained close friends until William's death in 1928. Philip also revered his father and often accompanied him on house visits to his congregation. The boy basked in the prestige and respect shown his father throughout the community. His father's moving speeches and effective sermons taught young Philip the value of having a social consciousness. Contributing to the family income, Philip worked at a number of jobs including store clerk, newsboy, errand runner, boxcar loader, and railroad section hand. He attended Cookman Institute High School in Jacksonville (later Bethune-Cookman College), where he took the classical course. A diligent student, he developed his elocution skills and did much reading both in and outside class. After graduation he decided to leave the South and go North; his move was an individual example of the great migration undertaken by thousands of other African Americans at the turn of the century to improve themselves economically.

LIFE'S WORK

In 1911, Randolph arrived in New York City and found residence in the Harlem section of Upper Manhattan. During the day he worked odd jobs as a porter, waiter, elevator operator, and switchboard operator. In the evenings he enrolled in courses at the City College of New York; there he became interested in literature, especially the works of William Shakespeare, and honed his oratorical talent. He gave readings of the classics to church groups, to literary clubs, and at public forums. He took courses in history, political science, and economics. College life introduced him to socialism, the cause of the Industrial Workers of the World, the ideas of William D. ("Big Bill") Haywood, Eugene V. Debs, and Elizabeth Gurley Flynn. While growing up in Jacksonville, he had read the works of Booker T. Washington and W. E. B. Du Bois, but now he discovered Marxism and other radical approaches to ameliorating the difficulties facing the laboring classes.

Tall and handsome, he was a meticulous, clean-cut dresser who paid careful attention to his grooming. As he matured into a confident yet disciplined young man, his baritone voice and sharp intellect presented a figure of considerable dignity whose presence commanded one's undivided attention. He married Lucille Campbell Green in 1915, an attractive, socially exuberant manager of a Madam C. J. Walker beauty salon. Although six years his senior, she shared his interest in socialism, the classics, the welfare of African Americans, and concern for the working poor. They remained together until her death in 1963.

The seminal event that launched Randolph's career as a labor and political activist occurred when he took a job as a waiter on the Fall River Line, which transported people from New York to Boston. Appalled at the cramped, squalid quarters of the employees, the long hours, and the low pay, he attempted to organize his fellow workers, whereupon he was fired by the steamboat company. Undaunted, he joined the Brotherhood of Labor Organization and helped to establish the Independent Political Council (1912).

In 1915, Randolph met Chandler Owen, a brilliant young intellectual who studied

Randolph, A. Philip

social sciences at Columbia University. They held similar political views and became great friends. It was a time of radical protest against brutal, intolerable working conditions in mills, mines, factories, and railroads across the nation. They joined the Socialist Party and believed that the only way to end black racial oppression in America was to attack the capitalistic economic system, which exploited both white and black workers by pitting them against one another, driving wages and living conditions down. Appeals to religious sentiment or humanistic ideals of fair play and equity were viewed as vacuous and pusillanimous. The majority of blacks were politically disfranchised. A successful strategy, they reasoned, must appeal to the economic self-interests of the parties involved. The solution was to forge black-white labor unity, have the laboring masses take control of the economic system from the capitalist classes, and establish a more equitable social system. Pragmatic and militant, their plan of action was to educate and organize African American workers. Randolph spoke from street-corner soapboxes, rallied opponents in social clubs, and debated opponents in public forums.

With Owen, Randolph published a monthly periodical, *Messenger*, subtitled "The Only Radical Negro Magazine in America." In editorials they treated many issues: the need for solidarity among black and white workers, impotent black leadership, the socialist critique of capitalism, and creative use of boycotts by blacks to achieve their goals. For example, one 1919 editorial succinctly put it, in part,

> Black and white workers should combine for no other reason than that for which individual workers should combine, viz., to increase their bargaining power, which will enable them to get their demands.
>
> Second, the history of the labor movement in America proves that the employing class recognize no race lines. They will exploit a white man as readily as a black man. They will exploit women as readily as men. They will even go to the extent of coining the labor, blood and suffering of children into dollars. The introduction of women and children into the factories proves that capitalists are only concerned with profits and that they will exploit any race or class to make profits, whether they be black or white men, black or white women or black or white children.

As a pacifist, Randolph opposed the United States' participation in World War I and was jailed for a short period of time because of his antiwar position. Randolph and Owen charged that W. E. B. Du Bois had failed as a theorist and offered no sound solutions to African American problems. They counseled blacks to eschew the National Association for the Advancement of Colored People (NAACP) because it was "controlled and dominated by a group who was neither Negro nor working people." The editors claimed that capitalism was the real culprit responsible for the lynchings of more than three thousand African Americans that occurred between 1890 and 1920; they advocated the use of armed resistance to end this barbaric extralegal practice. Despite having fundamental political differences with Marcus Garvey, Randolph worked for a while with him and his Universal Negro Improvement Association (UNIA). Although Randolph staunchly opposed communism, he believed that the Russian Revolution was "the greatest achievement of the twentieth century." Responding to Red-baiters who made no distinction between his support for socialism and disapproval of communism, he remarked,

> If approval of the right to vote, based on service instead of race and color is Bolshevism, count us as Bolshevists. If our approval of the abolition of pogroms is Bolshevism, stamp us again with that epithet. If the demand for political and social equity is Bolshevism, label us once more. . . .

For several years during and after the Great War, Randolph worked to organize several trade unions, with little success. In 1925, he took up the causes of the porters and maids on the Pullman railroad cars who had failed in their attempts to organize. The problems confronting these largely black workers were shocking. They labored between three and four hundred hours a month, barely earning seventy-five dollars monthly in good years. These workers had to pay for their dining-car meals, uniforms, lodging, and other expenses while supporting families and homes. To gain better wages and shorter hours, Randolph and less than a dozen men formed the Brotherhood of Sleeping Car Porters union, with *Messenger* as its official organization. By 1928, a majority of the maids and porters had joined the union. Randolph was labeled a dangerous agitator, Red, atheist, and radical—an outsider who never had worked as a Pullman porter. The American Federation of Labor (AFL) refused to support the union, and the Railroad Labor Board would not protect it. The Interstate Commerce Commission declined to investigate labor complaints. The Brotherhood lost its first attempt to win concessions from the Pullman Company. While a solid core remained loyal, membership in the union declined thereafter. During the Great Depression, when the New Dealers sought to protect the rights of labor to bargain collectively with their employers, porters once again began joining the Brotherhood and by 1935 voted to have the union represent them. By 1937, the union secured an important contract with the Pullman Company, reducing hours to 240 a month, better working conditions, and much higher pay. In less than twenty years, the union grew to become the most successful black labor organization in the nation, and Randolph was invited in 1957 to become a vice president of the newly merged AFL-CIO.

Randolph showed as much interest in politics as he had in labor organizing. While serving as president of the Joint Committee on National Recovery (JCNR) in 1935, he called for a united front of all black organizations (civic, labor, political) to abolish Jim Crow laws, attain civil rights, oppose fascism, and improve the economic status of African Americans. "True liberation," he maintained,

> can be acquired and maintained only when the Negro people possess power; and power is the product and flower of organization—organization of the masses, the masses in the mills and mines, on the farms, in the factories, in churches, in fraternal organizations, in homes, colleges, women's clubs, student groups, trade unions, tenant's leagues, in cooperative guilds, political organizations and civil rights associations.

With the coming of World War II, African Americans were still being denied fair employment opportunities, and those working were not receiving the same pay as their

Randolph, A. Philip

white counterparts for doing the same work. Randolph made a bold yet brilliant move by threatening a massive nonviolent march on Washington to protest job discrimination. As enthusiasm for the protest grew, fear of hampering the nation's war economy led President Franklin D. Roosevelt to issue Executive Order 8802, forbidding racial discrimination in employment by companies having defense contracts. A Fair Employment Practices Commission (FEPC) was established to monitor the order and investigate violations.

During the late 1940's, Randolph called for the complete desegregation of the United States armed forces. An ardent spokesperson for the Committee Against Jim Crow in Military Service and Training, he warned the government that he would lead a civil disobedience campaign to refuse registration and resist conscription into a Jim Crow army. Randolph's popular support no doubt influenced President Harry S. Truman to begin desegregation of the military. In 1950, Randolph, along with others, established the Leadership Conference on Civil Rights (composed of more than 157 national organizations representing blacks, Hispanics, Asians, labor, major religious denominations, women, the handicapped, and the aged) to guide President Truman's efforts to achieve racial equality. The Negro American Labor Council was founded in 1960 because Randolph, as its president (from 1960 to 1966), believed that the AFL-CIO was doing "little more than paying lip service to desegregation in unions." He was the prime mover behind the historic March on Washington for Civil Rights in 1963 involving a quarter of a million people.

Randolph retired from active political and labor work in 1968 to join for a brief period the A. Philip Randolph Institute, a labor research and information center directed by Bayard Rustin.

Significance

In numerous ways, A. Philip Randolph sought to secure economic opportunities, political power, and social justice for African Americans in particular and for all exploited and oppressed people in general. If the common people, the workers, unified and organized themselves, he believed that they would have the power in a democracy. In the early years, he had insisted that all ethnic groups and genders must fight together for their common rights. Although he continued to call for interracial solidarity throughout his life, he seemed to have lost faith that most white Americans would ever overcome their bigotry and racism. By the late 1930's, he put less emphasis on his earlier belief in a united labor party and urged the formation of a "tightly organized Negro non-partisan bloc."

With this concept, he galvanized the African American community for the threatened 1941 March on Washington. His masterful tactic was the most significant achievement initiated by any African American to achieve racial equality since emancipation. Extraordinary indeed, the federal government acceded to black demands. Although President Roosevelt's Executive Order 8802 was grossly undermined and the FEPC lacked strong enforcement power, for the first time in the nation's history African Americans by themselves had successfully compelled an administration to take action to improve their socioeconomic condition. It was a momentous event that marked a turning point in black-white relations. If for no other reason, this feat alone

Randolph, A. Philip

guaranteed Randolph an indelible place in the pages of United States history.

A. Philip Randolph was the consummate black political organizer of his age. He labored unrelentingly to get individuals and groups to put aside their divisive, parochial, and often petty concerns and close ranks in the formation of a mass movement for the common good. The foremost architect of the modern Civil Rights movement, he urged boycotts in the South against Jim Crow trains, buses, schools, and businesses. "Nonviolent Good Will Direct Action" is what he labeled his movement to gain social equality decades before Martin Luther King, Jr., and others emerged on the 1960's political scene. If not the man himself, then his influence and ideas were at home at the forefront of virtually every civil rights campaign from the 1930's through the 1960's, including desegregation of public accommodations and schools, ending of restrictive covenants, the Montgomery bus boycott, and the 1957 March on Washington. Randolph is to be credited for his role in passage of the 1957, 1960, and 1964 civil rights acts and the voting rights bill of 1965 as well. As one award stated: "No individual did more to help the poor, the dispossessed and the working class in the United States and around the world than A. Philip Randolph."

—*Lamont H. Yeakey*

FURTHER READING

Anderson, Jervis. *A. Philip Randolph: A Biographical Portrait.* New York: Harcourt Brace Jovanovich, 1973. This work is the most complete treatment of the life and work of Randolph. Although a sympathetic account, a wide variety of sources, particularly useful interviews with Randolph and others, was used. A strength of this biography is the author's conscientious effort to provide the historical background at each phase of Randolph's long and illustrious career.

Foner, Philip S., and Ronald L. Lewis, eds. *The Era of Post-War Prosperity and the Great Depression, 1920-1936.* Vol. 6 in *The Black Worker: A Documentary History from Colonial Times to the Present.* Philadelphia: Temple University Press, 1983. This volume and the following one in the set contain an invaluable collection of primary documents on a wide range of labor issues, not only those involving Randolph.

———. *The Black Worker from the Founding of the CIO to the AFL-CIO Merger, 1936-1955.* Vol. 7 in *The Black Worker: A Documentary History from Colonial Times to the Present.* Philadelphia: Temple University Press, 1983. Volume 7 of the set contains documents that give an indispensable account of the difficulties and aspirations of black trade unionism.

Garfinkel, Herbert. *When Negroes March: The March on Washington Movement in the Organizational Politics for FEPC.* New York: Atheneum, 1959, 1969. This is the first major treatment of the proposed March on Washington in 1941, initiated by Randolph. It is a well-reasoned, thoroughly documented examination of the central event in Randolph's career and should be read by all scholars of the period.

Harris, William H. *Keeping the Faith: A. Philip Randolph, Milton P. Webster, and The Brotherhood of Sleeping Car Porters, 1925-37.* Urbana: University of Illinois Press, 1977. Harris's study of the origins of The Brotherhood of Sleeping Car Porters is the best scholarly account of the creation and development of the union. The author's thorough research and thoughtful analysis of the problems, mistakes, and successes of this organization tell much about black trade unionism in particular and national opposition to it in general.

Kersten, Andrew E. *A. Philip Randolph: A Life in the Vanguard.* Lanham, Md.: Rowman & Littlefield, 2007. Examines Randolph's influences and accomplishments as both a civil rights and labor leader.

Marable, Manning. "A. Philip Randolph: A Political Assessment." In *From the Grassroots: Essays Toward Afro-American Liberation.* Boston: South End Press, 1980. Marable's essay is a critical analysis of Randolph, suggesting that the leader became increasingly cautious and conservative as he won modest victories for labor and achieved limited civil rights reforms. A provocative essay, it deserves a careful reading.

Meier, August, Elliott Rudwick, and Francis L. Broderick, eds. *Black Protest Thought in the Twentieth Century.* 2d ed. Indianapolis, Ind.: Bobbs-Merrill, 1971. Several primary documents spanning Randolph's career in labor and politics from 1919 to 1963 are made available in this collection. The volume is also useful for ideas and insights into other significant figures.

Rustin, Bayard. *Down the Line: The Collected Writings of Bayard Rustin.* Chicago: Quadrangle Books, 1971. This collection of essays has several partisan articles on various aspects of Randolph's philosophy and activities. Most of the selections on Randolph deal with his later years and offer an interesting, if not polemical, interpretation of the labor leader by his longtime colleague and friend.

Taylor, Cynthia. *A. Philip Randolph: The Religious Journey of an African American Labor Leader.* New York: New York University Press, 2006. Chronicles Randolph's life within the context of African American religious history and describes how Randolph, an African Methodist, held a wide spectrum of Protestant beliefs.

JEANNETTE RANKIN

❝ *You can no more win a war than you can win an earthquake.* ❞

U.S. congresswoman (1917-1919, 1941-1943) and social reformer

Rankin devoted her life to women's rights and peace. She was the first woman elected to Congress and the only member to vote against the entry of the United States into both world wars.

Born: June 11, 1880; near Missoula, Montana
Died: May 18, 1973; Carmel, California
Area of achievement: Government and politics

EARLY LIFE

Born in a ranch house near Missoula, Montana, Jeannette Rankin (RANG-kihn) was the eldest of seven children. Her father, John Rankin, the son of Scottish immigrants, moved to Montana in the late 1860's. After prospecting for gold, he settled in Missoula, became a builder and contractor, and played a central role in the town's political and economic development. Jeannette's mother, Olive Pickering, migrated from New Hampshire to Missoula in 1878 and served the town as its schoolteacher until her marriage to John Rankin the following year. John developed a lucrative business and purchased a ranch for cattle raising and farming.

The Rankin family was close-knit and loving but fostered each member's individuality. Evenings were often spent in lively discussion and hearing stories of gold prospecting and Indian warfare in the Montana Territory. The family was also very religious, and its beliefs formed the values by which Jeannette lived her entire life.

Although she loved to read, public school bored Jeannette. She found more satisfaction in learning practical skills from her parents. From her mother, Jeannette learned sewing, and she became an expert seamstress. She studied carpentry with her father and constructed a sidewalk in downtown Missoula.

Jeannette entered Montana State University in 1898, but her college experience was as frustrating as her earlier schooling had been. Because the university was located in Missoula, the change of scenery that she desired was impossible, and because the campus was regional, little opportunity existed to meet students from diverse backgrounds. Moreover, she frequently complained that her classes were uninteresting. She completed her studies, was graduated in 1902, and for a short time taught school.

Looking for something more challenging than teaching, Jeannette drifted from one job to another—dressmaker, sawmill supervisor, and furniture builder. In 1904, Jeannette visited her brother at Harvard College in Boston. She found the city exhilarating but was shocked by the slum conditions and the extent of poverty, overcrowded dwellings, and poor health among working-class residents. Repulsed by what she witnessed, Jeannette committed herself to social work.

Rankin, Jeannette

LIFE'S WORK

In 1908, Rankin enrolled in the New York School of Philanthropy to study social issues and social work. After completing the program in 1910, she secured employment in a Spokane, Washington, children's home. At that time the state of Washington was considering woman suffrage. Volunteering her services, she distributed leaflets, canvassed voters door-to-door, and delivered speeches in favor of the state suffrage amendment. Washington granted women the right to vote in November, and her participation sparked an enthusiasm that placed Rankin on a crusade for woman suffrage and social reform.

Rankin returned to Montana in December, 1910, for the Christmas holidays and learned that her home state had scheduled debate on a suffrage amendment for January. She quickly organized the Equal Franchise Society, requested and received an invitation from the state assembly to speak on behalf of the amendment, and presented a well-received argument for woman suffrage. Although the amendment was not passed until 1913, Rankin was instrumental in its eventual victory.

Having gained a taste for social reform politics, Rankin became a member of the National American Woman Suffrage Association (NAWSA) and joined organizations in several states. By autumn of 1914, she had lobbied and spoken before the legislatures of ten states, marched in rallies in major cities, and petitioned Congress for a national woman suffrage amendment. Rankin was quickly becoming a national personality.

In 1914, war erupted in Europe. Although the United States was not involved, Rankin feared that it might be unable to remain neutral. War, she reasoned, would shift the public's attention from social issues and slow the movement for woman suffrage. While in New York, Rankin helped to form the Women's Peace Party in January, 1915, and lobbied Congress to stay out of the European conflict. Although she spent the next summer in Montana organizing "good government clubs" designed to eliminate corruption and to increase women's rights, she devoted most of her time to speaking and writing against American entry into World War I.

In 1916, the likelihood of war led Rankin to take the boldest step of her career. Against the advice of Republican Party leaders, she announced her candidacy for election to the U.S. House of Representatives. Her personal platform reflected her professional goals—an amendment to the U.S. Constitution for woman suffrage, child protection laws, social justice, and good government. She was most demanding regarding continued American neutrality. Her antiwar views, which most Montana voters shared, brought her victory in November. Rankin was the only Republican to win office in Montana that year and the first woman in American history to take a seat in the U.S. Congress.

Rankin took the oath of office on April 1, 1917, but the warm welcome she received did not last long. On April 5, the House of Representatives commenced debate on the entry of the United States into the Great War. Special attention was focused on Rankin. She symbolically represented all women in the nation. Her vote for or against war would be interpreted as a woman's ability to deal with political crises.

The House debated the war resolution throughout the night. Rankin chose to remain silent but listened intently to the heated arguments. Tensions rose as opponents of war were jeered, hissed, and verbally branded as unpatriotic. When the House voted, Jeannette Rankin rose to her feet. "I want to stand by my country," she said, "but I cannot vote for war. I vote no." She found herself in the minority. Three hundred seventy-four representatives supported the resolution, while only fifty voted against war. On April 7, President Woodrow Wilson declared war on Germany.

Hannah Josephson stated in her biography *Jeannette Rankin, First Lady in Congress* (1974) that Rankin was warned before the vote that she might lose reelection because of her antiwar stance. Her opposition to war was far more important to her than her concern for reelection. The public's response was swift. Rankin was labeled unpatriotic and a disgrace to women nationwide. Even the NAWSA claimed that her vote against war would lose supporters for a constitutional suffrage amendment. Rankin later said that her vote against war was the most significant one she ever made. Women, she believed, had to take the lead to end war.

Once the nation was committed to war, Rankin supported American troops, worked in Congress to protect civil liberties, and pushed for social reform. She championed legislation authorizing the government to hire more women workers, to provide financial relief to families of soldiers, to improve conditions for imprisoned women, and to

Jeannette Rankin.
(Library of Congress)

guarantee food, clothing, shelter, and health care for children living in poverty. She participated in congressional debates on a federal amendment for woman suffrage, which Congress finally sent to the states for approval in 1918. As her term in the House of Representatives ended, however, Rankin's antiwar vote resurfaced and caused her defeat for reelection.

During the twenty years that followed, Rankin toured the nation promoting feminist issues. She worked with the National Consumers' League, which advocated federal child labor laws, better working conditions, and increased women's rights. Most of her energy, however, was directed toward achieving international peace.

The horrors of World War I still vivid in her mind and aware that social justice could never be attained as long as money was spent on defense and warfare, Rankin helped to form the Women's International League for Peace and Freedom and volunteered her services to numerous other peace organizations. She campaigned against Reserve Officers Training Corps programs on college campuses. She was a central figure at the Conference on the Cause and Cure for War, participated in the Peace March on Chicago, lobbied congressmen to introduce legislation to outlaw war, and advocated the creation of a National Peace Party to challenge both Republicans and Democrats in state and federal elections. As the 1930's drew to a close and the prospect for another world war seemed likely, Rankin intensified her efforts.

In November, 1940, at age sixty, Rankin was again elected to Congress on a peace platform. She proposed bills to prevent the sending of U.S. troops abroad and to require a national vote before war could be declared. Neither measure passed, but she persisted throughout 1941. Despite Japan's attack on Pearl Harbor on December 7, Rankin stood for peace regardless of personal consequences. On December 8, Congress voted for war. This time, Rankin cast the only vote in opposition. As before, Rankin received the brunt of public criticism and was not reelected the following year.

Until her death in 1973, Rankin traveled the world. The extent of global poverty and injustice she witnessed intensified her belief that only in a peaceful world could social problems be resolved. Based on this view, she condemned America's war in Vietnam throughout the 1960's. In January, 1968, she participated in an antiwar march on Washington. The Jeannette Rankin Brigade, so named by her admirers, petitioned Congress to end the war and "heal a sick society at home."

SIGNIFICANCE

Rankin pressed her demands for an end to war, protection of civil liberties, and direct popular vote on critical national issues. She never realized her dream to end war, but she was responsible, directly or indirectly, for the creation of many laws. Her efforts resulted in voting rights for women, support for dependents of servicemen, free postage for members of the armed forces, retention of citizenship for women who marry noncitizens, child labor and protection laws, and women's rights. Throughout her life she spoke on behalf of labor, for child welfare, for social justice and greater democracy, and against racial prejudice. She further advocated multimember congressional districts, a unicameral Congress, direct election of the president, and the restructuring of the U.S. military into a purely defensive force. Her two elections to Congress opened avenues for women nationally in politics and business. Although she was labeled an idealist and was criticized severely for her antiwar position, Rankin possessed the courage to remain true to her convictions and dedicated her life to the betterment of American society and the human race.

—Kenneth W. Townsend

FURTHER READING

Dedication of the Statue of Jeannette Rankin. Washington, D.C.: Government Printing Office, 1986. This publication includes a biographical sketch of Rankin and speeches given by prominent political figures in remembrance of her advocacy of women's rights and an end to war. Included is a time line of Rankin's life and accomplishments.

Josephson, Hannah. *Jeannette Rankin, First Lady in Congress.* Indianapolis, Ind.: Bobbs-Merrill, 1974. Although many prominent and influential women with whom Rankin worked receive limited attention and the broad context in which Rankin operated is somewhat vague, Josephson has presented a complete, well-researched biography. The author's twenty-year personal relationship with Rankin makes the work most insightful and revealing.

Libby, Frederick J. *To End War: The Story of the National Council for Prevention of War.* Nyack, N.Y.: Fellowship, 1969. Libby surveys the patterns of antiwar thought and peace organizations in twentieth century America.

Lopach, James J., and Jean A. Luckowski. *Jeannette Rankin: A Political Woman.* Boulder: University Press of Colorado, 2005. In this political biography, Lopach and Luckowski portray Rankin as a talented, driven, and deeply divided person.

Noble, David W. *The Progressive Mind, 1890-1917.* Rev. ed. Minneapolis, Minn.: Burgess, 1981. This work provides an overview of the intellectual foundations of the Progressive Era and the evolution in thought of Progressives themselves. One chapter devoted exclusively to women of the period adequately highlights the feminist movement.

Smith, Norma. *Jeannette Rankin: America's Conscience.* Helena: Montana Historical Society Press, 2002. Smith, a friend of Rankin, wrote this biography based on interviews she conducted with her friend in the 1960's.

RONALD REAGAN

> " *I will not make age an issue of this campaign. I am not going to exploit, for political purposes, my opponent's youth and inexperience.* "

President of the United States (1981-1989)

Reagan stemmed the general feeling of instability that surrounded the office of the U.S. president. Almost by sheer personality and by exuding an enormous self-confidence, Reagan reversed many of the negative images of the office. His tenure was marked by economic recession and recovery, problems of unemployment, complicated foreign affairs, a foreign policy scandal, expanding American military buildup, and silence regarding HIV-AIDS. However, his optimism appealed to voters, and his conservatism produced a number of programs that changed American government in fundamental ways.

Born: February 6, 1911; Tampico, Illinois
Died: June 5, 2004; Bel Air, California
Also known as: Ronald Wilson Reagan (full name); Dutch (nickname); the Gipper (nickname)
Areas of achievement: Government and politics; diplomacy; film; theater and entertainment

EARLY LIFE

Ronald Reagan (RAY-guhn) was born in Tampico, Illinois. He was the younger of two sons; his brother, John Neil Reagan, was born in 1909. His father, John Edward Reagan, was born in 1883 in Fulton, Illinois; his father's parents were born in County Cork, Ireland. The young Reagan's mother, Nelle Clyde Wilson Reagan, of English-Scottish ancestry, was born in 1885, also in Fulton. His father gave him the nickname Dutch because as a boy he had a stolid, chubby build and favored a Dutch-boy haircut.

When Reagan was ten years old, his family settled in Dixon, Illinois, after living in several other rural Illinois towns. His father was a shoe salesman who was troubled by alcoholism and had difficulty holding a job. His mother loved the theater, and it was in Dixon, while attending high school, that Reagan first began acting. In 1928, he graduated from high school, where he had played basketball and football and was on the track team; he also was president of the student body. For seven summers during his high school and college years, he worked as a lifeguard at Lowell Park near Dixon.

Reagan won a scholarship that paid half of his living expenses, tuition, and fees at Eureka College, where he majored in sociology and economics. At Eureka, he participated in student politics, athletics, and theater, playing the lead in several college productions and winning honorable mention in a drama competition sponsored by Northwestern University. He won varsity letters in football, swimming, and track, and, as in high school, was elected president of the student body.

After receiving a bachelor's degree in 1932, Reagan was hired as a sports announcer for station WOC in Davenport, Iowa. WOC was a five-thousand-watt station that shared its wavelength with WHO in Des Moines; both stations became part of the NBC network within a year after Reagan's initial employment. By 1937, his coverage of major-league baseball, Big Ten Conference football, and other sports events had earned for him a national reputation as a sportscaster. While covering the Chicago Cubs' training camp at Catalina Island, he was introduced to a Los Angeles motion picture agent who succeeded in getting him a screen test with Warner Bros. In 1937, Reagan signed a $200-per-week, seven-year contract with Warner Bros.

Reagan was married for the first time, in 1940, to actor Jane Wyman, who he had met while they were both appearing in films for Warner Bros. From that marriage, which ended in 1949, they had a daughter, Maureen Elizabeth, and an adopted son, Michael Edward. In 1952, Reagan married actor Nancy Davis, the daughter of Loyal Davis, a prominent Chicago neurosurgeon. They had two children, Patricia Ann and Ronald Prescott. Reagan was the first U.S. president to have been divorced.

Life's Work

Reagan's first career, then, was in film. His first picture was *Love Is on the Air* (1937), in which he played a radio commentator. He would act in more than twenty B-pictures before his performance as George Gipp, the famous Notre Dame football star, in *Knute Rockne, All American* (1940). This role established his reputation as a serious actor, and it was from this film that he got his second nickname, the Gipper. In 1940-1941, he was chosen one of the "stars of tomorrow" in an exhibitor's poll.

Reagan's most memorable film role was probably that of Drake McHugh, the victim of a sadistic surgeon, in *King's Row* (1942), a film directed by Sam Wood. Reagan's performance was described as excellent by many reviewers. Overall, Reagan was considered a competent but not outstanding actor. He made fifty-five feature-length films, mostly for Warner Bros., between 1937 and 1964. He left Warner Bros. in the 1950's and freelanced among several studios for a few years.

On April 14, 1942, Reagan became a second lieutenant with the cavalry of the U.S. Army Reserve; poor eyesight disqualified him from combat duty. Until his discharge as a captain on December 9, 1945, he made training films for the Army in California. It was after his years in the Army that Reagan began to give serious attention to the politics of the film industry. He took fewer roles as an actor after he was elected president in 1947 of the Screen Actors Guild (SAG), one of the major labor unions in the industry. He was elected to six one-year terms as president, and in that position he successfully negotiated several significant labor contracts. In October he appeared before the House Committee on Un-American Activities (better known as HUAC) as a friendly witness in its investigation of communist influence in the film industry. He came to view HUAC and its chair, Congressman J. Parnell Thomas, along with their questionable tactics, with enough wariness that he did not "name names" of suspected communists.

Reagan started his political life as a liberal Democrat who ardently supported President Franklin D. Roosevelt (FDR). In the 1940's, however, his political outlook became much more conservative. His movement to the right of center politically came during his experience from 1954 to 1962 when he was employed by General Electric, as host, program supervisor, and occasional actor on the weekly television show *Gen-*

eral Electric Theater. Between television appearances, Reagan traveled throughout the country for General Electric's personnel relations division. He spoke at the company's 135 plants and addressed thousands of its workers. In these speeches he often repeated two themes, that of America's need for free enterprise and of the evils of big government. In 1962, Reagan became the host of the weekly television program *Death Valley Days*. He remained with that show until he entered the race for governor of California in 1965.

Reagan switched to the Republican Party in 1962, although he had campaigned as a Democrat for Dwight D. Eisenhower in 1952 and 1956, and again for Richard Nixon in 1960. He also supported Harry S. Truman in 1948. However, in the early 1960's he felt that the Democratic Party had abandoned its roots in the ideas of Thomas Jefferson and had created a bloated federal government. In October, 1964, Reagan's prerecorded speech on behalf of Barry Goldwater, "A Time for Choosing," was well received by viewers and resulted in a huge surge in campaign contributions. Reagan's friendly, low-key delivery suggested a reassuring, plain patriotism that became a hallmark of his appeal to voters.

In November, 1966, Reagan defeated the incumbent Democratic governor of California, Edward G. "Pat" Brown, by more than one million votes. Reagan stumped the state with his basic speech, essentially unchanged from his days with General Electric. He called on voters to bring "common sense" back to government. He was reelected four years later when he defeated Democratic state assembly speaker Jesse Unruh by more than a half-million votes.

As governor of California, Reagan mastered the art of compromise with state legislators and was more restrained and pragmatic than his conservative rhetoric suggested. He took a hard line toward dissident students in the state's educational system, particularly at the University of California, Berkeley. He also reduced expenditures in a number of areas, including social services and education, to fulfill his campaign promise to reduce the size of government. These cuts, along with a prosperous state economy, resulted in substantial surpluses in the state government's revenues. In 1973, he was able to begin generous programs of income tax rebates and credits as well as significant property tax relief. A major tax law was passed during his tenure as governor, which corrected a regressive state revenue system. A major achievement of Reagan's second term was the passage of the California Welfare Reform Act of 1971. This law reduced the numbers of people on the welfare rolls while increasing payments to those in need, notably those recipients of Aid to Families with Dependent Children. His successes as a governor led many political observers to regard him as a leading contender for the Republican presidential nomination in 1968.

Reagan's first run for the presidency, however, was too tentative to stop Nixon in 1968, and, accordingly, he requested that the convention make Nixon's nomination unanimous. He next campaigned for the presidency against Gerald R. Ford, beginning with the New Hampshire primary in February, 1976. Reagan narrowly lost the nomination to Ford at the Republican National Convention in Kansas City, Missouri; the delegate vote was 1,187 for Ford to Reagan's 1,070. Nevertheless, Reagan had laid the groundwork for 1980 by his strong showing, especially with voters in the South, and in July of that year he arrived unopposed at the Republican convention. In his acceptance speech, Reagan pledged to support a conservative platform that called for voluntary prayer in public schools, credits for private-school tuition, and strong opposition to school busing, abortion, and the Equal Rights Amendment. Reagan overcame questions about his age with a vigorous campaign against incumbent Jimmy Carter, and his disarming and engaging performance in televised debates helped him to defeat Carter at the polls on November 4, 1980. His margin in the popular vote was substantial, and he received 489 votes to Carter's 49 in the electoral college.

On Tuesday, January 20, 1981, Reagan was inaugurated as the fortieth president of the United States, with Chief Justice Warren E. Burger administering the oath of office. For the first time in the nation's history, the ceremony was held at the West Front of the Capitol, in a symbolic allusion to Reagan's Western roots. The president gave a twenty-minute address calling for "an era of national renewal." Minutes afterward, he fulfilled a campaign promise by placing a freeze on government hiring. As the president concluded his address, at 12:33 P.M., the Iranian government released the American hostages whom they had held for 444 days. The news added to the festive spirit of the occasion.

A few months into his first term, Reagan was shot in the chest as he left the Washington Hilton Hotel at about 2:30 P.M. on March 30, after addressing a group of union officials. His assailant, John Hinckley, Jr., was overpowered and arrested at the scene of the crime. The president was rushed to nearby George Washington University hospital, where he later was operated on to remove a bullet from his left lung. On April 11, after a remarkably quick recovery, he returned to the White House.

During his first term, Reagan concentrated on a strategy of cutting taxes for economic growth stimulation (a strategy popularly known as Reaganomics), holding back increases in government spending, an expensive buildup of American defenses throughout the world, and a so-called War on Drugs to combat adolescent drug use. He asserted the government's authority during a strike of air traffic controllers in 1981 by firing more than ten thousand controllers who disobeyed his order to return to work. He asserted the nation's power abroad to protect American lives and interests in 1983, first in Lebanon and then on the Caribbean island of Grenada. By 1984, inflation was under control, interest rates moved down (though not low enough), employment was up significantly, and generally the economy was upbeat. Difficult problems remained, however, such as the huge size of the federal deficit, a somewhat myopic view of government's role in domestic matters, and a U.S. Supreme Court that was perhaps too conservative in such a complex, modern world. There remained to be found solutions to the problems of racism and to the concerns of American farmers. Nevertheless, the Reagan presidency set standards against which present and future programs were judged.

Buoyed by a landslide victory over former vice president Walter Mondale in the 1984 presidential election, Reagan began his second term with as much popular backing as any president since FDR. However, his age began to show. He underwent two surgeries during this term and appeared to many to have problems with his memory. Moreover, criticism of his policies began to mount, especially the administration's slow response to the epidemic of acquired immunodeficiency syndrome (AIDS) and his siting of Pershing II intermediate range nuclear missiles in Europe to counter Soviet military might.

It was the Iran-Contra affair that most overshadowed his second term. Members of the government's clandestine services illegally sold missiles to the Iranian government and used the money to finance an insurgency of Nicaraguan former military and brigands, called Contras, against the Central American country's leftist government after it won a civil war. When the operation became public, Reagan denied knowledge of it, yet high-ranking members of his administration were indicted for wrongdoing, some convicted, others forced to resign.

Another controversy grew from Reagan's decision to build a missile defense system, officially the Strategic Defense Initiative but popularly known as Star Wars because it required new technology. The research program escalated tensions with the Soviet Union, whose own military technology was beginning to equal in sophistication that of the United States. At the same time, Reagan persevered in diplomatic initiatives with the Soviets. At the last of four summits with Soviet leader Mikhail Gorbachev, the two leaders signed the Intermediate-Range Nuclear Forces Treaty, intended to eliminate thousands of nuclear weapons.

Reagan left office on January 11, 1989, succeeded by his vice president, George H. W. Bush. At age seventy-seven, he was America's oldest president. The Reagans moved into an exclusive suburb of Bel Air in Los Angeles but also spent part of their retirement on their ranch, Rancho del Cielo, near Santa Barbara, California. Reagan was six feet one inch tall, with light-brown hair and blue eyes. He wore contact lenses for many years, was a nonsmoker, and drank only on occasion. He enjoyed horseback riding, chopping wood, and watching television, and he privately screened motion pictures.

Reagan's health steadily deteriorated. In 1994, he was diagnosed with Alzheimer's disease and thereafter made few public appearances. He made his last public appearance on April 27, 1994, at the funeral of former president Nixon.

Alzheimer's disease slowly took away Reagan's memory and vitality. He died of pneumonia in his Bel Air home on June 5, 2004. Private funeral services took place at the Ronald Reagan Presidential Library in Simi Valley, California, and his body was flown to Washington, D.C., where he lay in state in the Capitol. A state funeral was held June 11 at the Washington National Cathedral and was attended by heads of state from throughout the world. The body was then returned to California for burial at the Reagan Library.

Among the many honors accorded to Reagan was the dedication of the Ronald Reagan Building and International Trade Center in Washington, D.C., in 1998, the renaming of Washington's airport as Ronald Reagan Washington National Airport (actually located in Virginia) the same year, and the christening of the aircraft carrier USS *Ronald Reagan* in 2001. He also received the Presidential Medal of Freedom in 1993. Many Americans place him with FDR and Abraham Lincoln in the front rank of the nation's leaders.

SIGNIFICANCE

Reagan fashioned two careers in his long years in the public eye. He was well known to the public before he undertook a career in public service in the 1960's. His first career was in film and television, and most voting-age Americans encountered him first in the darkened film theater or at home on television. It was during the Hollywood years that Reagan's vision of the United States was formed. He learned more than simply acting from the film world: He acquired an easy way with an audience, and he also experienced the competition and studio politics that led him into the larger arenas of the New Deal, SAG, and HUAC—all of which constituted the apprenticeship for his second career.

In his second career, that of public office, Reagan began at the top. His years in the governor's mansion in Sacramento coincided with an era of national protest, foreign war, and social change; his years in the White House were marked by economic recession and recovery, problems of unemployment, complicated foreign affairs, a foreign policy scandal, and expanding American military buildup.

Reagan's optimistic attitude appealed to voters, and his conservatism produced a number of programs that changed American government in fundamental ways. By June, 1986, public approval of his performance in office was higher than ever before, according to a Gallup poll. The poll also found that Reagan was more popular than any previous second-term, second-year president since World War II. A crest of public support in 1981, when 58 percent of Americans approved of his performance, had tapered off in 1982 and 1983 to 44 percent, rising again in 1984 to 56 percent approval and 61 percent in 1985.

Despite the Iranian arms scandal that marred the later half of Reagan's second term, few presidents in the twentieth century demonstrated such staying power in the polls, including Eisenhower and FDR. Indeed, Reagan's greatest achievement, perhaps, was to have restored the office of president of the United States to a position of power and prestige, especially in the eye of the public. Democratic senator Edward Kennedy, despite his frequent criticism of Reagan's economic, social, and civil rights policies, acknowledged nonetheless that Reagan "contributed a spirit of good will and grace to the presidency and American life generally and turned the presidency into a vigorous and forceful instrument of national policy."

—*Arthur F. McClure*

FURTHER READING

Bosch, Adriana. *Reagan: An American Story*. New York: TV Books, 1998. Bosch recounts Reagan's life in this compact, objective narrative work, a solid first source for general readers. Includes photographs.

Cannon, Lou. *Reagan*. New York: G. P. Putnam's Sons, 1982. This substantial and highly critical biography is the work of a veteran reporter and White House correspondent for *The Washington Post*. Although dated, it provides a perspective on Reagan to be considered with other, more positive viewpoints. Illustrated and well documented, with an extensive bibliography.

Colacella, Bob. *Ronnie and Nancy: Their Path to the White House—1911 to 1980*. New York: Warner Books, 2004. This book treats the Reagans' lives as a combination love story, social history, and political saga. The author is especially interested in identifying the background that shaped them into a sociable, steadfast force in American culture. Photographs and extensive bibliography.

Diggins, John Patrick. *Ronald Reagan: Fate, Freedom, and the Making of History*.

New York: W. W. Norton, 2007. In this full, scholarly work about Reagan's intellect and beliefs, Diggins argues that he was the most influential president after FDR, especially because of his views on the economy and his refreshing optimism.

Gelb, Leslie H. "The Mind of the President." *The New York Times Magazine*, October 6, 1985. The author concludes that Reagan is unique in the history of American presidents because he alone possessed the mind of both an ideologue and a politician. Reagan had "all the moral force and power that swell from absolute conviction." His success stemmed from being a "natural horsetrader" who mastered the art of political compromise to achieve his own political ends.

Reagan, Ronald, with Richard G. Hubler. *Where's the Rest of Me?* New York: Dell, 1981. Reagan originally wrote this autobiography in 1965, long before he dreamed of becoming president. It is a frank, witty, and moving account of his life. The title comes from his most famous line from his best movie, *King's Row*. The book reveals much of the charm, optimism, and common sense that made him such a phenomenally successful politician.

Spada, James. *Ronald Reagan: His Life in Pictures*. New York: St. Martin's Press, 2000. A pleasant, easygoing introduction to Reagan's life. The broadly written text accompanies a wealth of photographs that treat him as the embodiment of the American Dream.

Strober, Deborah Hart, and Gerald S. Strober. *The Reagan Presidency: An Oral History of the Era*. Rev. ed. Washington, D.C.: Brassey's, 2003. A sympathetic history of the Republican president that draws on interviews with those who knew him best. An updated edition of *Reagan: The Man and His Presidency*.

Thomas, Tony. *The Films of Ronald Reagan*. Secaucas, N.J.: Citadel Press, 1980. A study of Reagan's film career. Reagan took his acting seriously, in spite of what his political opponents have argued. He was an able actor usually assigned to poor roles. Workmanlike in his professional duties, he was seldom criticized for being less than convincing within his acting range. The author concludes that Reagan's career was a respectable one.

Weber, Ralph E., and Ralph A. Weber, eds. *Dear Americans: Letters from the Desk of President Ronald Reagan*. New York: Doubleday, 2003. Provides the full range of Reagan's letters to Americans and to people around the world. Recommended as a collection of primary sources.

RED CLOUD

" They made us many promises, more than I can remember, but they kept only one; they promised to take our land, and they did. "

Native American leader

Red Cloud led the Lakota (Sioux) Indians through a difficult period, effectively resisting the onrush of American westward advance and later helping the Lakota make the transition to reservation life under American rule.

Born: 1822; Blue Creek, near North Platte (now in Nebraska)
Died: December 10, 1909; Pine Ridge, South Dakota
Also known as: Makhpíya-Lúta (birth name)
Area of achievement: Native American affairs

EARLY LIFE

Red Cloud was born into the Oglala subtribe of the Teton branch of Lakota, or Dakota people (more popularly known as Sioux) on the high plains of what is now Nebraska. His father, a headman in the Brulé subtribe, was named Lone Man, and his mother was Walks-as-She-Thinks, a member of the Saone subtribe. There is disagreement over the origins of the name Red Cloud. Some sources contend that it was a family name used by his father and grandfather, while others claim that it was coined as a description of the way his scarlet-blanketed warriors covered the hills like a red cloud.

Little is known about Red Cloud's early life. His father died when he was young, and he was reared in the camp of Chief Old Smoke, a maternal uncle. He undoubtedly spent his boyhood learning skills that were important to Lakota men at the time, including hunting, riding, and shooting. Plains Culture Indians sometimes conducted raids against enemies, and Red Cloud joined his first war party and took his first scalp at the age of sixteen. Thereafter, he was always quick to participate in expeditions against Pawnee, Crows, or Ute. Other Oglala frequently retold Red Cloud's colorful exploits in battle. During a raid against the Crows, he killed the warrior guarding the ponies and then ran off with fifty horses. This was a highly respected deed among Plains Indians, whose horses were central to their way of life. On an expedition against the Pawnee, Red Cloud killed four of the enemy—an unusually high number in a type of warfare in which casualties were normally low.

During the early 1840's, most Oglala bands camped around Fort Laramie on the North Platte River, where they could obtain a variety of goods from white traders. Red Cloud was part of a band known as the Bad Faces, or Smoke People, under the leadership of his uncle, Old Smoke. Another band in the area, the Koya, was led by Bull Bear, the most dominant headman among the Oglala and commonly recognized as their chief. The two groups frequently quarreled. One day in the fall of 1841, after young men of both sides had been drinking, a member of the Bad Faces stole a Koya woman. Bull Bear led a force to the Bad Face camp and shot the father of the young man who had taken the woman. The Bad Faces retaliated, and when a shot to the leg downed

Red Cloud

Bull Bear, Red Cloud rushed in and killed him. This event led to a split among the Oglala that lasted for many years. It also elevated Red Cloud's standing among the Bad Faces, and shortly after the incident he organized and led a war party of his own against the Pawnee.

Soon after recovering from wounds suffered in that raid, Red Cloud married a young Lakota woman named Pretty Owl. Sources disagree as to whether he thereafter remained monogamous or took multiple wives, a common practice among prominent Lakota. There is no agreement on how many children he fathered, although five is the number most accepted by scholars. Over the next two decades, Red Cloud's reputation and status continued to grow. By the mid-1860's, he was a ruggedly handsome man of medium stature with penetrating eyes and a confident and commanding presence. He was also a band headman and a leading warrior with an increasing following among the Bad Faces. Lakota social and political structure was decentralized; no one person had authority over the whole group. Instead, certain leaders were recognized as chiefs on the basis of ability and achievement. An important member of his band, at this time Red Cloud was not yet a chief.

Life's Work

In the several decades before the Civil War, traders began operating in Lakota territory, followed by wagon trains, telegraph construction, and more. The Lakota welcomed most of the traders and at least tolerated most of the wagon trains, even though whites disrupted hunting by killing indiscriminately and chasing many animals away from traditional hunting grounds. By the closing years of the Civil War, American traffic across the northern plains increased even further. The discovery of gold in the mountains of Montana in late 1862 enticed more whites to cross Lakota land, leading to friction and occasional clashes. The final straw came when the government sent soldiers in to build forts and protect passage along a popular route known as the Bozeman Trail that linked Montana with the Oregon Trail.

In 1865, many Lakota, including Red Cloud, took up arms in resistance. Several Lakota leaders signed a treaty in the spring of 1866 that would open the Bozeman Trail, but Red Cloud and his many followers held out, insisting on a removal of soldiers. The government tried to ignore Red Cloud for a time, but the Lakota almost completely closed down travel and obstructed efforts to construct the forts. This was the high point in Red Cloud's career as a military strategist. He led his men to a number of victories, most notably the annihilation of Captain William J. Fetterman and eighty-two soldiers in an incident known to whites as the Fetterman Massacre and to Indians as the Battle of a Hundred Slain. In November of 1868, when, after negotiations, the army withdrew the troops and abandoned the forts, Red Cloud finally ended the war.

This victory increased Red Cloud's standing among his people, although he still was not the Lakota's exclusive leader. The U.S. government, however, assumed that he was the head chief and dealt with him as such. During the late 1860's, there was talk of creating a reservation for the Lakota, and Red Cloud surprised everyone by announcing that he would go to Washington, D.C., and talk about the idea.

Some have argued that Red Cloud was motivated by a desire to gain the status among the Lakota that he already enjoyed in the view of federal officials. On the other hand, he may have realized that since many white Westerners opposed a reservation and preferred the extermination of Indians, a reservation, combined with the withdrawal of troops from all Lakota lands, an important objective to Red Cloud, might be the best compromise he could achieve. He and twenty other Lakota leaders were escorted to the nation's capital in 1870 with great ceremony. Red Cloud did not win everything he wanted, but he clearly emerged as the most famous Native American of his time. He was applauded by many Easterners who sympathized with Indians and saw Red Cloud as a symbol of justifiable response to white advance.

In 1871, Red Cloud settled on the newly created reservation, at the agency named after him. Then, only a few years later, gold was discovered in the Black Hills portion of the reserve, and the government pressured the Lakota to sell the area. When negotiations broke down, events quickly escalated into the Sioux War of 1876-1877. With one eye on the government, Red Cloud publicly opposed the armed action undertaken by some Lakota to stop the flood of prospectors onto their lands, but privately he seemed to sanction such moves.

Red Cloud frequently became embroiled in political battles with federal agents on the reservation. He tried to win whatever provisions and concessions he could to ease his people's suffering, and he resisted government efforts to break down traditional cultural and political life. When many Lakota became involved in the controversial Ghost Dance in 1889-1890, Red Cloud avoided early commitment to or open encouragement of participation. Many dancers, however, believed that they indeed had his support. Red Cloud's frequent compromise position and his seeming cooperation with government agents sometimes made him suspect among some of his people, and, as a consequence, his influence steadily eroded. He died on the reservation on December 10, 1909.

SIGNIFICANCE

Red Cloud emerged as a military and political leader at a dramatic and tragic time in the history of the Lakota people. Onetime powerful nomadic buffalo hunters, they were going through far-reaching changes. American westward advance constricted their land base, destroyed the buffalo upon which their economy depended, and ultimately brought about their impoverishment. Moreover, government attempts to destroy traditional Lakota ways of life on the reservation, while never completely successful, resulted in cultural shock.

For a time, Red Cloud resisted militarily as effectively as any Native American leader ever had. Then, when American domination became clear, he attempted delicately to balance the two worlds of Indian and white, hoping to win the best results possible for his people under the circumstances. This was a difficult task, and he did not satisfy everyone. He was attacked from both sides—by whites for not doing more to encourage his followers to assimilate into the white world and by some Lakota for being too willing to give in to government authorities.

Red Cloud stood as a symbol to many Indians (and some whites) of strong defense of homelands and culture, while to other whites he epitomized the worst in Indian treachery and savagery. For both sides, the name Red Cloud conveyed immense power and meaning. During the 1960's and 1970's, with the rise of the Red Power movement

Red Cloud

and a rejuvenation of Indian culture, he again became a symbol—this time to a generation of young Indian (and sometimes white) political activists who found inspiration in what they saw as his defiance in the face of unjust authority.

—*Larry W. Burt*

FURTHER READING
Allen, Charles Wesley. *Autobiography of Red Cloud: War Leader of the Oglalas*. Edited by R. Eli Paul. Helena: Montana Historical Society Press, 1997. Red Cloud gave an oral account of his life to a historian in 1893, and Allen later prepared a manuscript with Red Cloud's recollections. The manuscript languished in the offices of the Nebraska State Historical Society for decades until it was published by the Montana Historical Society in 1997.
Cook, James H. *Fifty Years on the Old Frontier*. New Haven, Conn.: Yale University Press, 1923. Neither scholarly nor complete in its coverage of Red Cloud, it does contain some interesting, colorful, and firsthand descriptions of the Lakota leader and some of his exploits by a prominent frontiersman and close friend.
DeMallie, Raymond J., ed. *The Sixth Grandfather: Black Elk's Teachings Given to John G. Neihardt*. Lincoln: University of Nebraska Press, 1984. Does not focus on Red Cloud's life specifically but provides direct accounts of various events in his life, especially surrounding the 1875-1876 Black Hills controversy, as told by Black Elk and other Lakota participants to poet John Neihardt.
Goodyear, Frank H., III. *Red Cloud: Photographs of a Lakota Chief*. Lincoln: University of Nebraska Press, 2003. Red Cloud was photographed many times because he believed these photographs helped him serve as a mediator between the Oglala Lakota and the federal government. This book contains more than eighty photographs by Mathew Brady, Edward Curtis, and other photographers. It also features a biographical and historical analysis written by Goodyear.
Hyde, George E. *Red Cloud's Folk: A History of the Oglala Sioux Indians*. Norman: University of Oklahoma Press, 1937. Less complete and authoritative than the more recent book by James C. Olson but generally well written and reliable. Focuses on the earliest period of which historians have any knowledge of Lakota history to about the end of the Sioux War of 1876-1877.
_____. *A Sioux Chronicle*. Norman: University of Oklahoma Press, 1956. A continuation of *Red Cloud's Folk* that carries the story of the Oglala to the tragedy at Wounded Knee in 1890. Contains less information about Red Cloud, because his role was diminishing by the end of the nineteenth century. However, it does offer useful material on Red Cloud's part in Lakota history after the creation of the reservation during the 1870's.
Olson, James C. *Red Cloud and the Sioux Problem*. Lincoln: University of Nebraska Press, 1965. The best and most complete account of Red Cloud. Except for some background information on the Lakota and Red Cloud's early life, it begins with the period immediately after the Civil War and ends with the death of Red Cloud in 1909.
Robinson, Doane. *A History of the Dakota or Sioux Indians*. Aberdeen, S.Dak.: News Printing, 1904. Reprint. Minneapolis, Minn.: Ross and Haines, 1958. First printed

by the South Dakota State Historical Society in 1904, this book bears the mark of scholarship in an earlier era in its attitude toward Indians. It is so factually solid and complete that it still stands as an important source for information on Red Cloud.

Utley, Robert M. *The Last Days of the Sioux Nation.* New Haven, Conn.: Yale University Press, 1963. An excellent history of the events surrounding the famous Massacre of Wounded Knee, including material about Red Cloud's participation in that event that reveals something about his role in Lakota society in 1890.

WALTER REED

" If it happens, it happens. . . . We can't stop living. "

Physician

Reed served as the head of the commission that designed and conducted the experiments that proved that yellow fever was transmitted by mosquito bites, thus making control of this terrible disease possible and enabling the construction of projects such as the Panama Canal.

Born: September 13, 1851; Belroi, Virginia
Died: November 22, 1902; Washington, D.C.
Areas of achievement: Public health; medicine

EARLY LIFE

Walter Reed was the youngest of five children. His mother, Pharaba White, was the first wife of his father, Lemuel Sutton Reed, a Methodist minister. From the first, it seemed as if Reed were destined to live a gypsylike existence. As an adult, he would reside in a nearly endless series of army camps; as a child, his family moved frequently as his father was sent to parish after parish in the regions of southeastern Virginia and eastern North Carolina. In 1865, however, the Reeds achieved some stability with a move to Charlottesville, Virginia, and Walter was able to attend school with some regularity. In 1866, he entered the University of Virginia, receiving a medical degree in 1869.

Feeling the need for more clinical experience, Reed next enrolled in the medical school of Bellevue Hospital in New York City, where, at the age of nineteen, he completed study for his second medical degree. A year's internship followed in New York's Infant's Hospital, after which he became a physician in two other hospitals in the New York area while also serving as a sanitary inspector for the Brooklyn Board of Health.

LIFE'S WORK

Unhappy with the insecurity of life as a public physician yet having no good prospects for private practice, Reed decided upon a career in the military and, in 1875, passed the examinations that earned for him a commission as first lieutenant in the Army Medical Corps. He married Emilie Lawrence in 1876, and shortly afterward was transferred to

Reed, Walter

Walter Reed.
(Library of Congress)

Fort Lowell in Arizona. His wife soon joined him, and their son Lawrence was born in 1877. A daughter, Blossom, followed in 1883. The Reed children lived much the same restless life as their father had as a youngster as they followed him in almost annual moves from army post to army post in Arizona, Nebraska, Minnesota, and Alabama.

These wanderings in the West were interrupted briefly in 1889, when Reed was appointed surgeon for army recruits in Baltimore. While stationed there, he sought and was given permission to work in Johns Hopkins Hospital where he took courses in bacteriology and pathology. It was not, however, until 1893, when Reed returned to the East to stay, that his career finally began to flourish. In that year, he was promoted to the rank of major, assigned the position of professor of bacteriology and clinical microscopy at the recently established Army Medical School in Washington, D.C., and given the position of curator of the Army Medical Museum as well.

In 1896, Reed received his first real opportunity to demonstrate his ability as a medical investigator when he tracked down the cause of near-epidemic malaria among troops in the Washington barracks and in nearby Fort Myer, Virginia. In addition, in 1898, he chaired a committee that investigated the spread of typhoid fever in army camps. All this was excellent preparation for the task that Reed was about to undertake, and the task for which he is famous—that of resolving the riddle of yellow fever's transmission.

Yellow fever had been the scourge of the Caribbean Islands and the regions bordering on the Gulf of Mexico, as well as other port cities in North America and Brazil, for more than two centuries and had claimed hundreds of thousands of lives. Its abrupt but mysterious appearances and disappearances had long been the subject of controversy among physicians. Many believed the disease to be contagious, while many others were convinced that it was caused by local climatic conditions that created poisoned air (miasmata). By the end of the nineteenth century, much of the medical world had accepted the contagionists' view, believing that the disease was spread by fomites (items such as clothing or bedding used by a yellow-fever victim).

For at least a century, a few physicians had been skeptical of both explanations. Dr. John Crawford of Baltimore is sometimes credited with advancing a mosquito theory toward the end of the eighteenth century, as are Josiah Nott of Mobile, Alabama, and the French naturalist Louis Daniel Beauperthuy at about midpoint in the nineteenth century. The real credit for a mosquito theory, however, belongs to the Cuban physician Carlos Juan Finlay, who, in 1881, not only suggested that mosquitos were responsible for the transmission of yellow fever but also narrowed the focus to the *Aëdes aegypti* (then called *Stegomyia fasciata*) mosquito. Finlay's difficulty was that he could not prove his theory.

In 1896, an Italian physician, Giuseppe Sanarelli, claimed to have isolated the causative agent of yellow fever, and Reed, along with army physician James Carroll, was assigned the task of investigating that claim. They soon demonstrated it to be groundless, but this was only the beginning of Reed's work on yellow fever. He volunteered for duty during the war with Spain over the question of Cuban independence, but only got to Cuba after the war was over, arriving in Havana in 1899, to investigate a typhoid outbreak, and again in 1900, as the head of a commission sent to investigate the reasons for an outbreak of yellow fever among American troops still stationed on the island. Carroll, Aristides Agramonte, and Jesse Lazear made up the remainder of the commission.

At first, they made little progress with yellow fever, for their efforts were directed toward showing that the bacillus that Sanarelli believed to cause yellow fever was actually part of the group of hog cholera bacillus. It was only after Reed had investigated an outbreak of a disease originally thought to be malaria among soldiers in Pinar del Rio, that the commission settled down to its task. The disease in question turned out to be yellow fever, and the circumstances surrounding the death of one of the soldiers who had been a prisoner and locked in a cell particularly intrigued Reed because none of his cellmates had got yellow fever, not even the one who had taken his bunk and bedding. This fact seemed to discredit the fomite theory, and Reed wrote later that at this point he began to suspect that some insect was capable of transmitting the disease.

It was also at this point that several important findings began to converge. In 1894, Sir Patrick Manson had suggested that mosquitoes might be responsible for the transmission of malaria, and in 1897, Sir Ronald Ross had proved it. On the other hand, malaria was a very different disease from yellow fever. One of the reasons why Finlay had been unable to prove that the *Aëdes aegypti* mosquito was responsible for spreading yellow fever was that he (and everyone else) was unaware of the long period (generally nine to sixteen days) of incubation the yellow fever virus requires in the stomach of a mosquito before that mosquito is capable of passing the disease along to a human host.

Reed, Walter

In May of 1900, Henry Rose Carter of the United States Marine Hospital Service published his observations on outbreaks of the disease in Mississippi that for the first time revealed the lengthy incubation period.

Then, in the summer of 1900, the members of the commission met with Finlay, who placed the records of his experiments at their disposal. They had decided to test Finlay's theory using human subjects for the experiments.

Reed returned to Washington but was back in Cuba in September, upon learning that Lazear, who had permitted himself to be bitten by an infected mosquito, was dead from yellow fever and that Carroll was seriously ill with the disease. It seemed that Finlay had indeed been correct, and Reed at this juncture designed and conducted the experiments that produced twenty-two more cases in soldier volunteers, proving once and for all that the female *Aëdes aegypti* mosquito was responsible for epidemic yellow fever. Armed with this knowledge, Major W. C. Gorgas was able to free Havana of the disease quickly and then eradicate it in Panama (making construction of the canal possible), while others wiped out yellow fever in urban centers elsewhere in the hemisphere. More than three decades would elapse before another form of the disease called jungle yellow fever would be discovered in some of the monkey populations of that area and in those of Africa. With this discovery came the realization that the disease could not be completely eradicated but only controlled.

Reed did not live long enough to see the whole of this triumph of humankind over yellow fever. After completing his experiments in Cuba, he returned, in 1901, to Washington, a hero and the recipient of many honors. He resumed his teaching duties but died in late 1902 of complications that developed following surgery on his ruptured appendix.

Significance

In no small part because of a sensationalist American press, Reed (as Cuban physicians and historians in particular have pointed out) has probably received too much credit for the solution of the age-old mystery of yellow fever's transmission. However, Reed himself was always modest about his role in the matter and quick to pass along that credit to Finlay, and to his associates Carroll, Lazear, and Agramonte.

In truth, however, Reed was entitled to a lion's share of the credit. Finlay had not been able to prove the truth of his mosquito hypothesis, and Reed's colleagues were narrow specialists; Carroll was a bacteriologist, Lazear, a mosquito specialist, and Agramonte, a pathologist. Thus, it was Reed who successfully drew the work of these and others together and organized the experiments that made the final definitive breakthrough.

Although his early career gives no hint of this kind of ability, his activities in investigating malaria and typhoid outbreaks during the years immediately prior to his yellow fever work surely prepared him well for that work. In all these undertakings, Reed revealed a fine scientific mind, and his success in the tropical medicine field, heretofore dominated by Europeans, brought much prestige to American science and American scientific education. Thus, it is fitting that the small monument over his resting place in Arlington National Cemetery bears the inscription, "He gave to man control over that dreadful scourge Yellow Fever."

—Kenneth F. Kiple

FURTHER READING

Bean, William B. *Walter Reed: A Biography*. Charlottesville: University Press of Virginia, 1982. Despite its lack of documentation, it is clear that this study, by the leading authority on Reed, has been extensively researched, and as a full-length biography it has the virtue of providing a balanced account of Reed's life rather than concentrating excessively on his yellow fever work alone. Thus, it provides an excellent description of medicine and the military between the Civil War and the war with Spain.

Carter, Henry Rose. *Yellow Fever: An Epidemiological and Historical Study of Its Place of Origin*. Edited by Laura Armistead Carter and Wade Hampton Frost. Baltimore: Williams and Wilkins, 1931. The author, himself one of the major actors in the drama of the conquest of yellow fever, provides a thorough examination of the history of the disease as well as an account of its ultimate surrender to science.

Chappell, Gordon S. "Surgeon at Fort Sidney: Captain Walter Reed's Experiences, 1883-1884." *Nebraska History* 54 (1973): 419-443. Focuses on Reed's year of service as the chief medical officer at Fort Sidney, a Nebraska military post. An interesting glimpse of a slice of Reed's early career.

Dormandy, Thomas. *Moments of Truth: Four Creators of Modern Medicine*. Hoboken, N.J.: Wiley, 2003. Part 4 of this book contains six chapters examining Reed's life, career, and contributions to modern medicine.

Gilmore, Hugh R. "Malaria at Washington Barracks and Fort Myer." *Bulletin of the History of Medicine* 29 (1955): 346-351. This is a brief description of the careful epidemiological investigation of a malaria outbreak among soldiers in the Washington, D.C., area carried out by Reed in 1896.

Kelly, Howard A. *Walter Reed and Yellow Fever*. 3d rev. ed. Baltimore: Norman, Remington, 1923. The first scholarly and satisfactory biography of Reed despite its uncritical nature. It traces his life from birth to death, but, as the title indicates, it places most of the emphasis on the work done by Reed and his associates on yellow fever.

Pierce, John R., and Jim Writer. *Yellow Jack: How Yellow Fever Ravaged America and Walter Reed Discovered Its Deadly Secrets*. Hoboken, N.J.: Wiley, 2005. Chronicles the rise and fall of yellow fever, focusing on the impact of the disease in America. Describes Reed's successful efforts to eradicate the disease.

Truby, Albert E. *Memoir of Walter Reed: The Yellow Fever Episode*. New York: Paul B. Hoeber, 1943. This work, as the title indicates, is not biographical in nature but rather concentrates on the methods and techniques employed by Reed and his colleagues to demonstrate that the mosquito was indeed the carrier of yellow fever. In the process, the study also provides a fine background sketch of the Army Medical Corps and the conditions in Cuba with which Reed met upon his arrival.

Revere, Paul

PAUL REVERE

❝ *The regulars are coming out!* ❞

Revolutionary War hero

An American revolutionary patriot, Revere also was a prominent silversmith, engraver, and industrialist. He is remembered especially for his service as a civilian messenger, warning the military of British troop positions and movements, and as a propagandist, producing satirical engravings that criticized British authority.

Born: January 1, 1735; Boston, Massachusetts
Died: May 10, 1818; Boston, Massachusetts
Area of achievement: Government and politics

EARLY LIFE

Paul Revere (reh-VEER) was the third of twelve children born to Paul Revere and Deborah Hichborn Revere. Revere's father, a French Protestant Huguenot who at an early age had gone to live with an uncle on the Isle of Guernsey in the English Channel, anglicized his name from Apollos De Revoire. After arriving in Boston in 1715, the thirteen-year-old Revere was apprenticed as a silversmith; he eventually opened his own shop and taught the craft to his son.

From age seven to thirteen, the younger Revere attended the North End Writing School in Boston, then devoted himself to learning silversmithing from his father. Even as a boy, Revere exhibited a strong sense of individual responsibility and dedication to community service, both Calvinist traits. He and several other boys formed a bell-ringers association dedicated to the principle that no member should beg money from any person. Revere, though he would become a wealthy craftsperson, would always be regarded as a member of the "mechanicks" class, a social status ranked below Boston's elite. Of middling height, strong, and stocky, Revere displayed great energy and willingness to assume risks. Upon his death, a Boston newspaper described him as always "cool in thought, ardent in action" and "well adapted to form plans and carry them into successful execution—both for the benefit of himself and the service of others."

At age twenty-one, Revere served as a second lieutenant in a Massachusetts militia expedition against the French in western New York. He did not see any action, however, and after being stationed at Fort William Henry on Lake George from May through November, 1756, he returned to Boston. On August 17, 1757, Revere married Sarah Orne; five months after her death on May 3, 1773, he married Rachal Walker. Each marriage produced eight children; of the sixteen, five died as infants and five in childhood.

Revere, who took over his father's shop upon his father's death in 1754, ran a prodigious business as a silversmith, drawing clientele from his father's network of customers and from organizations to which he belonged. Revere, who like most silversmiths worked in both gold and silver, has been described as the foremost master craftsman of his time. Before the Revolutionary War, his shop produced ninety kinds of silver and gold pieces, all reflecting creative design and skilled craftsmanship, and repaired various items. Although the shop specialized in silver tableware such as tea sets, cups, trays, casters, and candlesticks, it also produced pieces ranging from small items such as thimbles, rings, buttons, and buckles to surgeon's instruments. Revere never sacrificed simplicity of design for elaboration; however, many of his pieces before 1785 carried some rococo-style ornamentation, usually in the form of scrolls and shells.

Always versatile, Revere practiced dentistry, chiefly in the wiring in of false teeth (he never made dentures) and cleaning teeth, and he sold goods imported from England. He also became an accomplished engraver, using copper plates to produce trade cards, book plates, mastheads, and illustrations for broadsides, newspapers, and magazines.

Revere participated in the emerging protest movement against Great Britain from the mid-1760's to the mid-1770's. An active member of Boston's North End Caucus, the Long Room Club, and the Sons of Liberty Whig Club, he was in the thick of every protest. Apparently content simply to make a contribution, he never rose to a high rank of leadership in the revolutionary movement and never ran for public office.

Revere served as an influential propagandist for the revolutionary cause from the passage of the Stamp Act in 1765 to the beginning of the war, publishing satirical engravings that ridiculed British authority. The best-known copper-plate engraving reads "The BLOODY MASSACRE perpetuated in King Street, BOSTON, on March 5th 1770, by a party of the 29th REGT." Though inaccurately depicting the event and appropriating a drawing of the scene by British artist Henry Pelham without giving Pelham credit, the engraving, by placing blame for shedding first blood upon British troops, stirred hearts of patriots everywhere.

In Boston Harbor on December 16, 1773, Revere joined other patriots barely disguised as American Indians and dumped overboard casks of tea belonging to the British East India Company. He then carried the news of the Boston Tea Party to New York City, becoming the official courier of the Massachusetts Provincial Assembly and the Boston Committee of Correspondence. In May, 1774, he rode to New York City and Philadelphia, bringing word of the parliamentary law that closed the port of Boston. In September, 1774, he carried the radical Suffolk Resolves, drawn up by delegates from Boston and other towns in Suffolk County, to the Continental Congress in Philadelphia; Congress quickly committed all the colonies to the document, which called for the colonies to cease trade with Great Britain and to prepare for armed defense. In December, 1774, Revere relayed news to patriots in New Hampshire that the Massachusetts governor and general, Thomas Gage, was planning to reinforce the small British garrison at Fort William and Mary at Portsmouth; this information led patriots to seize the garrison and its munitions, which were later used by the Americans at the Battle of Bunker Hill (1775).

LIFE'S WORK

Paul Revere was almost unknown in the annals of American history until the publication of Henry Wadsworth Longfellow's narrative poem, "Paul Revere's Ride," in *The Atlantic* in January, 1861. The poem's publication gave Revere an esteemed place in the pantheon of American heroes. On that fateful night of April 18-19, 1775, Revere rowed across the Charles River, with his oars muffled by petticoats wrapped around them, then galloped by horseback toward Concord to warn of the approach of the British. William Dawes and Samuel Prescott joined him; only Prescott made it to Concord. A less well-known fact is that two days earlier, Revere had ridden to Concord to warn John Hancock, Samuel Adams, and others of the British troops' plan to march out of Boston, enabling the removal of much of the munitions from Concord before the British arrived.

Involvement in the war effort distracted Revere from his business enterprises from 1775 to 1779. In 1775, Revere manufactured paper money for the Massachusetts government and the Continental Congress, engraving the plates and building a printing press for the task. He also designed coins, medals, and the first seal of the United States and the state of Massachusetts (the latter remains in use).

Commissioned a major in April, 1776, and lieutenant colonel six months later, Revere was in charge of three artillery companies in the Massachusetts militia. During 1778-1779, he commanded the patriot garrison at Castle William in Boston Harbor. Revere served in the expedition of July-August, 1778, commanded by General John Sullivan, which was unsuccessful in ousting British forces from Newport, Rhode Island. His military career came to an end with the Penobscot expedition of July 19-August 15, 1779. A Massachusetts land and naval force was to attack a British base at Castine, Maine, at the mouth of the Penobscot River. When an unexpected and large British reinforcement arrived, the Americans abandoned their ships and fled. Revere was accused of disobedience of orders, unsoldierlike conduct, and cowardice and was relieved of his command at Castle William. Revere insisted upon a court-martial, and in February, 1782, he was acquitted on all charges.

After the revolution, Revere's silversmith shop increased production, creating pieces in the neoclassic style, more restrained than before, and incorporating some classical designs, such as fluted teapots. More table items were produced, especially flatware, and fourteen types of spoons were cast. In 1783, Revere opened a hardware store.

The Revere enterprises expanded in 1788 with the establishment in Boston of an iron and brass foundry that cast cannon for the state and the federal government and produced a variety of other items such as nails and bolts. When the bell of the Second Congregational Church in Boston cracked in 1792, Revere offered to cast a new one himself rather than have the church order a replacement from England. His offer led to the creation of the first large-scale bell manufactory in America. From 1792 to 1828, the foundry (the bell operation was moved to Canton, Massachusetts, in 1804) produced 950 bells of all sizes and functions, weighing from a few pounds to about 3,000, and cast with 75 percent copper and 25 percent tin. Revere bells can still be found at many New England churches, including King's Chapel in Boston.

Revere also discovered a process for rolling sheet copper. In 1801, he built a mill at Canton for copper rolling and brass casting. The copper works eventually became one of the largest industries in the United States. While Revere was in charge, the Revere Copper and Brass Company made copper boilers for steamships and the copper sheeting for the dome of the Massachusetts State House and for the bottom of the USS *Constitution* (Old Ironsides). In 1811, Revere turned over management of his businesses to his son, Joseph Warren Revere. The Revere Copper Company was chartered in 1828 under his son's direction. The company went through major reorganizations and mergers in the twentieth century and is now known as Revere Copper Products. Over the years, Revere copper has been used in the making of warships, shells, torpedoes, tanks, telephones, radios, plumbing, and many other items.

An avid joiner, Revere belonged to many community groups. He joined the Masonic Order in 1760 and was a founder of the Massachusetts Grand Lodge and served as its grand master (1795-1797). He helped establish the Massachusetts Fire Insurance Company and presided over the Massachusetts Charitable Mechanic Association from 1795 to 1799. He served as Suffolk County coroner (1794-1800) and assisted in setting up the Boston Board of Health, acting as its president (1799-1800).

In early 1788, when it appeared that Massachusetts might fail to ratify the U.S. Constitution, Boston mechanics held a mass meeting, unanimously adopting resolutions in favor of ratification. Revere led a delegation from the group to the home of Samuel Adams, a member of the ratifying convention whose support of the Constitution had been wavering. Adams, impressed by the show of support, voted in favor of the Constitution. The action taken by Revere and his associates may well have been the deciding factor for the acceptance of the Constitution in Massachusetts.

After the Constitution went into effect, Revere expected to be appointed director of the mint or a customs house official, but his ambitions were denied, probably because he was a Federalist, opposed to the Jeffersonian Republicans. He thought of himself as a conservative who believed in the liberal principles of the American Revolution, chiefly liberty and opportunity within the confines of law and order. In an 1804 letter to a friend, Revere called himself a "warm Republican," saying "I always deprecated Democracy as much as I did Aristocracy." Revere may be regarded as "one of the last of the Cocked Hats." His conservatism was evident in his persistence in publicly wearing clothes of the revolutionary era—cocked hats, ruffled shirts, knee breeches, long stockings, large shoe buckles, and the like—long after such dress had fallen from fashion.

SIGNIFICANCE

Paul Revere was a true patriot hero. He was willing to serve in any capacity—courier, agitator, soldier, propagandist, or artisan—to further the revolutionary cause. When patriot leaders wanted something done, they could depend on Revere. Longfellow's stirring poem brought Revere a fame that he never sought to achieve.

A master silversmith, Revere operated a shop that produced an astounding amount and variety of silver pieces, setting a high standard of quality for the craft. He was a pioneer in copper-plate engraving and metallurgy and one of America's earliest large-scale industrialists, running iron and brass foundries and a copper-sheeting mill. Revere, one of the first to inaugurate a factory system in America, put investment capital to use for production, employed new technology, organized and managed a large labor force, made arrangements for acquisition of raw materials needed for production, and provided for transportation of goods to market. Revere founded an enduring, major segment of the copper industry. Daring, persistent, and hardworking, he exemplified what could be attained in a land of opportunity.

—*Harry M. Ward*

Revere, Paul

FURTHER READING

Buker, George E. *The Penobscot Expedition: Commodore Saltanstall and the Massachusetts Conspiracy of 1779*. Annapolis, Md.: Naval Institute Press, 2002. A reexamination of the expedition, including the roles of Revere and Commodore Dudley Saltanstall.

Fischer, David H. *Paul Revere's Ride*. New York: Oxford University Press, 1994. A lively, well-researched narrative focusing on the events of the spring of 1775. Includes copious annotation and a definitive bibliography.

Forbes, Esther. *Paul Revere and the World He Lived In*. Boston: Houghton Mifflin, 1942. This Pulitzer Prize-winning book presents a full biography and a description of the Boston community during Revere's life. Contains a short section of expository footnotes and a bibliography.

Gettemy, Charles F. *The True Story of Paul Revere: His Midnight Ride; His Arrest and Court-Martial; His Useful Public Services*. Boston: Little, Brown, 1905. Mainly a general survey, this volume contains some family letters and quotations from documents. No bibliography.

Goss, Elbridge H. *The Life of Colonel Paul Revere*. 2 vols. Boston: Joseph Cupples, 1891. This work contains a large section on the Penobscot expedition. The Revere family correspondence reproduced in this book is of great value.

Leehey, Patrick M., et al. *Paul Revere—Artisan, Businessman, and Patriot: The Man Behind the Myth*. Boston: Paul Revere Memorial Association, 1988. Essays and illustrations relating primarily to Revere's business and industrial life in the context of an exhibition at the Museum of Our National Heritage at Lexington, Massachusetts, 1988-1989.

Triber, Jayne E. *A True Republican: The Life of Paul Revere*. Amherst: University of Massachusetts Press, 1998. A biography describing Revere's role in the American Revolution, the evolution of his political thought, and his transformation from artisan to entrepreneur. Triber uses Revere's life to illustrate the attraction of republicanism for artisans, social life in colonial and postrevolutionary United States, the importance of Free Masonry, and the development of political parties in the new nation.

Sally Ride

> *All adventures, especially into new territory, are scary.*

Astronaut

NASA astronaut Ride was the first American woman to fly in space when she flew aboard space shuttle Challenger *in 1983 as a mission specialist. She was one of the first of a new breed of astronauts who were, primarily, scientists, and who were called mission specialists. Ride later founded NASA's Office of Exploration.*

Born: May 26, 1951; Encino, California
Also known as: Sally Kristen Ride (full name)
Areas of achievement: Aviation and space exploration; sports; physics

Early Life

Sally Ride was born in Encino, a suburb of the city of Los Angeles. She was the older of two daughters born to Joyce Ride and Dale B. Ride, a member of the faculty at Santa Monica City College. Ride's parents were active as elders in their Presbyterian church, and Joyce often volunteered her time as an English tutor to students from outside the United States and as a counselor at a women's prison.

Ride's parents encouraged her competitive spirit in academics and in athletics. She was a born athlete and often played the rough-and-tumble games of football and baseball with the neighborhood boys. Ride began playing tennis, a less hazardous sport, at the request of her mother. Under the tutelage of tennis great Alice Marble, Sally quickly excelled in this sport and became proficient enough to rank eighteenth nationally. Her excellence in tennis earned her a partial scholarship to Westlake School for Girls (now Harvard-Westlake School), a private preparatory school in Los Angeles. At the preparatory school, Sally became interested in the study of physics through the influence of her science teacher, Elizabeth Mommaerts, and, for the next five years, science and tennis competed for Sally's time and attention.

In 1968, Sally enrolled at Swarthmore College in Pennsylvania as a physics major but left after three terms to concentrate on her tennis game after winning a national collegiate tennis tournament. Although she was a top-ranked college player, she realized that she did not have the talent to advance to professional tennis. Sally returned to college in 1970 and completed a double major in English literature and physics at Stanford University in California in 1973. After graduation, she briefly considered studying Shakespeare in graduate school but settled on astrophysics to further her dream of working for the National Aeronautics and Space Administration (NASA).

Life's Work

Ride began her path to fame while completing work on her doctoral dissertation at Stanford with research into free-electron laser physics. One day she read an announcement in the campus newspaper indicating that NASA was seeking young scientists to serve as mission specialists. Acting on impulse, she applied to join the astronaut program, which had lifted its long-standing policy against women astronauts to attract ad-

Ride, Sally

ditional qualified scientists willing to forgo high salaries and work on the new space shuttle program. To Ride's surprise, she made it through the preliminary screening process to become one of the finalists. In 1977, she was flown to the Johnson Space Center outside Houston, Texas, for exhausting interviews and fitness and psychiatric evaluation tests. After three months of rigorous testing, Ride officially became an astronaut. In 1978, shortly after earning her Ph.D., she reported to the Johnson Space Center to begin the intensive training required of NASA mission specialists.

In the first year of training, Ride learned parachute jumping and water survival techniques, the latter for the possibility that the shuttle might have to be aborted into the ocean. She also acclimated to increased gravity forces, the force encountered during acceleration and deceleration back to Earth, as well as to weightlessness. She had courses in radio communication and navigation and learned to fly a jet. Piloting a jet proved to be an enjoyable experience for Ride, and she eventually acquired a pilot's license. From 1982 until 1987, she was married to fellow astronaut Steven Hawley.

Throughout Ride's preparation time, NASA maintained its bureaucratic composure regarding its inclusion of women in the space shuttle program. There was no flamboyant talk about "one giant step for womankind." Indeed, team player that she was, Ride insisted that her participation in the flight was "no big deal." Whether she liked it or not, news of her flight brought her instant celebrity. Newspapers and television reporters interviewed her again and again, and U.S. president Ronald Reagan gave her extra attention at a White House luncheon. Composer Casse Culver wrote and recorded a song, "Ride, Sally, Ride," and T-shirts urged the same.

Ride was asked to join the shuttle program by U.S. Navy captain Robert L. Crippen, a veteran astronaut who had piloted the first shuttle mission in 1981. Crippen said, of his choice of Ride, that "she is flying with us because she is the very best person for the job. There is no man I would rather have in her place." Ride, in her unassuming manner, simply stated that she had not become an astronaut to become "a historic figure" and that she believed it was "time that people realized that women in this country can do any job that they want to do." Ride's special virtue was that she was so much like the male astronauts and so utterly and convincingly their equal. She was just as determined, just as disciplined, just as fearless, and just as predictable.

On June 18, 1983, Ride blasted off from the Kennedy Space Center in Florida, aboard space shuttle *Challenger* (STS-7) as one of five crew members. On board, she had general mission duties in addition to performing her scientific work. She was chosen to sit behind mission commander Crippen and copilot Frederick Hauck to act as flight engineer during takeoff and landing. During the ninety-six orbits, she and her fellow mission specialist, John Fabian, worked in weightless conditions with the complex Canadarm—a fifty-foot remote "arm" used to move payloads in and out of the shuttle cargo bay. Ride and Fabian trained for two years on the ground with the computerized arm and became experts in its operation. Another task on the mission was to start *Anik-C*, a Canadian domestic communications satellite, on its way to a geosynchronous orbit hovering above Earth's equator. This satellite was designed to handle thirty-two color television channels. A second communications satellite, named *Palapa-B* and owned by the Indonesian government, was launched into orbit to carry voice, video, and telephone signals to Southeast Asia.

Sally Ride. (NASA)

Forty other experiments were conducted by the *Challenger* crew. These included studies of metal alloy manufacture, solar cell testing, growth of semiconductor crystals, and glass production. One experiment, devised by high school students, was a project sending 150 carpenter ants into orbit in the shuttle cargo bay to see how weightlessness affected their social structure. The California Institute of Technology sent an experiment in which radish seedlings were subjected to simulated gravity to find the right gravitational force for best growth. Purdue University's experiment investigated how sunflower seeds germinated in zero gravity. The highlight of the mission was the deployment of a huge free-floating satellite to document its position with the first in-space color photographs before recapturing it. The satellite was then released again and snared once more. The crew repeated this procedure for nine and one-half hours before Ride captured the satellite for the last time and stowed it in the cargo bay for the trip home. *Challenger* landed at Edwards Air Force Base in California on June 24.

Sally's ride (a pun often used by the media) marked major changes in what could no longer be called the United States "manned" space program. Much of the daredevil aspect was now gone from space travel. The object of the space program was not simply getting into orbit but working there. In fact, Ride had recommended to NASA administrator James Fletcher that space be used to study planet Earth.

Two Soviet women preceded Ride into space, but their feats did not leave a lasting mark. In 1963, in the early days of piloted spaceflight, twenty-six-year-old textile mill worker and amateur skydiver Valentina Tereshkova was put on a rocket by the Soviet Union in what was considered by many to be a propaganda coup. Reports of that flight indicate that Tereshkova was sick for most of the three-day flight. In August of 1982, the Soviets launched into space the second woman cosmonaut—thirty-four-year-old test pilot Svetlana Savitskaya. Her presence in space, however, was taken lightly by her colleagues.

Ride went into space a second time aboard the *Challenger* on October 5, 1984, as part of the seven-person crew of STS-41-G. Again, Crippen was the commander. She was joined by Kathryn D. Sullivan, marking the first time that two women had flown on the same space mission. Before landing on October 13, the crew deployed the Earth Radiation Budget Satellite, tested an orbital refueling system, and performed oceanography observations. At the end of the trip, Ride had 343 hours in space.

Ride had been training for a third shuttle trip when the *Challenger* explosion occurred in January, 1986. She was named to the presidential commission that investigated the accident and was chair of a subcommittee on operations. She later worked at NASA's headquarters in Washington, D.C., as special assistant to Fletcher for long-range and strategic planning. As part of her research brief, she produced an influential report entitled "Leadership and America's Future in Space." She also founded NASA's Office of Exploration. In 2003 she served on the Columbia Accident Investigation Board, which studied the accident involving space shuttle *Columbia*.

Ride left NASA in 1987 to be part of Stanford University's Center for International Security and Arms Control. Two years later she moved to the University of California, San Diego (UCSD), as a professor of physics and director of the California Space Institute. Her research focused on the theory of nonlinear beam-wave interactions.

One of Ride's principal interests involved encouraging young people to study science. In 1999 she inaugurated and directed EarthKam, a program permitting school children to take photographs from space and download them to the Web. In 2001, she founded Sally Ride Science, a company dedicated to science education. Her programs encouraged girls in the fifth through eighth grades to pursue science, mathematics, and technology. The company sponsored science camps, a national toy-design competition, festivals, and workshops and provided instruction for teachers, reading packets about individual sciences for public schools, and other publications. Ride also wrote five science books for children about astronomy and space exploration.

Ride received numerous awards and honors. Among them are the Space Flight Medal (twice), Von Braun Award, Lindbergh Eagle, Jefferson Award for Public Service, Theodore Roosevelt Award (the highest honor bestowed by the National Collegiate Athletics Association), and UCSD's Chancellor's Associated Recognition Award for Outstanding Community Service. She was inducted into the National Women's Hall of Fame, Astronaut Hall of Fame, International Scholar-Athlete Hall of Fame, and California Hall of Fame.

Ride, Sally

SIGNIFICANCE

For all the merits of the scientific and experimental aspects of the voyages of the space shuttle *Challenger*, Ride was the one who provoked the world's curiosity. Cool, calm, and controlled in all circumstances, Ride hurtled through space aboard the one-hundred-ton white-and-blue shuttle, proving that she was certainly made of "the right stuff."

Ride's legacy as an astronaut-scientist also came to signify the ascendancy of the mission specialist over the pilot. The close-knit brotherhood of test and fighter pilots who made up the original astronaut corps was diluted by those having a new kind of skill—the ability to do quadratic equations and conduct scientific experiments instead of fancy flying alone. Under these developing guidelines, Ride became the ideal candidate—and the ideal NASA astronaut—because of her scientific background and because she was able to learn and readily solve new problems.

Being a respected space pioneer was more important to Ride than achieving celebrity as a woman astronaut. Her space shuttle career earned for her the trust and high regard of her colleagues as well as the admiration of an entire nation. Following her work with the space shuttle program, she would continue to encourage young people, especially girls, to pursue careers in science.

—*Jane A. Slezak*

FURTHER READING

America's Space Shuttle: Shuttle Mission Reports and Astronaut Biographies, Documents on the Past, Present, and Future of the Shuttle. Mt. Laurel, N.J.: Progressive Management, 2001. A massive, 12,305-page CD-ROM collection of documents chronicling the history of the space shuttle program and shuttle astronauts. The disk includes the complete Johnson Space Center mission reports for each flight up to 2001.

Begley, Sharon. "Challenger: Ride, Sally Ride." *Newsweek*, June 13, 1983. An overview of Ride's life and the results of her crucial decision to join the elite NASA astronaut group in preparation for missions on the space shuttle.

Camp, Carole Ann. *Sally Ride: First Woman in Space*. Springfield, N.J.: Enslow, 1997. For young adult readers, this biography supplies a wealth of information about Ride's NASA career, emphasizing her dedication and the fascination of spaceflight. Includes a chronology and bibliographical references for further study.

Fox, Mary Virginia. *Women Astronauts: Aboard the Shuttle*. Rev. ed. New York: J. Messner, 1987. Chronicles the experiences of women selected for the space shuttle program. Aimed at young readers, this work discusses Ride's experiences as the first American woman to fly in space as well as the women who followed.

Golden, Frederic. "Sally's Joy Ride into the Sky." *Time*, June 27, 1983. In the magazine's section on space, Golden tells of Ride's experiences on the second orbiting flight of the space shuttle *Challenger* and includes Ride's observations regarding the public's reaction to her flight.

Harland, David M. *The Space Shuttle: Roles, Missions, and Accomplishments*. New York: John Wiley & Sons, 1998. Covers the complete history of the shuttle program up to the late 1990's, with a section on exploration and discussion of shuttle operations. Includes glossary, bibliography, and index.

Robeson, Paul

Kevles, Bettyann. *Almost Heaven: The Story of Women in Space.* Cambridge, Mass.: MIT Press, 2006. Excellent history of female astronauts that provides details, photographs, and quotations from the astronauts about their pioneering accomplishments in space.

Ride, Sally, and Tam O'Shaughnessy. *Exploring Our Solar System.* New York: Crown, 2003. This splendidly vivid book exemplifies Ride's campaign to intrigue pre-teens and teens in science. It provides them with a tour of the solar system, emphasizing both fact and the adventure of discovery. Accompanied by more than one hundred color photographs and graphics.

Shayler, David, and Ian Moule. *Women in Space—Following Valentina.* New York: Springer, 2005. A history of women in space, from balloonists to astronauts, with updated accounts based on interviews with women with careers in flight.

PAUL ROBESON

❝ *As an artist I come to sing, but as a citizen, I will always speak for peace, and no one can silence me in this.* **❞**

Athlete, actor, and activist

A Renaissance man, Robeson made unprecedented contributions to American and world history as an athlete, intellectual, performer, and internationally renowned peace advocate. In politics, he championed the cause of human rights for African Americans and other oppressed people throughout the world.

Born: April 9, 1898; Princeton, New Jersey
Died: January 23, 1976; Philadelphia, Pennsylvania
Also known as: Paul Bustill Robeson (full name)
Areas of achievement: Sports; theater and entertainment; film; oratory; diplomacy; civil rights; social reform

EARLY LIFE

Paul Bustill Robeson (ROHB-suhn) was born at a time when African Americans were politically disenfranchised, economically exploited, excluded from the mainstream of American life, and suffering the worst racial hostility since the abolition of slavery. Paul was the youngest of six children born to the Reverend William Drew Robeson and Maria Louisa Bustill Robeson. His mother was a member of the prominent Bustill family of Philadelphia, some of whom were patriots in the American Revolutionary War. The Bustills helped to establish the Free African Society and produced a long line of teachers, artisans, and ministers to the Northern free black community. Paul's father, William Drew Robeson, was born a slave in Martin County, North Carolina. He fled to the North and, with the outbreak of the Civil War, joined the Union army. After the war, William Robeson attended Lincoln University and received a divinity degree.

Paul was six years old when his mother died; the family moved to Sommerville,

New Jersey, where Paul received most of his early education. The greatest influences on Paul for the remainder of his life were his family tradition, the environment of Jim Crow America, and the experience of being reared by his father. At an early age, Paul, who often worked with his father after school, sang in his father's church, listened to stories about slavery, and became imbued with several basic principles: to labor diligently in all endeavors, pursue worthwhile goals, maintain high standards, be of service to his people, and maintain his integrity.

At age seventeen, Robeson won a state scholarship to Rutgers University in New Brunswick, New Jersey. Those who knew him described him as a good-natured person who loved life. Striving for perfection in his work, this handsome six foot three inch man maintained a sense of quiet, modest self-confidence. While attending Rutgers, he established an unprecedented academic record, achieving the highest grades in his class. He was also considered to be without equal in athletics.

Although football was his favorite sport, he participated in basketball, track and field, and baseball, winning an astonishing twelve major letters in four years. He was honored as the greatest athlete in Rutgers's history, elected to the All-American team twice (in 1917 and 1918), and has been called the greatest defensive back ever to tread the gridiron. Robeson brought the school national recognition by being the first player ever named All-American in any sport at Rutgers.

Robeson also loved public speaking and debate. A master in elocution contests, for four consecutive years he won first-place honors in many speaking competitions, excelling in oratory, in extemporaneous speaking, and in forensics.

Robeson won admission to Rutgers's exclusive Cap and Skull honor association and the prestigious Phi Beta Kappa society. His senior thesis, "The Fourteenth Amendment: The Sleeping Giant of the American Constitution," by identifying several ways in which the law could be used to secure civil rights for black Americans, presaged by nearly forty years ideas adopted by the United States Supreme Court in the landmark decision, *Brown v. Board of Education* (1954). At commencement, he delivered the class oration, and afterward Rutgers honored him as the "perfect type of college man."

LIFE'S WORK

In 1920, Robeson began law school at Columbia University and played a few games of professional football to finance his education. While at Columbia, he met and married Eslanda Goode Cardozo. They had a son, Paul, Jr., in 1927. After his graduation, Robeson worked briefly for a New York law firm; after encountering considerable hostility in the legal profession, however, he took up acting as a career.

During his law-school days, Robeson played Simon in a benefit play, *Simon the Cyrenian* (1921), staged at the Harlem Young Men's Christian Association by the Provincetown Players, a Greenwich Village theater group. His successful performance led to other parts, and he was offered the lead in two plays by Eugene O'Neill, *All God's Chillun Got Wings* (1924) and, in 1924, *The Emperor Jones* (1920). Robeson's acting was immediately acclaimed. He also made theater history, for that production of *All God's Chillun Got Wings* was the first in which a black man played the leading role opposite a white woman on the American stage. The young actor

Robeson, Paul

starred in numerous plays, including *Black Boy* (1925) by Jim Tully and Frank Dazey, *Porgy* (1927) by DuBose and Dorothy Heyward, and *Show Boat* (1927) by Jerome Kern and Oscar Hammerstein II. He successfully toured Europe in the late 1920's and throughout the 1930's, drawing massive, enthusiastic crowds. Robeson played Othello in William Shakespeare's play at London's Savoy Theatre in 1930, where the opening performance received twenty curtain calls. He reached the pinnacle of his stage career in 1943-1944, with his New York performance in *Othello*, which holds the record for the longest run of any Shakespearean play produced on Broadway. His ovations were among "the most prolonged and wildest . . . in the history of the New York theatre."

In one scene from the 1924 production of Eugene O'Neill's *The Emperor Jones*, Robeson was asked to whistle; instead, he sang a black spiritual. To his listeners' delighted surprise, he had a marvelous voice. This event launched an illustrious musical career that brought additional celebrity. Robeson began augmenting his acting by singing spirituals. He was the first person to give entire programs of exclusively African American songs in concert to white audiences. This innovation made Robeson one of the most popular concert singers for more than a quarter of a century. Later, he broadened his repertoire to include the music of other nationalities. Accompanied on piano by Lawrence Brown, Robeson's magnificent baritone voice thrilled audiences around the world. Jerome Kern's "Ol' Man River" became his personal signature, concluding every concert.

Paul Robeson.
(Library of Congress)

Robeson made several films, the more significant being *The Emperor Jones* (1933), *Sanders of the River* (1935), *Show Boat* (1936), *The Song of Freedom* (1937), *King Solomon's Mines* (1937), *Jericho* (1937), and *Big Fella* (1938). He was particularly pleased with *Proud Valley* (1939), which depicted the harsh life of Welsh coal miners and gave a fair and accurate portrayal of black people, and his narration for *Native Land* (1942), a moving documentary on contemporary American life. Although British filmmakers, unlike their American counterparts, were willing to feature Robeson in major roles, with few exceptions these films depicted blacks in a demeaning manner. Disgusted at the results, Robeson picketed his own films, abandoned the cinema, and focused attention on the stage, where he could control and determine the images in every performance.

As Robeson became more successful in the theater and on the concert stage, he committed himself to improving the plight of blacks. He believed that with his singing and acting he could increase the white world's respect, knowledge, and understanding of his people. "They will," he said in 1932, "sense that we are moved by the same emotions, have the same beliefs, the same longings—that we are all humans together." Moreover, his prominence motivated him to reaffirm his black identity, and he started a campaign to educate black people about the virtues of their own cultural heritage, arguing that African history was as old and significant as that of the Chinese or Persians. Uncompromisingly, he maintained that "it should be the mission of Negro artists to earn respect as Negroes as a step toward making the white race eventually respect the black." He believed that blacks had a unique and valuable contribution to make in humanizing the world through their philosophy and art.

Robeson developed a sophisticated concept of cultural pluralism that had at its roots a deep respect for his own nationality. Living in Europe during the 1930's, he determined to use art to advance the cause of his own people and to use it on a grander scale to build a more humane world. Art would be the vehicle to unite all people against the common foes of poverty, exploitation, bigotry, political violence, and war. He began studying world cultures, history, politics, and economic and social systems, and he became fluent in more than two dozen languages, including Ashanti, Mande, Swahili, Yoruba, Hindustani, Arabic, Chinese, German, Russian, French, Spanish, and Finnish.

Robeson's cultural philosophy led him to more direct political activity. In 1934, at the invitation of film director Sergei Eisenstein, he made the first of several trips to the Soviet Union. He spoke out against the fascist politics of the Nazis and was the only American entertainer to go to Spain and sing to Loyalist troops. At a rally sponsored to aid Spanish refugee children held in 1937 at London's Royal Albert Hall, he remarked, "The artist must take sides. He must elect to fight for freedom or slavery. I have made my choice." He raised money to fight the Italian invasion of Ethiopia and opposed all forms of colonialism. Robeson supported the Committee to Aid China, denounced Japanese imperialism, and made a special album of Chinese songs, *Chee Lai* (1940), which he recorded in the language to raise money for Chinese relief. The foremost spokesperson against European colonialism, he led the campaign for African independence and became chair of the Council on African Affairs, which he helped establish in 1937. With the outbreak of World War II, he supported the American effort by entertaining soldiers in camps and laborers in war industries. Many of his concerts were greeted by some of the largest audiences of military personnel and civilian workers ever assembled during wartime.

By 1946, Robeson became more determined than ever to work for an end to colonialism in Africa, Asia, and the Caribbean. For the second time in his life, black soldiers were returning from a war to preserve democracy only to be greeted with racism and bigotry. Robeson could no longer tolerate the status of second-class citizenship imposed on blacks. Jeopardizing his career and spending more than $100,000 a year, he devoted his time to campaigning for black civil rights. He spoke on behalf of trade unions who found their wartime, New Deal economic gains eroded; defended Native Americans; denounced sexism; backed Henry Wallace and the Progressive Party; and confronted President Harry S. Truman, demanding that he put an end to lynchings in the South and segregation in the armed forces and that he enforce fair employment practices for minority laborers.

Disturbed by Robeson's militance, opponents labeled him a Communist to undermine his legitimate dissent and weaken his mass appeal. When Cold War tensions and McCarthyistic hysteria mounted, Robeson's detractors tried to discredit him, and on several occasions he was called to testify before government committees regarding his loyalty to the United States. Repeatedly he challenged the officials, reminding them of the unconstitutionality of these proceedings, and refused to be baited into identifying anyone of his associates or activities as being un-American.

As the fear of war between the United States and the Soviet Union escalated, Robeson, at the 1949 Paris Peace Conference, called for a cessation of hostilities and an end to the arms race. A cogent and powerful speaker, he articulated the similarities in attitude between many domestic and international policies, suggesting that the black people of the world, whether in the South or in colonies abroad, had no quarrel with Russia. Their grievance was more immediate; it was with those who oppressed them: "the senators who have just filibustered them out of their civil rights. . . . Milan in South Africa who, just like Hitler, is threatening to destroy eight million Africans and hundreds of thousands of Indians through hunger and terror."

In the 1950's, Robeson was viciously attacked for his statements. Riots occurred, disrupting his concerts in Peekskill, New York. His opposition to the United States' participation in the Korean War brought a barrage of criticism. Books and information about his achievements were removed from library circulation and stricken from histories, anthologies, and bibliographic references. Blacklisting and intimidation cost him his theatrical and concert bookings and a domestic audience. His passport was revoked, and he was barred from travel outside the United States. According to the State Department's brief, action was taken "solely because of his recognized status as a spokesman for large sections of Negro Americans . . . in view of his frank admission that he has been for years active politically in behalf of independence of the colonial people of Africa."

The government offered to return his passport if he signed a statement that he would not make any speeches while abroad; Robeson refused. He lost the lucrative income from concerts and an international forum. In the meantime, he continued to accept invitations to speak and sing before labor organizations, civic groups, and black churches.

One amazing concert was mounted in 1953, when Canadians arranged to meet Robeson near the border at Blain, Washington, where he spoke and sang to nearly thirty thousand people who jammed the Peace Arch Park.

With the Supreme Court ruling in 1958, Robeson's passport was reinstated. He published his autobiography, *Here I Stand* (1958), and resumed a vigorous speaking and concert tour, traveling to Great Britain, the Soviet Union, Germany, New Zealand, and Australia. Dispelling any misconceptions about his actions, he stated, "The truth is, I am not and never have been involved in any international conspiracy or any other kind, and do not know anyone who is."

Whenever he spoke crowds gathered. Yet the physical strain of the previous decades had taken its toll. In 1961, illness caused him to retire from singing and acting, and in 1963 he returned to the United States, where he remained in seclusion until his death in 1976.

SIGNIFICANCE

During his life, Paul Robeson received hundreds of awards and tributes for his superlative artistic achievements, phenomenal intellectual contributions, and unparalleled political sacrifices on behalf of world freedom and international peace. The British parliament set aside a day to honor him. He won the Donaldson Award for Best Acting Performance, received the American Academy of Arts and Sciences' Gold Medal for Best Diction, and was awarded numerous honorary degrees from colleges. He was honored with the Badge of the Veterans of the Abraham Lincoln Brigade, for those who fought for Republican Spain against Francisco Franco, the Thirtieth Annual Spingarn Medal, and the National Federation for Constitutional Liberties' award. Further, he received the Lenin Peace Prize and the African Freedom Award, as well as other international honors. His prodigious career included eleven films, five documentaries, nearly two dozen plays, and hundreds of records. His meticulous and constant scholarship resulted in three dozen articles, one book, and hundreds of addresses and speeches.

Robeson believed that he could show the world through the media of entertainment that racism and exploitation of all people had to end. For him, art had a definite purpose. Aside from offering pleasure and joy, art was enhanced when it enlightened people; this was the true essence of art's potential to uplift the human spirit.

During the 1930's, Robeson integrated his artistic career with that of a political activist, a socialist cultural philosopher, and a peace advocate. Seeing German fascism at firsthand compelled him to fight against it. He called for "immediate action" to save the Jews of Europe even though it might mean "heavy sacrifice and death." His interest in labor organization grew out of his pioneering effort as a founder of the Unity Theatre in England.

Robeson supported popular liberation movements in Asia, Africa, and the Caribbean in the 1930's and 1940's. He wrote on behalf of Philippine independence from the United States and was the most prominent voice against colonial rule in Africa. Robeson pioneered in the antiapartheid movement, counseling in the 1940's that "we cannot afford to tolerate the advocates of White Supremacy in South Africa, any more than we can agree to the activities of the Ku Klux Klan in Georgia or Mississippi."

Robeson, Paul

Robeson was without peer in championing the cause of worldwide democracy, yet he became one of the greatest casualties of the Cold War. Actions that won approval and praise in the 1920's and 1930's brought derision and enmity in the late 1940's and 1950's. (Earl Schenck Miers, at the height of Robeson's vilification, wrote in *The Nation* that, "as a product of his times, Robeson today is perhaps more All-American than he was as a member of his college.") His constitutional rights were violated, and a torrent of hostility was directed against him.

A new generation of Americans, rediscovering Robeson in the 1970's, brought increasing recognition of his achievements. No doubt they would be reassured by his last public statement just before his death: "Though I have not been able to be active for several years, I want you to know that I am the same Paul, dedicated, as ever, to the worldwide cause of humanity, for freedom, peace and brotherhood." As William Shakespeare's Othello said in his last speech before they took him away: "Soft you; a word or two before you go. I have done the state some service, and they know't." With his genius and his humanism, Paul Robeson did indeed serve the state extraordinarily well.

—*Lamont H. Yeakey*

FURTHER READING

Boyle, Sheila Tully, and Andrew Bunie. *Paul Robeson: The Years of Promise and Achievement*. Amherst: University of Massachusetts Press, 2001. Tracing Robeson's life from his birth through 1939, this biography describes how his radical politics were a response to racism and how these political views affected his life and career.

Davis, Lenwood G. *A Paul Robeson Research Guide: A Selected Annotated Bibliography*. Westport, Conn.: Greenwood Press, 1982. All Robeson scholars must consult this very fine bibliography. Given the difficulty in identifying foreign and obscure domestic material on Robeson, this rather large compendium is a timely and essential reference.

Foner, Philip S., ed. *Paul Robeson Speaks: Writings, Speeches, Interviews, 1918-1974*. New York: Brunner/Mazel, 1978. This is an extremely valuable reader containing most of Robeson's major published material. Those interested in twentieth century history and politics must include this volume on their reading lists.

Freedomways Associates. *Paul Robeson: The Great Forerunner*. New York: International, 1985. This anthology contains a number of short articles on various aspects of Robeson's life. Also included are a few documents and numerous tributes to the man from friends, associates, and admirers, who appreciated his contributions to humanity.

Gilliam, Dorothy Butler. *Paul Robeson: All-American*. Washington, D.C.: New Republic, 1976. This thoughtful biography of Paul Robeson is the best of the recent surveys of his life. The author, however, fails to explain adequately political events in the 1930's or Cold War issues that shaped his thinking.

Robeson, Paul. *Here I Stand*. New York: Othello, 1958. Although short and succinct, this autobiography covers Robeson's life, beginning with his family and concluding with his sixtieth birthday. This fascinating personal account should be read by everyone.

Robeson, Paul, Jr. *The Undiscovered Paul Robeson: An Artist's Journey, 1898-1939*. New York: Wiley, 2001. In the first book of a projected two-volume biography, Robeson's son explores his father's life, career, and intellectual development. Robeson is the owner and archivist of his parents' archives, and he uses materials from that collection to provide new information about his father and mother.

Seton, Marie. *Paul Robeson*. London: D. Dobson Books, 1958. Seton, a longtime friend of Robeson since the early 1930's, has written the best biography of the man to date. Filled with many colorful insights, Seton endeavors to explain the origin of Robeson's radicalism in the 1930's. The work should be updated to cover the period from 1958 until his death in 1976.

Stuckey, Sterling. "'I Want to Be African': Paul Robeson and the Ends of Nationalist Theory and Practice, 1914-1945." *Massachusetts Review* 17 (Spring, 1976): 81-138. This stimulating article treats the development and expression of Robeson's cultural nationalism in the 1930's. The author is correct in asserting that the actor had a profound understanding of African culture and its possibilities as a humanistic approach to life that, if accepted by the West, might benefit the entire world.

Walwik, Joseph. *The Peekskill, New York, Anti-Communist Riots of 1949*. Lewiston, N.Y.: Edwin Mellen Press, 2002. Recounts the violent demonstrations staged by veterans' groups and others to protest Robeson's comments about American racism.

Wright, Charles H. *The Peace Advocacy of Paul Robeson*. Detroit, Mich.: Harlo Press, 1984. This short pamphlet provides valuable insight into a hitherto misunderstood aspect of Robeson's political activities: his role as one of the world's leading antiwar pioneers at the start of the nuclear age.

_____. *Robeson: Labor's Forgotten Champion*. Detroit, Mich.: Balamp, 1975. Although much has been written about Robeson, this book stands alone as the only treatment of his trade union activities, a vital commitment to which the artist devoted much of his life. Another virtue of the book is its insight into labor's views and support for this champion of the working class.

JACKIE ROBINSON

" *Life is not a spectator sport.* **"**

Baseball player

Robinson was the first black to play in the major leagues and as such is known for breaking the "color line" in baseball. A hero for his brilliant career with the Brooklyn Dodgers, he was elected to the Baseball Hall of Fame.

Born: January 31, 1919; Cairo, Georgia
Died: October 24, 1972; Stamford, Connecticut
Also known as: Jack Roosevelt Robinson (full name); Dark Dasher (nickname)
Area of achievement: Sports

EARLY LIFE

Jackie Robinson was the fifth child born to Mallie Robinson and Jerry Robinson, sharecroppers of Cairo, Georgia. Robinson's grandparents had been slaves. When he was six months old, his father abandoned the family, and a year later his mother took the family to Pasadena, California, where Robinson grew up. Although poor, Robinson's mother saved money and ultimately purchased a house in a previously all-white neighborhood. This was Robinson's first experience as a pioneer in integration. As a child, Robinson excelled in all sports. In high school, community college, and at the University of California, Los Angeles (UCLA), Robinson starred in baseball, basketball, football, and track. In 1938, at Pasadena Junior College, he broke the national community college record for the broad jump, previously set by his older brother, Mack Robinson, who himself had won a silver medal at the 1936 Olympics. In 1939, he entered UCLA, where he became the school's first letterman in four sports. Robinson's best sport was football; in 1941, he was named an All-American. That year, he dropped out of college to earn money for his family.

In 1941, Robinson played professional football with the Honolulu Bears. Drafted in 1942, Robinson applied for Officer's Candidate School at Fort Riley, Kansas. Although admitted to the program, Robinson and the other black candidates received no training until pressure from Washington forced the local commander to admit blacks to the base training school. Robinson's reputation as a sports hero helped to generate that pressure. As a second lieutenant, Robinson successfully challenged some of the Jim Crow policies at the base post exchange. He quit the base football team in protest when the Army agreed to keep him out of a game with the nearby University of Missouri, because that school refused to play against black opponents. Transferred to Fort Hood, Texas, Robinson protested segregation on an Army bus. His protests led to a court-martial; he was acquitted and honorably discharged. The Army had little desire to keep the person who kept fighting against racism, and for his part, Robinson was, as he later wrote in his autobiography, "pretty much fed up with the service."

LIFE'S WORK

Out of the Army, Robinson secured a tryout with the Kansas City Monarchs, a leading team in the segregated Negro Leagues. He was quickly offered four hundred dollars a month. In August, 1945, while playing for the Monarchs, Robinson was approached by a scout for the Brooklyn Dodgers. Dodger president Branch Rickey was publicly calling for a new black baseball league, with a team to be called the Brooklyn Brown Dodgers. Rickey wanted Robinson for the team and asked him to come to Brooklyn for a meeting.

Robinson traveled to Brooklyn to meet Rickey. The twenty-six-year-old Robinson was just under six feet tall and weighed 195 pounds. He was handsome, agile, and a natural athlete of almost limitless potential. He was also intelligent and articulate and one of the best-educated black baseball players in the United States. He had grown up in an integrated world and played on integrated teams in high school and college. He was the perfect candidate for Rickey's great experiment: the integration of the major leagues.

The meeting between Robinson and Rickey is a classic in American sports. Robinson expected to talk about a new black baseball team. Instead, Rickey asked him if he had a girlfriend, and on hearing about Robinson's college sweetheart, Rachel Isum, Rickey told him to marry her. Robinson was puzzled. Rickey continued the conversation, asking Robinson if he knew why he was there. Robinson mentioned the Brown Dodgers. No, Rickey told him, Robinson was brought there to play for the real

Jackie Robinson. (National Baseball Library, Cooperstown, New York)

Dodgers, to integrate baseball. Rickey then began to detail Robinson's life for him. Robinson had not been scouted simply for his baseball skills; he had been scouted for his character. Rickey wanted to know if he had the courage to be the first black athlete to play in the major leagues—if he could stand the insults, the racial slurs, the beanballs, without fighting back. Rickey swore at Robinson, called him the worst possible names, and tried in other ways to anger him. The meeting was "tough" according to Robinson, but necessary, because for Robinson, baseball would not simply be a matter of box scores. That day, he signed a contract for six hundred dollars a month with a thirty-five-hundred-dollar bonus. Rickey, who was a businessman as well as a man with a strong sense of social justice, knew that Robinson had only an oral contract with the Monarchs, which was renewed monthly. Thus, Rickey never offered to pay the Monarchs for the rights to Robinson's contract.

On October 23, 1945, the Brooklyn Dodgers shocked America by announcing that Jackie Robinson would be playing for their number-one farm team, the Montreal Royals. Southerners asserted that they would never play on the same team as Robinson; white sports reporters declared that he had few baseball skills and would never make it to the major leagues; owners of other baseball teams complained about Rickey's breaking the unwritten rule against hiring blacks. The manager of the Royals, a Mississippian, privately begged Rickey not to send Robinson to his team. In spring training in Florida, Robinson faced segregation as he had never seen it before. Buses, restaurants, hotels, and all other public facilities were rigidly segregated. On the way to Florida, Robinson and his new wife were twice asked to leave their airplane seats to make room for white passengers. Later, they were forced to move to the back of a bus. These were common experiences for southern blacks but had been unknown to the California couple. During training, Robinson could not stay with the team at a local hotel but had to live with a local black family. Tensions were high throughout the spring.

Despite a poor spring training, Robinson started at second base for the Montreal Royals in the opening game. His performance was masterful. He had four hits, including a three-run home run, scored four times, and stole two bases. His baserunning so unnerved opposition pitchers that twice they balked with Robinson on third base, which allowed him to score. This was the beginning of a promising career.

That first year, Robinson faced hateful racist crowds and opponents in a number of cities. Often this only spurred Robinson on. For example, at Syracuse, the opposing players threw a black cat on the field, yelling, "Hey, Jackie, there's your cousin." Robinson then hit a double and shouted to the Syracuse bench, "I guess my cousin's pretty happy now." Robinson was totally unnerved by the crowd, however, when he played in Louisville in a postseason championship game. The southern crowd mercilessly booed him with "a torrent of mass hatred," as he later described it. In Montreal, on the other hand, Robinson, nicknamed the Dark Dasher for his baserunning skills, was a star and a hero. When he made the game's winning hit in the last game of the "little world series," he was carried off the field by his teammates and had to run from an adoring crowd. One sportswriter noted that it was "probably the only day in history that a black man ran from a white mob with love instead of lynching on its mind."

In 1947, Robinson started for the Brooklyn Dodgers. Enormous pressures and ra-

Robinson, Jackie

cial insults hampered his playing. A few Dodgers, most notably Fred "Dixie" Walker, asked to be traded. The St. Louis Cardinals, playing in a segregated city, threatened to boycott Dodger games. The manager of the Philadelphia Phillies, Ben Chapman of Alabama, became so abusive that the commissioner of baseball, himself a southerner, intervened. By the end of the season, most of Robinson's teammates were behind him, as were many opponents. Robinson smothered his temper, absorbed insults, and fought back only with his bat, glove, and baserunning. He led the league in stolen bases that year, batted .297, and electrified fans with his baserunning, including his ability to steal home. The *Sporting News*, which had initially predicted that he would never make it to the major leagues, voted him Rookie of the Year. More significant, a public opinion poll found him the second most popular man in America, behind the singer Bing Crosby.

Two years later, in 1949, Robinson led the National League in hitting with a .342 average and was named Most Valuable Player. By then, a few other blacks, including Roy Campanella, Don Newcombe, Larry Doby, and the legendary pitcher LeRoy "Satchel" Paige, had entered the major leagues. Most major-league teams were beginning to scout black ballplayers. In 1950, Hollywood gave its stamp of approval to the experiment by hiring Robinson to star in a film about himself entitled *The Jackie Robinson Story*. Robinson was now making the rather princely sum of thirty-five thousand dollars a year from the Dodgers, as well as additional income from endorsements and promotions. The Dodgers were the dominant team in their league, and Ebbets Field was attracting large crowds. The experiment seemed to be paying off for all concerned. The owners of teams in the Negro Leagues, however, complained that their players were being stolen from them by the major-league teams and that, with one or two exceptions, they were never compensated. The complaints were justified as Negro League stars such as Paige, Campanella, and Monte Irvin, and future great stars such as Hank Aaron and Willie Mays, were indeed being hired by forward-thinking, previously all-white baseball teams. By the early 1950's, all but a few teams—most notably the New York Yankees and the Boston Red Sox—would have black players.

After the 1950 season, Rickey left the Dodgers and was replaced by Walter O'Malley. Robinson feuded with his new boss for the next six years. O'Malley seemed uninterested in challenging the status quo, while Robinson would no longer quietly accept racist insults. For example, O'Malley was unsympathetic to Robinson's demand that he be allowed to stay at the same hotels as his teammates. Robinson contemplated leaving baseball in 1954 and finally did so after the 1956 season. Robinson secretly sold the exclusive story of his retirement to *Look* magazine. Meanwhile, the Dodgers sold Robinson's contract to the New York Giants, their crosstown rival. Despite an offer of sixty thousand dollars a year, Robinson stuck to his plans and left baseball.

Robinson did not, however, fade from public life. He accepted a job with a New York restaurant chain and continued to work actively in civil rights causes. He became a major fund-raiser for the National Association for the Advancement of Colored People in the 1950's. In the 1960 presidential election primaries, he campaigned for Hubert H. Humphrey, but in a decision he later regretted, he supported Richard M. Nixon in the general election. Henry Cabot Lodge, Nixon's running mate, promised Robinson that Nixon would appoint a black person to a cabinet position. In addition,

Robinson, Jackie

Robinson was unimpressed with John F. Kennedy's record on civil rights. Robinson later wrote: "The Richard Nixon I met back in 1960 bore no resemblance to the Richard Nixon as President." After the 1960 election, Robinson became closely associated with Nelson Rockefeller, the liberal New York Republican governor. In 1964, he became one of Rockefeller's advisers on civil rights and a deputy director of his presidential campaign. After the nomination of Barry Goldwater, however, Robinson became a national leader of the Republicans for Johnson. At about this time, Robinson also became involved in the formation of a black-owned bank in Harlem, the Freedom National Bank. Robinson correctly noted that white-owned banks offered few services to blacks, and he believed that the situation could be remedied only with black-controlled capital. In 1966, he accepted an appointment from Governor Rockefeller as a special assistant to the governor for community affairs.

While Robinson became involved in politics and business, he was never fully divorced from baseball. In 1962, he was elected to the Baseball Hall of Fame. In the early 1950's, he had publicly attacked those teams, such as the New York Yankees, which had not yet hired black players. In the late 1960's, he began to campaign for the hiring of a black manager. He accused the men of professional baseball of hypocrisy and of maintaining a double standard in allowing blacks to play but not to manage. In 1972, Robinson threw the first ball out at the World Series. Given a public forum, he declared, on national television, "I'd like to live to see a black manager; I'd like to live to see the day when there is a black man coaching at third base." When asked why he had to use the World Series to raise this issue, he responded, "What better place? What better time?" Nine days later, Robinson died at age fifty-three of complications caused by diabetes.

SIGNIFICANCE

Robinson's significance is twofold. First, he was an outstanding athlete and one of the most exciting baseball players of his time. In the late 1970's, the New York Mets would use pictures of Robinson in their advertising campaigns, knowing that the memory of his playing could still thrill fans. In an age of power-hitters, Robinson brought back base-stealing, bunting for hits, and finesse. His ability to unnerve pitchers was uncanny. His daring in stealing home, even in a tight World Series game, brought spectators to their feet. He was a trusted player who came through with the big hit, or the big stolen base, at a crucial moment in the game. He was a star with charisma and class. He was truly one of the greatest sports heroes of his age.

Second, Robinson was a pioneer. While he had the backing of Rickey and the help of many players and fans when he integrated baseball, it was Robinson who had to bear the racial slurs, duck the beanballs, and dodge spikes aimed at his body. Robinson did this with grace and dignity, but he also did it with fire. Moreover, he was able to make the transition from turning the other cheek to fighting back verbally. He was the ultimate competitor, for after his baseball career he continued to fight for racial justice and equality. To the end, Robinson spoke out against all forms of segregation.

—Paul Finkelman

FURTHER READING

Eig, Jonathan. *Opening Day: The Story of Jackie Robinson's First Season.* New York: Simon & Schuster, 2007. Focuses on 1947, Robinson's first season with the Brooklyn Dodgers, describing his relationship with his teammates, fans, and players from other teams and how his hiring by a major-league team affected his family and other African Americans.

Erskine, Carl, with Burton Rocks. *What I Learned from Jackie Robinson: A Teammate's Reflections on and off the Field.* New York: McGraw-Hill, 2005. Erskine recalls his days as a member of the Brooklyn Dodgers, reminiscing about Robinson and other teammates.

Frommer, Harvey. *Rickey and Robinson: The Men Who Broke Baseball's Color Line.* New York: Macmillan, 1982. Excellent dual biography of Branch Rickey, the owner of the Dodgers who hired Robinson, and Robinson. Follows careers of both beyond their years in baseball, to their deaths.

Lamb, Chris. *Blackout: The Untold Story of Jackie Robinson's First Spring Training.* Lincoln: University of Nebraska Press, 2004. Chronicles Robinson's 1946 spring training with the Montreal Royals, a farm club for the Brooklyn Dodgers, detailing his experiences during his six weeks in segregated Florida.

Lowenfish, Lee. *Branch Rickey: Baseball's Ferocious Gentleman.* Lincoln: University of Nebraska Press, 2007. This biography of Rickey recounts how and why the Brooklyn Dodgers' manager signed Robinson to the team and the results of this decision.

Peterson, Robert. *Only the Ball Was White.* Englewood Cliffs, N.J.: Prentice-Hall, 1970. History of black baseball. Contains important information on early black players and the organization of the Negro Leagues.

Robinson, Jackie. *Baseball Has Done It.* Edited by Charles Dexter. Philadelphia: J. B. Lippincott, 1964. Part autobiography, part history of the integration of baseball, and part a history of the blacks who played in the Negro Leagues, this book is also Robinson's first long statement about race relations and integration after he left baseball. Written during the early years of the civil rights revolution, this is an important book that links civil rights to baseball. The book also gives important details about the events leading up to Robinson's breaking of the color line.

———. *I Never Had It Made.* New York: G. P. Putnam's Sons, 1972. Robinson's autobiography, published just before he died. A key source for Robinson's life, especially after he left baseball.

Rogosin, Donn. *Invisible Men: Life in Baseball's Negro Leagues.* New York: Atheneum, 1983. Study of black baseball before the integration of the major leagues. Based on extensive interviews with former players. Readable yet scholarly.

Tygiel, Jules. *Baseball's Great Experiment: Jackie Robinson and His Legacy.* New York: Oxford University Press, 1983. Skillfully written, this is the best study of the integration of baseball. Written by a professional historian, based on archival work and interviews, this book is a joy to read and the place to start when reading about Robinson.

JOHN D. ROCKEFELLER

" *Charity is injurious unless it helps the recipient to become independent of it.* **"**

Industrialist and philanthropist

One of the major industrialists and philanthropists in American history, Rockefeller pioneered in raising the scale of business organization through his phenomenally successful Standard Oil Company; he also raised the scale of philanthropic giving.

Born: July 8, 1839; Richford, New York
Died: May 23, 1937; Ormond Beach, Florida
Also known as: John Davison Rockefeller (full name)
Areas of achievement: Business; philanthropy

EARLY LIFE

John Davison Rockefeller (RAW-keh-fehl-lur) was the son of Eliza Davison and William Avery Rockefeller. His father owned a farm and traded such commodities as salt and lumber. The family, which included John's older sister, two younger sisters, and two younger brothers, moved frequently: first to Moravia, New York; then to Owego, New York; and finally, to Cleveland, Ohio. John's education was irregular, but he studied hard and did attend two years at Cleveland High School. His father, who by that time had become a wandering vendor of patent medicine, encouraged him to go into business. John especially liked mathematics, and he took a three-month course in bookkeeping at Folsom's Commercial College.

In selecting a job, Rockefeller was not as much interested in the salary as he was in the possibilities a position offered for learning about the business world. He selected a large and diversified merchant firm and started as a bookkeeper at a salary of $3.50 per week. After three and a half years, he left to form his own wholesale grain and grocery business with Maurice B. Clark. Together, the two had only $4,000; during their first year, however, they grossed $450,000 and netted a $1,400 profit. The following year, the Civil War began. The war gave Rockefeller, along with a number of other leading postwar industrialists, the opportunity to make his initial pile of money. Business at Cleveland-based Clark and Rockefeller boomed with major orders coming in from the army, other cities, and Europe. Rather than miss these business opportunities fighting in the Civil War, Rockefeller avoided the draft by paying for a substitute to fight in his place.

During these early business years, Rockefeller displayed the character traits and personal lifestyle that would be with him throughout his life. A devout Baptist, Rockefeller remained active in that church, even after becoming fabulously successful in business. For years, he taught Sunday school and served on church boards with streetcar conductors and other working-class people. He also took seriously the biblical injunction to give away one-tenth of what he earned, even when starting out at a low salary. He lived simply, had few pleasures, and was devoted to his family.

In 1864, Rockefeller married Laura Celestia Spelman, whose father was a prosper-

Rockefeller, John D.

ous businessperson. Eventually, they had four children who lived to adulthood: three daughters, Bessie, Alta, and Edith, and a son, John D. Rockefeller II, of whom his father was quite proud. The family lived in a large, comfortable, but not ostentatious house in Cleveland until moving to New York during the 1880's. Rockefeller instilled a sense of industry and public responsibility in his offspring that extended down to the third and fourth generations, producing one vice president (Nelson) and three state governors (Nelson of New York, Winthrop of Arkansas, and John D. IV of West Virginia). Of all the leading American industrial families, the Rockefeller dynasty became the most remarkable.

LIFE'S WORK

It was possible for John D. Rockefeller to gain a monopolistic fortune in the oil business because of certain conditions that existed at that time. Oil was first used for medicinal purposes. Oil strikes in Pennsylvania during the 1850's greatly increased the supply. To find other uses for the product, the Pennsylvania Rock Oil Company hired Benjamin Silliman, Jr., a Yale chemist. Silliman discovered that oil could be distilled into kerosene for burning in lamps, and he also noted its lubricating qualities. At the time, oil was obtained by skimming off what floated on the surface of water-filled ditches and springs.

With other uses, however, drilling quickly became economically productive. Independent oil wells and small-scale refineries sprang up in great profusion in northwestern Pennsylvania, and refineries also proliferated in Cleveland. The oil business was chaotic, with numerous small operators, overproduction, cutthroat competition, and alternating periods of boom and bust. Rockefeller perceived that whoever could bring order to this industry could make a fabulous fortune.

In 1863, Rockefeller began his involvement with the oil business. He and his wholesale grocery partners, along with refining expert Samuel Andrews, built a refinery in Cleveland. His wholesale grocery partners proved too cautious for Rockefeller's taste. In 1865, he decided to buy out the three Clark brothers, get entirely out of the wholesale grocery business, and devote himself to oil. By the end of the year, the firm of Rockefeller and Andrews had an oil refinery that was producing at least twice as much as any other single refinery of Cleveland's nearly thirty refineries.

Rockefeller prospered more than his competitors because of his foresight, attention to detail, emphasis on efficiency, lack of toleration for waste, and growing reputation as a successful businessperson. These qualities allowed him to borrow heavily from bankers and to attract partners who brought additional capital to his firm. Henry M. Flagler joined Rockefeller in 1867, bringing with him a substantial amount of money and the ability to negotiate ever-lower railroad shipping rates. Railroad rates were unregulated then, with railroads commonly giving favored shippers rebates on their publicly stated rates. The larger the shipper, the more favorable the rate. Rockefeller was able to play two railroads off against each other and water transportation off against the railroads. In turn, his lower shipping rates allowed him to undersell his competitors, steadily driving them out of business.

Meanwhile, Rockefeller implemented a policy of vertical integration. To cut his firm's dependence on related businesses, he began making his own barrels and then

Rockefeller, John D.

bought his own timber tracts to supply his cooperage plant. He owned his warehouses, bought his own tank cars, and, to the extent possible, owned or produced the raw materials and transportation he needed to operate. Finally, he fought waste by using kerosene by-products to become the oil industry's leading producer of paraffin and machine lubricants.

In 1870, to accommodate additional growth, Rockefeller converted his partnership into a joint-stock corporation, the Standard Oil Company of Ohio. Meanwhile, Thomas A. Scott of the Pennsylvania Railroad began organizing certain railroads, oil refiners, and well owners into the infamous South Improvement Company. The purpose was to form a monopoly and get rebates on their competitors' shipments. The public reaction was hostile, and the South Improvement Company quickly lost its charter. Rockefeller had been part of this scheme, which badly tarnished his reputation. However, through the South Improvement Company, he acquired another wealthy partner, Cleveland refiner Oliver H. Payne.

Furthermore, Standard Oil decided to proceed on its own to create a monopoly in the oil business. Early in 1872, Rockefeller offered to buy out nearly all remaining Cleveland oil refineries. Owners could either accept a cash offer, take the offer in Standard Oil stock, or be driven out of business. With the South Improvement Company still a live entity and given the size of Standard Oil itself, most refiners sold out. Some claimed that they had been pressured into taking less than their businesses were worth, but those who acquired Standard stock did make small fortunes. Rockefeller accomplished this takeover of his Cleveland competitors in three months. From Cleveland, Standard then proceeded to acquire refineries in Pittsburgh, in Philadelphia, and on Long Island. By 1875, the firm was refining half of the oil products in the United States. Rockefeller's next step was to gain control of pipelines, oil terminals, kerosene distributors, and additional plants. He also attracted rival oilman John D. Archbold to his firm. By 1878, Rockefeller had secured his monopolistic position.

During the 1880's, Standard Oil continued to grow. The firm acquired new oil fields, built new refineries, and developed new refining methods. Under the direction of John's brother, William Rockefeller, the firm also expanded into the international market. Standard Oil products were a familiar sight in Asia, Africa, South America, and even central Europe, where Standard encountered stiff competition from cheap Russian oil. Also, Standard Oil pioneered in corporate organization. Rockefeller employed the best legal talent to devise the concept of the trust. That meant that the stock of Standard's subsidiaries and related companies was combined with Standard's stock, new certificates were issued, and an executive committee with Rockefeller at the head assumed control. During 1883-1884, he transferred the corporate headquarters to New York City. However, Standard Oil never took total control of the oil industry. While accounting for 80 to 90 percent of oil produced in the United States and making substantial profits, Standard did lower the price of its products. Rockefeller had stabilized a chaotic industry.

In the process, Rockefeller became powerful and was feared and vilified. The lack of railroad rate regulation did much to make his monopoly possible. Unfair railroad rates upset many more people than Rockefeller's business competitors. The public began agitating for railroad rate regulation, first at the state level and then for the Inter-

Rockefeller, John D.

John D. Rockefeller.
(Library of Congress)

state Commerce Act, passed in 1887. Because that law was largely ineffective, agitation continued until railroad rates were finally effectively regulated in the twentieth century. Throughout this agitation, the outstanding example of how unregulated railroad rates could lead to powerful monopolies was Standard Oil.

The New York legislature investigated Standard Oil in 1879 and again in 1888. Henry Demarest Lloyd published an exposé in the *Atlantic Monthly* in March, 1881. Congress sought to dampen the public's concern with the Sherman Antitrust Act of 1890. When that law went initially unenforced, muckrakers again attacked. The best-known exposé was Ida M. Tarbell's *History of the Standard Oil Company* (1904). Rockefeller always refused to respond directly to these attacks. His attitude was that his products spoke for themselves. Not until 1905 did Standard Oil hire its first public relations expert. Nevertheless, the federal government proceeded to prosecute Standard Oil for violating the Sherman Antitrust Act. Under court order, the company broke into smaller, separate companies in 1911.

Rockefeller's wealth at one point approached $900 million. What to do with all this money posed a dilemma. He invested in the stock market and, during the 1890's, gained control of the Mesabi Range, the richest iron ore field in the United States. Within a few years, however, he sold his Range holdings to Andrew Carnegie. Increasingly, his interests were turning to philanthropy, where his impact was tremendous.

Rockefeller, John D.

At first, Rockefeller's gifts to hospitals, colleges, and other institutions were haphazard, and his gifts were sometimes misused. Soon, however, he began to apply some of his principles for making money—of attention to detail and organization—to giving away money. He virtually made the University of Chicago with a founding gift in 1889 of $600,000 and later gifts (some from his son) totaling $80 million. He created the Rockefeller Institute for Medical Research in 1901 and the General Education Board in 1902. The latter helped to revolutionize medical education, fought the spread of hookworm, and worked to improve southern agriculture. His philanthropy was further systematized with the creation of the Rockefeller Foundation in 1913. He gave away more than a half billion dollars, and the influence of his philanthropic institutions has continued to grow after his death. Rockefeller had turned over active leadership of the Standard Oil Company in 1897 but lived until 1937, dying at the age of ninety-seven.

Significance

John D. Rockefeller succeeded as a businessperson and a philanthropist in part because of his personal qualities and in part because of his times. He had an uncanny ability to identify and secure leading executive talent. The extreme care with which he made decisions was accompanied by a boldness of action and accuracy of vision unmatched in his field. Furthermore, he had the steadiness to compete in a rough, competitive, "survival of the fittest" environment where there were few laws and regulations. Indeed, he turned this freewheeling environment to his advantage.

Rockefeller was able to build Standard Oil because of conditions such as the general absence of effective railroad rate regulation and the lack of an income tax. He went into the oil business at a time when it was taking off, and good luck was with him when the gasoline-powered automobile came along to increase demand. He regarded himself as a trustee of his wealth and became, perhaps, the most outstanding philanthropist in the United States. Finally, he instilled in his descendants a devotion to public service. Of all the "robber barons" of his generation, his long-range impact may have been the greatest.

—*Judith Ann Trolander*

Further Reading

Abels, Jules. *The Rockefeller Billions: The Story of the World's Most Stupendous Fortune.* New York: Macmillan, 1965. Scholarly, readable, with a good selection of photographs of Rockefeller, his family, business associates, and houses. Generally, Abels is favorably disposed toward Rockefeller.

Carr, Albert A. *John D. Rockefeller's Secret Weapon.* New York: McGraw-Hill, 1962. Focuses on the role that the Union Tank Car Company, established by Rockefeller and the key to his transportation system, played in the success of Standard Oil. In 1891, the company became a separate corporation from Standard Oil in response to the Sherman Antitrust Act. Carr covers the history of Union Tank Car up to 1961.

Chernow, Ron D. *Titan: The Life of John D. Rockefeller, Sr.* New York: Random House, 1998. Well-written, meticulously researched biography based on newly acquired archival materials. Chernow recounts the details of Rockefeller's life and career, describing his human side as well as his misdeeds.

Collier, Peter, and David Horowitz. *The Rockefellers: An American Dynasty*. New York: Holt, Rinehart and Winston, 1976. The bulk of this book is on John D. Rockefeller's descendants, down through his great-grandchildren, the impact his fortune has had on them, and their sense of public responsibility.

Hawke, David F. *John D.: The Founding Father of the Rockefellers*. New York: Harper & Row, 1980. A chatty, popular account, this slim volume is not too extensively footnoted but is based on archival sources along with more detailed secondary sources, especially Nevins's 1940 biography.

Josephson, Matthew. *The Robber Barons: The Great American Capitalists, 1861-1901*. New York: Harcourt, Brace, 1934. Reprint. Harcourt, Brace, and World, 1962. In this critical account, Rockefeller is only one among many late nineteenth century industrialists, but the book is excellent for setting him in the context of his time. Josephson is critical of the business practices and extensive power of Rockefeller and his associates.

Nevins, Allan. *John D. Rockefeller: The Heroic Age of American Enterprise*. New York: Charles Scribner's Sons, 1940. Nevins is the scholarly authority on Rockefeller. This two-volume work was the most comprehensive, carefully researched, and balanced source on Rockefeller until Nevins's 1953 book appeared.

_____. *Study in Power: John D. Rockefeller, Industrialist and Philanthropist*. New York: Charles Scribner's Sons, 1953. More of a second biography of his subject than a revision, this book incorporates material based on a large amount of documents not available to Nevins in his earlier biography; it also reflects a maturing of Nevins's analysis. Both Nevins biographies can be profitably consulted.

KNUTE ROCKNE

> *" One man practicing sportsmanship is far better than fifty preaching it. "*

Football coach

One of the great sports innovators of the early twentieth century, Rockne revolutionized football by promoting the forward pass as a major part of game play. As a coach, Rockne devised innovative game strategies, including the shift formation-shift offense, which transformed Notre Dame University into one of the premiere college football programs. As a consequence, he became a legend in his own time, and his reputation was accentuated by his untimely death in a plane crash.

Born: March 8, 1888; Voss, Norway
Died: March 31, 1931; Chase County, Kansas
Also known as: Knute Kenneth Rockne (full name)
Area of achievement: Sports

EARLY LIFE

Knute Rockne (newt RAWK-nee) was born in Voss, Norway. His father, a master carriage maker who came to the United States to display his wares in 1891, became so enamored with the potential of America that he did not return to Norway. Instead, Rockne brought his family, including his son, Knute, to the Logan Square district of Chicago to begin a new life.

Rockne was a multisport athlete at North West Division High School, excelling in football, baseball, and track and field. He intended to go to college at the University of Illinois but lacked the financial resources. To earn money for his education, Rockne went to work for the post office; he continued to engage in track-and-field events with local Chicago clubs. After saving his money for four years, he was finally prepared to pursue a college degree, but he chose not to attend Illinois. Fellow members of his local track-and-field club who planned to attend Notre Dame University in South Bend, Indiana, persuaded him to enroll there instead. At the age of twenty-two, Rockne was finally a college freshman.

Football was not Rockne's primary emphasis at Notre Dame. He played sparingly as a freshman and devoted most of his time to the track-and-field team. He continued to excel at field events, setting school records in the pole vault. His athletic ability caught the attention of football coach Jesse Harper, who convinced Rockne to give football another chance. A swift and sure-handed receiver, Rockne earned All-American third-team honors the following year.

Members of the football team—officially known as the Fighting Irish since 1927—roomed together. Rockne's roommate was Charles "Gus" Dorais, the team's quarterback. The two players got jobs as lifeguards during the summer of 1913, passing the time by tossing the ball to each other, a seemingly trivial event in itself. However, they became so proficient at throwing and catching that they determined to use the forward pass more often in the upcoming season.

The forward pass had been legal in college football since 1906, but it was used only sparingly—until the fall of 1913, when Notre Dame would use the forward pass extensively and become the first program to do so. The Irish would win often and convincingly that season. Perhaps the greatest use of the forward pass came on November 1, when Notre Dame traveled to New York to play Army, the team from the U.S. Military Academy. Army was the powerhouse college football program of the day, but thanks to Notre Dame's passing attack, the Irish upset the heavily favored Army by a score of 35-13. The game not only established Notre Dame as a college football power but also made the forward pass a significant part of games thereafter.

LIFE'S WORK
Rockne graduated from Notre Dame in 1914, and the university asked him to stay, but not as football coach. Rockne had graduated magna cum laude with a degree in chemistry, and the university offered him a position as a graduate assistant to teach chemistry. Rockne, newly married and with a family to support, took the position on the condition that he also be allowed to serve as an assistant football coach. Notre Dame agreed, and Rockne taught chemistry and coached football until 1917, the year head coach Jesse Harper retired. Rockne became the head coach the following season, with his former teammate, Dorais, as one of his assistants.

Notre Dame became a football powerhouse as Rockne developed his team not only with an innovative offense but also with physical conditioning. Other coaches relied upon the innate talent of their players, but Rockne was one of the first to employ conditioning drills and calisthenics. He also instituted standardized practice drills designed to improve upon natural talent.

One of Rockne's greatest innovations, in addition to the forward pass, was the so-called shift offense. An offense would line up in the traditional T formation that most teams of the era used, but with Rockne's plan the offense would shift into a box formation just before the quarterback received the snapped ball. The box formation gave Notre Dame an advantage, as the last-moment movement of the offense stymied the defense and prevented it from reacting in time to compensate. The shifting formation was a staple of Notre Dame football for years, both during and after Rockne's tenure as coach. The team's offensive schemes under Rockne would help to popularize college football by the end of the 1920's. Football now deftly combined running and passing plays, which created a varied and exciting sport that became immensely popular by the end of the decade.

Rockne also helped the program at Notre Dame by attracting talented players, including George Gipp, better known as the Gipper. Gipp was Notre Dame's first player to achieve All-American status, but he died tragically in his senior season in 1920. Locked out of his lodgings and forced to sleep outside one night, Gipp contracted pneumonia and developed a strep infection. According to legend, Gipp, while lying on his deathbed, asked Rockne to have the Irish players "win one for the Gipper." Rockne's other fabled players were Harry Stuhldreher, Don Miller, Jim Crowley, and Elmer Layden. Playing in the same backfield, the talented quartet was dubbed the Four Horsemen by famed sportswriter Grantland Rice, who drew upon the biblical imagery of the four horsemen of the apocalypse. Between 1923 and 1924, the Four Horsemen powered Notre Dame to a 28-2 record, their only losses coming against the University of Nebraska.

In 1931, Rockne was hired as a consultant for the Hollywood film *The Spirit of Notre Dame* (1931). However, he would never make it to Los Angeles to aid in the production. The aircraft in which he was a passenger crashed soon after takeoff from Kansas City, Missouri, killing everyone on board. In 1940, Warner Bros. released a film portraying Rockne's life titled *Knute Rockne, All American*, with Pat O'Brien as Rockne and Ronald Reagan as the Gipper.

SIGNIFICANCE

Success as a coach made Rockne a sporting legend in his own time. His fame made him a popular public speaker as well, as he presented speeches on the benefits of teamwork, a theme Rockne knew well. In thirteen years as head coach at Notre Dame, he compiled a record of 105 wins, 12 losses, and 5 ties. He coached the team to five undefeated seasons and won six national championships.

In addition to changing how football was played and coached, Rockne was one of the first sports celebrities in the United States. During the 1920's, sports figures such as Rockne, Babe Ruth, and Jack Dempsey were the first athletes to gain nationwide celebrity and to earn the riches and accolades that fame brought with it. Unlike other early sports celebrities, however, Rockne strove to project a persona of strength, preparation, and personal integrity and in doing so made himself a football legend when the game was first reaching national popularity.

—*Steven J. Ramold*

FURTHER READING

Maggio, Frank P. *Notre Dame and the Game That Changed Football: How Jesse Harper Made the Forward Pass a Weapon and Knute Rockne a Legend*. New York: Carroll & Graf, 2007. A detailed discussion of the famed 1913 game between Notre Dame and Army, the contest that defined Rockne's early career and set him on his path as a future coach.

Robinson, Ray. *Rockne of Notre Dame: The Making of a Football Legend*. New York: Oxford University Press, 1999. The best general biography of Rockne. Fully describes the legend around Rockne but also reveals some less complimentary elements of his personality.

Rockne, Knute, and Bonnie Skiles Rockne. *The Autobiography of Knute K. Rockne*. Indianapolis, Ind.: Bobbs-Merrill, 1931. Rockne was in the middle of writing this autobiography when he died, so his wife, Bonnie Skiles, completed the task. A broad discussion of Rockne's life, with the most in-depth discussion of his childhood available in any biography.

Sperber, Murray A. *Shake Down the Thunder: The Creation of Notre Dame Football*. New York: Henry Holt, 1993. A history of Notre Dame University's role in the rise of college football, with Rockne's career as the book's centerpiece.

ELEANOR ROOSEVELT

" *It is better to light one small candle than to curse the darkness.* "

First Lady of the United States (1933-1945)

As First Lady and as a private citizen, Roosevelt worked for civil rights, women's rights, and domestic and international peace and justice.

Born: October 11, 1884; New York, New York
Died: November 7, 1962; New York, New York
Also known as: Anna Eleanor Roosevelt (birth name)
Areas of achievement: Government and politics; women's rights; diplomacy

EARLY LIFE

Anna Eleanor Roosevelt (ROH-zeh-vehlt) was the first child of Elliott Roosevelt and Anna Livingston Ludlow Hall Roosevelt. Her beautiful and aristocratic mother, who was only twenty years old when Eleanor was born, was more involved in the social life of her contemporaries than in the needs of her daughter. Elliott Roosevelt, although handsome and charming, was troubled by problems associated with alcoholism. As a result of her parents' self-absorption, Eleanor's early childhood was lonely and somber despite her family's wealth and social position.

Anna Roosevelt died of diphtheria in 1892, depressed and discouraged by her husband's drinking and irresponsibility. Eleanor idolized her father and imagined that she would live with him and that they would travel to exciting places together. In reality, however, Elliott's attitude toward Eleanor, although expressed in loving words, was characterized by thoughtlessness. Elliott died on August 14, 1894, of complications related to his drinking.

After her father's death, Eleanor lived with her maternal grandmother Mary Livingston Ludlow Hall. A strict disciplinarian, Hall insisted on a regimented life for her grandchildren. Despite her grandmother's insistence that she wear unfashionable clothes and a back brace to improve her posture, and despite the dreary atmosphere of Hall's New York townhouse, Eleanor's childhood was not as miserable as some writers have suggested. She had, for the first time in her life, a stable and orderly home. Her grandmother and aunts were sympathetic and supportive of her academic and athletic activities, and the family's country estate at Tivoli was a pleasant place with spacious grounds for a child to roam.

Eleanor remained in this environment until the age of fifteen, when she was sent to Allenswood, a girls' boarding school in England. Presided over by Mademoiselle Marie Souvestre, Allenswood provided a rigorous academic environment that encouraged young women to think and act independently. Eleanor came into her own at boarding school. She was an outstanding student, was active in sports, was held in the highest esteem by her fellow students, and was a protégée of Mademoiselle Souvestre. She took from Allenswood an intellectual self-possession, an increased sense of tolerance, and a commitment to public activity.

Roosevelt, Eleanor

Eleanor Roosevelt.
(Library of Congress)

LIFE'S WORK

At eighteen, Eleanor Roosevelt returned to New York, at her grandmother's insistence that she make her debut. Although in her own memoirs Eleanor describes herself as shy and awkward at this period of her life, her contemporaries remembered her as attractive and sought after by the more thoughtful young men. One young man who was particularly interested was Eleanor's fifth cousin once removed, Franklin D. Roosevelt (FDR), at the time a Harvard student. The two became secretly engaged in November, 1903, and were married in March, 1905, after a courtship during which his rather possessive mother tried to raise obstacles.

During the years before her marriage, Eleanor had become involved in volunteer work in New York City. There she had found a sense of usefulness and satisfaction that social life had never held for her. She worked with the Junior League to teach settlement house children, and she joined the Consumers' League, helping to investigate women's working conditions in factories and department stores. She had firsthand exposure to urban poverty, and her commitment to improving the lives of the less fortunate dates from this period of her life.

After their wedding, Eleanor and Franklin settled in New York City in a townhouse adjoining his mother's home. During the next eleven years, Eleanor had six children: Anna (1906); James (1907); Franklin (1909), who lived only seven months; Elliott (1910); Franklin, Jr. (1914); and John (1916). Her life was filled with domestic responsibilities and with her mother-in-law's interference in the younger Roosevelts' household. Those were years of little personal satisfaction for Eleanor. She had little involvement with friends or work outside her family.

In 1910, Franklin Roosevelt began his political career by winning a seat in the New York state legislature. Eleanor also began her public life. She enjoyed the role of political wife, especially because it brought her into contact with the issues and figures of the day. Contrary to some reports, she was not opposed to woman suffrage during this period. She had not given the issue much thought until FDR came out in support of votes for women in 1911. Then she realized that "if my husband were a suffragist I probably must be too."

In 1913, the Roosevelts moved to Washington, D.C., where Franklin served as assistant secretary of the Navy under President Woodrow Wilson. There, during World War I, Eleanor organized the Red Cross canteen and the Navy Red Cross. She knitted, entertained troops, and served food to servicemen. She visited soldiers in the hospital and raised money for a recreational center for wounded men. Her work often lasted from 9:00 A.M. until long past midnight.

The war years also brought Eleanor heartache and disillusionment when she learned of her husband's affair with her social secretary, Lucy Mercer. Eleanor offered to divorce Franklin at this time, but he refused. Certainly, the Roosevelts' decision to continue their marriage partly was made not only because divorce was a serious liability in politics in the early twentieth century but also because Franklin realized that Eleanor's special skills would be invaluable in his career. For Eleanor, the Lucy Mercer episode encouraged her to seek her own fulfillment in the world outside her marriage.

After an unsuccessful run for the vice presidency in 1920, Franklin Roosevelt developed polio in 1921. Spurred by these events, Eleanor became involved in politics both in women's issues and in the Democratic Party. During the 1920's, she became active in the League of Women Voters and the Women's Trade Union League, which supported protective legislation for women. She became acquainted with such activist women as Esther Lape and Elizabeth Read, who introduced Eleanor into a community of independent women. With her friends Marion Dickerman and Nancy Cook, Eleanor built a cottage called Val-Kill on the grounds of the Roosevelt family estate at Hyde Park. There they created a partnership that managed a furniture crafts factory and also published the *Women's Democratic News*. With her friends, Eleanor also purchased Todhunter, a private girls' school in New York City. She taught there three days a week until she became First Lady in 1933. Teaching fulfilled a dream from her days at Allenswood, gave her immense satisfaction, and brought her into contact with the young people she always loved.

With the phenomenal energy that characterized her whole life, Eleanor also entered Democratic politics, first as a representative of her husband during his convalescence and then in her own right as a spokesperson for women and social reform. She organized Democratic women in New York, traveled and spoke for Democratic Party candidates, and advocated the election of women to public office.

When Franklin was elected governor of New York in 1928 and president of the United States in 1932, Eleanor worked with the Women's Division of the Democratic National Committee to involve women in the election process and to ensure that women were appointed to positions in the administration. Among those whom Eleanor brought to her husband's attention was Frances Perkins, the secretary of labor, the first woman ever appointed to a presidential cabinet.

Eleanor had feared that the position of First Lady would mean curtailing her own political and reform activities, but she discovered new opportunities to promote her primary concerns, such as equal rights and the concerns of the poor and dispossessed. She held regular press conferences that were open only to women reporters, gave radio interviews and lectures, and wrote a syndicated newspaper column called "My Day." In addition, she supervised the responses to the thousands of letters she received, sometimes sending a personal note or a check. Eleanor also traveled throughout the country as the president's "eyes and ears," seeing for herself the conditions on farms, in mines and factories, and in the homes of the poor during the Depression. She brought representatives of excluded groups to the White House, frequently seating them next to the president so that he could hear their stories.

A primary commitment of Eleanor Roosevelt's adult life was to civil rights for African Americans. She had grown up in an isolated and prejudiced environment, but living in Washington, D.C., had made her aware of the evils of racism. Her advocacy took the form both of symbolic gestures, as when she insisted on placing her chair in the center of the aisle between black and white sections at a segregated meeting of the Southern Conference on Human Welfare in 1939, and of quiet lobbying, as in her role of messenger between her husband and the National Association for the Advancement of Colored People (NAACP). She supported federal legislation to outlaw lynching and, during World War II, worked to eliminate discrimination in the armed forces.

During the war, Eleanor endeavored to ensure women's participation in all aspects of the mobilization, visited troops in hospitals and in the field, and sought to continue the many New Deal social reforms jeopardized by the country's focus on the international crisis.

Franklin Roosevelt died in April of 1945, during his fourth term as president. Eleanor continued her public life, perhaps feeling freer because she was no longer perceived as a politician's wife. She turned many of her efforts to international matters, an extension of her long-standing interest in building a lasting peace. She had earlier been an advocate of the League of Nations and the World Court, and now President Harry S. Truman appointed her as a delegate to the newly formed United Nations, where she served until 1953. She chaired the committee that produced the 1948 Declaration of Human Rights and was nominated four times for the Nobel Peace Prize.

The "First Lady of the World" showed concern for the victims of war and oppression parallel to her continuing domestic interests in civil rights and women's issues. Her last public role was as the chairperson of President John F. Kennedy's Commission on the Status of Women, in which capacity she supported women's full access to economic and political opportunities. She died in New York City on November 7, 1962, of a rare type of tuberculosis.

SIGNIFICANCE

Eleanor Roosevelt's life bore out the advice she had written to women in 1930, "to be ready to go out and try new adventures, create new work for others as well as herself, and strike deep roots in some community where her presence will make a difference in the lives of others."

She defined a new role for women in American public life. Although during much of her life she filled a position as the wife of a prominent politician, her contributions stand on their own. With compassion and a commitment to humanitarian interests, Eleanor helped to place the issues of racial and gender justice on the national agenda. She was an advocate for all excluded groups, using her public visibility as a means to bring their concerns to national attention and using her influence to promote changes in attitudes and in legislation. On the international scene, she reached out to the victims of injustice and poverty, legitimizing and promoting their well-being.

To women of future generations, Eleanor Roosevelt became a model of energy, humanity, and courage. Always an example of impeccable courtesy, she could also confront leaders of the Soviet Union or the proponents of segregation and state her case. Eleanor Roosevelt demonstrated the need to redefine power as not only the authority to move armies or to control economic might but also the ability to inspire, to question the status quo, and to work for equality without the expectation of personal gain.

—*Mary Welek Atwell*

FURTHER READING

Cook, Blanche Wiesen. *Eleanor Roosevelt*. Vol. 1. New York: Viking, 1992. The first volume of a projected two-volume study, Cook's sensitive biography places Eleanor Roosevelt in the context of a rich emotional life and emphasizes her lifelong strengths.

Glendon, Mary Ann. *A World Made New: Eleanor Roosevelt and the Universal Declaration of Human Rights*. New York: Random House, 2001. Recounts how Roosevelt and others in 1947 began drafting the Universal Declaration of Human Rights, which was adopted by the United Nations the following year. Includes a legal analysis of the declaration and its applicability to the twenty-first century.

Hoff-Wilson, Joan, and Marjorie Lightman, eds. *Without Precedent: The Life and Career of Eleanor Roosevelt*. Bloomington: Indiana University Press, 1984. An excellent collection of articles on Roosevelt's character and contributions. The essays introduce fine scholarship dealing with the major themes in her life.

Lash, Joseph P. *Eleanor and Franklin*. New York: W. W. Norton, 1971. The first part of a two-volume biography of Roosevelt. Lash had full access to Roosevelt's papers.

———. *Eleanor: The Years Alone*. New York: W. W. Norton, 1972. The second volume of the biography looks at Roosevelt's life after her husband's death. Lash's personal friendship with Roosevelt enabled him to provide a warm and comprehensive picture of her life.

Roosevelt, Eleanor. *The Autobiography of Eleanor Roosevelt*. New York: Harper & Brothers, 1961. Three volumes consolidated into one, this autobiography is indispensable to the student but provides a picture that is too self-effacing.

———. *My Day: The Best of Eleanor Roosevelt's Acclaimed Newspaper Columns, 1936-1962*. Edited by David Emblidge and Marcy Ross. New York: Da Capo Press, 2001. A selection of Roosevelt's syndicated newspaper columns in which she expresses her views on the New Deal, World War II, human rights, and other issues.

Youngs, J. William T. *Eleanor Roosevelt: Personal and Public Life.* 3d ed. New York: Pearson/Longman, 2006. A biography that touches on Roosevelt's life at home and in the public eye.

FRANKLIN D. ROOSEVELT

" . . . the only thing we have to fear is fear itself. . . . "

President of the United States (1933-1945)

Displaying extraordinary personal courage and perhaps the most astute political leadership America has ever witnessed, Roosevelt dominated American government for a longer period than has any other president of the United States.

Born: January 30, 1882; Hyde Park, New York
Died: April 12, 1945; Warm Springs, Georgia
Also known as: Franklin Delano Roosevelt (full name); F. D. R.
Areas of achievement: Government and politics; diplomacy

EARLY LIFE

Franklin D. Roosevelt (ROH-zeh-vehlt) was a member of an American aristocratic family of great wealth. James and Sara Roosevelt, of Dutch and English ancestry, educated their only child with private tutors and European tours. At Groton School in Massachusetts, Roosevelt came under the influence of Rector Endicott Peabody, who prided himself on grooming future politicians and instilling in his charges a lifelong commitment to public service.

By 1900, when Franklin enrolled at Harvard University, he was an impressive young man—six feet two inches tall, handsome, with a patrician nose and majestically deep-set eyes. In his junior year, he fell in love with his fifth cousin, Eleanor Roosevelt, a tall, slender woman whose pleasing face was punctuated by a prominent set of Rooseveltian teeth. Eleanor was the daughter of President Theodore Roosevelt's younger brother, Elliott, who died from alcoholism when she was ten. In 1905, Franklin married Eleanor, over the objections of his mother, who tried to postpone the wedding.

Following Harvard, Roosevelt dabbled briefly with the practice of law before turning to the real love of his life: politics. In 1910, he entered the political arena for the first time, running for the New York State senate. Fellow Democrats skeptically observed his entrance into the race for several reasons: his aristocratic bearing, his tendency to look down his nose at people, his unfamiliarity with working-class voters in the Hyde Park-Poughkeepsie area, and the fact that he was a former Republican. The political climate, however, demanded a reformer, and Roosevelt, following in the footsteps of his cousin Theodore, could fill the bill by pointing to the ugly specter of corruption within the opposition party. During the campaign, F. D. R. (as he came to be known) showed he was different from the average "cheap-talking" politician, displaying a pragmatic unorthodoxy that later endeared him to the nation. He even campaigned for office in an automobile, an unusual political act for a time when most people eyed the horseless carriage with suspicion. Victory was his, however, and Roosevelt became only the second Democrat elected from his district to the New York State senate since the Civil War. He was on his way.

It was not an easy path to success. Experiences in the New York senate taught him the limits of progressive, reformist power. When he challenged Charles F. Murphy's Tammany machine of New York City over the Democratic nomination for the United States Senate, he met defeat. He gradually learned, however, to moderate his reform tendencies. This later proved to be his first major lesson in the school of politics. Following his reelection in 1912, Roosevelt jumped at the opportunity to join Woodrow Wilson's administration in the capacity of assistant secretary of the Navy under Josephus Daniels. In doing so, young F. D. R. may have imagined himself following the example of Theodore, who had achieved the governorship of New York, the vice presidency, and the presidency after serving in the same position. The Navy Department afforded Roosevelt a chance to hone his administrative skills and strengthen his political ties throughout the Democratic Party to the point that, by 1920, delegates to the national convention were willing to exploit his famous name by nominating him for the vice presidency as James M. Cox's running mate. Cox and Roosevelt suffered defeat in the Republican landslide that swept Warren G. Harding and Calvin Coolidge into office. F. D. R. remained basically unchanged throughout these events, still a somewhat immature young man who maintained very few strong convictions.

All this changed in August, 1921, when Roosevelt contracted polio while vacationing at Campobello Island, his family's resort off the Maine seacoast. His health was shattered, but a new Roosevelt slowly began to emerge. Paralyzed from the waist down, and wealthy enough to retire at the age of thirty-nine, he fought to regain his vigor. First, he had to overcome the frustration that resulted from the wearing of heavy steel braces that prohibited him from walking unaided. Second, he had to ignore the pleas of his mother (whom he worshiped but who urged him to withdraw from politics) and listen to his wife and his personal secretary, Louis McHenry Howe, who plotted to restore him to some semblance of health. During this period of recovery, Eleanor became his "legs," going where he could not go, doing what he could not do physically, and generally learning the art of politics.

LIFE'S WORK
In 1924, F. D. R. showed that Roosevelt the fighter had superseded Roosevelt the dedicated aristocrat when he appeared at the Democratic National Convention to give his "Happy Warrior Speech" nominating Alfred E. Smith for president. Smith lost the nomination, but Roosevelt did not lose his political career to polio. Instead, it seemed to give him a strength of character he had rarely shown before the Campobello incident. In 1928, while Smith was losing his home state of New York by 100,000 votes to Herbert Hoover, Roosevelt was winning the governorship by 25,000, thus becoming the front-runner for the 1932 Democratic presidential nomination. Reelected by an un-

Roosevelt, Franklin D.

precedented 725,000 votes in 1930, Roosevelt, aided by his national campaign manager, James A. Farley, began his first run for the presidency. Capturing the nomination on the third ballot, Roosevelt pledged himself to create, if elected, a "new deal" for the American people.

The 1932 presidential campaign pitted Roosevelt against the Republican incumbent, Herbert Hoover. With the country three years into the Great Depression, Roosevelt wisely ran a pragmatic campaign—fluctuating between alternative ideological positions, allowing Hoover's record to speak for itself, and leaving the decision to the American electorate. On November 8, 1932, the people spoke—giving him a 472-59 electoral victory over Hoover. When Roosevelt took office on March 4, 1933, the nation was mired in the worst depression in American history. There were approximately thirteen million unemployed people—25.2 percent of the workforce. As a mood of apprehension gripped the country, Roosevelt tried to calm the panic-stricken populace when he said,

> First of all, let me assert my firm belief that the only thing we have to fear is fear itself—nameless, unreasoning, unjustified terror which paralyzes needed efforts to convert retreat into advance. In every dark hour of our national life a leadership of frankness and vigor has met with that understanding and support of the people themselves which is essential to victory. I am convinced that you will again give that support to leadership in these critical days.

During the crucial one hundred days that followed his inaugural speech, Roosevelt began the New Deal. He quickly satisfied the public's overwhelming desire for leadership and action by issuing executive orders and introducing legislation that a frightened Congress quickly rubber-stamped. Roosevelt acted in four critical areas: finance, industry, agriculture, and relief (welfare). In combating the Depression, he gave the nation no panacea but offered the means through which it might be able to survive the crisis. He did not end the Depression—but many of his programs and the laws he signed got the country through the Depression and remained an effective part of the federal government long after his death. In finance, the Emergency Banking Act (1933) and the Glass-Steagall Banking Act (1933) saved the banking structure and helped prevent a future crisis by creating the Federal Deposit Insurance Corporation. The Truth-in-Securities Act (1933) and the Securities Exchange Act (1934) brought Wall Street under tighter public regulation. In industry, the National Industrial Recovery Act (1933) offered both business and labor opportunities for greater self-government. Later, through the National Labor Relations Act (1935), he concentrated more on allowing labor unions the right to organize. In agriculture, Roosevelt tried to restore farmers' prosperity through the Agriculture Adjustment Act (1933) by subsidizing certain farm products they could not afford to sell at market prices. In relief, FDR straddled the line between welfare and public works. At first, the New Deal doled out money to unemployed people through the Federal Emergency Relief Administration (1933) and sent young men to work camps through the Civilian Conservation Corps (1933).

After the one hundred days had passed, FDR turned away from welfare and made government jobs a primary goal of his administration. Listening to his advisers, Harry Hopkins and Harold L. Ickes, Roosevelt made the federal government the employer of the last resort through the Civil Works Administration (1933), the Public Works Administration (1933), and the Works Progress Administration (1935). In particular, the WPA, which averaged 2,112,000 on its monthly payrolls from 1935 to 1941, was the largest, most visionary, and probably most effective federal relief program ever created. Perhaps the most long-lasting reform achieved by Roosevelt was the Social Security Administration (1935), granting unemployment compensation and old-age pensions.

Roosevelt's New Deal programs generated billions of new dollars throughout the American economy, increasing incomes and causing tax revenues to "trickle up" to the federal and state governments. The jobs also raised the hopes of millions of voters who came to believe that Roosevelt had saved them from financial disaster. He was the man who put food on their tables, shoes on their feet, and a roof over their heads. In brief, the New Deal was political dynamite, and Roosevelt was the New Deal. The president's charismatic leadership, his inspirational speeches and informal "fireside chats," made him an unbeatable campaigner, as his 1936 Republican opponent learned. Roosevelt crushed Kansas Governor Alfred M. Landon by the largest electoral margin in recent American history, 523 to 8.

In less than three years, Roosevelt created an imperial presidency and vastly enlarged the federal bureaucracy, thus prompting criticisms from conservatives and the

Franklin D. Roosevelt.
(Library of Congress)

Supreme Court. When the Court began invalidating some New Deal programs such as the National Industrial Recovery Act *(Schechter v. United States*, 1935) and the Agriculture Adjustment Act *(Butler v. United States*, 1936), he struck back. In 1937, Roosevelt tried to pack the Court with New Dealers by introducing the Federal Judiciary Reorganization Bill. Although the bill failed to pass Congress, Roosevelt prevailed in this struggle, since the Court's later decisions proved more favorable to New Deal legislation. Still, the court-packing scheme suggested dictatorial ambitions and damaged Roosevelt's reputation in some circles. His popularity further declined as the nation slid deeper into the Depression in 1938, and the president, determined to keep his working majority in Congress, attempted to purge conservative Democrats from his party. This tactic also failed. By 1939, the New Deal, for all practical purposes, was dead.

As the New Deal passed into history, new dangers loomed on the horizon. Totalitarian regimes in Germany, Japan, and Italy threatened the position of the United States in the world. Roosevelt himself recognized that the leaders of these regimes, Adolf Hitler, Hideki Tōjō, and Benito Mussolini, would necessitate some changes in American foreign policy when he said that "Dr. Win the War" would have to replace "Dr. New Deal." In this way, he reluctantly began to shift American diplomacy in the direction of confronting these aggressors. After Germany invaded Poland on September 1, 1939, precipitating a declaration of war by England and France, Americans debated whether their country should maintain its isolation or aid its British and French allies. While Roosevelt was preaching neutrality, he won an unprecedented third term, a 449-82 electoral victory over his 1940 Republican opponent, Wendell Willkie.

When the war came to the United States, it struck with a fury. Possibly no aspect of Roosevelt's foreign policy has evoked more controversy than the role he played in leading the United States into World War II. On December 7, 1941, a little more than a year after he promised that "this country is not going to war," Japanese planes swept down on the American naval base at Pearl Harbor, Hawaii, nearly destroying the United States Pacific Fleet. The declaration of war that followed prompted his critics to complain that he had tricked his nation into war. While the Roosevelt administration made numerous errors in judgment, Roosevelt did not intentionally expose the military installation to attack in order to drag a reluctant and isolationistic American people into the war.

Shortly after the "day of infamy," Roosevelt met with British prime minister Winston Churchill in the first of several Washington conferences forming a "grand alliance" between the two world leaders and their nations. At the first meeting, Roosevelt agreed to the idea that the Allies should place top priority on defeating Germany and Italy, while fighting a holding action against Japan in the Pacific theater. In fact, throughout the war, Roosevelt actively planned and executed top military and diplomatic decisions that affected its outcome and the postwar world. Together with Churchill and Soviet premier Joseph Stalin, he agreed to the formulation of the United Nations. At the Yalta Conference (February, 1945), Roosevelt made another of his extremely controversial decisions that would affect public opinion long after he was gone. In return for Stalin's promise to enter the war against Japan and to allow free elections in the Soviet bloc nations, Roosevelt acquiesced to Russia's hegemony in

Roosevelt, Franklin D.

eastern Poland and other territories occupied by Soviet troops. Because these decisions were kept secret by the chief signatories, Roosevelt never felt the full fury of his critics before his death on April 12, 1945.

SIGNIFICANCE

In electing Roosevelt to an unprecedented four terms of office, the American people lent credence to the belief that Roosevelt was the greatest leader ever to hold the presidency. This view was further substantiated by the 1982 survey conducted by Professor Robert K. Murray of Pennsylvania State University among a thousand historians with doctoral degrees; only Abraham Lincoln ranked ahead of Roosevelt as the best president in American history. Nevertheless, Roosevelt certainly had his critics, and they made valid points: He seems to have had dictatorial ambitions when he circumvented the Constitution and tried to pack the Supreme Court. Roosevelt may have gravely damaged the national economy by allowing the national debt to grow to astronomical proportions. Other presidents followed him down the path of "deficit spending," enlarging on the problem that he had created to combat the Depression. Without a doubt, Roosevelt was one of the most controversial presidents in American history.

Roosevelt created the imperial presidency, in the process setting a precedent for leadership by which all his successors have been evaluated. He took the executive branch, which had lost much of its power and glory, and expanded it beyond the limits achieved by any twentieth century American chief executive. Circumstances such as depression and war, and the force of his indomitable personal character shaped by the adversity of polio, allowed him to restructure the office into its present form—one that casually encroaches on the normal powers and functions of Congress and the Supreme Court. In 1939, for example, in an act that escaped virtually unnoticed by the nation's press, he issued Executive Order 8248, creating the Executive Office of the President and shifting the powerful Bureau of the Budget from the Treasury Department to the White House. Then, when the time came to run for an unprecedented third term in 1940, Roosevelt occupied a perfect position to manipulate the federal economy for reelection purposes, and manipulate it he did—setting another example that his successors have followed.

Although Roosevelt's primary claim to greatness lay in domestic achievements, he made major contributions in foreign policy as well. He was the president who led America to victory over the Axis powers and then achieved the first détente with the new superpower: Soviet Russia. It was in the arena of American politics and government, however, that Roosevelt made his greatest imprint. Even his critics must concede that his impact on the nation was extraordinary.

—*J. Christopher Schnell*

FURTHER READING

Beschloss, Michael. *The Conquerors: Roosevelt, Truman, and the Destruction of Hitler's Germany, 1941-1945*. New York: Simon & Schuster, 2002. Chronicles how the United States and its Allies met before and after World War II to negotiate a vision of a postwar Germany and Europe.

Burns, James MacGregor. *Roosevelt: The Lion and the Fox*. New York: Harcourt

Roosevelt, Franklin D.

Brace, 1956. The best political biography of Roosevelt. Burns stresses FDR's Machiavellian tendencies and his failure to implement an enduring reform coalition.

_____. *Roosevelt: The Soldier of Freedom.* New York: Harcourt Brace Jovanovich, 1970. One of the best books analyzing Roosevelt's role as commander in chief during World War II.

Davis, Kenneth Sydney. *FDR, Into the Storm, 1937-1940: A History.* New York: Random House, 1993. This work provides a close look at the years that led to World War II and Roosevelt's role.

Freidel, Frank. *The Apprenticeship.* Boston: Little, Brown, 1952. The first of a four-volume biography of Roosevelt, this volume covers the period from Roosevelt's birth through his tenure as assistant secretary of the Navy. Some reviewers thought this volume suffered from an overemphasis on FDR's early life.

_____. *The Ordeal.* Boston: Little, Brown, 1952. The second volume covers the era from 1919 to 1928, including FDR's contracting polio in 1921, his comeback (firmly established by the "Happy Warrior Speech" in 1924), and his election as governor of New York in 1928.

_____. *The Triumph.* Boston: Little, Brown, 1956. The third volume addresses the subject of Roosevelt's two terms as governor of New York, culminating with his election as president of the United States in 1932. This is a very dispassionate analysis of Roosevelt's emergence as the master politician who crushed Herbert Hoover's hopes in the 1932 presidential election.

_____. *Launching the New Deal.* Boston: Little, Brown, 1973. The fourth volume focuses on the winter of 1932-1933 through the completion of the "One Hundred Days" Congress of June, 1933. This is a very detailed, well-documented study of the early New Deal, although it omits Harry L. Hopkins's Federal Emergency Relief Administration.

_____. *Franklin D. Roosevelt: A Rendezvous with Destiny.* Newtown, Del.: American Political Biography Press, 2006. A one-volume biography of Roosevelt that covers the entire life of the former president.

McElvaine, Robert S. *Franklin Delano Roosevelt.* Washington, D.C.: CQ Press, 2002. Concise overview of Roosevelt's life and career, focusing on his presidency. One in a series of books about the presidents that are published by the Congressional Quarterly Press.

Neal, Steve. *Happy Days Are Here Again: The 1932 Democratic Convention, the Emergence of FDR—and How America Was Changed Forever.* New York: William Morrow, 2004. Neal relates the events of the 1932 Democratic convention, describing the political maneuvers that enabled Roosevelt to win the party's presidential nomination.

Schlesinger, Arthur M., Jr. *The Age of Roosevelt.* 3 vols. Boston: Houghton Mifflin, 1957-1960. Three volumes focusing on the changes experienced by the United States during Franklin Roosevelt's career. The first volume analyzes the political, economic, and social currents of the 1920's, culminating with Roosevelt's first presidential election in 1932. Somewhat flawed by the author's tendency to allow his liberalism to prejudice his historical analysis of the period. The second volume analyzes the first two years of Roosevelt's presidency and the New Deal from

1933-1935. The problem of Schlesinger's pro-Roosevelt bias is less serious in this work than in his first volume. The third volume carries the analysis through Roosevelt's reelection in 1936. As with the first and second volumes, this work is characterized by Schlesinger's highly subjective analysis of political, economic, and social history, but it solidifies Schlesinger's major contribution to the literature on Roosevelt.

THEODORE ROOSEVELT

> *I have always been fond of the West African proverb: 'Speak softly and carry a big stick; you will go far.'*

President of the United States (1901-1909)

As twenty-sixth president of the United States, Roosevelt energetically led America into the twentieth century, promoting a larger role for the United States in world affairs as well as major domestic reforms and the conservation of natural resources and wilderness areas. In so doing, he added power to the presidential office.

Born: October 27, 1858; New York, New York
Died: January 6, 1919; Oyster Bay, New York
Also known as: Teddy Roosevelt; T. R.; Old Fifty-seven Varieties
Areas of achievement: Government and politics; military; environmentalism

EARLY LIFE

Theodore Roosevelt (ROH-zeh-vehlt) was born into a moderately wealthy mercantile family in New York City. His father, Theodore, Sr., was of mostly Dutch ancestry; his mother, Martha Bulloch of Georgia, came from a slaveholding family of Scots and Huguenot French. (During his political career, Roosevelt would claim an ethnic relationship with practically every white voter he met; among his nicknames—besides T. R. and Teddy—was Old Fifty-seven Varieties.) He was educated at home by tutors and traveled with his parents to the Middle East and Europe.

As a child, Roosevelt was puny, asthmatic, and unable to see much of the world until he was fitted with thick eyeglasses at the age of thirteen. He grew determined to "make" a powerful body, and by strenuous exercise and force of will, young Roosevelt gradually overcame most of his physical shortcomings. Shyness and fear were other weaknesses he conquered. "There were all kinds of things of which I was afraid at first," he later admitted in his *Theodore Roosevelt: An Autobiography* (1913). "But by acting as if I was not afraid I gradually ceased to be afraid." Insecurity, however, was one demon that he never exorcised.

While becoming athletic and assertive, young Roosevelt retained his wide-ranging intellectual curiosity. At Harvard, from which he was graduated in 1880, his absorption with both sports and books made him something of an oddity. Yet career plans remained uncertain. Dull science classes at Harvard dimmed his earlier interest in be-

Theodore Roosevelt.
(Library of Congress)

coming a naturalist. A year at Columbia University Law School (1880-1881) did not stimulate an interest in a legal career. While attending Columbia, he married Alice Lee, completed his first book, *The Naval War of 1812* (1882), and entered politics in the autumn of 1881 by election to the New York legislature as a Republican representative from Manhattan. For the remainder of his life, except for brief military glory in the Spanish-American War, writing and politics would absorb most of his overflowing energy.

LIFE'S WORK

At the age of twenty-three, Roosevelt, the youngest member of New York's legislature, attracted attention because of his anticorruption stance and his flair for the dramatic. He instinctively knew how to make his doings interesting to the press and the public. Personality flaws were obvious from the beginning of his political career (egotism, impulsiveness, a tendency to see everything in black or white, and occasional ruthlessness), yet Roosevelt's virtues were equally apparent and won for him far more admirers than enemies: extraordinary vitality and intelligence, courage, sincerity, conviviality, and, usually, a willingness to make reasonable compromises.

Roosevelt, Theodore

Family tragedy, the death of his young wife, prompted Roosevelt to retire from politics temporarily in 1884. During the next two years, he operated cattle ranches he owned in the Badlands of the Dakota Territory, where he found time to write *Hunting Trips of a Ranchman* (1885), the first of a trilogy of books on his Western activities and observations. Ranching proved financially unprofitable, but outdoor life made Roosevelt physically more robust and helped ease the pain of Alice's death. In 1886, he returned to New York and married Edith Kermit Carow, who would bear him four sons and a daughter and rear the daughter, Alice, born to his first wife. That same year, Roosevelt was the unsuccessful Republican nominee for mayor of New York City; he also commenced work on a six-volume history of America's Western expansion, *The Winning of the West* (1889-1896).

Roosevelt did not seek another elective office until he won the governorship of New York in 1898, but in the meantime he served in three appointive positions: member of the United States Civil Service Commission (1889-1895), president of New York City's Board of Police Commissioners (1895-1897), and assistant secretary of the Navy (1897-1898). He resigned the latter post when war with Spain broke out in 1898. Eager for combat, he organized a volunteer cavalry regiment known as the Rough Riders. Most of the land fighting between the United States and Spain occurred in Cuba; the image of Colonel Roosevelt leading a charge up San Juan Hill (in actuality, Kettle Hill) became a public symbol of this brief, victorious war. "Teddy" was a national hero. In November of 1898, he was elected governor of New York and quickly published a new book, *The Rough Riders* (1899), which a humorous critic said should have been titled "Alone in Cuba."

As governor of New York (1899-1900), Roosevelt pursued a vigorous program of political reform. The Republican state machine, wanting him out of New York, promoted his nomination for vice president on the national ticket in 1900. With reluctance, thinking that office might be a dead end, Roosevelt was finally persuaded to accept the nomination, thus becoming President William McKinley's running mate in 1900.

Within a year, McKinley died by an assassin's bullet, and Theodore Roosevelt, at age forty-two, was sworn in as the youngest chief executive in the nation's history. Physically, the new president had an aura of strength despite his average height, spectacles, small hands and feet, and high-pitched voice. His wide, square face; prominent, firm teeth; and massive chest overrode any hint of weakness.

The presidency, Roosevelt once observed, was a "bully pulpit," and he wasted no time in exhorting America toward new horizons in both domestic and foreign policy. Yet Roosevelt was painfully aware that he had become president by mishap. Not until his overwhelming election to a full term in 1904 did he believe that the office was truly his.

Within the nation, President Roosevelt called for a Square Deal for both capital and labor. He saw himself as chief arbiter of conflicts between economic groups; government, he believed, should represent everyone equitably. Believing in capitalism yet convinced that big corporations were too powerful and arrogant, he began a policy of "trust busting." Roosevelt's administration was the first to use successfully the Sherman Antitrust Act (passed in 1890) to break up business monopolies. Actually,

Roosevelt, Theodore

Roosevelt believed more in regulation than in "busting," but he hoped to frighten big business into accepting regulation. Privately, he was convinced that, for modern America, industrial and financial combinations were inevitable; he desired to subordinate both big business and labor unions to a stronger central government, which he viewed as the proper instrument for protecting the general interest.

The Hepburn Act, which for the first time gave the Interstate Commerce Commission regulatory power over railroads, was a signal accomplishment of Roosevelt's presidency as were the Pure Food and Drug Act and the Meat Inspection Act, all passed in 1906. Conservation of natural resources was another Roosevelt goal. Over both Democratic and Republican opposition, he cajoled Congress into limiting private exploitation of the nation's wilderness, mineral, and water resources. His administration doubled the number of national parks and tripled the acreage of national forests. Fifty-one wildlife refuges were established. Conservation was probably Roosevelt's most passionate cause and one of his most enduring legacies.

In foreign policy, Roosevelt is remembered by the proverb he once used: "Speak softly and carry a big stick." In practice, however, he bifurcated that approach; he spoke softly toward nations whose power he respected, while saving the big stick for small or weak countries. High-handedly, he "took Panama"—to use his own words—away from the nation of Colombia in 1903, so as to build an isthmian canal; the next year, he proclaimed a protectorate over all of Latin America—the Roosevelt Corollary to the Monroe Doctrine. As for the Far East, Roosevelt worried over but respected the rising power of Japan. He wanted the Japanese to thwart Russian expansionism but not to dominate Asia. He assumed that Great Britain and the United States would draw closer in worldwide interests; he viewed Germany, Japan, and Russia as probable enemies of a future Anglo-American alliance.

Roosevelt did not run for reelection. He had pledged after his 1904 triumph that he would not seek or accept another nomination. It was a promise he later regretted. The Republican Party in 1908 chose Roosevelt's close personal friend William Howard Taft who, with Roosevelt's blessing, easily won the presidency. Yet Taft's troubled term (1909-1913) split the Republicans into Progressive and Old Guard wings, and by 1910, Roosevelt angrily decided that Taft had capitulated to the Old Guard. Consequently, Roosevelt attempted to regain the White House in 1912. After losing a bitter contest to Taft for the Republican nomination, Roosevelt burst into the general election as a third party (Progressive, or Bull Moose Party) candidate, thus virtually guaranteeing victory for Democratic nominee Woodrow Wilson. Roosevelt's personal popularity allowed him to finish second in the 1912 presidential election, but, without a viable national organization, he lost heavily to Wilson in the electoral count. Taft ran third.

Roosevelt spent most of the remainder of his life writing books, exploring Brazil's backcountry, and criticizing President Wilson, whom he hated. He wanted to fight in World War I but was refused a commission. His health weakened by infections contracted in Brazil, Theodore Roosevelt died in his sleep on January 6, 1919, at the age of sixty.

Roosevelt, Theodore

SIGNIFICANCE

"The Republican Roosevelt," as one historian termed him, is usually ranked among the best American presidents. An inspirational leader and superb administrator, he revitalized the presidency. His career seemed to defy the adage that power corrupts. In mental prowess, he had few equals in American political history; indeed, Roosevelt ranks among the rarest of human types: an intellectual who was also a man of action.

Ideologically, Roosevelt defies simple definition. Whether he was an "enlightened" conservative or a "Progressive" liberal remains in dispute. Roosevelt himself refused to accept pat labels. He viewed himself as a moral leader who combined practicality and idealism for the purpose of unifying the nation's opposing economic and social interests into a mutually beneficial synthesis.

Coming to the presidency at the dawn of the twentieth century, Roosevelt understood that America was fast becoming a complex urban, industrial nation and that a new balance was needed between individualism and the collective good. In foreign policy, Roosevelt acted on his conviction that the old isolationism was no longer possible and that the United States, because of its growing strength, was destined to be a world power.

—*William I. Hair*

FURTHER READING

Beale, Howard K. *Theodore Roosevelt and the Rise of America to World Power.* Baltimore: Johns Hopkins University Press, 1956. Best study of Roosevelt's foreign policy. Beale demonstrates that Roosevelt had prophetic insights yet was blind toward the nationalistic aspirations of "backward" colonial peoples.

Cordery, Stacy A. *Theodore Roosevelt: In the Vanguard of the Modern.* Belmont, Calif.: Thomson/Wadsworth, 2003. Solid overview of Roosevelt's life and career aimed at high school students and college undergraduates.

Gould, Lewis L. *The Presidency of Theodore Roosevelt.* Lawrence: University Press of Kansas, 1991. Gould describes Roosevelt's presidency and touches on his earlier life.

Harbaugh, William Henry. *Power and Responsibility: The Life and Times of Theodore Roosevelt.* Rev. ed. New York: Oxford University Press, 1975. The most thorough full-length biography of Roosevelt. Judiciously balances his virtues and limitations.

Morris, Edmund. *The Rise of Theodore Roosevelt.* New York: Coward, McCann and Geoghegan, 1979. Splendidly written, insightful treatment of Roosevelt's life from birth to the beginning of his presidency in 1901. Especially good for Roosevelt's ranching days in the Dakota Territory and his exploits during the Spanish-American War.

_____. *Theodore Rex.* New York: Random House, 2001. The second volume in Morris's projected three-volume biography focuses on Roosevelt's years in the White House, providing a well-researched and exceptionally insightful account of his presidency.

O'Toole, Patricia. *When Trumpets Call: Theodore Roosevelt After the White House.* New York: Simon & Schuster, 2005. Chronicles Roosevelt's activities after his presidency.

Pringle, Henry F. *Theodore Roosevelt: A Biography*. New York: Harcourt Brace, 1931. This readable Pulitzer Prize biography of Roosevelt was long considered the definitive work, but later historians tended to fault Pringle for overemphasizing Roosevelt's immaturity and bellicosity.

Roosevelt, Theodore. *The Writings of Theodore Roosevelt*. Edited by William H. Harbaugh. Indianapolis, Ind.: Bobbs-Merrill, 1967. An excellent one-volume anthology of Roosevelt's own words, including excerpts from his autobiography.

Time 168, no. 1 (July 3, 2006). This issue contains several articles about Roosevelt that examine his life, career, loss of the 1912 presidential nomination, and other subjects.

JOHN ROSS

> ❝ *I have been actuated by a desire to promote the best interests of my people.* ❞

Native American leader

As a leader of the Cherokee nation during its ordeal of forced removal and civil war, Ross is the supreme example of nineteenth century Native American statesmanship.

Born: October 3, 1790; Turkey Town, Cherokee Nation (near present-day Center, Alabama)
Died: August 1, 1866; Washington, D.C.
Also known as: Coowescoowe (birth name)
Area of achievement: Native American affairs

EARLY LIFE

Born in a Cherokee settlement in Alabama, John Ross was by blood only one-eighth Cherokee. His mother, Mollie McDonald, was the granddaughter of a Cherokee woman, but his father, the trader Daniel Ross, and all of his mother's other ancestors were Scottish. His father, while securing a tutor for his children and sending Ross to an academy near Kingston, Tennessee, did not want to stamp out his children's Cherokee identity, and his mother gave him a deep sense of loyalty to the tribe, to their ancient lands and traditions, and to the ideal of Cherokee unity. As a son of three generations of Scottish traders, Ross early showed an interest in business. In 1813, he formed a partnership with Timothy Meigs at Rossville, near modern Chattanooga, and two years later another with his brother Lewis Ross; during the Creek War of 1813-1814, when Cherokee warriors fought in Andrew Jackson's army, Ross did a lucrative business filling government contracts. During the Creek War, he served as adjutant in a company of Cherokee cavalry.

By the mid-1820's, his increasing involvement in the political affairs of the Cherokee nation caused him to abandon business. In 1827, he settled at Coosa, Georgia, thirty miles from the new Cherokee capital at New Echota, and established himself as a planter, with a substantial house, orchards and herds, quarters for his twenty slaves, and a lucrative ferry.

Ross served as a member of four Cherokee delegations to Washington between 1816 and 1825 and was president of the tribe's National Committee in 1818, when it resisted the attempt of Tennessee to persuade the tribe to surrender their lands in that state. In 1822, he was a cosigner of a resolution of the National Committee that the Cherokee would not recognize any treaty that surrendered Cherokee land. In 1823, Ross earned for himself the undying loyalty of the majority of the tribe when he rejected a bribe offered by federal commissioners and publicly denounced them in a meeting of the National Committee.

LIFE'S WORK

Ross was president of the convention that in 1827 produced the Cherokee constitution. This document, in its assignment of powers to three branches of government, its bicameral legislature, and its four-year term for the principal chief, was modeled on the Constitution of the United States. In 1828, he was elected principal chief, an office that he held until his death, and in 1829 he went to Washington on the first of many embassies that he undertook in that capacity.

The Cherokee established their republic within the context of an ongoing struggle to maintain their traditional claims against state governments, particularly that of Georgia. In 1802, Georgia had ceded to the United States its western territory (what later became Alabama and Mississippi) in exchange for a promise that all Native Americans would be removed from Georgia. A substantial number of Cherokee, accepting removal, surrendered their land rights and moved west. (One of them was the great Cherokee genius Sequoya, who gave his people a syllabary for their language.)

With the inauguration of Andrew Jackson, who was determined to send the Cherokee west, and the discovery of gold on Cherokee land, it was clear that removal was almost inevitable. Ross was determined to exhaust every legal and political recourse, however, before submitting to the superior physical might of the U.S. government. Though Jackson was willing to assert the power of the federal government—even if it meant war—to put down any movement in South Carolina for "nullification" of the Constitution, he declared that in the Cherokee case he would not interfere with state sovereignty. As a result, his Indian Removal Bill of 1830 included the provision that any Native American who chose not to remove was subject to state law. Georgia therefore refused to recognize the legitimacy of the Cherokee republic and made no effort to prevent white squatters from moving into the Cherokee country. These official attitudes and the chaos caused by the gold rush produced a state of anarchy in which, on one occasion, Ross himself barely escaped assassination.

By 1833, pressure by the government of Georgia and by the Jackson administration was producing dissension among the Cherokee themselves. John Ridge, son of an influential Cherokee family, and Elias Boudinot, editor of the *Cherokee Phoenix*, were both working for acceptance of removal and were thus undermining the efforts of Ross, who wanted the tribe to resist removal and, if it were inevitable, to accept it only on the best possible terms.

Ross, John

In 1835, returning from a trip to Washington, Ross found his land and house occupied by a white man, who was able to present a legal title granted by Georgia. In the same year, the Ridge faction signed the Treaty of New Echota, accepting removal. In spite of the fact that it was signed by only a handful of Cherokee, in spite of opposition by the Cherokee who had already settled in the West, in spite of a protest signed by fourteen thousand Cherokee, and in spite of Henry Clay's opposition in the Senate, it was approved by the Senate in May, 1836, and signed by Jackson.

Under the conditions of the treaty, the Cherokee were given two years to prepare for removal, and Ross spent that time in further hopeless efforts to persuade the government to give the entire Cherokee people opportunity to accept or reject the treaty. The removal itself was flawed by looting, arson, and even grave-robbing by white squatters; disease was inevitable in the stockades that served as holding pens; of the thirteen thousand people who were removed, probably four thousand, including Ross's wife, died on the "Trail of Tears."

In his first years in Oklahoma, Ross devoted all of his energies to his efforts to unite three Cherokee factions: his own Nationalist followers, the Ridge-Boudinot faction that had accepted removal, and the Old Settlers, who had formed their own government and did not want to merge with the easterners. In July, 1839, a convention wrote a new constitution, virtually the same as that of 1827, and passed the Act of Union, which was ratified by all parties.

In spite of Ross's efforts for Cherokee unity, extremists in his own party exacted the traditional Cherokee penalty for selling tribal lands when they murdered Ridge and Boudinot. Ross was not involved in these crimes and did not condone them, but they were a source of disharmony in the tribe as long as he lived, and they were the primary reason that he had difficulty negotiating a new treaty with the government in an attempt to guarantee Cherokee claims to their Oklahoma lands. Ross had opposed removal because he knew that if the government were allowed to confiscate the Georgia lands they could confiscate lands in Oklahoma later. The government refused to agree to guarantees, however, because the followers of Ridge and Boudinot claimed that Ross was responsible for the murders; finally, in 1846, the Polk administration signed a treaty acceptable to all parties.

On September 2, 1844, Ross married Mary Bryan Stapler, daughter of a Delaware merchant, who bore him two children. The period from the 1846 treaty until the Civil War was a relatively happy time for Ross and for his people. He prospered as a merchant, raised livestock, and contributed much of his wealth to charities on behalf of poor Cherokee; under his guidance, seminaries and a Cherokee newspaper were established.

Though, by 1860, Ross owned fifty slaves, he opposed slavery on principle, and this issue during the 1850's was another source of tribal dissension, his full-blood followers opposing it and the mixed-bloods favoring it. When the war began and agents were working among the Oklahoma tribes on behalf of the Confederacy, Ross favored neutrality and adherence to the 1846 treaty. Only when the neighboring tribes accepted a Confederate alliance and the Cherokee nation was virtually surrounded was Ross willing to accept an alliance. However, in June, 1862, when Union forces finally arrived from Kansas, he welcomed them, though he and his family were forced to leave the Cherokee country as refugees when the Union forces withdrew. His four sons by his first wife served in the Union army, and one of them died in a Confederate prison.

For the next three years, Ross was in the East working to persuade the Lincoln administration to send federal troops to the Cherokee country and to feed the six thousand pro-Union Cherokee who had taken refuge in Kansas. The last year of the war was a particularly unhappy time for him because of the illness of his wife, who died in July, 1865.

When Ross died on August 1, 1866, he was in Washington, D.C., negotiating a peace treaty with the U.S. government and fighting the efforts of the Cherokee faction that had been pro-South in the war to get federal approval of a permanently divided tribe. The treaty that was proclaimed ten days after his death was his last contribution to the cause of Cherokee unity.

SIGNIFICANCE

John Ross was passionately devoted to the ancestral homeland of the Cherokee and to their cultural traditions, but when he recognized that removal might be inevitable he submitted to it in order to reestablish a unified Cherokee nation on the frontier; his people's achievement of a remarkable blend of tribal traditions and white man's political and economic methods was his greatest monument. Though he was "by blood" only one-eighth Cherokee, he grew up as a Cherokee, identified with the Cherokee people, and devoted his life to the great cause of tribal unity. The Cherokee tragedy, which remains permanently fixed as one of the most disgraceful acts of the American people, stands in contrast to the life of the man who was probably the most distinguished Native American political leader of the nineteenth century and who resembles Lincoln both in his political skills and in his vision of union as the only basis for peace and justice.

—*Robert L. Berner*

FURTHER READING

Eaton, Rachel Caroline. *John Ross and the Cherokee Indians*. Chicago: University of Chicago Press, 1921. A doctoral dissertation that concentrates on the Cherokees' political ordeal during Ross's lifetime. Essentially accurate, though apparently written without access to all the early documents.

Jahoda, Gloria. *The Trail of Tears*. New York: Wings Books, 1995. Recounts the Cherokees' forced removal and resettlement west of the Mississippi River.

McLoughlin, William G. *After the Trail of Tears: The Cherokees' Struggle for Sovereignty, 1839-1880*. Chapel Hill: University of North Carolina Press, 1993. Examines the social, cultural, and political history of the Cherokee Nation in the forty years after the tribe was forced to resettle in Oklahoma. Describes Ross's leadership during this period.

Meserve, John Bartlett. "Chief John Ross." *Chronicles of Oklahoma* 13 (December, 1935): 421-437. A brief but balanced account of Ross's life, though flawed by several errors in detail.

Moulton, Gary. *John Ross: Cherokee Chief*. Athens: University of Georgia Press, 1978. The best and most nearly definitive account of Ross's life and political struggles. Most useful because of its copious notes, which provide all the apparatus necessary for further study.

Starkey, Marion L. *The Cherokee Nation.* New York: Alfred A. Knopf, 1946. A semipopular account of Cherokee history from the beginnings to removal, with a final chapter devoted to later events. Written from the point of view of the missionaries to the Cherokee and perhaps overly sympathetic to the Treaty Party.

Wardell, Morris L. *A Political History of the Cherokee Nation, 1838-1907.* Norman: University of Oklahoma Press, 1938. A scholarly account of the Cherokee from removal to Oklahoma statehood. Refers to Ross in passing.

Woodward, Grace Steele. *The Cherokees.* Norman: University of Oklahoma Press, 1963. The best general account of the full range of Cherokee history, from first white contact to the late twentieth century. A fuller and much more balanced history than Starkey's book.

BILL RUSSELL

> *Concentration and mental toughness are the margins of victory.*

Basketball player

Revolutionizing the strategy of basketball with an emphasis on aggressive defense, Russell introduced to the sport a style of play never before used or advocated. His defensive play made him one of the most celebrated players in the history of the game.

Born: February 12, 1934; Monroe, Louisiana
Also known as: William Felton Russell (birth name)
Area of achievement: Sports

EARLY LIFE

Bill Russell (RUHS-sehl) was born in Monroe, Louisiana. His mother, Katie, who died when Russell was twelve years old, exerted a strong, lasting influence. She named Bill for William Felton, president of Southeastern Louisiana College, and made it clear that her children would be college graduates. Russell's father, Charles Russell, was a hardworking wage earner who held several jobs: factory laborer, truck driver, construction worker, hauling business owner, and ironworker in a foundry. He was also a semiprofessional baseball player, as had been his brother, Robert. Robert Russell, just short of making the Negro Major Leagues, blamed his failure on his being right-handed. Robert insisted that his nephew do everything with his left hand.

When Russell was nine years old, the family left Louisiana for better economic opportunities in Detroit, Michigan, but soon afterward moved to West Oakland, California. Bill's brother, Chuck, proved to be an outstanding athlete in baseball, football, basketball, and track and later became a successful playwright. Two years older than

Bill, Chuck cast a shadow over Bill through high school. Unlike Chuck, Bill was not gifted with coordination and muscle until late in his senior year. His gawkiness and awkwardness gave him a self-admitted inferiority complex which, through later athletic stardom, was replaced by an outgoing, although enigmatic, personality.

Russell, six feet ten inches tall and 215 pounds in his prime, had a fierce integrity, frequent cackling laugh, incisive wit, competitive intensity, and far-ranging, intellectual mind. His interests included music appreciation and reading as well as assembling electric trains and investing in a Liberian rubber plantation. His ego was described by Boston Celtics teammate Tom Heinsohn as the largest on the team, while another Celtics teammate, Tom Sanders, emphasized Russell's capacity to needle people and keep them slightly off balance.

Russell was married twice, to Rose Swisher and then to Dorothy Anstett. He had three children from his first marriage—William Felton, Jr. (called Buddha), Jacob Harold, and Karen Kenyatta.

LIFE'S WORK
Russell's older brother, Chuck, was named to Bay Area all-star teams in basketball, football, and track, playing for Oakland Tech. When Bill enrolled at McClymonds High School, he intended to escape Chuck's shadow. However, coaching personnel and students expected Russell to lead McClymonds in similar fashion. Russell proved instead to be skinny and awkward. One sport in which Russell became proficient, however, was table tennis, which improved his reflexes and coordination. As his height and weight increased, Russell's efforts in basketball and track improved.

In his senior year, Russell was a starter, and McClymonds won the Bay Area basketball championship. A winter graduation enabled him to play with a California high school all-star group that toured northward into Canada, playing against top high school and even small college competition. The trip was a turning point for Russell, as his play dramatically improved and his mind constantly analyzed the game. He also gained his first insight into his jumping ability.

Despite Russell's starting role on a championship team and his noticeably improved play with the touring group, only the University of San Francisco (USF) offered a basketball scholarship. Russell had never heard of the school. While waiting for USF head coach Phil Woolpert to contact him, Russell took a job as an apprentice sheet-metal worker. Playing in a McClymonds alumni game, Russell experienced a first that was enjoyable and terrifying at the same time: He jumped high enough to look down into the basket. A new dimension entered Russell's expanding range of skills.

Russell's freshman coach at USF, Ross Giudice, introduced him to the hook shot and spent innumerable post-practice and weekend hours helping Russell sharpen his game. During that season, Russell averaged twenty points per game and started to develop remarkable, one-of-a-kind defensive skills. Giudice was so impressed that he told Woolpert that the potential was there for Russell to become the greatest player in history.

Another great help to Russell was K. C. Jones, his dormitory roommate and teammate. Jones and Russell decided that basketball was a geometric game, and repeated analyses led them to develop and redevelop concepts and strategies from that time throughout their careers. Their approach eventually revolutionized theories of rebounding and defense, but it did not result in instant success. The USF varsity fell well short of championship-level play. A ruptured appendix removed Jones as soon as the season started, and other illnesses and injuries depleted the roster. Russell looked back with no excuses, however, and ascribed the squad's mediocrity to lack of teamwork.

In Russell's junior year, everything changed. Jones was back, Russell was the acknowledged leader, and tough team defense keyed San Francisco to an amazing year. After losing to the University of California, Los Angeles (UCLA) in its third game of the season, the USF Dons swept its next twenty-six games to win the National Collegiate Athletic Association (NCAA) championship. By then, Russell had been tabbed by Howard Dallmar, coach of Stanford and a former standout player in the National Basketball Association (NBA), as one player who could stop George Mikan, who was professional basketball's best player at the time. The Eastern press was not convinced, though, calling Tom Gola, senior leader of defending champion La Salle, college basketball's best player. The issue was settled in the NCAA title game. Russell scored twenty-three points, had twenty-two rebounds, and constantly harassed La Salle shooters, while teammate Jones kept Gola scoreless from the field for twenty-one minutes, in an 89-77 win. Russell tallied 118 points in five play-off games, breaking Gola's NCAA record of 114, and was named the tournament's Most Valuable Player.

Russell's superior defensive play led to significant rule changes. He was a jumper, able to redirect many of his teammates' arrant shots to the basket. The NCAA rules committee responded by instituting a rule against what came to be called goaltending. Also, to keep tall players from establishing an unyielding position under or too near the basket, the free-throw lane, or key, was extended from six to twelve feet, a rule quickly referred to as the Bill Russell rule.

After his junior year, Russell was invited by U.S. president Dwight D. Eisenhower to the White House to discuss a national fitness program and was designated the college basketball representative on a physical-fitness council, joining Willie Mays and Bob Cousy, among others. Russell, by this time, had tried varsity track and became a friend and intense rival of another USF high jumper, Johnny Mathis, who was destined to be a popular singer. At the Modesto Relays, Russell outjumped Mathis, six feet, seven inches to six feet, six inches. Russell's interest in track lasted past his graduation when, intent on being a 1956 U.S. Olympian, he entered both the basketball and high-jump trials. The high jump narrowed to four contestants for three spots, and Russell tied Charlie Dumas—who would later be the first person to leap seven feet—for first place. Since Russell had already been selected as one of only three collegians on the twelve-person U.S. Olympic basketball team, he withdrew his name from the high-jump ranks.

Prior to the Olympics, Russell had led San Francisco to an undefeated season and a second consecutive NCAA title. In the process, the Dons had won fifty-five games in a row, then an NCAA record. When the NBA draft came around, Russell discovered that the Boston Celtics had dealt veteran scorer Ed Macauley and rugged Kentucky all-American Cliff Hagan to the St. Louis Hawks for their draft rights. The Rochester Royals selected first, taking Sihugo Green, a top-rated guard, bypassing Russell because they believed that Maurice Stokes, the NBA Rookie of the Year, supplied them with the same kind of rebounding strength. Additionally, Russell's presence on the

Olympic team would remove him from much of the regular season. It was rumored, too, that the Harlem Globetrotters would outbid any NBA team to get Russell.

Arnold "Red" Auerbach, coach of the Celtics, picked Russell anyway. His Celtics had always been a high-scoring team but needed a strong center. Russell led an undefeated Olympic team that bested the Soviet Union's team 89-55 in the gold medal game and then rejected a Globetrotter offer which was well above Boston's offer. By the end of his first NBA season, Russell proved to be the Celtics' long-needed ingredient. They celebrated their first NBA championship, and Russell had turned pivot play around forever. Thus, in one year, Russell had been the dominant force on three championship teams, in the NCAA, in the Olympics, and in the NBA.

In his second year, Russell was severely injured during the third game of the championship finals. Boston, without its shot-blocking, rebounding genius, lost to the Hawks in six games. During that season, Russell set a single-game rebounding record of forty-nine, which he later increased to fifty-one, set a play-off single-game rebounding record, a single season's rebounding record, and was the runaway choice as the league's Most Valuable Player. Curiously, he was bypassed for the All-League Team.

In the following season, Russell broke his own season's rebounding record, enjoyed a .598 shooting percentage from the field (the best of his career), and led Boston to a sweep of the Minneapolis Lakers for the league crown. He was named All-League center. Over the next seven seasons, Russell led the Celtics to eight league championships in a row and nine out of ten. During that period, Russell was constantly compared to Wilt Chamberlain, the seven foot two inch record-breaking scorer whose style of play contrasted sharply with Russell's. Opinion was divided as to which powerful center was better, but Russell wore the championship rings.

In 1966-1967, Russell succeeded Auerbach as head coach and, though leading the Celtics to a 60-21 overall season record, finished behind the Chamberlain-powered Philadelphia 76ers, whose 68-13 mark set an NBA record (now held by the Chicago Bulls for its 72-10 season in 1995-1996). The 76ers handily beat Boston four games to one in the play-offs, and many believed that Russell and the Celtics were items of the past. Instead, Boston came back in 1967-1968 to beat Philadelphia in three straight play-off games, after being down three games to one, and then beat the Los Angeles Lakers in six games for its tenth NBA title in twelve years. *Sports Illustrated* chose Russell as its Sportsman of the Year. When Russell took the team to another title in 1968-1969, the Celtics claimed the best championship streak in sports history, eleven titles in thirteen tries, and Russell had been the central figure in each. Russell retired after this season. The personal statistics for his thirteen-year career reflects his dominance in the NBA: 14,522 points and 21,620 rebounds, second in NBA history. He won the Most Valuable Player award five times, led the league in rebounds four times, and participated in twelve All-Star games.

Russell faced hostile, racist crowds while playing and coaching in the NBA, similar to the hostility and hatred he faced as a youth in Oakland. In an interview with *Sports Illustrated* in 1999, Russell remembered how the police routinely harassed him with racial epithets in the streets of Oakland when he was a teenager. As the first African American to manage an NBA team, many Celtics fans boycotted the team's games,

Russell, Bill

and the press was sometimes hostile. Teammate Heinsohn remarked that Russell led the league in regrets. Russell remembered that while he was a player, the mayor of Marion, Indiana, presented each of the Celtics with a key to the city, but after the ceremony, Russell and K. C. Jones were refused service in a restaurant. He spoke of receiving honors in Reading, Massachusetts, which was followed by the citizens of a wealthy section of that town circulating a petition to keep him out when they learned he planned to move there. In spite of it all, Russell told *Sports Illustrated* that, even in the face of racism, "I never permitted myself to be a victim."

Sam Schulman, principal owner of the then-hapless Seattle SuperSonics, lured Russell back into NBA coaching in 1973. In Russell's initial season, the SuperSonics won ten more games than in the previous year, and in 1974-1975, Seattle made the play-offs for the first time in its history. The team repeated that achievement in 1975-1976, but Russell had already started to lose faith in too many of his players. He began a fourth and final season with little determination and regretted that he had not resigned earlier. That regret, however, did not keep him from re-entering the NBA as manager of the Sacramento Kings more than a decade later in 1987. After leading the team to a dismal record of seventeen wins and forty-one losses, he resigned midseason in 1989 and retired permanently from basketball.

Russell began a second career on the lecture circuit, advising businesses how best to achieve success. Russell took up golf, ventured into films, did several radio shows for the American Broadcasting Company (ABC) and basketball broadcasts for ABC-TV, and later held television contracts with the Columbia Broadcasting System and the Turner Broadcasting System. He also did Bell Telephone commercials and even served as a substitute for talk-show host Dick Cavett.

In 2007, Russell gained the attention of basketball fans once more by persuading basketball superstars—and former Lakers' teammates—Shaquille O'Neal and Kobe Bryant to end their long feud. That same year, with his daughter, Karen, Russell recorded public service announcements for the Foundation for Sarcoidosis Research to raise national awareness of the disease; both Russell and his daughter have sarcoidosis, an inflammatory autoimmune disorder of unknown cause that can affect any organ, although usually the lungs, and may be fatal.

Russell received many honors during his career. He was named to the Basketball Hall of Fame in 1975, the National Collegiate Basketball Hall of Fame in 2006 (one of the first five to be chosen), and the Fédération Internationale de Basketball (FIBA) Hall of Fame in 2007. He was placed among the fifty greatest players in NBA history in 1996. He holds two honorary doctorates, one from Suffolk University and one from Harvard University, both presented in 2007.

Significance

Russell's fame was a result of his consistently superb efforts as an unselfish team player who intimidated opposing shooters, who blocked shots that almost always triggered fast breaks for his team, who believed in and used a psychology that worked to his team's advantage, and who led in a style that went unchallenged. Coach Auerbach, knowing the importance of winning in professional sports, guaranteed Russell that he would never talk statistics at contract time. This was exactly what Russell, the ultimate

Russell, Bill

team player, wanted to hear. In his own view, he never graded himself as a player higher than sixty-five against a perfect game standard of one hundred. Posterity thought differently. In 1980 the Basketball Writers Association of America chose him as the greatest player in the history of the NBA. Although that accolade came before the arrival of Michael Jordan, many still believe Russell to be, at minimum, the greatest defensive player as well as team player.

More important, Russell recognized that there was far more to life than basketball. From his pedestal of fame he stood tall on matters that counted. Teammate Cousy referred to Russell as a crusader. Certainly, he was among the first African Americans in sports to speak out on racism in the league, in sports in general, and in society. Russell remembered how his grandfather had cried when, in the Celtics locker room, he had seen John Havlicek, a white player, showering alongside Sam Jones, who was black. Russell remained politically active, speaking about blacks nationally as well as locally, such as in the case of Boston schools.

Russell spoke out against the NBA's unwritten, but patently obvious, "quota" rule, and was fined for doing so. He was among those who defended boxer Muhammad Ali while condemning newspapers and magazines for their yellow journalism. When he was the first black person selected to the Basketball Hall of Fame, already in its fifteenth year at the time, he refused to be inducted, criticizing the organization's standards and its racist leadership. Likewise, when the Celtics held a ceremony to retire his uniform number in 1972, he did not attend out of resentment toward racist fans and his wariness of the media. However, in a 1999 reenactment of the ceremony that he attended, he received a long standing ovation.

—*John E. DiMeglio*

FURTHER READING

Bjarkman, Peter C. *The Biographical History of Basketball*. Chicago: Masters Press, 2000. This biographical history compares Russell with NBA greats Wilt Chamberlain, Michael Jordan, and Oscar Robertson.

Havlicek, John, with Bob Ryan. *Hondo: Celtic Man in Motion*. Englewood Cliffs, N.J.: Prentice-Hall, 1977. Candid descriptions of the Boston Celtics plus interesting insights into Russell's youth make this a worthwhile book. As with all books by Celtics personnel, Russell's personality, as well as his value to the club, is assessed.

Heinsohn, Tommy, with Leonard Lewin. *Heinsohn, Don't You Ever Smile?* Garden City, N.Y.: Doubleday, 1976. Easily the most humorous of all Celtics literature. In his discussion of Russell, Heinsohn may get closer to the truth of how Russell and his teammates related than any other work yet written.

Heisler, Mark. *Giants: The Twenty-Five Greatest Centers of All Time*. Chicago: Triumph Books, 2003. Heisler places Russell second on his list, behind Wilt Chamberlain and ahead of Kareem Abdul-Jabbar for reasons explained in brief annotations. A separate text describes Russell's talents as a player and offers photographs of him in action.

Linn, Ed. "I Owe the Public Nothing." *Saturday Evening Post*, January, 1964. An article which, because Russell spoke out so candidly, created controversy. Permits a quick study of Russell's pride and philosophy.

Nelson, Murray R. *Bill Russell: A Biography*. Westport, Conn.: Greenwood Press, 2005. Nelson emphasizes Russell's ability to analyze basketball and engage other team members, traits which made him a successful lecturer and businessman as well. Includes an extensive bibliography and a chronology.

Russell, Bill, and Taylor Branch. *Second Wind: The Memoirs of an Opinionated Man*. New York: Random House, 1979. The second of two Russell autobiographies, this concentrates considerably more on his private life and behavior and rearticulates his philosophy. The better book of the pair.

Russell, Bill, with David Faulkner. *Russell Rules: Eleven Lessons on Leadership from the Twentieth Century*. New York: Dutton, 2001. This book offers eleven "rules of success" that Russell presented to businesspeople during his lectures. Also discusses his basketball career and personal life.

Taylor, John. *The Rivalry: Bill Russell, Wilt Chamberlain, and the Golden Age of Basketball*. New York: Random House, 2005. Taylor focuses on the difference in temperaments between the two great centers and how their rivalry accelerated professional basketball's metamorphosis into a major media attraction.

BABE RUTH

" Never let the fear of striking out get in your way. "

Baseball player

A remarkably talented athlete with a great flair for showmanship, Babe Ruth has come to symbolize baseball, the American national pastime.

Born: February 6, 1895; Baltimore, Maryland
Died: August 16, 1948; New York, New York
Also known as: George Herman Ruth (birth name); the Babe (nickname)
Area of achievement: Sports

EARLY LIFE

George Herman Ruth, later known as Babe Ruth (rewth), was the son of George H. Ruth, Sr., and Kate Schamberger Ruth. Some confusion exists about the younger Ruth's actual date of birth. For many years, George Ruth believed that he had been born on February 7, 1894, but his birth certificate gives February 6, 1895, as his date of birth. George Ruth was the eldest of the eight children born to the Ruths, although only he and a sister (later Mrs. Wilbur Moberly) survived to adulthood. George Ruth's mother (whose maiden name is sometimes spelled Schanberg) lived until her eldest son was thirteen. His father survived until young George's second year in the major leagues.

The Ruths attempted to support their family through the operation of a barroom. Of his childhood, the dying Ruth told his biographer Bob Considine in 1947, "I was a bad kid. I say that without pride but with a feeling that it is better to say it." Having discovered that their eldest child, George, was a fractious youth, George and Kate enrolled him in St. Mary's Industrial School in Baltimore, Maryland, in 1902. Under the direction of the Xaverian Catholic Brothers, St. Mary's served as a vocational school as well as an orphanage, boarding school, and reform school. It was at St. Mary's that young Ruth studied to become a tailor and also learned to play baseball. Brother Matthias of St. Mary's would hit fungoes to Ruth, who quickly seized on the game as a release from the studies and chores at St. Mary's as well as a chance to demonstrate what Brother Matthias recognized as a remarkable skill in the popular game. To Ruth, Brother Matthias was not only a fielding, hitting, and pitching coach, but also "the father I needed." Years later, at the height of his fame and popularity, Babe Ruth never forgot St. Mary's or the Xaverian Brothers who had taught him so well.

In Baltimore, in 1914, there was a professional baseball team named the Orioles. At the time, the Orioles were a minor-league team, owned and managed by Jack Dunn, who, after learning about Ruth's great baseball promise, signed the young athlete to a contract. Ruth discovered that he did not have to become a tailor; he could make a living doing what he enjoyed most: playing baseball. On February 27, 1914, George Ruth left St. Mary's to join the Baltimore team. During his first few days of spring training, Jack Dunn's new "babe" was the subject of some good-natured baseball pranks. Eventually, the new arrival on the team became Babe Ruth, arguably the greatest and most colorful player in the history of the sport he loved so well.

LIFE'S WORK

Young Babe Ruth was a left-handed pitcher, and the high prices being offered for Ruth's pitching ability soon proved too tempting for the financially distressed Orioles to resist: Ruth was sold to the Boston Red Sox in July, 1914. On July 11, 1914, Babe Ruth pitched and was victorious in the first major-league baseball game he had ever played. With his tremendous speed and sharp breaking ball, Ruth impressed Red Sox manager Bill Carrigan. Still, it was clear by August that the Red Sox would not win the American League pennant from Connie Mack's Philadelphia Athletics. Ruth was therefore sent down to the Red Sox minor-league team in Providence, Rhode Island, to help them win the International League pennant. Providence manager "Wild Bill" Donovan was credited by Ruth for his effective pitching coaching, later of value to Ruth in his Red Sox career.

Throughout his long and colorful career, Ruth was criticized for financial, gastronomic, and sexual excesses. As with other legendary personalities, however, his sins as well as his successes may have been exaggerated. In his major-league career, spanning 1914 to 1935, the Babe (as he was called) was an exciting, intelligent, and astonishingly well-rounded ballplayer, suggesting that the tales about his endless hedonism were largely, if not entirely, fictitious. On October 17, 1914, Babe Ruth married Helen Woodford, a waitress whom he had met in 1914, while with the Red Sox. In 1922, the Ruths adopted a baby girl named Dorothy. In 1926, the Ruths separated; in January, 1929, Helen Ruth was killed in a tragic fire. Three months later, Ruth married a beautiful widow named Claire Merritt Hodgson and adopted her daughter Julia. Ruth remained with his second wife until his death in August, 1948.

In 1915, the Boston Red Sox won the American League pennant, winning 101

Ruth, Babe

games, of which Ruth had won 18, and losing only 50. In the 1915 World Series, the Red Sox defeated the Philadelphia Phillies, 4 games to 1. In 1916, Ruth won 23 games—a figure he matched in 1917. Overall, Babe Ruth won 92 games as a pitcher, and lost only 44; his earned run average was a remarkable 2.24. Ruth pitched for Boston in three World Series: 1915, 1916, and 1918. He won 3 World Series games, lost none, and sported an earned run average of 0.87. Had he continued as a pitcher, Ruth's pitching record could have been as remarkable as his hitting record.

The Red Sox now faced a problem with Ruth. In 1918, Ruth was recognized as one of the finest pitchers in baseball. He also hit eleven home runs, knocked in sixty-four runs, and batted .300. Ruth was too good a hitter to pitch every four days, resting between starts. He was too good a pitcher, however, to play the outfield or first base every day. It is some indication of Ruth's phenomenal baseball ability that from 1914 to 1919, while he was principally a pitcher, Ruth had 342 hits in 1,110 at-bats, with 49 home runs and 230 runs batted in. He simply had become too powerful as a hitter to keep as a pitcher. He also had become too expensive. Babe Ruth's 1917 salary was five thousand dollars, in 1918 it was seven thousand, and by 1919, it had grown to ten thou-

Babe Ruth.
(Library of Congress)

sand. In January, 1920, Babe Ruth was sold again—this time by the Red Sox to the New York Yankees. The price tag was $100,000 and a loan of $350,000.

The season of 1920 was a turning point in the history of baseball. In that season, Ruth smashed an incredible 54 home runs, driving in 137. A new national hero was born, and the game of baseball began to change from a short game (meaning a game of bunts, sacrifices, and steals) to a long game (meaning home runs and big-scoring innings). There had been great concern for the future of the national pastime when it was revealed that some Chicago White Sox players had been bribed in the 1919 World Series, which they lost to Cincinnati. Ruth's amazing feats, however, drove the 1919 scandal from fans' minds. As *The New York Times* reported: "Inside of a fortnight the fandom of the nation had forgotten all about the Black Sox, as they had come to be called, as its attention became centered in an even greater demonstration of superlative batting skill by the amazing Babe Ruth." In 1921, Ruth hit an astounding 59 home runs and drove in 170, while batting .378. Ruth's Yankees won ninety-eight games in that season and beat their cross-town rivals, the New York Giants, five games to three, in the World Series. It was no wonder, *The New York Times* reported, that "the baseball world lay at his feet."

The Yankees won the pennant again in 1922, 1923, 1926, 1927, 1928, and 1932; they won the World Series in 1922, 1923, 1927, 1928, and 1932. In the World Series games in which he played as a Yankee, Ruth hit fifteen home runs, drove in twenty-nine runs, and hit .347. Obscured by his extraordinary totals as a hitter (and pitcher) are Ruth's fielding, throwing, and baserunning abilities. Numerous baseball fans and analysts testify to Ruth's superb skills as an outfielder and daring, aggressive base runner. Ruth's attempted steal of second base in the final game of the 1926 World Series, which the St. Louis Cardinals won, is part of baseball folklore. With two outs in the ninth inning of the deciding Series game, Ruth walked. Trailing 3-2 in the ninth inning, the Yankees had two outs, but powerful Bob Meusel was at bat. With one strike on Meusel, Ruth attempted a delayed steal of second but was thrown out. The game was over, and the Cardinals were world champions. Baseball fans still argue the wisdom of Ruth's attempted steal. There is another Ruth legend associated with the 1926 World Series, the validity of which is still debated by baseball mythologists. A young boy, John Sylvester, was seriously ill during the 1926 series. When he asked his father for a ball autographed by Ruth, the older Sylvester wired that request to the Babe. Players of both teams autographed balls that were sent to the Sylvester home. Johnny Sylvester did recover, but reports that Ruth promised to hit a home run for Johnny that, when executed, led to the boy's recovery, are in error.

In 1927, the New York Yankees, led by Ruth's herculean hitting (60 home runs, 164 runs batted in, batting average of .356), won the World Series in a four-game sweep of the Pittsburgh Pirates. The 1927 Yankees are properly regarded by baseball historians as the greatest of all baseball teams. Ruth had by that time accumulated 416 home runs, batted in 1,274, and was batting .349. He was regarded as the great turnstile whirler, and it seemed as though people everywhere knew of Babe Ruth. In 1927, the Yankees paid Ruth an unbelievable seventy thousand dollars—a figure they matched in 1928 and 1929. In 1930 and 1931, he received eighty thousand dollars per season. Ruth's earnings over twenty-two seasons in the majors were estimated to be $896,000, in addition to World Series shares of $41,445 and approximately one million dollars from endorsements and barnstorming tours. Despite the high cost, Ruth was an asset to the Yankees: He attracted so many fans to Yankee Stadium, which opened in 1923, that it was nicknamed the House That Ruth Built.

Although 1927 will always be associated in sports history with Babe Ruth, the years 1928-1933 are equally, perhaps even more, impressive. In those years alone, Ruth batted .341, hit 270 home runs, and drove in 852 runs. It was spectacular. It was the golden age of sports, and Babe Ruth came to symbolize it all. Americans needed a diversion: The Depression had hit, and Prohibition was not repealed until December, 1933. The public followed Ruth's successes and his failures, his heroics and his occasional misconduct, with enthusiasm.

In 1934, Babe Ruth spent his last full year in the major leagues. His average sank to .288; he hit twenty-two home runs and batted in eighty-four. It would have been an excellent season for most players, but it signaled the end for Babe Ruth. In 1934, the Yankees failed again (as in 1933) to win the pennant. Ruth left the Yankees and signed on for the 1935 season with the Boston Braves of the National League. He played in only twenty-eight games for the Braves, hitting six homers, driving in twelve runs, and batting .181. Ruth never attained his goal of becoming a major-league manager, although he did coach in 1938 for the Brooklyn Dodgers. Statistics do not always reliably convey the value of a ballplayer, but, in Ruth's case, the evidence is clear: In his major-league career, he played in 2,503 games; he batted 8,396 times and had 2,873 hits, of which 714 were homers. His lifetime batting average was .342. At the time of his death in 1948, Babe Ruth held fifty-four major-league records. Although some of those records have now been captured by more recent players, Babe Ruth, the famous Number Three of the Yankees, is still the standard against which ballplayers are measured.

In June, 1948, Ruth, a dying man, stood in Yankee Stadium to say good-bye to thousands of fans. About two months later, he died of cancer at a New York City hospital. On the evening of August 17, 1948, Ruth's body lay inside the main entrance to Yankee Stadium. It is estimated that more than 100,000 fans passed by to pay their respects. The Babe was dead, but, as Marshall Smelser put it, "one with ears tuned and eyes alert will hear or read his name almost monthly. Even without any imposing monument his memory will last in this country till memory be dead."

SIGNIFICANCE

In March, 1944, during the bitter fighting on Pacific Islands, Japanese soldiers attacked U.S. Marine positions, screaming in English: "To hell with Babe Ruth." Babe Ruth had come to symbolize not only American baseball but also America. As Robert Creamer, the baseball historian, reported, Ruth once said of himself: "I swing big, with everything I've got. I hit big or I miss big. I like to live as big as I can." Here was an indigent boy who rose from the obscurity of a Maryland boys' home to become one of the most famous Americans, whose death was reported in the headlines of *The New York Times*. Although he died when he was only fifty-three, Ruth's life seemed curiously long and complete. Ruth had a remarkable flair for the spectacular and the flamboyant. He lived his life with a zest that his countrymen seemed able to share. As he was dying, he told Considine that "I want to be a part of and help the development of the greatest game God ever saw fit to let man invent—Baseball." Smelser summarized the importance of Babe Ruth in American life thus: "[H]e is our Hercules, our Samson, Beowulf, Siegfried. No other person outside of public life so stirred our imaginations or so captured our affections."

—James H. Toner

FURTHER READING

Creamer, Robert W. *Babe: The Legend Comes to Life*. New York: Penguin Books, 1974. A very well-written and well-researched biography. A balanced account of Ruth's life, neither iconoclastic nor hagiographic. Probably the best general account of Ruth's life, although there is little documentation for the close reader.

Montville, Leigh. *The Big Bam: The Life and Times of Babe Ruth*. New York: Doubleday, 2006. Comprehensive biography based on new documents and interviews in which Montville separates the facts from the myths of Ruth's life.

Reisler, Jim. *Babe Ruth: Launching the Legend*. New York: McGraw-Hill, 2004. Recounts the 1920 baseball season, Ruth's first season with the Yankees, to examine the team's impact on the game of baseball.

Ruth, Babe. *Babe Ruth's Own Book of Baseball*. New York: G. P. Putnam's Sons, 1928. No credit is given in this volume to any assistant writer, although there very probably was at least one. This is an interesting book because it contains details about Ruth's life—as well as about his baseball beliefs—which are rarely referred to elsewhere. Anecdotal. It provides an interesting view of baseball strategy in the 1920's.

Ruth, Babe, as told to Bob Considine. *The Babe Ruth Story*. New York: E. P. Dutton, 1948. A surprisingly well-done and frank account of Babe's life, written in the last months of that life. Although bowdlerized, the book contains the Babe's views of many important episodes in his life and is enjoyable reading for the Ruth fan.

Smelser, Marshall. *The Life That Ruth Built*. New York: Quadrangle/New York Times Books, 1975. By far the best study of Ruth yet to emerge. Balanced account, if rather forgiving of Ruth in certain areas. Superbly researched and documented. Thoughtful and analytical. Thorough. Attempts to place Ruth into his historical context. Indispensable for those wishing a deeper study of the Ruth legend.

Wagenheim, Kal. *Babe Ruth: His Life and Legend*. New York: Praeger, 1974. A very good popular account, overshadowed by Creamer's when both appeared at about the same time. Although this volume is not as thorough as Creamer's—and certainly not as thorough as Smelser's—it is a useful and readable account.

Weldon, Martin. *Babe Ruth*. New York: Thomas Y. Crowell, 1948. A book appearing about the same time as *The Babe Ruth Story*, this book was never given close attention, but it is a short, readable account without documentation. Tends to be rather flattering of the Babe. This book, like Claire Ruth's memoir *The Babe and I* (with Bill Slocum), published by Prentice-Hall in 1959, becomes a philippic against organized baseball for not embracing Babe as a manager after his playing career was done. Useful if read with other accounts.

SACAGAWEA

> *I saw at a distance Several Indians on horseback coming towards me. The interpreter and [Sacagawea], who were before me at some distance, danced for the joyful sight, and she made signs to me that they were her nation....*
> (journal of William Clark, August 17, 1805)

Native American explorer

Sacagawea was the only woman who accompanied the Lewis and Clark expedition in its exploration of the territory acquired through the Louisiana Purchase, but as the expedition's primary guide and interpreter, she played a major role in its success.

Born: c. 1788; central Idaho
Died: December 20, 1812; Fort Manuel, Dakota Territory (now in South Dakota)
Also known as: Sagagawea; Sakakawea; Sacajawea; Bird Woman; Boat Pusher
Area of achievement: Exploration

EARLY LIFE

Sacagawea (SAH-kah-jah-WEE-ah) was born into a band of northern Shoshone Indians, whose base was the Lemhi Valley of central Idaho. Her name translates as "Bird Woman" (Hidatsa) or "Boat Pusher" (Shoshonean). The northern Shoshone, sometimes referred to as Snake Indians (a name given them by the French because of the use of painted snakes on sticks to frighten their enemies), were a wandering people, living by hunting, gathering, and fishing. As a child, Sacagawea traveled through the mountains and valleys of Idaho, northwest Wyoming, and western Montana. In 1800, at about age twelve, Sacagawea and her kin were encamped during a hunting foray at the Three Forks of the Missouri (between modern Butte and Bozeman, Montana) when they were attacked by a war party of Hidatsas (also called Minnetarees), a Siouan tribe; about ten Shoshone were killed, and Sacagawea and several other children were made captives. Sacagawea was taken to reside with the Hidatsas at the village of Metaharta near the junction of the Knife and Missouri Rivers (in modern North Dakota).

Shortly after her capture, Sacagawea was sold as a wife to fur trader Toussaint Charbonneau. A French-Canadian who had developed skills as an interpreter, Charbonneau had been living with the Hidatsas for five years. At the time that Sacagawea became his squaw, Charbonneau had one or two other Indian wives.

All that is known of Sacagawea for certain is found in the journals and letters of Meriwether Lewis, William Clark, and several other participants in the expedition of the Corps of Discovery, 1804-1806, along with meager references in other sources. The Lewis and Clark party, commissioned by President Thomas Jefferson to find a route to the Pacific and to make scientific observations along the way, traveled on the first leg of their journey up the Missouri River to the mouth of the Knife River, near which they established Fort Mandan (near modern Bismarck, North Dakota) as their winter headquarters. The site was in the vicinity of Mandan and Hidasta villages. Here the expedition's leaders made preparations for the next leg of their journey and collected information on the Indians and topography of the far West.

LIFE'S WORK

Sacagawea's association with the Lewis and Clark expedition began on November 4, 1804, when she accompanied her husband to Fort Mandan. She presented the officers with four buffalo robes. Charbonneau was willing to serve as interpreter, but only on condition that Sacagawea be permitted to go along on the journey. After agreeing to those terms, Lewis and Clark hired Charbonneau. At Fort Mandan on February 11, 1805, Sacagawea gave birth to Jean-Baptiste Charbonneau. Thus, along with the some thirty men, the "squaw woman" and baby became members of the exploring group.

The expedition set out from Fort Mandan on April 7, 1805. Charbonneau and Sacagawea at different times were referred to in the journals as "interpreter and interpretess." Sacagawea's knowledge of Hidatsa and Shoshonean proved of great aid in communicating with the two tribes with which the expedition primarily had contact. Later, when the expedition made contact with Pacific Coast Indians, Sacagawea managed to assist in communicating with those peoples even though she did not speak their language. Her services as a guide were helpful only when the expedition sought out Shoshone Indians in the region of the Continental Divide in order to find direction and assistance in leaving the mountains westward. Carrying her baby on her back in cord netting, Sacagawea stayed with one or several of the main groups of explorers, never venturing out scouting on her own. Little Baptiste enlivened the camp circles, and Clark, unlike Lewis, became fond of both baby and mother.

Several times on the westward journey Sacagawea was seriously ill, and once she and Baptiste were nearly swept away in a flash flood. In May of 1805, Sacagawea demonstrated her resourcefulness by retrieving many valuable articles that had washed out of a canoe during a rainstorm. Lewis and Clark named a stream "Sâh-câ-ger we-âh (*Sah ca gah we a*) or bird woman's River," which at a later time was renamed Crooked Creek. Not the least of Sacagawea's contributions was finding sustenance in the forests, identifying flora that Indians considered edible. She helped to gather berries, wild onions, beans, artichokes, and roots. She cooked and mended clothes.

On reaching the Three Forks of the Missouri, Sacagawea recognized landmarks and rightly conjectured where the Shoshone might be during the hunting season. A band of these Indians was found along the Lemhi River. Sacagawea began "to dance and show every mark of the most extravagant joy . . . sucking her fingers at the same time to indicate that they were of her native tribe." The tribe's leader, Cameahwait, turned out to be Sacagawea's brother (or possibly cousin). Lewis and Clark established a cordial relationship with Sacagawea's kinsmen and were able to obtain twenty-nine horses and an Indian guide through the rest of the mountains.

As it came down from the mountains, the exploring party made dugout canoes at the forks of the Clearwater River and then followed an all-water route along that stream, the Snake River, and the Columbia River to the Pacific coast. At the mouth of the Columbia River, just below present Astoria, Oregon, the adventurers built Fort Clatsop, where they spent the winter. Sacagawea was an important asset as the expedition covered the final phase of the journey. "The wife of Shabono our interpreter,"

Sacagawea

wrote William Clark on October 13, 1805, "reconciles all the Indians, as to our friendly intentions a woman with a party of men is a token of peace."

Besides her recognition of topography that aided in finding the Shoshones, Sacagawea's other contribution as guide occurred on the return trip. During the crossing of the eastern Rockies by Clark's party (Lewis took a more northerly route), Sacagawea showed the way from Three Forks through the mountains via the Bozeman Pass to the Yellowstone River. Lewis and Clark reunited near the junction of the Missouri and the Yellowstone. Sacagawea, Charbonneau, and infant Baptiste accompanied the expedition down the Missouri River only as far as the Hidatsa villages at the mouth of the Knife River. On April 17, 1806, they "took leave" of the exploring group. Clark offered to take Sacagawea's baby, whom Clark called "Pomp," with him to St. Louis to be reared and educated as his adopted son. Sacagawea, who consented to the proposal, insisted that the infant, then nineteen months old, be weaned first.

With the conclusion of the Lewis and Clark expedition, details about Sacagawea's life become sketchy. In the fall of 1809, the Charbonneau family visited St. Louis. Charbonneau purchased a small farm on the Missouri River just north of St. Louis from Clark, who had been named Indian superintendent for the Louisiana Territory. In 1811, Charbonneau sold back the tract to Clark. Sacagawea yearned to return to her homeland. Charbonneau enlisted in a fur-trading expedition conducted by Manuel Lisa. In April of 1811, Sacagawea and Charbonneau headed upriver in one of Lisa's boats. One observer on board at the time commented that Sacagawea appeared sickly.

Sacagawea left Jean-Baptiste Charbonneau with Clark in St. Louis. On August 11, 1813, an orphan's court appointed Clark as the child's guardian. Sacagawea's son went on to have a far-ranging career. At the age of eighteen, he joined a western tour of the young Prince Paul Wilhelm of Württemberg and afterward went to Europe, where he resided with the prince for six years. The two men returned to America in 1829, and again explored the western country. Jean-Baptiste thereafter was employed as a fur trapper for fifteen years by the American Fur Company. He later served as an army guide during the Mexican War. Joining the Gold Rush of 1849, Jean Baptiste set up residence in Placer County, California. Traveling through Montana in May of 1866, he died of pneumonia.

There has been a lively controversy over the correct determination of the date and place of Sacagawea's death. Grace Raymond Hebard, a professor at the University of Wyoming, published the biography *Sacajawea* in 1933, in which she went to great lengths to prove that Sacagawea died April 9, 1884. Hebard traced the alleged wanderings of the "Bird Woman" to the time that she settled down on the Wind River Reservation in Wyoming. Hebard made a substantial case, based on oral testimony of persons who had known the "Bird Woman"; the hearsay related to known details of the Lewis and Clark expedition. Hebard also relied upon ethnological authorities.

At the heart of the controversy is a journal entry of John Luttig, resident fur-company clerk at Fort Manuel. On December 20, 1812, he recorded: "This Evening the Wife of Charbonneau, a Snake Squaw died of a putrid fever she was a good and the best Women in the fort, aged about 25 years she left an infant girl." It is known that Sacagawea had given birth to a daughter, Lizette. The Luttig journal was not published until 1920. Hebard claimed that the death notice referred to Charbonneau's other Shoshone wife, Otter Woman. The issue, however, seems put to rest by the discovery in 1955 of a document in William Clark's journal dated to the years 1825 to 1828. Clark's list of the status of members of his expedition states: "Se car ja we au Dead." Nevertheless, the notion that Sacagawea lived until the 1880's continues to have support.

SIGNIFICANCE

Sacagawea had a fourfold impact on the Lewis and Clark expedition. Though she viewed much of the country the group traversed for the first time, her geographical knowledge was most important in locating the Shoshones in the Rocky Mountains and directing Clark's party through the Bozeman Pass. At crucial instances her services as a translator were essential, and she served as a contact agent. Perhaps, most of all, as an Indian mother with a young baby, she dispelled many of the fears of the Indians encountered on the journey, particularly the fear that the expedition might harm them.

Sacagawea may be credited as a primary factor in ensuring the success of the Lewis and Clark expedition. Sacagawea also contributed to the uplifting of morale. Throughout the venture she exhibited courage, resourcefulness, coolness, and congeniality. The presence of mother and baby encouraged a certain civilized restraint among the members of the party. Henry Brackenridge, who met Sacagawea in April of 1811, said that she was "a good creature, of a mild and gentle disposition." Clark expressed regrets at the end of the expedition that no special reward could be given to Sacagawea. In many ways she was more valuable to the expedition than her husband, who ultimately received compensation for their efforts.

Sacagawea's place in history was long neglected. Interest in her life, however, gained momentum with the centenary celebrations of the Lewis and Clark expedition during the early twentieth century and especially with the rise of the suffrage movement, which saw in Sacagawea a person of womanly virtues and independence. Eva Emery Dye's novel, *The Conquest: The True Story of Lewis and Clark* (1902), did much during the course of its ten editions to popularize an exaggerated role of Sacagawea on the famous journey of discovery.

Sacagawea attracted new attention in 2000, when the U.S. Mint began issuing a new dollar coin with her image on the front. Images of American Indians had been used on many earlier coins—such as the "Indian head" penny and the "buffalo" nickel—but the new Sacagawea dollar was the first coin to feature the image of a specific Indian person.

—*Harry M. Ward*

FURTHER READING

Anderson, Irving. "A Charbonneau Family Portrait." *American West* 17 (Spring, 1980): 4-13, 58-64. Written for a popular audience, this article provides a thorough and reliable account of the lives of Sacagawea, her husband Toussaint, and her son Jean-Baptiste.

Chuinard, E. G. "The Actual Role of the Bird Woman." *Montana: The Magazine of Western History* 26 (Summer, 1976): 18-29. Emphasizes the role of Sacagawea as a guide and contact agent and challenges the exaggeration of her actual accomplishments.

Clark, Ella E., and Margot Edmonds. *Sacagawea of the Lewis and Clark Expedition.* Berkeley: University of California Press, 1979. Includes discussion of Sacagawea's life and the efforts made to popularize her legend. Although they provide a relatively accurate account, the authors choose to accept the discredited theory that Sacagawea lived until 1884.

Howard, Harold P. *Sacajawea.* Norman: University of Oklahoma Press, 1971. A balanced biography aimed at a general audience, this work attempts to sort out fact from legend in the life of Sacagawea.

Hunsaker, Joyce Badgley. *Sacagawea Speaks: Beyond the Shining Mountains with Lewis and Clark.* Guilford, Conn.: Two Dot Books, 2001. Sacagawea recounts her experiences with the Corps of Discovery. Hunsaker uses oral tradition, scholarly research, anecdotes, and other materials to compile Sacagawea's first-person narrative.

Jackson, Donald, ed. *Letters of the Lewis and Clark Expedition, with Related Documents, 1783-1854.* 2d ed. 2 vols. Urbana: University of Illinois Press, 1978. Contains a variety of letters, journal entries, and other papers relevant to the activities of the expedition. Sheds some light on the contribution of the Charbonneau family.

Nelson, W. Dale. *Interpreters with Lewis and Clark: The Story of Sacagawea and Toussaint Charbonneau.* Denton: University of North Texas Press, 2003. Examines the contributions of Toussaint and Sacagawea to the Lewis and Clark expedition. Nelson seeks to rehabilitate Toussaint's character and reputation.

Perdue, Theda, ed. *Sifters: Native American Women's Lives.* New York: Oxford University Press, 2001. Chapter 4 in this collection of biographies focuses on the myth and reality of Sacagawea's life.

Ronda, James P. *Lewis and Clark Among the Indians.* Lincoln: University of Nebraska Press, 1984. This scholarly study examines the contact made between the Lewis and Clark expedition and the Indians. Provides insights into Sacagawea's contributions to the success of the expedition. Includes an appendix that evaluates various books and articles about Sacagawea.

Jonas Salk

> *" I have had dreams, and I've had nightmares. I overcame the nightmares because of my dreams. "*

Physician and immunologist

Salk developed the first effective vaccine for polio, and he marshaled the nation's resources to help eradicate the disease.

Born: October 28, 1914; New York, New York
Died: June 23, 1995; La Jolla, California
Also known as: Jonas Edward Salk (full name)
Areas of achievement: Medicine; public health; biology

Early Life

Jonas Salk (JOH-nehs sahlk) was the firstborn child of Daniel B. Salk and Dora Press. His father was a garment maker, and both of his parents encouraged their children to do well in school. Salk attended Townsend Harris High School for the gifted and received his B.A. from College of the City of New York in 1934. He received his M.D. from New York University in 1939 and interned at Mount Sinai Hospital, where he studied immunology. Salk was recognized as an able scientist by his teachers, and during World War II he was a participant in the U.S. Army's effort to develop an effective vaccine for influenza. He continued this interest in his first academic appointment at the University of Michigan, developing such a vaccine with his more senior colleague and former mentor, Thomas Francis, Jr. This established Salk's reputation professionally as an ambitious, bright, and innovative scholar who could organize a laboratory and work well under pressure.

Salk was restless and wanted independence from the projects of his senior colleagues so that he could try out some of his own unconventional ideas. He astounded his peers by accepting a position at the University of Pittsburgh Medical School, which, at that time, had no record of basic research in medicine. Salk got the space he needed and rapidly put together a team of laboratory workers to help him study infectious diseases. Not intimidated by authority, Salk used his managerial skills and cultural breadth to convince philanthropists and university administrators to equip his laboratory. His driving energy resulted in the publication of many important papers that caught the attention of the National Foundation (March of Dimes) and its director, Daniel Basil O'Connor. The National Foundation had for many years supported treatment and rehabilitative programs for paralytic polio victims. Salk was one of many younger investigators whom O'Connor hoped to recruit for the research that would lead to a vaccine for that dreaded disease.

Life's Work

Salk's greatest contribution to immunology was his insight that the killing of a virus by chemical treatment need not profoundly alter the antigenic properties of the virus. Any foreign material in a body can serve as an antigen and provoke the body's immune system to form antibodies to attack it. This is one of the body's major defenses against the invasion of bacteria and viruses. A virus may have complex proteins that coat its deadly infectious nucleic acid. Chemical treatment by formaldehyde may damage some of the genes of the virus so that they cannot multiply in the body, but they may not appreciably change the shape of the surface proteins of the virus. It is the surface proteins, and not the inner core of genes contained in the viral nucleic acid, that provoke antibody formation.

Salk's success in developing a vaccine for polio depended on the discoveries of many other researchers in immunology and virology. Originally polio could only be grown in live monkeys. Attempts in the 1930's to use a vaccine prepared from the killed extracts of infected monkey brains resulted in the deaths of several children from meningitis and other reactions. It was also erroneously thought that polio grew only in nerve tissues, but infected humans produced large amounts of viruses in their feces, suggesting that it also grew in the intestines. John F. Enders and his colleagues succeeded in growing polio virus in tissue culture using embryonic cells, a major breakthrough that led to their being awarded a Nobel Prize in 1954. Polio also turned out not to be one virus but at least three different types of viruses, each type having many different strains, some highly infectious and others only weakly so. It was this need to type the polio viruses that brought O'Connor to Pittsburgh. Salk developed new methods to type the viruses rapidly and new methods to grow the viruses in large quantities. He realized that this work could not be done with a few animals, and so he organized a large laboratory, heavily funded, to maintain and use thousands of monkeys for his experiments. Salk made good use of the facilities and support; he soon proved his hunch that the antigenic properties of killed polio virus were not impaired by the formaldehyde treatment of the viruses.

Two additional findings were important for Salk's future work in developing a polio vaccine. Isabel Morgan Mountain succeeded in immunizing monkeys against polio by using formaldehyde-killed virus. Hilary Koprowski used live viruses whose properties had been attenuated or weakened by passage through rats; he fed twenty-two human subjects with the altered virus, and none showed symptoms, although all had developed antibodies against the fully infectious strain of polio virus.

Salk rejected two prevailing views at the time. Many immunologists believed that purified antibody, gamma globulin, would be effective in preventing polio. Gamma globulin, however, was expensive, and it afforded protection for only a short time. Many other immunologists were convinced that a killed virus would not work or that it could not be purified without contamination of the proteins from the cells on which it grew. Salk proved that these two views were mistaken; with the backing of the National Foundation, he prepared the purified killed polio virus vaccines against all three types of polio. Although the virus was rendered inactive after three days, Salk kept the virus in formaldehyde for thirteen days to guarantee that no live virus was present. By 1954, all the difficulties were resolved, and Salk began the crucial human experimentation to confirm the results obtained on monkeys. He and his laboratory workers immunized themselves and their families and then began field-testing the vaccine. The virus proved better than 90 percent effective. The first seven million doses of the vaccine were administered in 1955. A contaminated source from a California pharmaceutical firm was noticed, and the trials were held up until the purification procedures

Jonas Salk.
(Courtesy, March of Dimes)

were standardized. Salk then initiated a nationwide program from 1956 through 1958. Almost immediately after this massive program of immunization, the United States was polio-free.

Salk's killed virus vaccine required four injections, one for each type plus a booster. Additional boosters were necessary as the antibody levels gradually fell. The National Foundation, aware of this possibility, had also backed Albert Sabin to develop a live polio vaccine. The live vaccine, which then required fewer visits to a physician for booster doses, replaced the Salk vaccine. The killed virus vaccine does not cause polio in its recipients or in individuals who have never been vaccinated; the live vaccine, however, occasionally does cause polio in family members or neighbors who have never been vaccinated. For this reason, Salk urged the use of killed vaccine in areas where compliance with vaccination requirements was inadequate. Although live vaccine was more frequently used in the years following Salk's campaign, polio had already been defeated, and in the public's mind Salk had become a national hero. Among the many honors showered on him was the Lasker Award in 1956 and the Presidential Medal of Freedom in 1977.

Salk's popularity with the National Foundation and with philanthropists led him to a second major venture. He proposed an institute for biological research that would permit the most talented scientists in the world to carry out research that would lead to new advances in knowledge beneficial to health and human happiness. The Salk Institute for Biological Studies was founded in 1960, and a building for it opened in 1963. The building, chiefly funded by the National Foundation, was constructed in La Jolla, California, a suburb of San Diego noted for its beautiful scenery and beachfront. The Salk Institute attracted many Nobel laureates; the freedom to do full-time research and thinking was a major feature of its design. Salk thought of the institute as an experiment in the sociology of science, with a primary mission to study and initiate modern trends in biology tempered with a conscience for humanity. Among the seven original resident fellows of the Institute was Jacob Bronowski, a mathematician turned philosopher, whose television series *Ascent of Man* reflected the optimism of the Salk Institute—the conviction that knowledge of the universe enriches both human understanding and human welfare. Salk maintained a laboratory to study multiple sclerosis, and he also devoted much of his energy to writing books about the philosophy and social role of science. In 1995, Salk emerged from retirement to develop a therapeutic AIDS vaccine for HIV-positive patients.

Significance

Salk's national immunization campaign in 1956-1958 administered more than two hundred million doses of killed vaccine without a single individual becoming infected with the disease. This remarkable achievement reflected Salk's talent for establishing quality control as he shifted from a single laboratory to the national level in carrying out his project. The disease was particularly frightening to parents, who witnessed the devastating paralysis it produced in schoolchildren and the helplessness of its most severely affected survivors, who had to live in "iron lungs," expensive and bulky machines that kept them breathing. The disease had also taken on national importance as Americans admired the courage of President Franklin D. Roosevelt, who had survived polio and went on to guide the nation through the Great Depression and World War II while confined to a wheelchair.

Salk represented a new generation of scientists who required funded research to accomplish their goals. Directing a large laboratory with many technical assistants and advanced students involves management skills, inspired leadership, the ability to write convincing grant applications and progress reports, and a personality that thrives on hard work and the occasional successes that careful scientific research yields. Salk was a model of this new type, but he was also unique in extending his efforts to involve an entire nation in his enterprise.

—*Elof Axel Carlson*

Further Reading

Carter, Richard. *Breakthrough: The Saga of Jonas Salk.* New York: Trident Press, 1965. This popular biography covers Salk's life through 1965. Salk's energy and personality are well depicted, although specific experiments are only mentioned and not analyzed.

Kluger, Jeffrey. *Splendid Solution: Jonas Salk and the Conquest of Polio.* New York: G. P. Putnam Sons, 2004. Although the book focuses on Salk, Kluger also describes the widespread fear of polio and the effects of the disease in the years before a vaccine was created and details the efforts of other scientists who sought to eradicate the disease.

Oshinsky, David M. *Polio: An American Story*. New York: Oxford University Press, 2005. Oshinsky's history of polio in the United States focuses on the 1950's, when Salk and Albert Sabin were embroiled in an intense competition to discover a cure for polio.

Salk, Jonas. *Anatomy of Reality: Merging of Intuition and Reason*. New York: Columbia University Press, 1983. Salk relates metabiological ideas to biological and cultural evolution. He proposes more efforts to view life and the universe from both rational and intuitive, especially value-laden, perspectives.

_____. *Man Unfolding*. Edited by Ruth N. Anshen. New York: Harper & Row, 1972. Salk introduces the idea of biological dualisms as attributes of the human condition, whose unresolved conflicts lead to social unrest and conflict. He uses biological processes as guides or analogies for constructing psychological and social models that attempt to resolve the conflicts.

_____. *The Survival of the Wisest*. New York: Harper & Row, 1973. Salk greatly extends his concept of dualisms and introduces the idea of metabiology, a philosophic extension of the life sciences. From this perspective, Salk argues that resolution of conflicts arising from dualisms is not only possible but also necessary.

Salk, Jonas, and Jonathan Salk. *World Population and Human Values: New Reality*. New York: Harper & Row, 1981. The ideas of Salk's metabiology are applied to the problem of overpopulation. Each concept is accompanied by a separate diagram. Provides a global perspective by using United Nations vital statistics and population trends in different continents and cultures.

PETE SAMPRAS

> *The difference of great players is at a certain point in a match they raise their level of play and maintain it.*

Tennis player

Widely considered one of the greatest tennis players of all time, Sampras was known for his powerful and accurate serve and his volley. He won fourteen Grand Slam titles and finished as the top-ranked player in the world six consecutive times, a record for men's professional tennis.

Born: August 12, 1971; Washington, D.C.
Also known as: Peter Sampras (full name)
Area of achievement: Sports

EARLY LIFE

Pete Sampras (SAM-prus) was born in Washington, D.C., to Greek immigrants Sam and Georgia Sampras. He spent his early years in Potomac, Maryland, where his father

Sampras, Pete

worked as a civil aerospace engineer for the U.S. Air Force, then moved to Rancho Palos Verdes in Southern California when his father took a job in the civilian aviation industry.

Sampras was an outstanding athlete as a child, and he had a naturally powerful tennis game. By age eleven he learned a game tactic that would mark him as a player to watch: the serve and volley. His coach was Pete Fischer, a pediatrician, who would encourage Sampras to change his two-handed backhand into a one-handed shot, increasing his chances of winning at a tournament as demanding as Wimbledon in England.

By the time Sampras was twelve years old he was playing in a division for older boys and was winning. In 1987 he played in the Boys 18 Tournament, sponsored by the United States Tennis Association (USTA), and placed second in singles but lost in the finals to Michael Chang. After making it to the third round of the Newsweek Championship Cup several weeks later, Sampras accepted $7,000 in prize money, which changed his status from amateur to professional. At age sixteen, in 1988, Sampras began his professional career ranked 311 among professional male players.

LIFE'S WORK

After a slow start as a professional player, Sampras made it to the fourth round of the Australian Open in January, 1990, and earned his first professional victory in February at the U.S. Pro Indoors in Philadelphia. Several months later he defeated Andre Agassi and became, at age nineteen, the youngest men's singles player to win the U.S. Open tournament. The rivalry between Sampras and Agassi captured the attention of the tennis world for the next ten years. Sampras followed up his 1990 U.S. Open victory by winning the first Grand Slam Cup, an event that features the top-sixteen finishers of the year's Grand Slam events.

In 1992, Sampras began working with a new coach, Tim Gullikson, a former top-ten player who insisted that Sampras spend more time on the slower clay courts, where he would be less dependent on his serve and could focus instead on winning points with good ground strokes and strategy. Sampras reached the quarterfinals of the Australian Open and made it to the semifinals at Wimbledon before losing to Goran Ivanisevic. At the U.S. Open, Sampras lost to Stefan Edberg in the finals after playing with a stomach problem. Although he did not win a Grand Slam during 1992, he did win five titles and seventy matches, and he earned more than $1.5 million for the year.

Sampras reached the number-one ranking for the first time in 1993, then won Wimbledon and the U.S. Open. He also became the first male player to serve more than one thousand aces in a season. The following year, 1994, he won a career-high ten titles and compiled a personal best twenty-nine-match winning streak. From 1993 to 1998, he won ten Grand Slam titles, including three U.S. Opens and two Australian Opens.

The fast-playing grass courts favored Sampras's style of tennis, and it was on the grass courts at Wimbledon that he felt most at home. He would win seven Wimbledon titles in his career, the most of any male player. For his last championship victory at Wimbledon, he defeated Pat Rafter in an exciting final. His seventh Wimbledon victory was also his thirteenth Grand Slam title, breaking Roy Emerson's record of twelve Grand Slam titles.

Sampras's career also included numerous injuries, and he revealed that he was living with a genetic trait predisposing him to thalassemia, which is common to those with a Mediterranean family background. Although the thalassemia made him anemic and fatigued at times, he did not reveal the condition until very late in his career. In 1995, Sampras was faced with a personal tragedy while playing at the Australian Open. Prior to his quarterfinal match with Jim Courier, Sampras found out that Gullikson, his coach and good friend, had been diagnosed with terminal brain cancer. A fan in the stands had called out for Sampras to "do it for your coach," and Sampras answered with an emotional comeback, defeating Courier in five sets. Unfortunately, Sampras lost in the semifinals.

The Sampras-Agassi rivalry, which began when the two were just children, often brought out the best in both players. They had played against each other in a 1979 junior tournament in Northridge, California. Sampras's career matchups with Agassi proved to be a contrast in styles. Sampras was low-keyed in his behavior, dress, and demeanor, whereas Agassi had long hair, wore nontraditional clothing, and had a gregarious personality. Notable Sampras-Agassi matches of 1995 included the finals of the Australian Open, Indian Wells, Rogers Cup, and the U.S. Open, with Sampras winning at Indian Wells and the U.S. Open. The two players traded the number-one ranking several times that year.

The 1995 U.S. Open men's singles final between Sampras and Agassi was the highest-rated tennis match for an American television audience. However, the most memorable Sampras-Agassi match came in a U.S. Open quarterfinal in 2001. Sampras battled to a 6-7, 7-6, 7-6, 7-6 victory. There were no breaks of serve during the entire match. The second highest-rated match between the two was the final of the U.S. Open in 2002, in which Sampras won, recording his fourteenth and final Grand Slam victory. This match also was his last as a player. After much speculation, Sampras retired from tennis in 2003.

During his fifteen years on the tennis circuit, Sampras compiled a 762-222 record, winning more than 77 percent of all the professional matches he played. He won singles titles in eleven different countries. He won sixty-four top-level singles titles, including fourteen Grand Slams, eleven Association of Tennis Professionals (ATP) Masters Series titles, and two doubles titles. With seven titles at Wimbledon, five at the U.S. Open, and two at the Australian Open, only the slower clay courts of the French Open denied Sampras a Grand Slam championship there. *Tennis* magazine named him the greatest player of the years 1965 through 2005, and he earned a record $43 million in prize money over his career.

Whether Sampras was the greatest male player in the history of tennis remains a topic of discussion. Jimmy Connors played over a longer period and won many more titles, and John McEnroe compiled a better Davis Cup record. Rod Laver won two Grand Slams—one as an amateur and one as a professional—and won the French Open twice, while Sampras failed to win the French Open in thirteen attempts. However, Sampras's record of fourteen Grand Slam wins will be difficult to match, or even top. Finally, he was inducted into the International Tennis Hall of Fame on January 17, 2007.

Sampras married American actor and former Miss Teen U.S.A. Bridgette Wilson in 2000. Their first son, Christian Charles, was born in 2002, and their second son, Ryan Nikolaos, was born in 2005.

Sampras, Pete

SIGNIFICANCE

Sampras likely will be remembered for his dominating style of tennis. His trademark move was the running cross-court forehand, and he had an excellent volley. His serve is considered to have been of the most powerful and most accurate. Also, he possessed perhaps the best overhead smash in the history of the men's game. His unemotional but powerful game was built on a serve that crossed the net at up to 130 mph and was backed up by excellent ground strokes and precise serve-and-volley skills. Added to his physical abilities was the single-minded determination to win, which made him one of the greatest players in the game.

As an individual, Sampras was humble, polite, professional, and provided no controversial distractions on or off the court. His low-key demeanor and sportsmanlike behavior kept him from becoming a major celebrity, and the press believed that he lacked charisma, but his stature as one of the greatest of tennis players and his determined work ethic prove best his significance to the history of not only professional tennis but also professional sports.

—*Mary McElroy*

FURTHER READING

Bauman, Paul. *Agassi and Ecstasy.* New York: Bonus Books, 2000. While the book focuses on the life of Andre Agassi, it provides a good discussion of the longstanding rivalry between Sampras and Agassi.

Boughn, Michael. *Pete Sampras.* London: Warwick House, 1999. Discusses the early career of Pete Sampras and includes many action photographs. The book was written especially for young readers.

Branham, H. A. *Sampras: A Legend in the Works.* New York: Bonus Books, 2000. Published before the end of Sampras's career. Measures only a part of his total contribution to the game of tennis.

Drucker, Joel. "Match Point: His Glory Days Fading, Tennis's Pete Sampras Seeks One Last Hurrah." *Los Angeles Times Magazine*, September, 2002, 50-54. A brief but informative article covering Sampras's impending retirement.

Margaret Sanger

> *No woman can call herself free who does not own and control her body.*

Health educator

Through the establishment of low-cost birth control clinics, including the first such clinic in the United States, Sanger made birth control information and contraceptive devices available to American women of all social classes.

Born: September 14, 1879; Corning, New York
Died: September 6, 1966; Tucson, Arizona
Also known as: Margaret Louisa Higgins (birth name)
Areas of achievement: Public health; women's rights; social reform

Early Life

Margaret Sanger (SAN-gur) was the sixth of eleven children born to poor Irish parents. Her mother died at the age of forty, and Sanger always believed that her mother's premature death was a consequence of excessive childbearing. During her mother's illness, Sanger acted as a nurse and also helped care for her younger siblings. Sanger enjoyed a close relationship with her father, who worked as a headstone carver. Higgins advised his resourceful children to use their minds to make a contribution to the world and to try to leave it better than they found it.

As a young girl, Sanger formed the conclusion that poverty, illness, and strife were the fate of large families, whereas small families enjoyed wealth, leisure, and positive parental relationships. Being from a large family, Sanger always felt inferior, and she longed to be rich and comfortable.

After the death of her mother, Sanger decided to become a nurse. During her final training at a Manhattan hospital, she met an architect named William Sanger, who fell in love with her at first sight. Margaret married Bill Sanger in 1902 after a six-month courtship. Over the next few years, Bill continued his work as an architect and Margaret stayed home with their three children. Sanger's restlessness and boredom in her role as a housewife led to her return to obstetrical nursing in 1912. She felt a need to regain her personal independence, and her mother-in-law agreed to move in and take care of the children. At the same time, Sanger began attending socialist meetings in Greenwich Village. She observed forceful speakers, such as Emma Goldman, who were rethinking the position of women and the future of worldwide political and economic systems. Sanger was considered a shy, delicate woman who rarely voiced her opinion at meetings.

Sanger's speaking debut was as a substitute before a group of working women. Her topic was family health. The working women liked Sanger's demeanor and believed what she said. Throughout her life, much of Sanger's impact was attributable to her personal appearance: She was petite, feminine, and demure. Sanger invariably gained support after the publication of her picture in the newspaper. Although her appearance was described as Madonna-like, Sanger was single-minded, stubborn, and intolerant;

893

she was also charming, personable, and energetic. Sanger's personality was such that people either worshiped her or despised her.

LIFE'S WORK

During her years as an obstetrical nurse, Sanger frequently made house calls to the Lower East Side of New York City to attend to poor women who were giving birth or experiencing complications from self-induced abortions. These women were worried about the health and survival of the children they already had and were desperate to find a way to stop having more children. They would beg Sanger to tell them "the secret" of the rich women and would promise that they would not tell anyone else. Sanger would suggest coitus interruptus or the use of condoms, but she quickly realized that the women rejected initiating these methods, placing contraceptive responsibility on men. Sanger herself never believed in male-oriented contraceptives because she saw men as opponents, rather than partners, in the struggle for conception control.

A turning point in Sanger's life occurred when she met a young mother of three named Sadie Sachs. Sanger was called to nurse Sadie during the sweltering summer of 1912. Sadie had attempted an abortion and was near death when Sanger was called to the apartment. Two weeks later, Sadie was finally out of danger. Sadie believed that another pregnancy would kill her, and she pleaded with the attending physician to help prevent another pregnancy. The doctor callously told Sadie that she could not expect to have her cake and eat it too. His only suggestion, jokingly added, was that she have her

Margaret Sanger.
(Library of Congress)

husband, Jake, sleep on the roof. After the doctor left, Sadie turned to Sanger, who was more sympathetic than the doctor but who had no better suggestion for contraception. Sanger promised the anguished woman that she would return at a later date and try to provide helpful information. Sanger did not return, and three months later she was again summoned to the Sachs apartment. Sadie was in critical condition from another abortion attempt, and this time she died minutes after Sanger arrived. Sanger was burdened with guilt over the death of Sachs and resolved that she would find out how to prevent conception so that other women would be spared the pain, suffering, and heartache of unwanted pregnancies.

After two years of research, including a trip to France, Sanger decided to publish a journal aimed at working women that would encourage them to rebel and to insist on reproductive freedom. It was at this time that Sanger coined the term "birth control." In 1914, the first issue of *The Woman Rebel* was published. Although Sanger advocated that women limit births, she was prohibited by Anthony Comstock from explaining to women the precise methodologies for limiting births. Comstock was the head of the New York Society for the Suppression of Vice, and Sanger had experienced problems with him several years earlier when she wrote articles for *The Call*, a labor publication. Sanger's health-oriented column on venereal disease was aimed at adolescent girls, but Comstock refused to allow the column to be published. He had been instrumental in seeing that no obscene materials were distributed through the United States mail, and Comstock made it clear to publishers of *The Call* that he considered Sanger's article obscene and that its publication would result in immediate revocation of their mailing permit. Both Sanger and Comstock wanted to protect America's young people. Comstock sought to protect the young by distancing them from information on venereal disease, while Sanger thought that the protection of the young could best be achieved by exposing them to and educating them about the realities, dangers, and treatment of venereal disease.

Thousands of women responded to Sanger's articles in *The Woman Rebel*, once again pleading for information about the prevention of pregnancy. Sanger wrote a pamphlet called *Family Limitation* that provided practical, straightforward information in language that women of all social classes could understand. Sanger included descriptions and drawings of suppositories, douches, sponges, and the cervical pessary. Sanger also advocated sexual fulfillment for women, which was a radical idea in the early 1900's. After twenty refusals, Sanger found a printer for *Family Limitation*. With the help of friends, Sanger began distributing the pamphlet and was arrested immediately. The possibility of prison was overwhelming to Sanger at this time, so she sailed for Europe before she came to trial, leaving her husband and children behind. She settled in London and was accepted into the intellectual circle of people on the vanguard of sexual and contraceptive thought. Sanger discovered that the Netherlands, because of an emphasis on child spacing, had the lowest maternal death rate and infant mortality rate in the world. In addition, contraceptive clinics had been in operation for thirty years. When Sanger visited the Netherlands, she received trained instruction on the fitting and insertion of the diaphragm, which came in fourteen sizes. Sanger became convinced that she not only would have to overcome the restraint on free speech in the United States but also would have to provide women with access to trained people, preferably physicians, who could fit them with contraceptives.

Sanger returned to the United States to stand trial, but the charges against her were dismissed. Anthony Comstock had died while she was away, and the mood of the people was now supportive of Sanger.

In October of 1916, Sanger opened the nation's first birth control clinic. The clinic provided birth control and venereal disease information and birth control instruction. Most important, the clinic kept detailed medical records and case histories of patients. Although Sanger and her sister Ethel Byrne were imprisoned for their role in the new birth control clinic, public sentiment was in their favor. In the next few years, Sanger began publishing the *Birth Control Review*, a scientific, authoritative journal intended for health care professionals. In 1921, Sanger organized the first national birth control conference, which attracted physicians from all over the country.

Margaret and Bill Sanger were divorced in 1920, and in 1922 Margaret married a wealthy businessman named Noah Slee. Slee contributed many thousands of dollars to his wife's cause but always stayed in the background of her life. Sanger was a national figure by this time and a frequent speaker who enthralled her audience. She traveled internationally and made a great impact on the birth control movements in both Japan and India. In her efforts to establish international unity, Sanger established a World Population Conference, and years later, in 1952, the International Planned Parenthood Federation.

Throughout her career, Sanger lamented the absence of a safe, easy, effective contraceptive. She believed that some sort of contraceptive pill would best meet the needs of women, and she called such a pill her "holy grail." When she discovered that scientists John Rock and Gregory Pincus were experimenting with hormonal methods of contraception, Sanger convinced Mrs. Stanley McCormick, a wealthy widow, to provide funding for Rock and Pincus to continue their research for a contraceptive pill.

Sanger continued to be an active force in the birth control movement until very late in her life. As a nursing home patient in Tucson, Arizona, she was irascible and stubborn and insisted that since she was rich and smart she would do exactly as she pleased. She did just that until she died in 1966 of arteriosclerosis, one week before her eighty-seventh birthday.

SIGNIFICANCE

In her lifetime, Sanger was jailed eight times, yet she never relented in her efforts to promote, and democratize access to, birth control. The medical records of patients visiting Sanger's birth control clinic provided the basis for the initial studies on the effects of child spacing on maternal health and marital satisfaction. These records also yielded information on the efficacy of various birth control methods for different groups of women.

Sanger's early efforts to disseminate contraceptive information were condemned by the church, the press, and the medical profession. Her belief that sex is a normal part of human life that requires a rational response led her to search for easy and safe contraceptives that would allow women to choose maternity while attaining freedom through control of their bodies. Sanger believed that in some way every unwanted child would be a social liability and that a society should try to maximize its social assets by having children that are wanted by their parents. Sanger insisted that the best measure of the success of her work was in the reduction of human suffering.

Availability of contraceptive information and birth control devices has had widespread implications for Americans, both individually and collectively. Maternal death rates and infant mortality rates have declined, child spacing spans have increased, and total family size has decreased. Control of conception is a subject taught in classes throughout the country, and American women and men take for granted the fact that contraceptives are sold in drugstores and are easily obtained from physicians. As a result of the achievements of Sanger, control of conception has become a reality for many women throughout the world.

—*Lesley Hoyt Croft*

FURTHER READING

Chandrasekhar, Sripati. *"A Dirty Filthy Book": The Writings of Charles Knowlton and Annie Besant on Birth Control and Reproductive Physiology*. Berkeley: University of California Press, 1981. Includes essays by Sanger's American and British predecessors who laid the foundation for her work. Provides an account of the Bradlaugh-Besant trial in 1877 and its impact on the British birth rate.

Davis, Tom. *Sacred Work: Planned Parenthood and Its Clergy Alliances*. New Brunswick, N.J.: Rutgers University Press, 2005. Recounts how Planned Parenthood allied with members of the clergy, beginning with Sanger's efforts to include clergymen in the organization's efforts to dispense public information about contraceptives.

Douglas, Emily Taft. *Pioneer of the Future*. New York: Holt, Rinehart and Winston, 1970. A thorough work documenting the milestones of Sanger's life. Good in-depth account of research, events, and individuals who gave Sanger the basic knowledge, ideas, and encouragement from which to proceed.

Franks, Angela. *Margaret Sanger's Eugenic Legacy: The Control of Female Fertility*. Jefferson, N.C.: McFarland, 2005. Describes Sanger's ideas—many of which are still debated—about birth control, eugenics, sterilization, and population control.

Gray, Madeline. *Margaret Sanger: A Biography of the Champion of Birth Control*. New York: Richard Marek, 1979. Excellent, well-researched biography with one of the few in-depth examinations of Sanger's later years, including her addiction to Demerol.

Kennedy, David M. *Birth Control in America: The Career of Margaret Sanger*. New Haven, Conn.: Yale University Press, 1970. Focuses on Sanger's public career in the United States and illuminates American society in the years prior to 1945. Describes the social context in which Sanger worked and the attitudinal, behavioral, and institutional responses she evoked.

Sanger, Margaret. *Margaret Sanger: An Autobiography*. New York: Dover, 1971. A factual description of the life of the author without much insight and introspection. Describes people who influenced Sanger, including the C. V. Drysdales and Havelock Ellis in England, and Aletta Jacobs, birth control pioneer in the Netherlands.

_____. *Motherhood in Bondage*. New York: Brentano's, 1928. Reprint. New York:

Pergamon Press, 1956. Composed of letters written to Sanger by women desperate to discover a method of preventing conception. Tragic, heart-wrenching accounts.
_____. *Woman and the New Race.* New York: Brentano's, 1920. Attempts to convince working-class women that control of reproduction is the key to a healthier, more satisfying life and a better world. Advocates rebellion to gain access to contraceptive information.

Junípero Serra

> *We have seen Indians in immense numbers, and all those on this coast of the Pacific contrive to make a good subsistence on various seeds, and by fishing.*

Franciscan missionary

A Catholic missionary, Serra supervised the founding of the first nine missions in California. Although his association with the conquest and cruel treatment of American Indians makes him a controversial figure, his key role in the settlement of California and his lifelong dedication to teaching California's indigenous peoples and "preparing souls for heaven" led the Franciscans to recommend him for canonization.

Born: November 24, 1713; Petra, Mallorca, Spain
Died: August 28, 1784; Carmel, Alta California (now California), New Spain
Also known as: Miguel José Serra (full name); Blessed Junípero Serra
Areas of achievement: Religion and theology; exploration

Early Life

Junípero Serra (hoo-NEE-peh-roh SEHR-rah) was born on the Spanish island of Mallorca in 1713, the son of Antonio Serra and Margarita Serra, poor farmers without formal education. Some of his ancestors were *conversos*, or Jews who had been forcibly converted to Christianity. He attended the local elementary school taught by Franciscan friars, where he decided at a young age to join their religious order. His baptismal name was José Miguel, but when he joined the Franciscan order at the age of sixteen he took the name Junípero in honor of Saint Francis of Assisi's companion, known for humility and compassion. While studying for the priesthood in Palma de Mallorca, Serra earned a reputation for oratorical excellence and personal piety.

Following ordination in 1738, Serra earned a doctorate in theology at Lullian University in Palma, where he was appointed to the John Duns Scotus chair of philosophy in 1744. Five years later, at the age of thirty-five, he decided to give up his secure and prestigious position to devote his life to missionary activities in the New World. Like other committed clerics of the century, he firmly believed that converting pagans to Christianity was the noblest of endeavors and was influenced by the tradition of Franciscan mysticism, which valued suffering as the path to spiritual enlightenment.

LIFE'S WORK
After receiving permission to become a missionary, Serra sailed to Mexico in 1749. En route, he preached his first sermon as a missionary at San Juan, Puerto Rico. Arriving in Mexico City, he spent several months at the Franciscan College of San Fernando. Beginning in 1750 he worked for eight years as a missionary among the Palmés Indians in the Sierra Gorda region north of Mexico City. He learned to speak the local language and helped to build a large stone church in the town of Jalpan. In 1758 he was assigned to the Mexican capital, where he served as administrator of the College of San Fernando while also assuming the duties of a traveling missionary priest.

In 1767, when King Charles III of Spain expelled the Jesuits from Spain and its colonies, the Spanish government requested the Franciscan friars take over the missions in Baja (lower) California. Hoping to stop Russian expansion southward along the Pacific coast, the government also charged the Franciscans with the task of founding missions in Alta (upper) California. Serra was selected to serve as *presidente* (or chief administrator) of both projects, with his headquarters located at Loreto.

In 1769, when General José de Gálvez, inspector general of New Spain (now Mexico), ordered the military invasion of Alta California, Serra personally accompanied the troops of Don Gaspar de Portolá, the governor of California who commanded the so-called Sacred Expedition to establish Franciscan missions in Alta California. Serra was fifty-five years old and in very poor health, having long suffered from an ulcerated leg and foot. Some historians think his health had been damaged by his practice of self-mortification, which consisted of flogging his back with a whip, beating his breast with a stone, and burning his flesh with candles. Whatever the reasons, Serra had to be lifted onto the saddle of his horse. His friend and biographer, Francisco Pálou, observed Serra's frail condition and tried to discourage him from making the arduous journey, but Serra rebuked his friend for a lack of faith in divine providence.

Serra founded the first mission in Alta California, located in what is now the city of San Diego, on July 16, 1769. In June, 1770, he established a second mission at Carmel, San Carlos Borromeo, which henceforth served as his permanent headquarters. Of the twenty-one missions that the Franciscans founded in California, Serra was directly responsible for nine, including San Antonio de Padua (1771), San Gabriel Arcángel (1771), San Luis Obispo de Tolosa (1772), San Francisco de Asís (1776), San Juan Capistrano (1776), Santa Clara de Asís (1777), and San Buenaventura (1782). By the time of his death the mission system contained about five thousand American Indians from at least six linguistic stocks, more than thirty-five friars, and approximately five hundred settlers and soldiers.

The missions were separated from one another by about a day's trip on horseback. Serra personally visited each mission several times, often performing baptisms and confirmations. He walked thousands of miles, although at times he traveled by mule, carriage, or packet boat. He usually traveled with a page, sometimes accompanied by military escort. While his main objective was to "prepare souls for heaven," he understood that conversion would not be permanent unless Indians acquired the means to earn their livelihood. In addition to religious instruction, therefore, the Franciscan friars did their best to teach methods of European agriculture and construction as well as other practical skills. The missions operated as miniature empires with farming as the principal industry. American Indian families within the compound were assigned small apartments, and the friars supervised their work schedules.

Serra's critics usually concede that he desired the well-being of the American Indians under his jurisdiction. He frequently came into conflict with political and military officials over issues of rightful payment for labor and proper punishment. He particularly denounced Spanish soldiers for raping indigenous women. In 1773 he presented Viceroy Antonio María de Bucareli de Ursúa, the highest Spanish official in Mexico, with a *representación* containing thirty-two points for increasing the protection of Indians. Bucareli accepted most of the suggestions and incorporated them into California's regulatory code. Serra, however, shared the typical biases of the time, looking upon the Indians as childlike and in need of strict discipline. In several of his letters he instructed his friars about the necessity of using corporal punishment when confronted with disobedience or rebellion.

Despite his deteriorating health, Serra continued to work until his death at the age of seventy in his headquarters on the Carmel River.

Significance

In 1931, a statue of Father Serra, representing the state of California, was placed in the Capitol Building in Washington, D.C. Still, Serra is a controversial figure. His admirers look upon him as a holy man worthy of canonization, and Franciscan leaders in California recommended him as a candidate for sainthood. In 1985, the first hurdle in the three-stage process of canonization was passed when the pope named Serra "venerable," meaning that his life met the Catholic standards of "heroic virtue." Proponents of his sainthood maintain that he converted many American Indians to Christianity and, with his fellow Franciscans, educated and improved the life conditions of indigenous peoples. Detractors, on the other hand, denounce Serra for his active involvement in a brutal conquest that decimated the American Indian population and destroyed much of American Indian culture.

One of the major issues in this debate is whether Serra should be judged by eighteenth century standards or by modern conceptions of human rights. Despite strong protests by American Indians and others, he was beatified in 1988, but years later, in the early twenty-first century, it remains unclear whether he would ever be proclaimed a saint.

Regardless of one's conclusions, it is impossible to deny that Serra played an important role in the early history of California. He will always be remembered as the founder of the first mission in California, San Diego de Alcalá, which became the basis for the development of the first permanent European settlement in the province. It is impossible to understand the Spanish Empire in the New World without considering the work and ideas of missionaries such as Serra.

—*Thomas Tandy Lewis*

Further Reading

Cook, Sherburne. *The Conflict Between the California Indian and White Civilization.* Berkeley: University of California Press, 1976. Polemical but scholarly essays emphasizing the thesis of biological conquest while also criticizing Serra and other missionaries for using excessive cruelty in punishing American Indians.

Costo, Rupert, and Jeannette Costo, eds. *The Missions of California: A Legacy of Genocide*. San Francisco, Calif.: Indian Historian Press, 1987. Collection of passionately written articles opposing Serra's canonization, edited by California Indian activists.

DeNevi, Don, and Noel Moholy. *Junípero Serra*. San Francisco, Calif.: Harper & Row, 1987. Scholarly biography that is highly favorable to both Serra and his religious beliefs.

Fogel, Daniel. *Junípero Serra, the Vatican, and Enslavement Theology*. New York: Ism Press, 1996. Fogel's criticisms of Serra reflect a strong animus against traditional Catholic beliefs and practices.

Geiger, Maynard. *The Life and Times of Junípero Serra*. 2 vols. Monterrey, Mexico: Siempre Adelante, 1959. Detailed biography written by an admiring Franciscan scholar who devoted many years to the subject.

Morgado, Martin. *Junípero Serra: A Pictorial Biography*. Monterrey, Mexico: Siempre Adelante, 1991. A short account with many beautiful illustrations of buildings and artifacts.

Pálou, Francisco. *Life of Fray Junípero Serra*. Translated by Maynard Geiger. Washington, D.C.: Academy of American Franciscan History, 1955. Hagiographic biography written by Serra's good friend and fellow Franciscan missionary.

Sandos, James. "Junípero Serra's Canonization and the Historical Record." *American Historical Review* 93 (1988): 1253-1269. Analyzing the historical evidence, Sandos concludes that, despite Serra's sincere love for the American Indians, he probably was responsible for excessive punishment and other abuses.

Tibesar, Antonine, ed. *Writings of Junípero Serra*. 4 vols. Washington, D.C.: Academy of American Franciscan History, 1955-1966. Dealing almost exclusively with mission affairs, these factual reports, instructions, and commentaries provide much insight into Serra's character.

Tinker, George. *Missionary Conquest: The Gospel and Native American Cultural Genocide*. Minneapolis, Minn.: Fortress Press, 1993. Written by a Cherokee Lutheran theologian, the book examines Serra and three other respected missionaries, arguing that they inadvertently did great harm to American Indians and their cultures.

ALAN SHEPARD

> " *You may not have any extra talent, but maybe you are just paying more attention to what you are doing.* "

Astronaut

Shepard flew the first U.S. piloted spaceflight in 1961 and became the only Project Mercury astronaut to walk on the Moon, only the seventh human to have done so.

Born: November 18, 1923; East Derry, New Hampshire
Died: July 21, 1998; Monterey, California
Also known as: Alan Bartlett Shepard, Jr. (full name)
Area of achievement: Aviation and space exploration

EARLY LIFE

Alan Shepard (SHEH-purd) was born to Colonel Alan B. Shepard and his wife in East Derry, Hew Hampshire. After attending primary school in East Derry, Shepard graduated from Pinkerton Academy in Derry. He spent a year studying at Admiral Farragut Academy in Toms River, New Jersey, prior to his acceptance into the United States Naval Academy. After several years of distinguished military service, Shepard studied at the Naval War College in Newport, Rhode Island, graduating in 1958.

The National Aeronautics and Space Administration (NASA), created on October 1, 1958, received primary authority for Project Mercury, which attempted to send the first humans into space. As a result, astronauts were required. Military service files of test pilots were studied, invitations for application were sent, and NASA accumulated a large set of candidates. Following rigorous medical examinations, psychological tests, and personal interviews, seven individuals were selected as the original Mercury astronauts. Shepard was among that select group.

NASA announced on February 22, 1961, that three astronauts—John Glenn, Gus Grissom, and Shepard—had been selected to train for the first suborbital Mercury flight. Which astronaut would make that first flight was not revealed until Shepard emerged from the Astronaut Quarters on May 2, 1961, fully suited, only to have poor weather prevent launch that day. By that time, NASA had lost the race to send the first human into space. On April 12, 1961, Soviet cosmonaut Yuri Gagarin had orbited Earth once in *Vostok 1* before landing within the Soviet Union.

LIFE'S WORK

Shepard's next launch attempt came on May 5, 1961. Before sunrise, Shepard rode out to Pad 5-6. Leaving his transfer van, he paused to look up at the Redstone rocket about to hurtle him down the Atlantic Missile Range. Shepard slipped into his Mercury-Redstone 3 (*Freedom 7*) spacecraft and was hooked up to life-support and communications systems therein. Technicians bolted closed the hatch. Minor difficulties were encountered during the remainder of the countdown. Each was overcome, but each delayed liftoff. The last, a faulty pressure-gauge reading, surfaced less that three minutes before liftoff. Once resolved, the countdown continued until, at 9:34 A.M. eastern daylight time (EDT), the Redstone rocket rose from its pedestal. Shepard was on his way.

The Redstone exhausted its fuel a little over two minutes into flight. *Freedom 7* separated from the spent booster, and the escape tower jettisoned. Shepard assumed manual control and reoriented his spacecraft for retrofire.

Shepard briefly viewed the Earth below using a periscope extended from *Freedom 7*'s hull. He experienced five minutes of weightlessness before reentry, reaching a maximum altitude of 115 miles. Three retrorockets fired in turn, and then the retropack on which they were located separated from *Freedom 7*. The spacecraft hit the upper atmosphere at over five thousand miles per hour, slowing down to about three hundred miles per hour over the next minute, the result of which was to subject Shepard to ten times normal Earth gravity.

Parachute deployments occurred normally, and, at 9:50 A.M., *Freedom 7* splashed down about one hundred miles from Grand Bahama Island. NASA's first piloted spaceflight lasted fifteen minutes, twenty-two seconds. The spacecraft traveled 302 miles downrange from Cape Canaveral (now Cape Kennedy). Based on Shepard's success, a prior chimpanzee (Ham) flight, and a subsequent suborbital flight by Virgil "Gus" Grissom (*Liberty Bell 7*), NASA was confident to move ahead with orbital missions, beginning with John Glenn's three-orbit flight on February 20, 1962.

Later, as Project Gemini (the stepping-stone between Mercury missions and Apollo lunar flights) evolved from design to test-flight stages, Shepard was consid-

Alan Shepard.
(NASA-HQ-GRIN)

ered for an early flight assignment. However, he was dropped from active astronaut status in 1963 and restricted to flying conventional aircraft only with a copilot, having developed Ménière's syndrome, an inner-ear condition capable of inducing nausea, ringing ears, and vestibular disturbances. Shepard assumed the role of chief of the Astronaut Office but clung to hopes of flying in space again. In 1968 he secretly underwent an experimental surgical procedure. Detailed postsurgical testing by NASA doctors found no evidence of Ménière's syndrome, and Shepard lobbied for active flight status restoration and assignment to a lunar landing. He received command of Apollo 13. NASA management did not approve and suggested that Shepard needed additional training time because he had been inactive so long. He and fellow crew members Edgar Mitchell and Stuart Roosa were bumped back to Apollo 14, and James Lovell, Fred Haise, and John Swigert moved up to the ill-fated Apollo 13 mission.

Apollo 13's lunar landing site, the Fra Mauro highlands, was considered too scientifically significant to be missed. Fra Mauro held promise for sampling bedrock material excavated from deep below the lunar surface during the formation of Cone Crater. Originally, Apollo 14 was to land near the crater Censorinus in Mare Tranquilitatis relatively close to where Apollo 11 landed. Fra Mauro became Apollo 14's landing site. Apollo 14 carried tremendous responsibility for continuing Moon flights in the aftermath of Apollo 13. Budget considerations had already cut three previously planned landings. NASA could not survive another aborted flight and maintain sufficient congressional support for the remaining Apollo missions.

Apollo 14 launched from Cape Canaveral at 4:03 P.M. on January 31, 1971, the thirteenth anniversary of Explorer 1, United States' first orbital satellite. Ascent into orbit and subsequent translunar injection to boost Apollo 14 toward the Moon were both normal. A series of serious problems arose shortly thereafter, the first when the command and service module (*Kitty Hawk*) attempted to dock with the lunar module (*Antares*). Contact was made, but not a latched mating. If the two vehicles could not rigidly dock, Apollo 14's lunar landing was impossible. On the sixth attempt, *Kitty Hawk* and *Antares* achieved hard dock and separated from their Saturn 5 rocket's spent third stage.

Apollo 14 entered lunar orbit on February 4 amid concern over a suspect docking apparatus. Examination of the command module's probe failed to relieve that concern or identify the cause of earlier difficulties. *Kitty Hawk* dropped down to an orbital low point of only eleven miles above the surface, the point from which *Antares* would begin its powered descent to touchdown.

On February 5, *Antares* separated from *Kitty Hawk*, but before its braking engine could fire, a major computer problem required resolution. A false signal was being sent to *Antares* guidance computer, one that would automatically trigger an abort twenty-six seconds after power descent initiation and send the astronauts back up to orbit. After two hours, Massachusetts Institute of Technology (MIT) computer specialists devised a software patch that circumvented that action. Then, as *Antares* steadily descended toward the lunar surface, the radar altimeter failed to lock on and provide critical altitude data to the guidance computer. After technicians recycled the radar's circuit breaker, critical data started flowing at an altitude of just twenty-five hundred feet.

Antares touched down at 4:17 A.M., resting in a small depression tilted 8 degrees. Five and one-half hours later, Shepard and lunar module pilot Mitchell stood on the surface at Fra Mauro to begin the first of two moonwalks, the primary focus of which was to assemble a small science station that would provide data for months after the astronauts returned home. One experiment required active data collection. Shepard and Mitchell fired small pyrotechnics while a seismometer registered subsurface vibrations. Before concluding the first moonwalk, there was time for collecting geological samples.

The second moonwalk began at 3:10 A.M. on February 6, this one dedicated to careful geological sampling during a traverse to the rim of Cone Crater. Shepard pulled behind him a special rickshawlike transporter in which he stored tools and samples during the climb up Cone Crater's slope. The slope of the crater proved steeper than anticipated, and determination of position among the boulders and depressions was difficult. Shepard and Mitchell terminated their ascent and settled for sampling a promising boulder field just short of Cone Crater's rim. Before returning to *Antares*, Shepard, an avid golfer, took time to chip a pair of golf balls using a sample-collecting tool affixed with a club head. With limited moon-suit mobility, Shepard could only swing one arm, but the balls went quite far in the reduced lunar gravity.

Antares lifted off from the Moon carrying Shepard, Mitchell, and 108 pounds of lunar samples at 1:49 P.M. on February 6. This time, docking was trouble free, and the journey home was devoid of nagging problems. Apollo 14 ended after slightly more than nine days with a gentle ocean splashdown.

Shepard returned to his post of chief astronaut, remaining in that capacity from June, 1971, until August 1, 1974. Shepard retired simultaneously from NASA and the Navy (at the rank of rear admiral) to enter private enterprise, joining the Marathon Construction Company in Houston, Texas. Shepard had other business ventures in his post-Apollo period and served as president of Seven-Fourteen Enterprises in Houston. He was instrumental in several different efforts to both memorialize early spaceflights and educate young people. Shepard, along with the other Mercury, Gemini, and Apollo astronauts, was inducted into the Astronaut Hall of Fame in Titusville, Florida, where the *Kitty Hawk* is on display.

Shepard had planned to be present at the Kennedy Space Center to view his former colleague John Glenn's historic return to space after thirty-six years when the space shuttle *Discovery* launched in late 1998. Unfortunately, the United States' first human in space succumbed to leukemia and passed away at age seventy-four on July 21, 1998. That passing was noted by all major Western media news services with great nostalgia and respect for Shepard's contributions to the early years of the U.S. space program.

SIGNIFICANCE

The name and contributions of Shepard loom large in the U.S. space program's early history. His laurels include being the original Mercury astronaut, the first American in space, the seventh human to walk on the Moon, and the first astronaut to be posted as chief of the Astronaut Office. Shepard's suborbital Mercury flight came three weeks after Russian cosmonaut Gagarin became the first human to orbit the Earth. Although Shepard's flight only lasted fifteen minutes, *Freedom 7* provided enough confidence

Shepard, Alan

for President John F. Kennedy to challenge the Soviets to achieve a piloted lunar landing before the end of the 1960's. That challenge was issued nine months before NASA was even able to match Gagarin's orbit with John Glenn's *Friendship 7* flight.

—David G. Fisher

FURTHER READING

Caidin, Martin. *Man Into Space.* New York: Pyramid, 1961. Perhaps somewhat difficult to locate, this book provides an excellent account of the early days of the space program leading up to and including Shepard's suborbital *Freedom 7* flight told from that period's viewpoint. The author is a noted writer of historical spaceflight books for the general audience.

Carpenter, M. Scott, et al. *We Seven.* New York: Simon & Schuster, 1962. The original Mercury astronauts provided insight from personal experience as part of the first U.S. piloted space program. Four sections and one entire chapter were provided by Shepard. The chapter chronicles his *Freedom 7* suborbital flight.

Shepard, Alan, et al. *Moon Shot: The Inside Story of America's Race to the Moon.* Atlanta, Ga.: Turner, 1994. Plenty of texts chronicle the United States' race to the Moon from an engineering, exploration, or political viewpoint. Written by two astronauts instrumental in the rich story of Apollo, assisted by two of the most experienced space journalists, this book provides the inside story of NASA's golden age of piloted spaceflight, detailing Shepard's participation in and supervision of that effort. A video version of this material is also available.

Slayton, Deke, with Michael Cassutt. *Deke! U.S. Manned Space: From Mercury to the Shuttle.* New York: Forge, 1994. Although an autobiography of Deke Slayton, this book also provides plenty of insight into the life of Alan Shepard, who, like Slayton, was an original Mercury astronaut and suffered a long period during which a medical condition forced him off active flight status. Slayton and Shepard developed a close friendship working together in the Astronaut Office.

Thomson, Neal. *Light This Candle: The Life and Times of Alan Shepard, America's First Spaceman.* New York: Crown, 2000. Comprehensive biography based on exclusive access to Shepard's private papers and interviews with his family and fellow astronauts.

WILLIAM TECUMSEH SHERMAN

❝ *War is cruelty. There's no use trying to reform it.* **❞**

Military leader

Sherman was one of the architects of the Union victory in the Civil War and a significant contributor to the development of modern warfare.

Born: February 8, 1820; Lancaster, Ohio
Died: February 14, 1891; New York, New York
Also known as: Tecumseh Sherman (birth name); Cump; Uncle Billy
Area of achievement: Military

EARLY LIFE

William Tecumseh Sherman (teh-KUHM-zeh SHEHR-muhn) was born Tecumseh Sherman. His father, Charles R. Sherman, was a lawyer and Ohio supreme court justice. His mother, Mary Hoyt, was a graduate of an eastern school for women. They migrated from Connecticut to Ohio in 1811 and produced there a family of eleven children, including later senator and federal cabinet member, John Sherman. Tecumseh (Cump) was their sixth child.

When Tecumseh was nine years old, his father died suddenly, and his family was broken up. He was taken up the street to live with the family of Thomas Ewing, later a U.S. senator and a cabinet member. There he was baptized in the Roman Catholic Church and received the Christian name William to go with his Indian one. From that moment he was William Tecumseh Sherman. Ewing never adopted him but always treated him like a son.

Sherman had a happy childhood, enjoying his friends and relatives and often participating in innocent pranks. He received the best education Lancaster had to offer, and, at the age of sixteen, Ewing arranged a West Point appointment for him. Sherman endured the military academy boredom and was graduated sixth in his 1840 class.

During these early years, Sherman came to admire his foster father and adopt many of his Whig Party attitudes. At the same time, he always felt a need to prove himself capable of survival without Ewing's help. At West Point, he accepted the aristocratic concept of the superiority of the professional soldier over the volunteer. Sherman came to view his military friends as his family and throughout his life always felt most comfortable around them.

Upon his graduation, Sherman received a commission in the artillery and assignment to Florida, where he participated in the Second Seminole War. Though combat was rare, he came to see the Indians at first hand and developed the mixture of admiration and repugnance toward them that he was to hold all of his life. In March, 1842, he was sent to Fort Morgan, in Mobile Bay, where he first experienced the pleasures of polite society. His June 1, 1842, transfer to Fort Moultrie, near Charleston, allowed him to continue his socializing, of which he soon tired. For four years, he lived a boring existence, brightened only by his passion for painting, a furlough back to Ohio high-

Sherman, William Tecumseh

lighted by his first trip down the Mississippi River, and investigative duty in the area of his later march on Atlanta. He also became engaged to Ellen Ewing, his foster sister, with whom he had corresponded since his 1836 departure for West Point. Sherman never painted much after he left Fort Moultrie in South Carolina, but all these other experiences were to have a profound effect on his later life.

When the Mexican War erupted, Sherman hoped to participate in the fighting. He was instead sent to Pittsburgh on recruiting duty. He chafed under his bad luck and jumped at the chance to travel around the Horn to California. By the time he arrived, however, the war there was over, and he found himself adjutant to Colonel Richard B. Mason, spending long hours battling correspondence, not Mexicans. He became depressed. The 1849 discovery of gold provided him with new excitement, and he absorbed all he could of the gold fever, though the inflation almost ruined him. In 1850, he was sent East with messages for General Winfield Scott, and on May 1 he married Ellen Ewing. Their wedding was an important Washington social event, as Thomas Ewing was then a member of President Zachary Taylor's cabinet.

During the decade of the 1850's, Sherman fathered six children and tried unsuccessfully to support them. From 1850 to 1853, he served in the Army Commissary Service in St. Louis and New Orleans, at which time he resigned his commission to open a branch bank in San Francisco for some St. Louis friends. The pressures of banking in the boom-and-bust California economy, his chronic asthma, and a homesick wife who wanted to return to her father's house caused Sherman to spend the years from 1853 to 1857 in recurring depression. When the bank closed in 1857, he took on as personal debts the unsuccessful investments he had made for army friends.

Sherman carried that financial burden to New York, where he opened another branch bank only to see it fail during the Panic of 1857. He was crushed; no matter what he tried, he met failure. Instead of establishing independence from his foster father, he repeatedly had to look to him for support. Thomas Ewing continued to hope that Sherman would agree to manage his salt interests in Ohio, but Sherman refused. Instead, he went to Kansas as part of a law and real estate business, along with two Ewing sons.

The business failed, and Sherman desperately tried to return to the army for his economic (and psychological) salvation. There were no openings, but an officer friend told him about a new Louisiana military seminary looking for a superintendent. Sherman applied and became founder of what became modern Louisiana State University. When secession came, duty persuaded him he had to leave the job and the people he had come to love. He believed that he had to sacrifice his economic well-being for the sake of the Union.

LIFE'S WORK

After leaving Louisiana in February, 1861, Sherman became angry over alleged northern nonchalance toward southern secession. He found a position with a St. Louis street railway company, determined to remain aloof from the national crisis until he could see a change. Thomas Ewing and John Sherman urged him to reenter the Union army, and, through their efforts, he was named a colonel of the Thirteenth Infantry Regiment in May, 1861. He stood over six feet tall, with long legs and arms, piercing blue eyes, sandy red hair that seemed always to be mussed, a grizzly reddish beard, and a generally unkempt appearance. He spoke rapidly and often, his mind able to reach conclusions before his charmed listeners understood his premises.

Before Sherman could serve with the Thirteenth Infantry, he was appointed to a staff position under Winfield Scott and, in July, 1861, commanded a brigade at Bull Run. He saw that fiasco as further proof that the North was not taking the war seriously enough.

Sherman was happy to leave chaotic Washington for Kentucky to help Fort Sumter hero Robert Anderson organize the Union war effort there. Upon arrival, he quickly convinced himself that the Confederate forces were much larger than his were and that it was only a matter of time before they would overrun him. He sank into depression and lashed out at newspaper reporters for allegedly publicizing his weaknesses. At his own request, he was transferred to Missouri in November, 1861, where his outspoken negativity convinced many that he was unbalanced. He took a twenty-day leave in December, 1861, and was mortified to see his sanity unfairly questioned in the press. When he returned to duty and was given command over a training facility in Missouri, his depression deepened and he even contemplated suicide. The Union war effort and his own career seemed hopeless.

Sherman's transfer to Paducah, Kentucky, in February, 1862, and his association with the successful Ulysses S. Grant slowly lifted his spirits. He distinguished himself as a division commander in the bloody Battle of Shiloh in April, 1862, and he then defended Grant and other generals against press and political criticism of their roles in the battle. When he was promoted to major general of volunteers and took part in Henry W. Halleck's capture of Corinth in May, 1862, he began to believe that the Union effort had hope and he could play an important role in any success.

In July, 1862, Grant appointed Sherman to the post of military governor of recently captured Memphis. Sherman was able to use both his banking and military experience to govern that hotbed of secession sentiment. It was there that the activities of Confederate guerrillas caused him to see at first hand that the war was not simply a contest between professional soldiers. The general populace had to be controlled if the Union effort was to be successful. When guerrillas fired on a boat in the Mississippi River, Sherman leveled a nearby town. He had long recognized the determination of the southern populace, and he now began to see that only a destruction of this stubborn intensity would resolve the conflict in the Union's favor. He would utilize this insight at the appropriate time.

In December, 1862, Sherman led an unsuccessful assault on the heights above Vicksburg. When the press resuscitated the insanity charge against him, he court-martialed a reporter, the only such event in American history. The trial, though it might have been an excellent exposition of the almost inevitable conflict between the military and the press in wartime, proved to be little more than a conflict of personality. It settled little.

Sherman was part of Grant's enormous army that captured Vicksburg in July, 1863, and he was made brigadier general in the regular army as a reward. He became commander of the Army of Tennessee when Grant became supreme commander in the West; he participated in the successful November lifting of the Confederate siege at

Sherman, William Tecumseh

Chattanooga. In January, 1864, he commanded the Meridian, Mississippi, expedition, which showed him yet again the effectiveness of the destructive activity he was later to use during his March to the Sea.

In the spring of 1864, Grant moved East to become general-in-chief of all Union armies, and Sherman took command over Western forces. On May 5, 1864, Grant attacked Lee in Virginia, and Sherman took on Joseph E. Johnston in Georgia. After first organizing railroads to supply his troops, Sherman battled Johnston throughout the spring and summer of 1864, slowly but inexorably pushing the Confederates from the Chattanooga region toward Atlanta. Jefferson Davis became nervous at Johnston's constant retreat and replaced him with offensive-minded John Bell Hood. The new Confederate commander attacked Sherman and was defeated. Atlanta fell in September, in time to influence the reelection of Abraham Lincoln that November.

Sherman then showed the Confederates that war had indeed become total. He ordered the civilian evacuation of Atlanta. When his order was met with shocked protests, he responded: "War is cruelty. There's no use trying to reform it." He did not: In November, he began his March to the Sea, revolutionizing warfare by cutting himself off from his base of supplies, living off the countryside, and destroying goods and property. His aim was to convince the Confederates that their war effort was doomed. He became the founder of psychological warfare. On December 21, 1864, his army reached Savannah and made contact with the Atlantic fleet. His presentation of the Georgia city to Lincoln as a Christmas present electrified the North.

On February 1, 1865, Sherman began his march through the Carolinas. On April 17, Johnston and his Confederate forces surrendered at Durham Station, North Carolina. Sherman, who had retained his affection for Southerners throughout the war and had only conducted his total warfare as the most efficient way to end the hostilities quickly, demonstrated his feelings in the peace agreement he made with Johnston. He negotiated political matters, neglected to insist that slavery was over, and, in general, wrote an agreement favorable to the South. In Washington, the administration, just then reeling from the assassination of Lincoln, was shocked. Secretary of War Edwin Stanton and General Henry W. Halleck led the opposition to the agreement, and Sherman was forced to change it, suffering sharp criticism from both the public and the press.

With the war over, Sherman became commander of troops in the West. He fought the Indians and helped construct the transcontinental railroad. When Grant became president in 1869, Sherman became commanding general, a position he held until his retirement in 1883. His tenure was filled with controversy as he battled secretaries of war and Congress over his authority, his salary, and sufficient appropriation for the troops. When he published his memoirs in 1875, the blunt directness of those two volumes created a controversy, including a bitter exchange with Jefferson Davis.

From his retirement in 1883 until his death in 1891, Sherman kept busy attending veterans' reunions and the theater, while also becoming a popular after-dinner speaker. In 1884, he categorically refused to run for the presidency, establishing a standard that allegedly reluctant office seekers have been measured against ever since. In 1886, he and his family moved from St. Louis to New York. On February 14, 1891, he died from pneumonia.

SIGNIFICANCE
William Tecumseh Sherman was one of the leaders of the successful Union war effort that prevented the disruption of the United States. He helped introduce the nation and the world to the concept of total war, his Civil War activities serving as a harbinger of the kind of conflict to be fought in the twentieth century. He devised his mode of warfare as a way to end the hostilities quickly, but it helped prolong Southern animosity toward the North into the twentieth century. However, when Sherman toured the South in 1879, he received a friendly greeting.

Sherman's life, apart from his Civil War years, is important in itself. Before the war, he attended West Point with many of the other military leaders of the Mexican and Civil wars. He served in the army in Florida during the Second Seminole War. In California, he composed a report to President James K. Polk that announced the discovery of gold and helped set off the famous gold rush of 1849. During the 1850's, as a banker, he was one of San Francisco's leading businesspeople during its formative years. In 1860, he helped found what is modern Louisiana State University. After the war, Sherman's tenure as general-in-chief of the United States Army from 1869 to 1883 allowed him to influence the direction of such events as the Indian Wars, Reconstruction, and the disputed election of 1876. Thus, Sherman influenced the development of American society throughout his life. He was one of the major figures of the nineteenth century.

—*John F. Marszalek*

FURTHER READING
Athearn, Robert G. *William Tecumseh Sherman and the Settlement of the West*. Norman: University of Oklahoma Press, 1956. A thorough study of Sherman's participation in the postwar Indian troubles and his role in the construction of the transcontinental railroad. Sherman was neither as harsh toward the Indians as the West desired nor as lenient as the East wished. He believed that the completion of the railroad would force the hostile Indians onto reservations.

Bailey, Anne J. *War and Ruin: William T. Sherman and the Savannah Campaign*. Wilmington, Del.: Scholarly Resources, 2003. Chronicles Sherman's March to the Sea, from its inception in Atlanta to its culmination in Savannah, describing its impact upon Georgians. Bailey contends that the physical damage was less severe than the psychological horror inflicted by the march; the campaign depleted Southerners' morale and spurred Confederate defeat.

Barrett, John G. *Sherman's March Through the Carolinas*. Chapel Hill: University of North Carolina Press, 1956. A detailed military history of Sherman's final campaign through North and South Carolina. Sherman reluctantly put his concept of total war into practice during this march from Savannah, Georgia, to Raleigh, North Carolina. His army inflicted special punishment on South Carolina because the soldiers blamed the Palmetto State for starting the war.

Glatthaar, Joseph T. *The March to the Sea and Beyond: Sherman's Troops in the Savannah and Carolinas Campaigns*. New York: New York University Press, 1985. An excellent analysis of the makeup and attitudes of the common soldier in Sherman's army during his marches. The author analyzes the soldiers' views about their cause, black Southerners, white Southerners, camp life, and pillaging.

Kennett, Lee. *Sherman: A Soldier's Life*. New York: HarperCollins, 2001. Generally sympathetic biography, focusing on Sherman's military career, including descriptions of his military training and Civil War battles.

Lewis, Lloyd. *Sherman: Fighting Prophet*. New York: Harcourt, Brace, 1932. Though dated and written without the benefit of all the now-available Sherman documentation, this is still a valuable and very readable biography. It puts special emphasis on Thomas Ewing's influence on his foster son. The vast bulk of the book details the Civil War years; coverage of the postwar years is brief.

Liddell Hart, Basil H. *Sherman: Soldier, Realist, American*. New York: Harcourt, Brace, 1958. A fine study of Sherman's Civil War military activities by a leading military historian. The author states that Sherman was far ahead of his time and that later generations of military men might have profited from his example had they paid attention.

Marszalek, John F. *Sherman's Other War: The General and the Civil War Press*. Memphis, Tenn.: Memphis State University Press, 1981. A thorough account of Sherman's battles with reporters during the war, this study also contains an extended analysis of his personality during this period. Argues that Sherman fought the press in a constitutional battle formed more by personality than by First Amendment principles.

Merrill, James M. *William Tecumseh Sherman*. Skokie, Ill.: Rand McNally, 1971. A detailed popular biography that has the benefit of the major Sherman manuscript collections. It discusses all aspects of Sherman's life but is especially valuable for its coverage of his postwar years.

Sherman, William T. *Memoirs of General William T. Sherman*. 2 vols. New York: D. Appleton, 1875. Reprint. Introduction by William S. McFeely. New York: Da Capo Press, 1984. Sherman's controversial and absorbing account of his life from 1846 to the end of the Civil War, originally published in 1875. This is an essential source for gaining an understanding of Sherman's perception of the battles in which he participated and the leaders with and against whom he fought.

SITTING BULL

> *Is it wrong for me to love my own? Is it wicked for me because my skin is red?*

Native American leader

One of the outstanding icons of nineteenth century Indian defiance of American expansion, Sitting Bull led his Lakota (Sioux) people from their zenith in the middle of the nineteenth century to the decline of their culture in the face of superior technology and numbers of the whites.

Born: March, 1831; near the Grand River, Dakota Territory (now in South Dakota)
Died: December 15, 1890; Standing Rock Agency, South Dakota
Also known as: Tatanka Iyotanka (birth name)
Area of achievement: Native American affairs

EARLY LIFE

Sitting Bull was born Tatanka Iyotanka in a village a few miles below where Bullhead, South Dakota, now stands. During his first fourteen years, his Lakota (Sioux) friends called him Slow, a name he earned because of his deliberate manner and the awkward movement of his sturdy body. The youth grew to manhood as a member of the Hunkpapa tribe, one of seven among the Teton Lakota, the westernmost division of the Sioux Confederation. His people thrived as a nomadic hunter-warrior society. As an infant strapped to a baby-board, he was carried by his mother, as the tribe roamed the northern Plains hunting buffalo. At five years, he rode behind his mother on her horse and helped as best he could around the camp. By the age of ten, he rode his own pony, wrapping his legs around the curved belly of the animal (a practice that caused him to be slightly bowlegged for the remainder of his years). He learned to hunt small game with bow and arrows and to gather berries. He reveled in the games and races, swimming and wrestling with the other boys. His was an active and vigorous life, and he loved it.

The warrior dimension of Lakota male life came more into focus as the boy grew. The Tetons concentrated most of their wrath on the Crow and Assiniboin Indians, at first, and the whites, at a later time. The hub of Lakota society centered on gaining prestige through heroic acts in battle. Counting coups by touching an enemy with a highly decorated stick was top priority. The Lakota lad learned his lessons well, and, at the age of fourteen, he joined a mounted war party. He picked out one of the enemy, and, with a burst of enthusiasm and courage, he charged the rival warrior and struck him with his coup stick. After the battle, word of this heroic deed spread throughout the Hunkpapa village. The boy had reached a milestone in his development; for the remainder of his life, he enjoyed telling the story of his first coup. Around the campfire that night, his proud father, Jumping Bull, gave his son a new name. He called him Sitting Bull after the beast that the Lakota respected so much for its tenacity. A buffalo bull was the essence of strength, and a "sitting bull" was one that held his ground and could not be pushed aside.

In 1857, Sitting Bull became a chief of the Hunkpapa. He had ably demonstrated his abilities as a warrior, and his common sense and his leadership traits showed promise of a bright future for him. Although his physical appearance was commonplace, he was convincing in argument, stubborn, and quick to grasp a situation. These traits gained for him the respect of his people as a warrior and as a statesman.

LIFE'S WORK

Sitting Bull's leadership qualities were often put to the test in his dealings with the whites. During the 1860's, he skirmished with the whites along the Powder River in Wyoming. He learned of their method of fighting, and he was impressed with their weapons. In 1867, white commissioners journeyed to Lakota country to forge a peace treaty. They also hoped to gain Lakota agreement to limit their living area to present-day western South Dakota. While his Jesuit friend Father Pierre De Smet worked to gain peace, Sitting Bull refused to give up his cherished hunting lands to the west and south and declined to sign the Treaty of 1868. Other Lakota, however, made their marks on the "white man's paper," and the treaty became official.

Developments during the 1870's confirmed Sitting Bull's distrust of the white men's motives. Railroad officials surveyed the northern Plains during the early 1870's in preparation for building a transcontinental railroad that would disrupt Lakota hunting lands. In 1874, the army surveyed the Black Hills, part of the Great Sioux Reservation as set up by the treaty, and in the next year thousands of miners invaded this sacred part of the Sioux reserve when they learned of the discovery of gold there. The tree-covered hills and sparkling streams and lakes were the home of Lakota gods and a sacred place in their scheme of life. The whites had violated the treaty and disregarded the rights of the Lakota. Sitting Bull refused to remain on the assigned reservation any longer and led his followers west, into Montana, where there were still buffalo to hunt and the opportunity remained to live by the old traditions.

As many other Lakota became disgruntled with white treatment, they, too, looked to Sitting Bull's camp to the west as a haven from the greedy whites. In this sense, he became the symbol of Lakota freedom and resistance to the whites, and his camp grew with increasing numbers of angry Lakota.

The showdown between Lakota and whites came in 1876. The U.S. government had ordered the Lakota to return to their reservations by February of 1876, but few Indians abided by this order. The government thus turned the "Sioux problem" over to the army with instructions to force the Indians back to the agencies. In the summer of 1876, General Alfred H. Terry led a strong expedition against Sitting Bull's camp. The Indian chief had a premonition of things to come when he dreamed of blue-clad men falling into his camp. Soon, he would learn the significance of this portent. A detachment of cavalry from Terry's column under the command of Lieutenant Colonel George A. Custer attacked Sitting Bull's camp. The forty-five-year-old chief rallied his men, and they defeated Custer, killing more than three hundred soldiers, including their leader.

Although the Lakota had won the Battle of the Little Bighorn, they decided that it was time to leave the area and divide up into smaller groups in order to avoid capture. Many additional soldiers were ordered into the northern Plains, and they spent the remainder of the summer and fall chasing and harassing the fleeing Lakota. While other groups of Lakota eventually returned to their agencies, Sitting Bull led his people to Canada, where they resided until 1881. Even though the Canadian officials refused to

Sitting Bull

feed the Lakota, the latter were able to subsist in their usual manner of hunting and gathering until 1881, when the buffalo were almost gone. Because of homesickness and a lack of food, Sitting Bull finally surrendered to United States officials, who kept him prisoner at Fort Randall for two years.

By 1883, Sitting Bull had returned to his people at Standing Rock Agency in Dakota Territory and soon became involved in unexpected activities. In that same year, the Northern Pacific Railroad sponsored a last great buffalo hunt for various dignitaries, and Sitting Bull participated. In the next year, he agreed to tour fifteen cities with Colonel Alvaren Allen's Western show. Sitting Bull was portrayed as the Slayer of General Custer, but the stubborn Indian chief found this label inaccurate and distasteful. In 1885, Sitting Bull signed with Buffalo Bill Cody's Wild West Show and traveled in the eastern United States and Canada during the summer. He sold autographed photographs of himself and eventually gave away most of the money he made to poor white children who begged for money in order to eat. At the end of the season, the popular Buffalo Bill gave his Indian friend a gray circus horse and large white sombrero as a remembrance of their summer together.

During the latter part of the decade, Sitting Bull returned to Standing Rock, where he settled into reservation life. The Hunkpapa still cherished him as their leader, much to the dismay of agent James McLaughlin, who sought to break the old chief's hold over his people.

In 1890, Wovoka, a Paiute Indian prophet from Nevada, began to preach a message that most Indians prayed was true. He dreamed that he had died and gone to Heaven. There, he found all the deceased Indians, thousands of buffalo, and no whites. The Indian prophet taught that, in order to achieve a return to the old ways of life, the Indians had only to dance the Ghost Dance regularly until the second coming of the Messiah, who would be in the form of an Indian. The Ghost Dance spread rapidly throughout much of the West, and soon Lakota were following Wovoka's teachings. Sitting Bull had his doubts about the new religion, but he realized that it disturbed the whites and in particular agent McLaughlin, and so he encouraged his people to dance.

The events that followed brought about the death of Sitting Bull as well as the military and psychological defeat of the Lakota. Cautious Indian officials deplored the fact that the Lakota were dancing again. Sitting Bull, the symbol of the old culture, was still their leader, and they decided to arrest him. McLaughlin chose Lakota Indians who served in the Agency Police Force to apprehend Sitting Bull. They came to his hut to seize him during the night of December 15, 1890, and a scuffle broke out. The fifty-nine-year-old chief was one of the first to be killed. In the dust and confusion of the struggle, fourteen others died. Several days later, other Lakota who had left their reservation were stopped at Wounded Knee Creek, and a scuffle again broke out with the white soldiers, who were trying to disarm them and to force them back to the agency. When the fighting was over on that cold December day, 153 Lakota had died and the dream of a return to the old way of life was lost forever.

SIGNIFICANCE

Sitting Bull, the proud leader of the Hunkpapa, had died along with many of his people. He had served his people well as a feared warrior and respected chief. He had

Sitting Bull

fought against Indians and whites, including sixty-three coups against unfortunate Indians. The whites had suffered their worst defeat when they attacked his village. Although the old chief was unable to fight, he proved his inspirational mettle to the people. During his last years, he continued to serve as a model for his followers, although in a losing cause.

Technology and the overwhelming white population were forces that even the stubborn Lakota leader could not subdue. Gone were the days of nomadic camp life, horseback riding, and buffalo hunting. Also gone were the memories of courtships and polygamous marriages: White Americans hoped to convert the Lakota tribesmen into Christian yeoman farmers. By 1890, the frontier phase of American history had passed, and citizens confronted the problems of immigration from southern and eastern Europe, the growing urbanization, and the massive industrialization that would make the United States a world leader. The Lakota life that was so well adapted to the plains environment was gone forever.

—*John W. Bailey*

FURTHER READING

Adams, Alexander B. *Sitting Bull: An Epic of the Plains*. New York: G. P. Putnam's Sons, 1973. A richly detailed popular account of Sitting Bull's life, with a good description of the various divisions and tribes of the Lakota.

Anderson, Gary Clayton. *Sitting Bull and the Paradox of Lakota Nationhood*. New York: Longman, Addison Wesley, 1996. Biography focusing on the challenges Sitting Bull faced in leading the Lakota people.

Bailey, John W. *Pacifying the Plains: General Alfred Terry and the Decline of the Sioux, 1866-1890*. Westport, Conn.: Greenwood Press, 1979. Follows Sitting Bull's career in the period after the Civil War, with particular emphasis on his role as the leader of the nonreservation Lakota and their conflict with the military during the 1870's.

Johnson, Dorothy M. *Warrior for a Lost Nation: A Biography of Sitting Bull*. Philadelphia: Westminster Press, 1969. A readable book based on limited research. Includes Sitting Bull's pictographs or calendar of winter counts that recorded his feats in battle.

Utley, Robert M. *The Lance and the Shield: The Life and Times of Sitting Bull*. New York: Ballantine Books, 1994. A definitive biography that portrays Sitting Bull as a complex leader.

_____. *The Last Days of the Sioux Nation*. New Haven, Conn.: Yale University Press, 1963. An excellent book that focuses on the death of Sitting Bull and the Wounded Knee battle of 1890. The author illustrates how the Lakota suffered a military and psychological conquest that saw their demise after the failure of the Ghost Dance.

Vestal, Stanley. *Sitting Bull: Champion of the Sioux, a Biography*. Boston: Houghton Mifflin, 1932. Rev. ed. Norman: University of Oklahoma Press, 1957. The most reliable biography of Sitting Bull, based on oral and documentary research. The author was closely associated with the Plains Indians since his boyhood and proved to be a careful student of their culture.

MARGARET CHASE SMITH

> **"** *Moral cowardice that keeps us from speaking our minds is as dangerous to this country as irresponsible talk.* **"**

U.S. congresswoman (1940-1949) and senator (1949-1973)

As the first leading American stateswoman to be elected in her own right to both houses of the U.S. Congress, Smith focused her attention on improving the status of women, military preparedness, and defense of free speech and democratic values.

Born: December 14, 1897; Skowhegan, Maine
Died: May 29, 1995; Skowhegan, Maine
Also known as: Margaret Madeline Chase (birth name)
Area of achievement: Government and politics

EARLY LIFE

Margaret Chase Smith was born in a mill and factory town in west-central Maine that provided a small-town atmosphere in which her parents George Emery and Carrie Murray Chase reared their six children. Margaret was the eldest of the four who survived. Her father, a barber from Irish and English background, was a hardworking family man whose own father had fought in the Civil War before taking his position as a Methodist minister in Skowhegan. Her mother took jobs occasionally to supplement the family income while instilling in her children the importance of family life and independence.

While pursuing a commercial course of study in high school, Smith worked as a clerk in the local five-and-dime store, was employed as a telephone operator, and was hired to record tax payments in the town books during her senior year. She shook hands with President Woodrow Wilson on her senior class trip to Washington, D.C. After her graduation from Skowhegan High School in 1916, Smith taught in the one-room Pitts School outside Skowhegan. Seven months later she returned to Skowhegan to accept a full-time telephone operator's job for Maine Telephone and Telegraph Company.

In 1919, she began an eight-year job at the town's weekly newspaper, the *Independent Reporter*, which Clyde H. Smith (her future husband) co-owned. Rising to circulation manager, she continued to meet influential people and cultivate her skills in public relations. She drew on these skills in 1922, when she organized the Skowhegan chapter of the Business and Professional Women's Club. Smith was named president of the Maine Federation of the Business and Professional Women's Clubs the following year. In 1928, she served as office manager for the Daniel E. Cummings Company, a Skowhegan woolen mill. Her early working experiences not only taught her how to get along with people but also instilled in her a respect for working people that influenced her subsequent pro-labor record in the United States Congress.

In 1930, Smith married Clyde H. Smith, a respected and experienced Maine politician who was twenty-two years her senior. From 1930 to 1936, she supported his energetic public career while learning the basic skills for campaigning and public service.

Smith, Margaret Chase

During this period, she also served as a member of the Maine Republican State Committee. Clyde Smith was elected to the United States House of Representatives in 1936. Margaret Smith served as his secretary in Washington, D.C., until his death in April, 1940.

LIFE'S WORK

Smith won a special election in the spring of 1940 to fill her husband's vacated seat in the House of Representatives. As a candidate for the succeeding full term in office, Smith scored an impressive electoral victory in the September general election. Her eight years as the congresswoman from Maine's Second Congressional District were highlighted by her interest in military affairs. In her first term she broke with the Republican Party and voted for the Selective Training and Service Act to draft men for the upcoming war. She was the only member of the Maine delegation to vote for Lend Lease in 1941, and she broke with her party to support a bill to arm American merchant ships. In 1943 she was appointed to the House Naval Affairs Committee, which was later merged into the Armed Services Committee.

Many of Smith's concerns focused on the status of women in the civilian workforce and in the military. In 1944, she was appointed by Secretary of Labor Frances Perkins to serve as technical adviser to the International Labor Organization, which explored the role of women in employment planning after World War II. Smith worked to improve the status of women in the military by introducing the Army-Navy Permanent Nurse Corps Bill to grant women permanent status in the military. This bill was signed into law by President Harry S. Truman in April of 1947. Smith toured the South Pacific naval bases and sponsored legislation that would permit women to serve overseas during war. She gained passage for the Women's Armed Services Integration Act of 1948, which gave women equal pay, rank, and privileges. Her desire to see the United States exert leadership in world affairs enabled her to support U.S. membership in the United Nations and the European Recovery Plan.

Senator Smith favored domestic legislation to improve the conditions of the working class and women. She helped to defeat the Tabor Amendment, which had proposed to halve the funds designated for community service programs such as child care. In 1945 and 1949 she cosponsored a proposed Equal Rights Amendment, which did not get the necessary two-thirds majority votes in Congress to be submitted to the states for ratification. She voted with the Democrats against the Smith-Connally Anti-Strike bill. In economic matters she opposed a bill to freeze the social security tax and voted for federal pay raises. In 1947 she voted against a Republican proposal to cut President Truman's budget. That same year she voted with her party in supporting the Taft-Hartley Act, which placed specific limits on labor. She had been named chair of the Maine State Republican Convention in 1944 to prepare her to chair the national Republican Party conference in 1967.

Smith ran for election to the U.S. Senate in 1948, winning by a record plurality. Though her opponents charged her with being a party maverick by calling attention to the votes that she cast contrary to her party, she produced a House voting record that aligned with her party 95 percent of the time. Her election to the United States Senate in 1948 made her the first woman in United States history to be elected in her own right

Smith, Margaret Chase

Margaret Chase Smith.
(Library of Congress)

without prior service by appointment to serve in the U.S. Senate and the first woman to be elected to both houses of Congress. Her four terms in the Senate from 1949 to 1973 acquainted her with six presidents, among whom were Dwight D. Eisenhower and John F. Kennedy.

In 1949, Senator Smith began a daily newspaper column, *Washington and You*, which was syndicated nationally for five years. She was named to the prestigious Senate Republican Policy Committee. She won the Associated Press award for Woman of the Year in politics in 1948, 1949, 1950, and 1957. She delivered her famous Declaration of Conscience speech on June 1, 1950, as a response to the abuses of Senator Joseph McCarthy's inquisitions into communism in the United States. She courageously opposed McCarthy's negativism and demeaning of Americans at a time when most Republicans in the Senate were either too afraid to oppose him or somewhat supportive of his extremist anticommunist activities. Her Declaration of Conscience speech still has appeal as a defense of American values and the importance of free speech to the maintenance of American democratic processes.

Smith traveled to Florence, Italy, in 1950 as U.S. delegate to the UNESCO conference. She was also appointed as a lieutenant colonel in the U.S. Air Force Reserve. After winning reelection to the Senate in 1954 she embarked on a twenty-three nation world tour to see how U.S. foreign aid money was being used. She interrupted her trip to return to the United States to cast her censure vote on McCarthy. In 1956, Senator Smith campaigned for Eisenhower, the Republican presidential candidate. She debated in his defense with Eleanor Roosevelt on CBS television's *Face the Nation*. As someone who enjoyed new experiences, Smith had by this time been the first woman to ride on an American destroyer in wartime, spend a day on an aircraft carrier at sea, and in 1957 to fly as a passenger in a F-100 jet fighter that broke the sound barrier.

In 1960, Smith won a hotly contested election over another female candidate, the first time two women had run against each other for a Senate seat. That same year she won *Newsweek* magazine's press poll rating as Most Valuable Senator. On resuming her duties in the Senate, she agonized over her vote on Kennedy's Limited Nuclear Test Ban Treaty. Her concern for national security won out in her vote against both the treaty and most of her party. Her vote put her on the same side as Barry Goldwater, who became the Republican Party presidential nominee for 1964. Although Smith was touted as a potential candidate for vice president in 1964, she earned the distinction that year of becoming the first woman nominated for president by a major U.S. political party.

She supported the 1964 Civil Rights Act using her influence in the Republican Conference to keep the provision barring sex discrimination in employment in Title VII intact. Smith won an unprecedented fourth term for a woman to the Senate in 1966. In 1967 she was elected chair of the Conference of Republican Senators. The next year she had to miss her first roll call vote in her thirteen years in Congress because of hip surgery. She held the record for 2,941 consecutive roll call votes. In the remaining two years of her tenure in the Senate, Smith cast important votes against President Richard M. Nixon's nominations of Clement F. Haynesworth and G. Harold Carswell for the U.S. Supreme Court. Demonstrations protesting the Vietnam War, especially on college campuses, led her to make her second Declaration of Conscience speech on June 1, 1970.

In her final campaign for reelection to the Senate in 1972, Smith was defeated by her Democratic opponent, William D. Hathaway. During her Senate career she served on the powerful Armed Forces, Appropriations, Government Operations, and Rules Committees and showed strong support for the space program as a charter member of the Senate Aeronautical and Space Committee. She also sponsored legislation for government support of medical research. Senator Smith used her considerable influence to look out for the seafaring interests and industries of the state of Maine and to cast votes on issues critical to the well-being of the Republican Party and the future course in world politics for the United States. After she left public office, Smith focused on a second career as a visiting professor and lecturer with the Woodrow Wilson National Fellowship Foundation and at numerous college and university campuses.

SIGNIFICANCE

In the course of her career, Smith received ninety-five honorary doctoral degrees and more than 270 other awards and honors. In 1989, she was awarded the Presidential Medal of Freedom, the nation's highest civilian honor. The Northwood Institute, Margaret Chase Smith Library in Skowhegan, Maine, was dedicated in 1982 to serve as a congressional research library and archives. This library houses the papers, political memorabilia, and documents that Smith accrued in her thirty-two years in Congress. In 1990 she was honored by the dedication of the Margaret Chase Smith Center for Public Policy at the University of Maine.

Smith's long and distinguished public service career furthered the interests of national security, especially military affairs. She pioneered legislation to further the status of women in domestic issues, in the military, and internationally. She was a model of decorum and earned a reputation for integrity, honesty, and independence of judgment. As a servant of the people in Congress, she put first priority on her duties in office. She campaigned vigorously and did not accept campaign contributions.

—*Willoughby G. Jarrell*

FURTHER READING

Fleming, Alice. *The Senator from Maine*. New York: Thomas Y. Crowell, 1969. This is a well-written book highlighting the life of Margaret Chase Smith from childhood through her work in Congress. Somewhat historically fictionalized, the book is suitable for grades six through eight.

Gould, Alberta. *First Lady of the Senate: Life of Margaret Chase Smith*. Mt. Desert, Maine: Windswept House, 1990. This work, written for younger readers, reviews the public career of Margaret Chase Smith. The author emphasizes Smith's personal values, public integrity, independent judgment, and contributions to public life.

Graham, Frank, Jr. *Margaret Chase Smith: Woman of Courage*. New York: John Day, 1964. This readable biography describes Smith's professional life in the Senate. The author emphasizes her accomplishments as a woman in national politics—at that time, an arena dominated by men. Presents clear explanations of how the U.S. government works.

Meisler, Stanley. "Margaret Chase Smith: The Nation's First Woman Senator Reflects Back over a Capitol Life." *Los Angeles Times*, December 8, 1991, p. M3. A brief interview with Smith in which she reminisces about her experiences as a politician in Washington, D.C. Places her accomplishments within the context of women's efforts to gain greater political representation during the 1990's.

Sherman, Janann. *No Place for a Woman: A Life of Margaret Chase Smith*. New Brunswick, N.J.: Rutgers University Press, 2000. Thoughtful, well-researched biography that examines the impact of Smith's gender on her political career.

_____. "'They Either Need These Women or They Do Not': Margaret Chase Smith and the Fight for Regular Status for Women in the Military." *Journal of Military History* 54 (January, 1990): 47-78. A scholarly analysis of Smith's stance on the issue of equitable status and treatment for women in the military. Amplifies her views on a topic that continues to generate interest among U.S. military leaders and the general public.

Smith, Margaret Chase. *Declaration of Conscience*. Edited by William C. Lewis, Jr. New York: Doubleday, 1972. This book, composed by Smith with the assistance of her legislative aide, William C. Lewis, Jr., focuses on her three decades of public service. It contains important source material including the text of her famous speeches and other important legislative statements.

Witt, Linda, Karen M. Paget, and Glenna Matthews. *Running as a Woman: Gender and Power in American Politics.* New York: Free Press, 1993. A journalist, a political scientist, and a historian collaborated on this sweeping narrative of the experiences of female candidates in American politics. Written from the vantage point of the so-called Year of the Woman in 1992, the book contains various references to Smith's trailblazing efforts in Congress and a telling assessment of public opinion regarding her chances of becoming president in 1964.

Elizabeth Cady Stanton

" *Self-development is a higher duty than self-sacrifice.* "

Social reformer

Stanton was one of the founders of the organized women's rights movement in the United States and served as one of its chief leaders during the second half of the nineteenth century.

Born: November 12, 1815; Johnstown, New York
Died: October 26, 1902; New York, New York
Also known as: Elizabeth Cady (birth name)
Areas of achievement: Women's rights; social reform

Early Life

Elizabeth Cady Stanton (KAY-dee STAHN-tuhn) was born Elizabeth Cady, the fourth of the six children of Daniel and Margaret Cady who survived childhood. Through her mother she was descended from a wealthy family, the Livingstons, who were part of the political elite of New York. Her mother's father, James Livingston, was an officer in George Washington's army during the American Revolution and a member of the New York state legislature. Elizabeth's father, Daniel Cady, was a successful lawyer who served in the New York state legislature and the U.S. House of Representatives, and, after 1847, he was a member of the New York State Supreme Court. Daniel Cady was a conservative in his political views and became an active member of the Federalist Party. Elizabeth's parents were strict Presbyterians who held firmly to traditional Calvinist doctrines of predestination and the depravity of human nature. As a child, Elizabeth found this version of religion frightening, even to the point of having nightmares that the Devil was attempting to possess her.

Several events in Elizabeth's childhood helped awaken her to the realization that women held a subordinate position in American society. Her father wanted very much to have a son, but each of Elizabeth's three brothers died young. At the death of his third son, Daniel Cady openly lamented to Elizabeth that she was not a boy. Part of the impetus for Elizabeth's refusal to accept a traditional female sex role may have stemmed from her attempt to be the son her father so fervently desired. A second instance that brought a new awareness of the disadvantage of being female occurred in her father's law office. Hearing of a case in which a female friend sought unsuccessfully to reclaim property she had purchased with her own money, but of which she had been deprived because of a state law transferring a woman's property to her husband when she married, Elizabeth became so upset that she attempted to cut the relevant pages out of her father's law books.

Even as a child, Elizabeth displayed intellectual ability considerably beyond that of the average youth. Believing that becoming a learned person was essential if she were to be equal to boys, she began the study of Greek at the age of eleven, later winning a prize at the Johnstown Academy for her achievements in this area. In spite of her outstanding academic record, she was not allowed to enroll at Union College, which admitted only boys, and had to be content with a girls' boarding school, Troy Female Seminary, which she attended from 1830 to 1833. Although most girls' boarding schools at this time were primarily finishing schools, concentrating on developing their students' social skills, Troy was unusual in that it attempted to provide academic training comparable to that which colleges provided men. The seminary encouraged its students to be self-reliant and provided careful training in writing skills, which Elizabeth later believed to have contributed to her success as an author.

After graduation from Troy Female Seminary, Elizabeth did not seek a career and at this point displayed little evidence that she would become a reformer. Even in this period, however, she occasionally displayed those qualities of independence and a militant opposition to efforts to place women in a subordinate position that marked her later life. She became the head of a young women's association that raised funds to enable an aspiring minister to attend seminary. When the recipient of their funds was invited to deliver a special sermon and chose to speak on women's inferiority, Elizabeth rose from her seat in the front pew and led the other young women out of the church in a gesture of protest.

During the 1830's, Elizabeth was increasingly drawn into the abolitionist reform effort by her cousin Gerrit Smith. Her cousin's home was a station on the Underground Railroad, and the accounts of their experiences by fugitive slaves made a lasting impression on Elizabeth. It was while attending an antislavery meeting that Elizabeth met the man who eventually became her husband. Henry Stanton was a member of the executive committee that directed the activities of the American Anti-Slavery Society. He was a gifted public speaker who had risked his life on several occasions by speaking against slavery to hostile crowds. When he proposed marriage to Elizabeth, her parents were totally opposed, because they considered abolitionists to be fanatics.

Marriage to Henry was an important turning point in Elizabeth's life, for he was not wealthy, and she knew that the social elite of New York would never accept them as long as he remained an abolitionist. Nevertheless—and even though her parents remained opposed and did not attend her wedding—Elizabeth married Henry in May, 1840. In two important respects, the marriage ceremony reflected her emerging feminist consciousness: At her request, the traditional bride's promise to obey her husband was deleted from the wedding vows, and, while adding her husband's name, she retained her own name.

Stanton, Elizabeth Cady

LIFE'S WORK
Almost immediately after their marriage, Elizabeth and Henry left for London to attend an international antislavery convention. This proved to be a traumatic experience for her. Many male delegates feared that association with feminism would harm the abolitionist cause and opposed allowing women to be delegates. The first major issue discussed at the conference was whether women delegates should be allowed to participate on an equal basis with men. It was eventually decided that women should not be allowed to sit on the convention floor with men and should not be permitted to speak at the conference. Stanton was deeply angered by the treatment accorded women and resolved to organize a women's rights convention when she returned to the United States. Although eight years passed before that conference was held, her treatment at the London convention was directly responsible for convincing her that women must join together in an organized effort if they were to progress toward equality.

After she and Henry returned to New York, Stanton became immersed in domestic activities. She had seven children between 1842 and 1859, and her husband considered it her responsibility to rear them. Partly because Henry was often away from home, sometimes for as long as eight months, Stanton was frequently depressed and resented the burdens of housework and child rearing. In her speeches and writings in later years, she often stressed birth control as of central importance in improving the position of married women; it is likely that her remarks at least partially reflected her own experiences.

After discovering that other women shared her sense of discontent, Stanton organized a women's rights convention at Seneca Falls, New York, at which women's grievances could be expressed. It was intended to be a local event, and she did not expect a large turnout. Nevertheless, more than three hundred persons came for the convention, including a number of prominent reformers from nearby Rochester. Stanton wrote the key document discussed by the convention, a list of women's grievances that she called the Declaration of Sentiments.

The declaration was modeled after the Declaration of Independence and drew upon the same natural-rights arguments to justify an end to discrimination based on sex. The list of grievances was lengthy and covered a wide spectrum: the admission of women to institutions of higher education, the right to enter professions such as law and medicine, the right of employed married women to retain their earnings, and an end to the double standard of sexual morality. Resolutions on these points received the unanimous support of those at the convention. A resolution proposing women's suffrage, however, proved far more controversial and passed by only a bare majority. Even Stanton's husband, Henry, opposed the suffrage resolution. After the convention, Stanton's father attempted to persuade her to remove her name from the list of those who had signed the Declaration of Sentiments, but she refused to do so. Her decision to persevere was an important turning point in her emergence as a nationally prominent feminist reformer.

During the years after the Seneca Falls convention, Stanton continued her activities on behalf of women's rights but was also active in other reform movements. In 1852, angry because the New York State temperance organization discriminated against women, she helped found the Women's State Temperance Society of New York. Her advocacy of temperance reflected a belief that excessive drinking by men often had serious consequences for women.

Because of the brutality often exhibited by drunken men toward their wives, Stanton urged that the grounds for divorce be expanded to include consistent heavy drinking. The majority of the women members were too conservative to consider Stanton's suggestion that the grounds for divorce be liberalized, and when they refused to reelect her as president, she withdrew from the organization. She also remained active in the abolitionist movement, urging the immediate emancipation of slaves, and opposed Abraham Lincoln's candidacy for the presidency in 1860 on the grounds that he was too moderate on the slavery issue and might compromise with the South. When, after the war, constitutional amendments were proposed extending the suffrage and civil rights to blacks, Stanton campaigned to have the amendments extended to women. Opposition to this step by her abolitionist friends contributed to its failure and drove a wedge between them; this was widened when she, in turn, argued against the Fourteenth and Fifteenth amendments because she feared the newly enfranchised black men would be hostile to women's suffrage.

In 1851, Stanton met Susan B. Anthony and initiated a friendship that had an important influence on the American feminist movement in the second half of the nineteenth century. Stanton persuaded Anthony to become involved in the campaign for women's rights, and the two worked closely on behalf of that cause for the next forty years. Stanton was a talented writer and public speaker but disliked the administrative work necessary to conduct a major campaign. Anthony excelled at such work, however, and thus the two formed an effective team. Although Anthony later received more public recognition for her role in bringing about women's suffrage, she was the junior partner in the relationship and acknowledged that Stanton was the true founder of the organized women's rights movement in the United States.

With the assistance of Anthony, Stanton promoted the cause of women's suffrage in a variety of ways. In 1866, she ran for Congress as an independent in order to test the constitutional right of a woman to hold public office. In the following year, she conducted an extensive campaign in Kansas, speaking throughout the state on behalf of a state constitutional amendment on women's suffrage.

In 1871, Stanton and Anthony made a speaking tour around the West, seeking to stimulate support for women's suffrage. In 1878, Stanton was responsible for the introduction of a women's suffrage amendment to the Constitution in Congress, a measure that was reintroduced in each subsequent Congress until it was passed in 1920. She appeared in Congress almost every year until late in her life to speak on behalf of the women's suffrage amendment. Perhaps her most important contribution to that movement was the major part she played in establishing and directing the National Woman Suffrage Association. Stanton and Anthony formed the NWSA in 1869, and Stanton served as its president until 1890, when it merged with the rival American Woman Suffrage Association. A prolific writer, Stanton joined with Anthony in coediting three volumes of *History of Woman Suffrage* (1881-1886), an invaluable source on the American women's suffrage movement.

Although women's suffrage was her major concern, Stanton never restricted her reforming efforts to one issue. She frequently shocked female audiences by her ideas on marriage and divorce. This caused friction between her and Anthony, who maintained that the cause of women's suffrage was being harmed by associating it with radical proposals for easier divorce. Stanton also alarmed Anthony with her criticisms of the Church. She believed that the Church was a major force maintaining the subordinate position of women, and from 1878, Stanton endeavored to persuade the NWSA to take a public stand against this.

Unsuccessful in that effort, Stanton then attempted to establish a committee of women to prepare a revised version of the Bible that would eliminate its sexist language. Eventually she proceeded on her own to write an extensive commentary on the biblical passages that directly discussed the status of women. Published in 1895 as *The Woman's Bible*, it defended women against the claim that they were responsible for Original Sin because of Eve's behavior in the Garden of Eden. Stanton was deeply hurt when the work was repudiated by other women's suffrage leaders, who feared that it would lead the public to dismiss the suffrage movement as irreligious.

Although her eyes began to fail during the last years of her life (she was completely blind by the time of her death), Stanton continued to write on women's issues until her death, on October 26, 1902, in New York City. She continued to enjoy life during old age, but her last years were marred by the breakdown of her friendship with Anthony and the efforts of women's suffrage leaders to distance themselves from her because of their belief that *The Woman's Bible* would prove harmful to their cause.

SIGNIFICANCE

The position of women in American society has changed considerably since the mid-nineteenth century, and Stanton was one of the central figures helping to bring about that change. As the founder of the organized women's rights movement in the United States and its recognized leader during the second half of the nineteenth century, she was a vital figure in an important and continuing reform movement. Although often remembered primarily in connection with the women's suffrage issue, she viewed suffrage as a means by which reforms could be instituted in other areas affecting women rather than an end in itself. Although she held important offices in women's organizations, Stanton was equally important as a publicist whose writings articulated the reasons that feminists wished to alter relationships between the sexes. Her writings on these issues were so extensive that it would be appropriate to consider her the chief theorist or intellectual of the late nineteenth century women's rights movement.

Since her death, Stanton's contribution to the American women's suffrage movement has been overshadowed by that of Anthony. This is in part because many of the women's suffrage activists in the generation immediately after Stanton's death did not share her views on issues other than suffrage. The revival of feminism in the United States since 1960, however, has brought a renewed interest in her life and work, partly because she did emphasize that the nonpolitical forces that kept women in a subordinate position were as important as those that were political.

—*Harold L. Smith*

FURTHER READING

Banner, Lois. *Elizabeth Cady Stanton: A Radical for Women's Rights*. Boston: Little, Brown, 1980. The best single volume on Stanton's life and thought. It presents her as the philosopher of the feminist movement and is especially helpful on her theories.

DuBois, Ellen Carol, ed. *Elizabeth Cady Stanton, Susan B. Anthony: Correspondence, Writings, Speeches*. New York: Shocken Books, 1981. This is an excellent collection of the correspondence between Stanton and Anthony, which also includes many of Stanton's more important speeches and articles. The critical commentary by DuBois is helpful in placing the documents in context.

Flexner, Eleanor. *Century of Struggle: The Woman's Rights Movement in the United States*. Cambridge, Mass.: Harvard University Press, 1959. Widely regarded as the best history of the campaign for women's suffrage. It includes some references to Stanton but focuses on the movement itself rather than on its leaders.

Forster, Margaret. "Elizabeth Cady Stanton, 1815-1902." In *Significant Sisters*. New York: Oxford University Press, 1984. A well-written chapter in a book about prominent feminists. It makes extensive use of Stanton's letters and other original sources in conveying a vivid sense of her personality.

Griffith, Elisabeth. *In Her Own Right: The Life of Elizabeth Cady Stanton*. New York: Oxford University Press, 1984. A detailed account of Stanton's life based on extensive research in primary sources. It is a psychological study that excels in discussing Stanton's private life.

Kern, Kathi. *Mrs. Stanton's Bible*. Ithaca, N.Y.: Cornell University Press, 2001. Examines Stanton's nonsexist Bible, published in 1895. Kern argues Stanton's biblical commentary alienated her from less radical feminists and may have delayed passage of the women's suffrage amendment.

Lutz, Alma. *Created Equal: A Biography of Elizabeth Cady Stanton*. New York: John Day, 1940. This was the first scholarly biography of Stanton. It is a clear, objective, narrative account that concentrates more on her political activities than on her thought.

Stanton, Elizabeth Cady. *Eighty Years and More: Reminiscences, 1815-1897*. London: T. Fisher Unwin, 1898. Reprint. New York: Schocken Books, 1971. Written near the end of her life, Stanton's autobiography provides the fullest account of her life from her own point of view. Although invaluable for its firsthand information, it is brief on some events in her life and omits others entirely and thus must be supplemented by other sources.

Wellman, Judith. *The Road to Seneca Falls: Elizabeth Cady Stanton and the First Women's Rights Convention*. Urbana: University of Illinois Press, 2004. Chronicles the events that took place during the historic women's rights meeting, describing how abolitionism, radical Quakerism, and the campaign for legal reform shaped the convention's proceedings—and Stanton's life.

ADLAI E. STEVENSON

" *A free society is one where it is safe to be unpopular.* "

Governor of Illinois (1949-1953) and U.N. ambassador (1961-1965)

Although unsuccessful in his repeated bids for the presidency, Stevenson inspired a new generation of liberals who would write the agenda for the New Frontier and Great Society during the 1960's. He brought to the American political scene an all too uncommon blend of integrity, high intelligence, and humane values.

Born: February 5, 1900; Los Angeles, California
Died: July 14, 1965; London, England
Also known as: Adlai Ewing Stevenson II (full name)
Areas of achievement: Government and politics; diplomacy

EARLY LIFE

Adlai Stevenson (AD-li STEE-vuhn-suhn) was born in Los Angeles, where his father, Lewis Stevenson, managed the Hearst mining and newspaper interests. Stevenson's family, however, was based in Bloomington, Illinois, and the marriage of his parents had united the town's leading Republican and Democratic families. The Stevensons and their relatives had long been active in Illinois political affairs. Jesse Fell, his great-grandfather, was a founder of the Republican Party and a political confidant of Abraham Lincoln. His grandfather, after whom he was named, was an Illinois Democrat who had served as Grover Cleveland's vice president during the 1890's.

This family history influenced Stevenson's formative years. In 1906, his family returned to Bloomington, where his father owned and managed several farms, became a noted agricultural reformer, and was active in state and national politics. Consequently, Adlai became acquainted with such political giants as William Jennings Bryan and, most notably, Woodrow Wilson, whose moral vision and internationalism became guideposts for his subsequent political career. Although he enjoyed a happy childhood in Bloomington, he became an indifferent student in the town's primary and secondary schools. This idyllic period was shattered in December, 1912, when he accidentally shot and killed his cousin. Stevenson was so shattered by the tragedy that he could never speak of it until it became part of the 1952 presidential campaign.

In 1916, Stevenson attended Choate School in Connecticut to prepare for the entrance examinations for Princeton University. He entered Princeton in 1918 and was graduated four years later with average grades. He was very active in student affairs and was managing editor of *The Princetonian*. At his father's insistence, Stevenson enrolled at Harvard Law School, where he was miserable; his grades declined accordingly. In 1926, he completed his legal training at Northwestern Law School. During this period, he met with Supreme Court Justice Oliver Wendell Holmes, Jr., which proved to be one of the most satisfying experiences of his life.

By this time, Stevenson had decided to make law his life's work. He had been seriously considering becoming a newspaper publisher, and he enjoyed working on the school press at Choate and Princeton as well as editing the family's Bloomington newspaper. In 1926, Stevenson made one last effort in the newspaper business by hiring out as a reporter for the International News Service to enter the Soviet Union and obtain an interview with Foreign Minister Georgi Chicherin. Stevenson traveled by train from the Black Sea through Kharkov and Kiev to Moscow, and his observations of life under the Bolshevik regime colored his attitude toward the Soviet system for the remainder of his life.

In 1927, Stevenson became a member of a prestigious Chicago law firm, and the following year he married Ellen Borden, a Chicago heiress with literary interests. They produced three sons, Adlai III, Borden, and John Fell, and established a home in the small community of Libertyville, Illinois.

Life's Work

In 1929, the United States suffered the greatest economic contraction in its history, with devastating social, economic, and political consequences. In 1932, voters turned to the Democratic Party under Franklin D. Roosevelt, who promised the country a "new deal." Stevenson became one of the New Deal's bright young attorneys who swarmed into Washington, D.C., to write, enact, and administer myriad administration programs. In 1933, he served as special counsel to the Agricultural Adjustment Administration under George Peek; then, a few months later, he joined the Alcohol Control Administration as special counsel to handle price codes and tax problems following the repeal of Prohibition. During the course of his brief service, Stevenson became acquainted with such figures as George Ball, Alger Hiss, James Rowe, and Tommy Corcoran, who played significant roles in American history.

Although Stevenson had left government service, he became increasingly active in politics. In 1930, he had joined the Council on Foreign Relations, where he honed his oratorical skills on behalf of Wilsonian internationalist principles. In 1939, he joined the Committee to Defend America by Aiding the Allies to counter the isolationist mood of the country. His support of Roosevelt's mobilization efforts, including the "destroyer deal" and the Lend-Lease program, reflected his belief that Great Britain was fighting the American fight against totalitarian aggression.

After the United States entered World War II in December, 1941, Stevenson became assistant secretary of the Navy under his close friend Frank Knox, a Republican newspaper publisher from Chicago. Stevenson handled the press, wrote Knox's speeches, and promoted desegregation of the Navy. In 1943, he led a mission to Italy to plan the Allied occupation of that country. As the war concluded, he was made a member of the United States Strategic Bombing Survey and then became assistant secretary of state under Edward L. Stettinius and James F. Byrnes, Jr. Finally, he became press officer of the United States delegation to the United Nations conference at San Francisco in 1945.

These posts served as a proving ground for Stevenson's meteoric rise in Illinois and national politics during the late 1940's and the 1950's. In Illinois, the incumbent Republican governor had been compromised by corruption in his administration, and Democratic boss Colonel Jacob M. Arvey of Cook County needed strong reform candidates to capture the state House and the Senate seat. Arvey selected Stevenson for governor and Paul H. Douglas for the Senate. In 1948, Stevenson campaigned as a political amateur and pledged honest government. He won by more than 500,000 votes, helping to bring in not only Douglas but also President Harry S. Truman in one of the country's greatest political upsets. This victory made Stevenson one of the "class of '48," a group of moderates and liberals who would dominate national politics into the 1970's.

Although his political career led to the breakup of his marriage, Stevenson was an effective liberal governor during a period of anticommunist hysteria known as McCarthyism. Stevenson appointed both Republican and Democratic businessmen to state positions, terminated commercial gambling, placed the Illinois state police on civil service, built new highways, streamlined state government, and increased education appropriations. On the debit side, however, was his failure to persuade the state legislature to enact a permanent fair employment practices commission and to authorize a state convention to revise an archaic state constitution.

As a result of his gubernatorial performance, Stevenson became a favorite for the Democratic presidential nomination in 1952. The Democrats had been in power since 1933, and the party's domestic record and Cold War policies made it vulnerable to a conservative attack. The Truman administration, in fact, had become so unpopular

Adlai E. Stevenson.
(Library of Congress)

Stevenson, Adlai E.

that the president declined to seek reelection. Instead, Truman placed strong private and public pressure on Stevenson to make the race. The problem was that Stevenson did not want the position; he wanted to be reelected governor of Illinois. Moreover, he believed himself to be too inexperienced for the office. Stevenson's hesitation led to the charge that he was indecisive, which was to haunt him for the rest of his career. In the end, he was nominated for president in a movement that came as close to a draft as any in the twentieth century.

The 1952 campaign between Stevenson and General Dwight D. Eisenhower, an enormously popular war hero, became a classic confrontation. Behind in the polls from the beginning, Stevenson pledged to "talk sense" to the American people and offered no panaceas for the nation's troubles. His position on the issues revealed him to be a moderate liberal on domestic matters and a cold warrior in foreign affairs. His penchant for writing his own speeches, his wit and erudition, his use of Lincolnian and Holmesian anecdotes, and his humility charmed millions of voters. When his opponents condemned him for appealing to intellectuals, he responded, "Eggheads of the world, unite! You have nothing to lose but your yolks!"

Although the early stages of the campaign showed promise, a number of factors combined to bring the Stevenson effort to a bitter conclusion. Stevenson's humor, intellectualism, and Hamlet-like posturing before the nominating convention made many voters suspect that he did not lust for the office. Moreover, the Republican attack of "K1C2" (Korea, communism, corruption) proved to be very effective with the voters. Stevenson's entanglement with the Hiss controversy did nothing to refute the charge that he was "soft on communism." Additionally, his support for federal over states' rights on the tidelands issue cost him significant support in such states as Louisiana, Texas, and California. The coup de grace to the campaign, however, proved to be Eisenhower's pledge to "go to Korea" and bring that stalemated conflict to an end. On election day, Stevenson lost by 33,936,252 to 27,314,992 votes, including the electoral votes of four southern states.

Stevenson declined to disappear from public view during the 1950's. He became a world traveler, met world leaders, and solidified his credentials in foreign affairs. He also maintained a rigorous speaking schedule at home, campaigned for Democrats in the congressional elections of 1954 and 1958, and published several books on contemporary issues. In 1956, he was renominated for president by his party and campaigned on the theme of a "New America." Although he proved to be more liberal on civil rights than was Eisenhower, he badly mishandled the *Brown v. Board of Education* decision (1954), which struck down segregation. Seeking to prevent national divisiveness on this issue, he declared that he would not use federal troops to desegregate public schools. He later recovered somewhat by pledging to enforce the decision if it were defied by state authorities. More controversial, however, were his proposals to end the draft and nuclear testing. Whatever chance he had for success was undermined in late October and November, 1956, by the Suez Canal and Hungarian crises. The electorate declined to change leaders, and Stevenson lost by an even greater margin, by 35,590,472 votes to 26,029,752.

By now, Stevenson's career had crested. In 1960, die-hard Stevenson loyalists made a "last hurrah" for their hero at the Democratic National Convention in Los Angeles, but the party turned to John F. Kennedy and a younger generation for leadership. Following Kennedy's narrow election victory, Stevenson hoped to be appointed secretary of state, only to be bitterly disappointed by his nomination for ambassador to the United Nations. Kennedy softened the disappointment by making the position cabinet-level and promising Stevenson a role in the National Security Council.

Stevenson's expertise on world affairs and his relationships with world leaders made him a popular and effective representative for the United States. His confrontations with his Soviet counterpart, Valerian Zorin, were tough and dramatic. In April, 1961, Stevenson's prestige tumbled when he denied that the United States had aided the Bay of Pigs invasion in Cuba by Cuban exiles. When President Kennedy took full responsibility for the incident, Stevenson was badly embarrassed and contemplated resignation. This action was averted when Kennedy promised to keep him fully informed on foreign policy decisions and even to seek his counsel.

This led to Ambassador Stevenson's superb performance in October, 1962, over the Cuban Missile Crisis when he successfully challenged Zorin's denial of Soviet insertion of missiles inside Cuba. His calm presentation of the evidence and his vow to wait until "hell freezes over" for the Soviet response won for him great praise at home and abroad. Unfortunately, this bravura performance was tarnished by administration insiders who leaked to journalists that Stevenson had acted the role of appeaser toward the Soviets. Although Stevenson and the Kennedy administration denied the story, it once again reinforced the public's perception of Stevenson's passivity.

Stevenson clearly was unhappy serving under Kennedy and Johnson. His admirers encouraged him to resign with a denunciation of their foreign policies, but he could not bring himself to take that step. While he did criticize Johnson's intervention in the Dominican Republic in 1965, he continued to support the containment, limited war, and collaborative aspects of American diplomacy developed during the Truman administration. He even supported basic American policies in South Vietnam. On the afternoon of July 14, 1965, Stevenson collapsed and died of a heart attack on a street in London.

Significance

Stevenson had acquired the reputation of a political loser, but his career should elicit admiration rather than contempt. He brought to public life the highest ideals and standards and never wavered in their defense. He did not seek easy answers to complex issues. He was an enigmatic political leader, a man who sought the nation's highest office yet appeared indifferent when it was within his grasp. It has been said that Stevenson lacked the ruthlessness to become president, but it may also be that he wanted the office on his terms. It seems ironic that he received his highest accolades not from his fellow citizens but from the people of the world who saw him as the best that America could produce.

A politician's success can be measured in many ways. Stevenson's "New America" campaign of 1956 anticipated much of the social and economic legislation of the New Frontier and Great Society in the 1960's. He inspired and brought into the political system millions of voters who had never before participated. He stood up to McCarthyism and practiced a disciplined civility in politics to which all politicians should aspire.

Stevenson, Adlai E.

Stevenson belongs to the tradition of pragmatic reform characteristic of the twentieth century. His admirers saw him as a political leader with a moral vision for economic and social justice at home and abroad. In foreign affairs, he represented the tradition of Wilsonian internationalism, with its respect for international law, collective security, nuclear arms limitation, and human rights. He was, at heart, an optimist, a gentle and wise man who believed in strong and compassionate government and the nurturing of democratic principles throughout the world.

—*Stephen P. Sayles*

FURTHER READING

Brown, Stuart Gerry. *Adlai E. Stevenson, a Short Biography: The Conscience of the Country.* Woodbury, N.Y.: Barron's Woodbury Press, 1965. A popular biography by a Stevenson admirer. Based on secondary sources as well as interviews with the subject and his friends and colleagues.

Cochran, Bert. *Adlai Stevenson: Patrician Among the Politicians.* New York: Funk and Wagnalls, 1969. Interprets Stevenson's life and career within the context of upper-class reform dating to the Gilded Age. Includes commentary on the role of intellectuals in the Cold War era.

Johnson, Wallace, and Carol Evans, eds. *The Papers of Adlai E. Stevenson, 1900-1965.* 8 vols. Boston: Little, Brown, 1972-1979. Correspondence and papers dealing with the life and career of Stevenson. Reflects his wit, intelligence, and character. A significant source of primary materials for students of post-World War II politics.

Liebling, Alvin, ed. *Adlai Stevenson's Lasting Legacy.* New York: Palgrave Macmillan, 2007. Collection of essays by Eugene McCarthy, Adlai Stevenson III, Arthur Schlesinger, Jr., and others examining Stevenson's past and current social significance.

Martin, John Bartlow. *Adlai Stevenson and the World: The Life of Adlai Stevenson.* Garden City, N.Y.: Doubleday, 1977. A scholarly two-volume biography of Stevenson by a longtime friend and associate. Volume 1 covers the formative years through the 1952 presidential campaign. Volume 2 discusses Stevenson's political decline and his influence in world affairs. A sympathetic portrait.

Ross, Lillian. "A Man for All Seasons." *Vogue*, November, 2003, 136-140. A profile of Stevenson surveying his career before he ran for the presidency in 1952, the 1952 election, and Ross's admiration for his writing.

Severn, Bill. *Adlai Stevenson: Citizen of the World.* New York: David McKay, 1966. A popular biography useful for readers with little background in modern American political history. An admiring treatment.

Stevenson, Adlai E. *Call to Greatness.* New York: Harper and Brothers, 1954. A candid nonpartisan assessment of the United States' position in world affairs during the 1950's. Emphasizes the destabilizing impact of nationalist and independence movements in the developing world. Urges Americans to be more mature in their hopes and aspirations for a stable and peaceful world order.

_____. *Friends and Enemies: What I Learned in Russia.* New York: Harper and Brothers, 1959. Commentary on Stevenson's observations while in the Soviet

Union in 1958. Notes that the Soviet regime is here to stay but states that the Soviet Union and the United States can maintain a peaceful coexistence. Typical of Stevenson's elegance of expression and clarity of style.

Whitman, Alden, and *"The New York Times." Portrait—Adlai E. Stevenson: Politician, Diplomat, Friend.* New York: Harper & Row, 1965. Drawn largely from the files of *The New York Times.* A flattering account of Stevenson's career, especially from his Illinois gubernatorial campaign until his death. Views Stevenson as a great, but flawed, man and emphasizes his growing estrangement from the Kennedy and Johnson administrations.

JAMES STEWART

> **"** *When I got back from the war in 1945, I refused to make war pictures.* **"**

Actor and bomber pilot

Stewart was one of the most successful and enduring actors in the history of American motion pictures.

Born: May 20, 1908; Indiana, Pennsylvania
Died: July 2, 1997; Beverly Hills, California
Also known as: Jimmy Stewart
Areas of achievement: Theater and entertainment; film

EARLY LIFE

James Stewart was born in the small town of Indiana, Pennsylvania. His father, Alex, owned a hardware store where Stewart worked as a young man. His mother, Elizabeth, was a homemaker and church organist. Stewart's only contact with the theater in his youth was the plays he staged in the family basement with his two younger sisters, Mary and Virginia. As a child, he attended Indiana's Model School, then Mercersburg Academy. On graduation from high school, he went to his father's alma mater, Princeton University, to study architecture.

While at Princeton, Stewart met future theatrical writer-producer Josh Logan, who encouraged him to appear in university main-stage productions. Shortly after graduation in 1932, Stewart accepted Logan's invitation to join him at a local theatrical group, the University Players, and played a number of small roles in summer stock productions. At the end of the summer, Princeton University offered Stewart a scholarship to pursue a master's degree in architecture. Instead, he traveled to New York with the University Players to appear in the Broadway opening of *Carry Nation*, a play loosely based on the life of the outspoken nineteenth century temperance leader. Though the play closed shortly after it opened, Stewart never returned to Princeton University.

LIFE'S WORK

Stewart stayed in New York after *Carry Nation* closed. He spent the next two years looking for stage work to help pay rent for the small apartment he shared with fellow struggling actors Josh Logan and Henry Fonda. Stewart's first successful stage appearance was as Sergeant O'Hara, a soldier volunteer for Walter Reed's malaria experiments, in *Yellow Jack*. Though *Yellow Jack* was also short-lived, Stewart received good critical reviews. He also received favorable notice from critics for his performance in *Divided by Three*. It was during the run of *Divided by Three* that a talent scout for Metro-Goldwyn-Mayer (MGM), the largest and most prestigious film studio in California, spotted Stewart's performance and arranged for a series of screen tests. Stewart signed a contract with MGM for $350 per week and moved to California.

In June of 1935, Stewart arrived in Hollywood and once again shared rent with Fonda and a series of other newly arrived actors. Over the next few years, Stewart appeared in a wide variety of roles while MGM tried to find a character type that would succeed with film audiences. He played a fugitive on the run in *Rose Marie* (1936), Jean Harlow's boyfriend in *Wife vs. Secretary* (1936), a murderer in *After the Thin Man* (1936), a sewer worker in *Seventh Heaven* (1937), a botany professor in *Vivacious Lady* (1938), and even sang a couple songs in *Born to Dance* (1936). He was also paired with former University Player Margaret Sullivan in a series of popular romantic comedies, including *The Shopworn Angel* (1938), *The Shop Around the Corner* (1940), and *The Mortal Storm* (1940). During this time, Stewart was also a frequent voice on radio, performing shortened versions of popular films and plays.

Stewart's screen personality—the sweet, small-town, dependable good guy—developed during the late 1930's. He made his mark with film critics in 1938 when he played Tony Vanderhoff in the screen adaptation of George Kaufman's Pulitzer Prize-winning play *You Can't Take It with You*. The film won the Academy Award for Best Picture, and Stewart's characterization of Tony charmed film audiences. In 1939, Stewart was paired with boisterous Marlene Dietrich as a sheriff in a comedy Western *Destry Rides Again*, which showed off Stewart's comedic flair. He received critical acclaim for holding his own against Dietrich's enormous screen presence.

In 1939, Stewart was cast as Jefferson Smith in *Mr. Smith Goes to Washington*, directed by Frank Capra. His performance as young and idealistic Jefferson Smith cemented Stewart's good-guy image. In the film, Smith is a small-town boy elected to serve in the United States Congress who is unjustly accused of criminal activity. Smith discovers corruption and loses his political innocence while sponsoring a bill to establish a boys' camp. The film was popular with audiences and critics alike, and Stewart received his first Best Actor Oscar nomination.

In 1940, Stewart appeared in *The Philadelphia Story* with Katherine Hepburn and Cary Grant. Hepburn played Tracy Lord, a rich divorcée on the eve of her second marriage who has difficulty deciding among her fiancé, her former husband, and Mike Conner, a visiting reporter played by Stewart. *The Philadelphia Story* was a huge box-office success, and Stewart received the 1940 Academy Award for Best Actor for his performance.

As Stewart's acting career reached new heights, his life took an unexpected turn. When conflicts that precipitated World War II erupted in Europe, Stewart enlisted in the U.S. Army. Initially turned down for service because he was underweight, Stewart went on a high-calorie diet and reported for duty on March 22, 1941. Already a licensed pilot, he was assigned to the Army Air Corps. Stewart received his wings and commission as a second lieutenant within weeks of the Japanese attack on Pearl Harbor that brought the United States into World War II. He received heavy-bomber instruction at Kirkland Field in New Mexico and trained as a B-17 commander at Hobbs Air Force Base. In 1943, Captain Stewart was transferred to Boise, Idaho, where he trained young bomber pilots. He also appeared on recruiting tours, traveled on bond drives to raise funds for the war effort, and made instructional films for the Army, a project he would continue for the next four decades.

In 1943, Stewart was transferred to Tibenham, England, to command the 703d Squadron of the 445th Bombardment Group of B-24 Liberators. He led nearly twenty bombing missions against the Germans in a total of 1,800 flying hours and was promoted to the rank of major. For his wartime service, Stewart was awarded the Air Medal, an Oak Leaf Cluster for leadership, the Distinguished Flying Cross, and the French Croix de Guerre. Early in 1944, Colonel Stewart became operations officer for the 453d Bombardment Group before returning to the United States in August of 1945. After the war ended, Stewart remained in the Air Force Reserve and eventually achieved the rank of brigadier general.

Stewart returned to Hollywood after the war, unsure of the status of his acting career. In 1946, he quickly accepted an invitation from director Frank Capra to star in a small black-and-white film for Radio-Keith-Orpheum (RKO). At the time of its release, the film received some critical favor but only mediocre audience response, yet years later, Stewart proclaimed *It's a Wonderful Life* (1947) to be his favorite motion picture. Stewart played George Bailey, a small-town man who longs for adventure but is seemingly stuck in an uneventful life. Matters degenerate, and George contemplates suicide before an angel named Clarence shows George what his family and friends would be like if he had never been born.

In the summer of 1948, Stewart met Gloria Hatrick at a dinner party given by Gary Cooper. Gloria was a recently divorced mother of two small boys. The two were married on August 9, 1949, at the Brentwood Presbyterian Church, ending the career of Hollywood's most eligible bachelor and beginning a long, successful marriage. In addition to Gloria's two boys, the Stewarts had twin girls in 1951.

After the release of *It's a Wonderful Life*, Stewart tried to find his place in postwar American film by playing a variety of characters through the late 1940's. He was a newspaper reporter in *Call Northside 777* (1948), a public relations man in *Magic Town* (1947), and a detective in *Rope* (1948), which teamed him with director Alfred Hitchcock for the first time.

Stewart was the summer Broadway replacement for Frank Fay, who played the part of Elwood P. Dowd in *Harvey* twice during the later 1940's. Stewart enjoyed the role and successfully campaigned to play Dowd in the 1950 film version. *Harvey* marked the beginning of the most successful decade of Stewart's life. Dowd is a quiet, tipsy man who spends his day with his best friend, an invisible rabbit named Harvey. Stewart received another Oscar nomination for the role and for years to come was associated with the harmless eccentric and his rabbit friend.

Stewart appeared in a number of Westerns during the 1950's and 1960's. The sweet, small-town man became a hardened cowboy, and audiences loved it. Stewart appeared in *Winchester 73* (1950), *Bend of the River* (1952), *The Naked Spur* (1953), *The Far Country* (1955), and *The Man from Laramie* (1955). Stewart teamed with director John Ford for *The Man Who Shot Liberty Valance* (1962) and played Wyatt Earp in *Cheyenne Autumn* (1964). For every Western, Stewart insisted on working with his favorite horse, Pie, which he credited with making him look like a real cowboy. In 1965, he played a stoic Virginia farmer determined to keep his six sons out of the Civil War in the popular film *Shenandoah*. The film was the number-one box-office draw for the year. He also portrayed a number of real-life heroes: He appeared as popular band leader Glenn Miller in *The Glenn Miller Story* (1954); baseball player Monty Stratton, who lost his leg in a hunting accident, in *The Stratton Story* (1949); and Charles A. Lindbergh in *The Spirit of St. Louis* (1957).

In 1954, Stewart and Hitchcock made the hugely successful film *Rear Window*. Stewart played a photojournalist who breaks his leg. Housebound and bored, he takes interest in the lives of the neighbors he watches through his rear window. Convinced that one neighbor has murdered his wife, he involves his girlfriend, played by Grace Kelly, and his nurse in the intrigue. He teamed with Hitchcock again for *The Man Who Knew Too Much* (1956), in which Stewart played Dr. Ben McKenna, a vacationer in North Africa who finds himself thrust into murderous events over which he has little control. He played a former police officer plagued by a fear of heights in *Vertigo* (1958) and received another Oscar nomination for the role of a small-town lawyer in *Anatomy of a Murder* (1959), directed by Otto Preminger.

Stewart appeared in fewer films during the 1970's and 1980's but starred in the television detective series *Hawkins*. He made frequent appearances at award ceremonies in his honor. He received an honorary Academy Award, was inducted into the American Film Institute, and was honored by the Kennedy Center. As a frequent guest on *The Tonight Show* with Johnny Carson, Stewart sometimes read poems he had written. They were so popular with audiences that he published a book of his poetry called *Jimmy Stewart and His Poems* (1989). Stewart's last film role was the voice of Wylie Burp in the animated *An American Tail 2: Fievel Goes West* (1991). Stewart's wife Gloria died of cancer in 1994, and Stewart remained reclusive until his death in 1997 at the age of eighty-nine.

SIGNIFICANCE

Stewart was one of the most popular and beloved actors of the twentieth century. Theater revivals and videotapes served to increase his popularity. *It's a Wonderful Life* was rediscovered in the 1970's and became a traditional Christmas favorite. Stewart's portrayal of small-town good guy George Bailey is perhaps his most memorable performance and creates a new generation of Stewart fans each year.

—*Leslie A. Stricker*

FURTHER READING

Bingham, Dennis. *Acting Male: Masculinities in the Films of James Stewart, Jack Nicholson, and Clint Eastwood.* New Brunswick, N.J.: Rutgers University Press,

Sullivan, Anne

1994. Bingham studies different acting styles and male portrayals among three leading actors.
Coe, Jonathan. *Jimmy Stewart: A Wonderful Life.* New York: Arcade, 1994. Coe focuses this work on Stewart's film and stage career.
Dewey, Donald. *James Stewart: A Biography.* Atlanta, Ga.: Turner, 1996. This book studies Stewart's life from his small-town upbringing to his life as an actor, father, and Army Air Corps pilot.
Eliot, Marc. *Jimmy Stewart: A Biography.* New York: Harmony Books, 2006. An exhaustive and generally admiring account of Stewart's life and career based on newly conducted archival research.
Fonda, Henry, with Howard Teichmann. *Fonda: My Life.* New York: New American Library, 1981. This book, written by Stewart's best friend, gives special insight into Stewart's personal life.
Munn, Michael. *Jimmy Stewart: The Truth Behind the Legend.* London: Robson, 2005. Munn seeks to debunk Stewart's image by citing the less pleasant aspects of his character. He maintains that Stewart was a "secret agent" for the Federal Bureau of Investigation (FBI) as part of an effort to crack organized crime in Hollywood and was manipulated into "flushing out" alleged Communists from the film industry.
Pickard, Roy. *Jimmy Stewart: A Life in Film.* New York: St. Martin's Press, 1992. Pickard focuses on Stewart's film work with a good chronology of film and television appearances.

ANNE SULLIVAN

> **"** *A miracle has happened! The light of understanding has shone upon my little pupil's mind, and behold, all things are changed!* **"**

Educator

With patience, determination, and knowledge of the manual alphabet for the hearing impaired, Sullivan taught Helen Keller to communicate. Encouraged by Keller's quick intelligence, Sullivan devoted her entire life to living and working with Keller in a partnership that inspired many and championed the causes of the blind and the deaf.

Born: April 14, 1866; Feeding Hills, Massachusetts
Died: October 20, 1936; Forest Hills, Long Island, New York
Also known as: Joanna Mansfield Sullivan (birth name); Anne Macy
Area of achievement: Education

EARLY LIFE
Anne Sullivan (SUH-lih-vuhn), born Joanna Mansfield Sullivan, experienced a childhood almost as difficult and tragic as that of her famous pupil Helen Keller. Sullivan,

the oldest child of Irish immigrants Thomas and Alice Sullivan, had trachoma, a bacterial infection that damaged her eyesight, when she was about five years old. When she was nine years old, her mother died of tuberculosis, leaving her alcoholic father to attempt to care for his three remaining children. Before long, Sullivan and her brother, Jimmie, who suffered from a tubercular hip, were sent to the Tewksbury Almshouse, where Jimmie died a few months later.

Jimmie's death meant that Sullivan was the only child at Tewksbury, an institution infamous for its slovenly living conditions. Despite almost total blindness, Sullivan was determined to escape, and in 1880 she caught the attention of the visiting chair of the Massachusetts Board of Charities, Frank B. Sanborn. Shortly thereafter, Sullivan was sent to the Perkins School for the Blind in Boston. She initially felt humiliated by her ignorance, and her temper caused friction with her teachers and fellow students, but eventually she settled down to her studies.

The significance of Sullivan's time at the Perkins School cannot be overstated. It was there that she came to know Laura Bridgman, a deaf-blind resident of Perkins for over forty years who communicated through the manual hand alphabet. In addition, a summer job that the school arranged for Sullivan led to her meeting the doctor who performed the first successful operation on her eyes, restoring some of her lost vision. Sullivan applied herself to her studies as never before and graduated from Perkins in 1886 as the valedictorian of a class of eight. Perkins director Michael Anagnos wrote to Sullivan about a job opportunity as governess for a deaf-mute (a common term at the time), and blind young woman named Helen Keller.

Life's Work

Sullivan arrived at the Keller home in Tuscumbia, Alabama, in March, 1887, having spent the preceding weeks reading teaching accounts by Samuel Gridley Howe, the first director of Perkins, who had taught Bridgman. Sullivan was relieved to find that Keller, who was not quite seven years old, was a robust if unruly child rather than frail and seriously disabled as she had feared.

Sullivan soon realized that she needed to calm Keller's robustness without breaking her spirit, before she could begin meaningful attempts to teach her language skills. Keller's family, however, was accustomed to giving the child her way, so Sullivan persuaded Keller's father to let the pair work together in a garden cottage away from the main house. Her initial progress with Keller was slow, but just over a month later, a breakthrough was reached when Sullivan finger-spelled the word "water" into Keller's hand while water from a pump poured over the girl's fingers, a scene that was famously re-created in the stage play *The Miracle Worker* (1956) by William Gibson, which also was produced as a play for television (1957) and as a film (1962).

Once Keller understood that the words Sullivan communicated represented objects, she progressed quickly, and Sullivan was able to convey to Keller not only nouns but also verbs, adjectives, and even abstract concepts. Sullivan concluded that she was meant to devote her life to Keller, and she soon accompanied the girl first on a visit to the Perkins School in Boston, then two years at the Wright-Humason School for the Deaf in New York City, and eventually to Radcliffe College, from which Keller would graduate in 1904. During these years, Sullivan spent several eye-straining hours every

Anne Sullivan (right) and Helen Keller.

day either reading to Keller or helping her write her autobiography, *The Story of My Life*, which was published in 1903 with assistance from Harvard professor John Macy.

In 1904, Keller and Sullivan purchased a farmhouse in Wrentham, Massachusetts, thus formalizing their increasingly interdependent relationship. During this period, Macy courted Sullivan, but she initially rejected his proposal, believing that her relationship with Keller would hurt any marriage, and vice versa. In 1905, Macy finally persuaded Sullivan to marry him, but her prediction proved correct. He eventually left Sullivan in 1914 after several strained years and faded out of her life, although she always cared for him.

In the meantime, in 1913, Sullivan and Keller had begun a lecture tour throughout New England. Partly because of Sullivan's poor health, the pair engaged Polly Thomson in 1914 as a secretary to Keller, taking some of the burden from Sullivan, who had weak eyes. Public interest in Keller continued unabated. Although Keller tried to direct some of the attention toward her teacher, Sullivan felt she did not deserve any special acclaim. Nonetheless, in 1915, she and Keller were both awarded Teacher's Medals at the Panama-Pacific Exposition in San Francisco.

In 1918, the trio traveled again to California to film *Deliverance*, a movie about Keller's life that was critically received but not commercially successful. In 1920,

Sullivan and Keller went on the vaudeville circuit, making appearances in which Sullivan asked prepared questions and Keller answered with witty comments. Again, however, Sullivan's health suffered, and they were forced to give up the tour. After a period of rest, all three women accepted positions with the American Foundation for the Blind, for which they gave speeches and raised public awareness of blindness. Thomson and Sullivan also continued to help Keller write and edit books, interspersed with trips abroad to improve Sullivan's health. In 1932, Sullivan reluctantly accepted an honorary degree from Temple University, which had been trying to bestow the honor upon her for more than a year.

Sullivan's failing eyesight and other maladies greatly depressed her; even the publication of Nella Braddy Henney's biography *Anne Sullivan Macy* (1933) did little to cheer her. Because she now felt assured that Thomson was a dependable companion for Keller, she almost seemed to welcome death, but she lived another three years before passing away on October 20, 1936, in Forest Hills, New York, due to a heart-related condition. Shortly before her death she dictated farewell messages to Keller and Thomson and spoke of her desire to see again her beloved husband, who had died a few years earlier, and her long-deceased brother.

SIGNIFICANCE

Although Sullivan had difficulty accepting the value of her contributions to society, the fact remains that with little formal training, she both utilized and improved upon the teaching techniques of those who came before her. In addition, although she herself was shy, she selflessly provided the means by which Keller could bask in the public's attention, thus offering thousands of disabled Americans the chance to see a shining example of what they themselves might achieve.

As testament to the skills Sullivan provided Keller, and in tribute to her teacher, Keller wrote the biography *Teacher: Anne Sullivan Macy* (1955). Sullivan believed that any teacher could have achieved the same feats with Keller, but Sullivan's inherent abilities, which allowed Keller not only to naturally acquire language skills the same way other children did but also to determine the direction of her own education, were truly miraculous.

—*Amy Sisson*

FURTHER READING

Garrett, Leslie. *Helen Keller: A Photographic Story of a Life*. New York: DK, 2004. Although this juvenile biography focuses primarily on Keller, it does address Sullivan's early life and contains many photographs of the teacher as well as facsimile reproductions of announcements pertaining to Sullivan's and Keller's many public appearances.

Henney, Nella Braddy. *Anne Sullivan Macy: The Story Behind Helen Keller*. Garden City, N.Y.: Doubleday, Doran, 1933. Although somewhat difficult to locate, this book is considered the definitive biography of Sullivan. The author's close relationship with Sullivan and Keller allowed her to examine and analyze the dynamics of the pair's relationship.

Keller, Helen. *The Story of My Life*. New York: W. W. Norton, 2003. Newly edited and published on the hundredth anniversary of the original edition, this autobiography by Keller, which provides extensive insight on her relationship with her teacher, also contains "supplementary accounts" by Sullivan and by John Macy. Includes an extensive index and a list for further reading.

_____. *Teacher: Anne Sullivan Macy, a Tribute by the Foster-Child of Her Mind.* Garden City, N.Y.: Doubleday, 1955. The last of Keller's published books, this volume consists of Keller's perceptions of the woman she called Teacher for the almost fifty years they lived and worked together.

Lash, Joseph H. *Helen and Teacher: The Story of Helen Keller and Anne Sullivan Macy.* 1980. New ed. New York: Addison-Wesley, 1997. In addition to an exhaustive examination of Keller and Sullivan's relationship, this book also discusses the influences of John Macy and Polly Thomson on the pair's lives. Includes a chronology and extensive index.

IDA TARBELL

> *Sacredness of human life! The world has never believed it! . . . We have held that a death toll was a necessary part of every human achievement, whether sport, war or industry. A moment's rage over the horror of it, and we have sunk into indifference.*

Journalist

Tarbell became a prominent leader in American magazine journalism in a period when women were almost entirely absent from the field. She is especially known for her investigative series on the Standard Oil Company in 1902, a report considered the first great work of the muckrakers of journalism.

Born: November 5, 1857; Erie County, Pennsylvania
Died: January 6, 1944; Bridgeport, Connecticut
Also known as: Ida Minerva Tarbell (full name)
Areas of achievement: Journalism; social reform

EARLY LIFE

Ida Tarbell (TAHR-behl) was born on her grandfather's farm in western Pennsylvania four years before the Civil War began. Her father, Franklin Sumner Tarbell, had earlier struck out for Iowa and its richer farming prospects; he would not see his daughter until she was eighteen months old. Ida's mother, Esther McCullough Tarbell, was a descendant of Massachusetts pioneers and had taught school for more than a decade before her marriage. She would ultimately bear four children, of whom Ida was the eldest.

When Tarbell was three, her father moved the family to the Pennsylvania oil region to take advantage of financial opportunities there. After the Civil War, the family would follow the oil boom to several towns in western Pennsylvania, settling ultimately in Titusville when Tarbell was thirteen. While her father made an increasingly comfortable living building wooden oil tanks, Tarbell studied in the local schools and attended Methodist church services and revival meetings with her family. When the time came for her to continue her studies, her father naturally selected Allegheny College, the Methodist coeducational college in nearby Meadville.

For the next four years, Tarbell combined diligent study in biology and languages with social activities, class offices, literary magazine editing, and public speaking. She was romantically linked with at least one young man, but the relationship did not survive college, and Tarbell never married. After her graduation, she embarked on a short-lived career as a teacher at the Union Seminary in Poland, Ohio. A low salary and high expectations placed on her ability to teach all subjects led to her return to Titusville after two years.

The opportunity that led to Tarbell's career in journalism appeared a few months after her return. She was hired as an editor for the *Chautauquan*, a magazine published to promote adult education and home learning by the Chautauqua Literary and Scientific Circle. Although the editorial work she was assigned initially was stultifying, she gradually expanded her responsibilities to include translating, reviewing manuscripts, and writing her own articles. The workload at first was light, and the magazine was located in Meadville, which enabled her to complete a master of arts degree at Allegheny College.

When Tarbell left the *Chautauquan* in 1891, she sailed to France determined to immerse herself in Parisian culture, support herself by submitting articles to American newspapers, and write a biography of Madame Manon Philipon de Roland, a hero of the French Revolution. She did all of this and more. After reading some of her work, Samuel S. McClure, the publisher of *McClure's* magazine, personally visited her in Paris to offer her a job. In the fall of 1894, she accepted his offer, which included money for the passage home.

Life's Work

Tarbell's first work at the magazine was the surprising assignment of producing a series of articles on the life of Napoleon, whose hundred-year-old military exploits produced a flurry of activity in the popular press of the 1890's. She had not expected to do a work of that sort, and she was astonished to be asked, after returning from Paris, to undertake a biography of a French subject using the comparatively limited sources to be found in American libraries. Nevertheless, her labors at the Library of Congress resulted in a distinctive and popular *McClure's* series that was subsequently published as a book, as was the practice at the time.

The resources of the Library of Congress were excellent, as Tarbell discovered, and so were the human resources in the nation's capital. She remained in Washington, D.C., until 1899, during which time she met influential politicians and public servants. She wrote articles about them and ghost-wrote the memoirs of other famous men. Her major work during her Washington years was another *McClure's* assignment, a biography of Abraham Lincoln. She conducted interviews in Washington and Illinois and established a wide network of correspondents who provided her with information. Her study of Lincoln's early years was published in 1896, with a complete two-volume bi-

Tarbell, Ida

ography following in 1900, after its serialization in the magazine.

Called to the *McClure's* New York staff in 1899 as managing editor, Tarbell joined a talented group of writers and editors. Although McClure himself was seldom in the office, his partner, John Phillips, shrewdly managed the publisher's affairs. Among the writers McClure and Phillips published regularly were Ray Stannard Baker and William Allen White, both of whom were poised on the brink of fame as preeminent journalists of their time. Also on the staff then or shortly thereafter were Willa Cather, Finley Peter Dunne, and Lincoln Steffens. This group took the lead in a new journalistic enterprise—muckraking—and Tarbell's series on the Standard Oil Company was in the forefront of that type of work.

The series that would later be published in book form as *The History of the Standard Oil Company* was launched in the November, 1902, *McClure's* magazine. Tarbell had undertaken it in response to McClure's idea of detailing the rise of the trusts in the late nineteenth century; she had formulated the idea of tracing the history of one such enterprise and the great entrepreneur associated with it, John D. Rockefeller. Growing up in the oilfield districts had acquainted her with the industry and the geographic area in which the boom began. Her industrious methods of working and her indomitable spirit in researching her subject ensured a thorough product. If anyone in *McClure's* talented group of writers could master such a vast (and elusive) body of information, it was Tarbell.

The Standard Oil series established two things: The first was that Tarbell was a formidable author and one of the outstanding journalists of her time; the second was that muckraking (as the reform journalists' movement was labeled in 1906 by Theodore Roosevelt) was a responsible enterprise that could produce thorough and dispassionate analyses of problems. Because of the efforts of Tarbell and her cohorts, *McClure's* became the leading voice of protest among the popular magazines.

This preeminence was short-lived, however, and Tarbell became the leader of a staff revolt against the magazine in 1906. At the center of the controversy was the mercurial McClure. The publisher was famous for his ability to produce ideas for articles at a rapid-fire pace, but his erratic behavior in 1905 and 1906 seemed to Tarbell, Phillips, and others to threaten the magazine they had helped to build. They questioned his new, risky publishing ventures and wondered whether his commitment to reform had been undercut by his commitment to making money. Tarbell resigned from the magazine in April, 1906.

By June, the old *McClure's* group had formed a new venture. They founded the Phillips Publishing Company, raised money to purchase a failed magazine, and launched it in the fall as their own, *The American Magazine*. Tarbell remained a regular staffer and contributor until the group sold its interests in 1915, although she also submitted articles to other magazines. Her major series in *The American Magazine* covered diverse topics: the protective tariff, the American woman, and the "golden rule" in business.

The first series highlighted the author at her best. She explained the complexities of the tariff to the general public, clarified controversies, and produced a reasoned analysis that clearly explained the costs of high tariffs to working people. Her golden rule series, her last extended writing for *The American Magazine*, was a defense of scientific man-

Ida Tarbell.
(Library of Congress)

agement in industry, a work that demonstrated how efficiency could blend with humane treatment of labor. The third series—on the American woman—proved to be the most controversial and caused a rift between Tarbell and some of her suffragist friends.

Like many reformers during the early years of the twentieth century, Tarbell believed that the government, through protective legislation, could act in the general interest of laborers, women, and minorities. Revolutionary change in the social or political system was not necessary. She was never truly a feminist. She did not support the woman suffrage movement, since she believed that a woman's influence was best exerted in the home, not in areas that were traditionally male preserves. Thus, for working women, she favored legislation that would limit their hours to allow them more time in the home. Raised by a suffragist mother, and herself a dominant force in a traditionally male profession, Tarbell espoused an apparently contradictory philosophy relating to women and their roles in society.

After the sale of *The American Magazine* in 1915, Tarbell remained active as a freelance writer. She also traveled and lectured on topics about which she had written earlier. She worked briefly in Washington during World War I until she was sidetracked by a diagnosis of tuberculosis and by the subsequent treatment. She spent much time during her later years tending to family members, often at her farm in Connecticut,

Tarbell, Ida

which she had purchased in 1906 with her book earnings. Projects she completed in her sixties and seventies included biographies of steel magnate Elbert Gary and General Electric head Owen D. Young, a history of American business during the late nineteenth century, and her autobiography, *All in the Day's Work*. Her major magazine writings were series on the Florida land boom and on Italian dictator Benito Mussolini.

Tarbell's work progressed more slowly as she aged, but she kept at it doggedly. In her eighties, she used her own declining health as the subject of a work she never completed, *Life After Eighty*. Old age, Parkinson's disease (diagnosed about two decades earlier), and pneumonia brought about Tarbell's death in early January of 1944. At her request, she was buried in Titusville.

Significance

Tarbell exerted both a specific and a general influence on her times. The specific influence related to Standard Oil, whose illegal operations she documented as thoroughly as if she were preparing a legal brief. Legal action, in fact, was the result. When the attorney general filed a 1906 case against Standard Oil for violation of the Sherman Antitrust Act, the charges were essentially those that Tarbell had made and documented in her book. The case was heard and appealed; when the U.S. Supreme Court made its ruling in 1911, it ordered the dissolution of the giant corporation.

Tarbell's general influence concerned the status of women in public life. Although she, ironically, did not participate in feminist or suffragist activities, her whole career exemplified what activist women attempted to achieve—the opportunity for women to enter the professions.

—*Richard G. Frederick*

Further Reading

Brady, Kathleen. *Ida Tarbell: Portrait of a Muckraker*. New York: Seaview/Putnam, 1984. The most thorough treatment of the contradictions in Tarbell's writings and of the contrast between her own achievements and her views on women and public life.

Conn, Frances G. *Ida Tarbell, Muckraker*. New York: Thomas Nelson, 1972. Written especially for juveniles, the book is anecdotal but informative. There is no systematic discussion of Tarbell's works, but there are numerous quotations from her writings.

Lyon, Peter. *Success Story: The Life and Times of S. S. McClure*. New York: Charles Scribner's Sons, 1963. Discusses Tarbell's writings in the context of the magazine muckraking movement generally considered to have begun in *McClure's* magazine. Examines the complex relationship between Tarbell and McClure.

Tarbell, Ida M. *All in the Day's Work: An Autobiography*. New York: Macmillan, 1939. An unassuming autobiography made rather bland by the author's saccharine approach to describing the controversies in which she was involved.

_____. *The History of the Standard Oil Company*. 2 vols. New York: Macmillan, 1904. Tarbell's magnum opus was not only the first great work of the muckrakers but also a solid history of the development of the oil industry in the United States. It is the main work on which her literary reputation rests.

Tomkins, Mary E. *Ida M. Tarbell*. New York: Twayne, 1974. This book in Twayne's United States Authors series mainly considers Tarbell's writings and evaluates her contributions to literature.

Treckel, Paula A. "Lady Muckraker." *American History* 61, no. 2 (June, 2001): 38. A tribute to Tarbell, focusing on her investigation of Standard Oil.

ZACHARY TAYLOR

❝ *I have no private purpose to accomplish, no party objectives to build up, no enemies to punish—nothing to serve but my country.* ❞

President of the United States (1849-1950)

After climaxing a nearly forty-year military career with major victories in the Mexican War, Taylor used his popularity as a war hero to win office as twelfth president of the United States but served only a little more than one year before he died.

Born: November 24, 1784; Orange County, Virginia
Died: July 9, 1850; Washington, D.C.
Also known as: Old Rough and Ready
Areas of achievement: Government and politics; military

EARLY LIFE

Born at a kinsman's Virginia country home, Zachary Taylor (ZA-kah-ree TAY-luhr) was the third of eight children of Richard and Sarah Dabney Strother Taylor, both members of prominent Virginia families. His father had been a lieutenant colonel in a Virginia regiment during the American Revolution; his paternal grandfather, also named Zachary Taylor, was a wealthy planter and surveyor general of Virginia.

During 1769 and 1770, Richard Taylor surveyed land in central Kentucky and around the Falls of the Ohio at the modern city of Louisville. In the spring of 1785, shortly after Zachary's birth, Richard Taylor moved his family to Jefferson County, Kentucky, where he carved out a farm known as Springfield, near Louisville. As a youth, Zachary studied under Kean O'Hara, who would become one of Kentucky's leading early nineteenth century educators, and Elisha Ayer, an itinerant Connecticut teacher. He also assisted his father with farmwork.

In 1806, possessing a youthful passion for a military career, Taylor got a brief taste of army life as a volunteer in the Kentuckian militia. His long career as an officer did not commence until June, 1808, however, when he received a commission as first lieutenant in the United States Army from Secretary of War Henry Dearborn. Appointed to the Seventh Infantry Regiment, he spent several months on recruiting duty in Kentucky, followed by temporary command of Fort Pickering, near modern Memphis, Tennessee, before reporting to General James Wilkinson at New Orleans in June,

Taylor, Zachary

1809. A short time later, he contracted yellow fever and returned to Louisville to recover. While at home, he met Margaret Mackall Smith, whom he married on June 21, 1810. They had six children, four of whom lived to maturity. Their daughter Sarah Knox Taylor was the first wife of Confederate president Jefferson Davis. Richard Taylor, their only son, became a lieutenant general in the Confederate army.

After his recovery and marriage, Taylor was promoted to captain and assigned to General William Henry Harrison, territorial governor of Indiana. In April, 1812, just before the War of 1812, Captain Taylor assumed command of Fort Harrison, near Terre Haute, which he successfully defended against an attack by some four hundred Indians the following September. Promoted to the rank of brevet major, he commanded several frontier posts during the second war with England.

In early 1815, Taylor won promotion to the full rank of major, but when the army was disbanded, he was reduced to his prewar rank of captain. Deciding to pursue private business, he declined reassignment, resigned his commission, and returned to his family's Kentucky farm.

Now thirty years old, Taylor epitomized neither the country gentleman nor the military hero. Five feet, eight inches in height, he was muscular and broad-shouldered with disproportionately long arms. He had a full-shaped head with an oval face; a wide, somewhat slanting brow; and prominent cheekbones. His long nose and hazel eyes gave him an eaglelike appearance.

LIFE'S WORK

Zachary Taylor was devoted to the soil, but his passion for military service was even stronger. Thus, in 1816, when President James Madison offered to reinstate him at his previous rank of major, Taylor accepted. His initial assignment was command of Fort Howard, near Green Bay, Wisconsin, where he remained for two years. After a furlough in Kentucky, he received a promotion to lieutenant colonel in 1819 and was assigned to the Fourth Infantry at New Orleans. A series of commands and special assignments followed over the next twelve years.

In 1822, Taylor built Fort Jesup, Louisiana, and the following year he served as commandant of Baton Rouge. In 1824, he was appointed superintendent general of the recruiting service at Cincinnati and Louisville and served until 1826, when he reported to Washington, D.C., to serve on a board chaired by General Winfield Scott to study militia organization. In May, 1828, Taylor assumed command of Fort Snelling, in the unorganized Minnesota Territory. Fourteen months later, he took command of Fort Crawford at Prairie du Chien in the Michigan Territory, now part of Wisconsin. There he remained until mid-1830.

In April, 1832, Taylor was promoted to colonel. Meanwhile, the Black Hawk War had erupted in Illinois. Colonel Taylor, on leave in Kentucky after recovering from an illness, sped to Galena, Illinois, and in May took charge of the First Infantry Regiment, under command of General Henry Atkinson. Three months later, Taylor participated in the decisive Battle of Bad Axe on the Mississippi River, north of Prairie du Chien. Black Hawk escaped the battlefield but was captured in late August. Taylor received custody of the defeated war chief and turned him over to Second Lieutenant Jefferson Davis, who escorted Black Hawk to Jefferson Barracks, Missouri.

Taylor, Zachary

With the end of the Black Hawk War, Taylor resumed command of Fort Crawford, where he remained until November, 1836. During this duty, he demonstrated a strong interest in the education of both white and Indian children and attempted to control the harsh practices of whiskey merchants and fur traders in their dealings with the tribes in the region. Upon relinquishing his command at Fort Crawford, the colonel reported to Jefferson Barracks and took charge of the right wing of the army's Western Department under General Edmund P. Gaines. In this capacity, Taylor exercised military authority over the entire Northwest.

Taylor's new command lasted less than eight months. In July, 1837, Taylor received instructions to take elements of the First Infantry from Forts Snelling and Crawford to Tampa Bay, Florida, where General Thomas S. Jesup was bogged down in the Second Seminole War. While the colonel was en route, Jesup violated a temporary truce and captured Seminole leader Osceola and about two hundred of his followers—but hundreds more waited deep in the Everglades.

Taylor and his troops arrived in Florida in the fall, and the colonel took command in the field. In early December, 1837, after weeks of preparation, Taylor left Fort Gardiner with a force of more than one thousand regular and volunteer troops. Pursuing the Seminoles into the vicinity of Lake Okeechobee, Taylor made contact with a large force on Christmas Day. In a fierce battle that cost the lives of several of his top officers, Taylor routed the Seminoles and drove them from the field. The victory won for Taylor a promotion to brevet brigadier general, and a short time later he replaced General Jesup as commander of the Florida theater.

General Taylor remained in Florida for two more years before assuming command at Baton Rouge. The following year, Taylor succeeded General Matthew Arbuckle as commander of the Second Department, Western Division, headquartered at Fort Smith, Arkansas. There, he remained until May, 1844, when he returned to Fort Jesup to assume command of the First Department. In June, 1845, after the United States annexed Texas, he received orders to move his troops to Corpus Christi, on the Nueces River, to protect the new state in case of attack by Mexico. The following January, President James K. Polk ordered Taylor to move to the Rio Grande, occupying territory whose possession was a source of dispute. In late March, Taylor established a position opposite the Mexican town of Matamoros. A month later, several American soldiers were killed in a skirmish with Mexican troops. On May 13, 1846, Congress declared war on Mexico.

Taylor, however, did not wait for the declaration of war. On May 8, he engaged and defeated a much larger Mexican force at Palo Alto. The next day, he defeated the Mexicans again at Resaca de la Palma. As a result, Polk promoted him to major general and gave him command of the Army of the Rio Grande. More victories followed as he captured Monterrey in September and crushed a force under General Antonio Lopez de Santa Anna at Buena Vista in February, 1847.

With the end of the Mexican War, Taylor returned to the United States, receiving a hero's welcome at New Orleans in December, 1847. A short time later, he retired to his home in Baton Rouge and began tending to the affairs of Cypress Grove, the Mississippi plantation he had acquired a few years earlier. His retirement was brief. In 1848, the Whig Party, starved for victory, nominated the military hero for president and secured his election over Democrat Lewis Cass and Free-Soiler Martin Van Buren.

Although a slaveholder, President Taylor was a staunch Unionist. Faced with the volatile issue of slavery in the territories acquired from Mexico, he supported California's admission as a free state in 1849 and the organization of New Mexico and Utah without consideration of the slavery issue. When Congress convened in January, 1850, Senator Henry Clay proposed a series of compromise resolutions designed to defuse these and related issues, including a Texas-New Mexico border dispute, the fugitive slave question, and the future of the slave trade in Washington, D.C.

While Congress debated the Compromise of 1850, delegates from nine southern states met in Nashville in June to consider the defense of southern rights and their section's future within the Union. Moderate voices prevailed, but more radical "Fire-eaters" raised the specter of secession. Taylor, however, continued to resist any compromise that would promote the expansion of slavery and promised to meet disunionist threats with force.

The political deadlock remained on July 4, when Taylor attended a ceremony related to construction of the Washington Monument. He became overheated and, according to tradition, tried to cool off by consuming large quantities of cherries and iced milk. During that same evening he contracted gastroenteritis, from which he died on July 9.

Significance

In many respects, Zachary Taylor symbolized both the aspirations and the anxieties of the American people during the mid-nineteenth century. In a period pervaded by the spirit of Manifest Destiny, his victories in the Mexican War contributed to the nation's acquisition of a vast new territory, including the future states of California, New Mexico, Arizona, Nevada, and Utah. Only four days before his death, President Taylor signed the Clayton-Bulwer Treaty with England, the first diplomatic step toward construction of the Panama Canal.

As president, however, the victor of Buena Vista had to deal with the practical consequences of Manifest Destiny. As both a Unionist and a plantation owner with more than one hundred slaves, he embodied the conflicting social and economic forces that confronted the nation during the decade before the Civil War, especially citizens of the border states and Upper South. In Taylor's case, Unionist sentiments formed during four decades in the nation's military service triumphed over his own economic interests. During the decade that followed his death, however, a growing number of his fellow southerners resolved the conflict between slavery and Union in the opposite direction. When the election of Abraham Lincoln as president in 1860 convinced many southerners that they no longer could protect their "peculiar institution" within the Union, they chose secession. They elected as their president Zachary Taylor's friend and former son-in-law, Jefferson Davis.

—*Carl E. Kramer*

Further Reading

Bauer, K. Jack. *Zachary Taylor: Soldier, Planter, Statesman of the Old Southwest*. Baton Rouge: Louisiana State University Press, 1985. This well-researched, well-written volume is the first account of Taylor's life to appear since 1951. Particularly useful for the general reader, Bauer's work gives a balanced view of Taylor's early life, military career, and brief presidency.

DeVoto, Bernard A. *The Year of Decision, 1846*. Boston: Little, Brown, 1943. Taylor fares poorly in this spectacular, almost theatrical saga of America's westward march. From the Mexican War to the Mormon immigration to Utah, DeVoto captures the profound national emotions that undergirded Manifest Destiny.

Hamilton, Holman. *Zachary Taylor: Soldier of the Republic*. Indianapolis, Ind.: Bobbs-Merrill, 1941. Volume 1 of Hamilton's magisterial biography, this remains the best single book on Taylor's early life and military career. Thoroughly researched and highly readable, it is sympathetic yet balanced, especially in regard to Taylor's dealings with his military and political rivals.

———. *Zachary Taylor: Soldier in the White House*. Indianapolis, Ind.: Bobbs-Merrill, 1951. A worthy companion to the preceding volume, this book explores the brief but important tenure of the nation's last slaveholding president. Thoroughly researched, it demonstrates that Taylor was a much more active president than is commonly believed.

Potter, David M. *The Impending Crisis, 1848-1861*. Completed and edited by Don E. Fehrenbacher. New York: Harper and Row, 1976. Taylor is one of the many important figures who appears in this excellent narrative of the political events leading from the Mexican War to the outbreak of the Civil War. An outstanding contextual volume, it synthesizes the vast literature dealing with the complex issues of slavery, expansionism, and sectional politics.

Singletary, Otis A. *The Mexican War*. Chicago: University of Chicago Press, 1960. This concise treatment of the war that climaxed American continental expansion is both historically sound and quite readable. Its emphasis is on military events and political intrigues at the expense of diplomatic relations between the United States and Mexico.

Smith, Elbert B. *The Presidencies of Zachary Taylor and Millard Fillmore*. Lawrence: University Press of Kansas, 1988. Smith maintains that Taylor and Fillmore are misrepresented and underrated presidents who acted responsibly by supporting the Compromise of 1850.

Weinberg, Albert K. *Manifest Destiny: A Study of Nationalist Expansionism in American History*. Baltimore: Johns Hopkins University Press, 1935. Zachary Taylor's name does not appear in this analytical study of American expansion from the Louisiana Purchase to the Spanish-American War, but the book is essential to understanding the policy motives behind the military ventures in which he participated.

Winders, Richard Bruce. *Mr. Polk's Army: The American Military Experience in the Mexican War*. College Station: Texas A&M University Press, 1997. Using diaries, journals, and reminiscences, Winders recounts the daily life of soldiers who fought the war, analyzing the cultural, social, and political aspects of the Army. He also contrasts the leadership styles of Generals Taylor and Winfield Scott.

TECUMSEH

" *A single twig breaks, but the bundle of twigs is strong.* **"**

Native American leader

Leading Indians of the Old Northwest in a united defense against the intrusion of white settlers, Tecumseh contributed significantly to the development of pan-Indianism in American history.

Born: March, 1768; Old Piqua, western Ohio
Died: October 5, 1813; Thames River, southeastern Canada
Area of achievement: Native American affairs

EARLY LIFE

Born in a Shawnee village in what is now western Ohio, Tecumseh (teh-KUHM-zeh) was the son of a Creek Indian woman. Her Shawnee husband, Puckeshinwa, had met her earlier, while staying with Creek Indians in Alabama. When Tecumseh was still a very young boy, Virginians began pushing into Kentucky onto lands used extensively for hunting by the Shawnee. The Indians resisted, and in 1774, Virginia governor Lord John Dunmore led troops into the area. Puckeshinwa died in one of the subsequent battles, leaving support of his family in the hands of relatives and in those of a war chief named Blackfish from a nearby village.

During the American Revolution, the Shawnee again went to war against whites. In 1779, local Kentuckians wrongly accused several Shawnee, including a popular leader known as Cornstalk, of some recent killings and senselessly killed them. The intense fighting that followed eventually led about a thousand members of the tribe to move for a time to southeastern Missouri. Methoataske was one of the migrants, but Tecumseh and his seven brothers and sisters did not accompany their mother. Instead, other family members took the children. Tecumseh moved in with his sister Tecumpease and her husband and eventually developed a close relationship with his older sibling.

The muscular young Tecumseh also became popular among his peers, distinguishing himself in games and in shooting skills. At the age of fifteen, Tecumseh experienced his first battle. American pioneers again started flooding onto Shawnee lands near the end of the revolution, many of them crossing the Appalachian Mountains and then descending the Ohio River in flatboats. In 1783, the young warrior accompanied his brother Chiksika on a war party in an effort to stop the flatboat traffic.

After winning independence, Americans considered themselves the owners of lands formerly claimed by Great Britain, including the Old Northwest (the area bordered by the Appalachian Mountains on the east, the Mississippi River on the west, the Ohio River on the south, and Canada on the north, comprising the modern states of Ohio, Indiana, Illinois, Wisconsin, and Michigan). Kentuckians attacked Shawnee villages in 1786 after blaming that group for raids actually launched by the Mingoes and Cherokee in opposition to settlement west of the Appalachians. The Shawnee hit back, with Tecumseh frequently taking part in the fighting. In 1787, he joined a war party led by his brother that went south and helped Cherokee attack settlements in Tennessee and southern Kentucky. Chiksika was killed in the action. The death of his brother greatly intensified Tecumseh's hatred for the expansionistic whites, and he stayed in the area for the next two years, seeking vengeance.

With Chiksika no longer in a position of leadership, Tecumseh was able to assert himself. Five feet, ten inches tall, with a powerful physical presence and a dynamic speaking ability, he quickly gained a large following, especially among the younger, more antiwhite members of his tribe. By the time the group of Shawnee warriors returned to the Old Northwest in 1790, Tecumseh had emerged as a popular war chief. In addition to his outstanding skills in warfare, however, he also gained a reputation for being kind and good-humored. He frequently demonstrated compassion for those who were weakest or least privileged and an aversion to the torture or murder of prisoners. These qualities made him exceptional at a time when indiscriminate brutality was common on both sides in frontier warfare.

Life's Work

Upon his return to the Old Northwest, Tecumseh found his antiwhite sentiments increasingly in tune with those of many Indians in the region. Settlers had been pouring into the southeastern Ohio River valley, and the frontier again erupted into violence. During the early 1790's, the U.S. government sent armies in on two occasions in attempts to counter Indian resistance, but in both cases, tribes united to hand the whites embarrassing defeats. Together with the prodding of the British to the north in Canada, these victories encouraged tribes to join in a common political front to negotiate a permanent Indian state in the Old Northwest. Differences among the groups, however, prevented success in the effort. The United States then tried a third time for a military solution, sending an army under Major General Anthony Wayne. This time the results were different, with the Americans claiming victory in the 1794 Battle of Fallen Timbers. The next year, some of the defeated Indians signed the Treaty of Greenville, giving up more than two-thirds of what became Ohio.

Tecumseh fought well in the last two of the three famous battles for control of the Old Northwest and thus added to his growing reputation. He refused to accept the outcome of the Treaty of Greenville, however, and soon was recognized as the dominant leader of those Indians who resolved to put an end to any further white incursions into the region. Over the next decade, Tecumseh and his followers traveled and lived throughout Ohio and Indiana.

In 1805, one of Tecumseh's brothers, who had failed at nearly everything he had attempted, claimed to have died, to have been taken to the Master of Life, and to have been appointed to lead his people to salvation. He renounced liquor and launched a fundamentalist spiritual movement that encouraged Indians to reject white influence and return to traditional values. He promised believers that the happier times of the past would be restored. He was known as Tenskwatawa, or the Prophet, and after Tecumseh's conversion to the new faith, the two brothers moved first to Greenville in western Ohio and eventually to Tippecanoe Creek in Indiana. There, in a village that would be named Prophet's Town, Indians from throughout the Old Northwest came to live and join the movement, including Wyandot, Kickapoo, Potawatomi, Miami, Wea, and Delaware.

Tecumseh

American officials such as William Henry Harrison, the governor of the Indiana Territory, watched events with apprehension. Harrison was well known for making treaties with individual tribes and winning much land for the government at low prices and through means that were not always ethical. In fact, his practices had deepened the antiwhite attitudes of many younger Indians who resented the loss of homelands and led them to join the Prophet's movement. Then, in 1809, Harrison gathered chiefs friendly to the government and persuaded them to cede more than three million acres of land in the Treaty of Fort Wayne. This event quickly elevated the status and position of Tecumseh, who had been developing a position that rejected the legitimacy of recent controversial treaties. Land was commonly owned by all tribes, according to the Shawnee war chief, and could not be sold individually.

Tecumseh traveled throughout the Old Northwest and even into the South, trying to win support for a political and military confederacy that would join many tribes under his leadership to stop white expansion. Then, just as Tecumseh was experiencing some success, Governor Harrison took advantage of his absence from Prophet's Town and in November of 1811 marched an army to within two miles of the Indian village. Tenskwatawa had been left in charge and decided to take the initiative and attack first. The subsequent Battle of Tippecanoe was not a dramatic Indian defeat, but the defenders withdrew and allowed the whites to destroy Prophet's Town.

Eventually, Tecumseh returned home, broke with his brother in anger over the way he had handled the situation, and struggled to put his broken movement back together. The coordinated attack that Tecumseh had hoped would stop the onrush of settlers became a series of random raids across the frontier. Many Americans blamed the British for the violence because they supplied the Indians with arms. This became one of several events that contributed to the outbreak of the War of 1812 against Great Britain. Tecumseh and many of his followers joined the British because the former mother country had tried several times to control American expansion and thus offered Indians the best hope for retaining their homelands. Tecumseh fought in a number of battles and was eventually killed in Canada on October 5, 1813, at the Battle of the Thames.

SIGNIFICANCE
In the last half of the eighteenth century, white expansion undermined the livelihood and lifestyle of Indians in the Old Northwest. Settlers destroyed game, treaties (many of them fraudulent or at least questionable) eroded the Indian land base, and alcohol disrupted social arrangements. Tribes grew dependent on European trade goods and eventually were used as pawns in the rivalries between the European superpowers over dominance in North America. The result was an almost constant state of war. This, in turn, elevated the importance of war chiefs among groups such as the Shawnee, who traditionally had separate political leadership for war and for peace.

As a war chief, Tecumseh emerged into a position of leadership in this environment. The movement that he would lead started as a primarily spiritual one under his brother, the Prophet. Tecumseh secularized and politicized the movement as Indians, under intense pressure to give up their lands, were increasingly attracted to his vision for stemming the tide of white advance. He encouraged Native American groups to forget their traditional hostilities toward one another and join in a common military and political effort.

Tecumseh's position has been called Indian nationalism, or pan-Indianism, and has been one of the most significant developments in the long term of Indian history. Identification on the basis of being Indian with less emphasis on tribal divisions remains a strong force in Native American affairs during the late twentieth century. Other Indian leaders before Tecumseh had attempted intertribal alliances but on more limited scales and without much success. Even though Tecumseh was a brilliant strategist, his movement ultimately failed in its immediate objectives as well. However, he undoubtedly contributed as much toward the evolution of pan-Indianism as any other single historical figure.

Tecumseh has enjoyed more admiration and respect, even among his contemporary foes, than any other Native American leader. As a result, he has attained an unparalleled status in legend and mythology. Evidence of this can be seen not only in the many biographies written about him but also in the many spurious or exaggerated stories about his life that have gained popularity and fooled even some of the best historians who have written about him.

—*Larry W. Burt*

FURTHER READING

Antal, Sandy. *A Wampum Denied: Procter's War of 1812*. East Lansing: Michigan State University Press, 1997. Chronicles the battle on the Detroit frontier, led by British commander Henry Procter, during the War of 1812. Details Tecumseh's role in assisting the British.

Edmunds, R. David. *The Shawnee Prophet*. Lincoln: University of Nebraska Press, 1983. Focuses on Tenskwatawa but contains much information on Tecumseh. Demonstrates how the stories of the two famous brothers are intertwined and have to be considered together and also describes the social and political milieu in which their movement thrived.

_____. *Tecumseh and the Quest for Indian Leadership*. Boston: Little, Brown, 1984. One of best complete biographies of Tecumseh. Scholarly yet relatively brief and very readable. It is also one of the most balanced accounts, discussing in a concluding chapter many of the myths surrounding the Shawnee leader's life to which other historians have fallen victim.

Josephy, Alvin M., Jr. "Tecumseh, the Greatest Indian." In *The Patriot Chiefs*. New York: Penguin Books, 1961. Reliable and well written, this stands as the best short summary of Tecumseh and his importance in history, although the author presents a slightly more romanticized version of the leader's life than most of the good later scholarship.

Klinck, Carl F., ed. *Tecumseh: Fact and Fiction in Early Records*. Englewood Cliffs, N.J.: Prentice-Hall, 1961. This useful anthology presents a variety of perspectives on Tecumseh's significance and on some of the controversies about his life through selections of both primary and secondary resource materials.

Sugden, John. *Tecumseh: A Life*. New York: Henry Holt, 1998. Definitive biography of Tecumseh, placing his life within the context of Shawnee and general Native

American history. Sugden details Tecumseh's failed attempts to create a pan-Indian resistance movement.

_____. *Tecumseh's Last Stand*. Norman: University of Oklahoma Press, 1985. A very good treatment of a narrow range of Tecumseh's life. It begins in the summer of 1813 and discusses in great detail his role in the War of 1812. It also deals with some of the later controversies, such as who actually killed Tecumseh and where he was buried.

Tucker, Glenn. *Tecumseh: Vision of Glory*. Indianapolis, Ind.: Bobbs-Merrill, 1956. A long and basically reliable biography, but it stands as perhaps the best example of the common tendency to overromanticize Tecumseh and accept too many of the questionable myths that shroud his life.

NORMAN THOMAS

> *If you want a symbolic gesture, don't burn the flag; wash it.*

Political reformer

Often called "the conscience of America," Thomas ran six times for president on the Socialist Party ticket and became one of the greatest critic-reformers of politics in the United States.

Born: November 20, 1884; Marion, Ohio
Died: December 19, 1968; Huntington, New York
Also known as: Norman Mattoon Thomas (full name)
Areas of achievement: Government and politics; social reform

EARLY LIFE

Norman Thomas was born in Marion, Ohio, the home of U.S. president Warren G. Harding, where he earned pocket money by delivering the *Marion Star*. He was the eldest of six children of the Reverend Welling Thomas, a Presbyterian minister whose father, also a Presbyterian minister, had been born in Wales. Norman's mother, Emma Mattoon, was also the child of a Presbyterian clergyman. The Thomas household was Republican in politics, devout in religion, and conservative in conduct, opposed to dancing, cardplaying, and Sunday merrymaking. Emma Thomas was acknowledged by the family as its dominant force, emphasizing a keen sense of personal and social responsibility that her firstborn practiced all of his life.

After his 1905 graduation from Princeton University as valedictorian of his class, Thomas took his first full-time job as a social worker at New York City's Spring Street Presbyterian Church and Settlement House, located in a poverty-stricken area. In 1907, he became assistant to the pastor of Christ Church in Manhattan. There he met Frances Violet Stewart, active in Christian social service and born into a moderately wealthy family of financiers. They were married September 1, 1910, and led a notably happy marital life, in their turn having six children and fifteen grandchildren.

From 1910 to 1911, Thomas attended the heterodox Union Theological Seminary. There he was most impressed by the writings of Walter Rauschenbusch, one of the leading figures of the Social Gospel movement, who argued that the ethical precepts of Jesus did not harmonize with the selfish materialism of a capitalist society. Thirty years later, Thomas wrote, "Insofar as any one man . . . made me a Socialist, it was probably Walter Rauschenbusch." Ordained in 1911, Thomas became pastor of the East Harlem Presbyterian Church and chair of the American Parish, a federation of Presbyterian churches and social agencies located in immigrant neighborhoods. In 1912, he declared, "The Christian Church faces no more burning question than the problem of making brotherhood real."

Life's Work

The agonies of World War I crystallized Thomas's social radicalism. He came to consider the war an immoral conflict between competing imperial powers, and in January, 1917, he joined the Fellowship of Reconciliation, a religious pacifist group with a commitment to drastic social reform. Thomas came to regard resistance to the war as a clear choice of individual conscience over the dictates of an amoral state. His militant pacifism led him to support Morris Hillquit, the socialist candidate, who ran on an antiwar platform in the 1917 New York City mayoral race.

Thomas joined another pacifist, Roger Baldwin, in the 1917 establishment of the Civil Liberties Union, later renamed the American Civil Liberties Union. In the spring of 1918, he resigned from his church and the parish, aware that his radicalism was jeopardizing these institutions' chances for outside financial assistance. In October, 1918, he applied for membership in the American Socialist Party; he was motivated, he recalled later, by "grotesque inequalities, conspicuous waste, gross exploitation, and unnecessary poverty all around me."

The party was led by three talented people: Victor Berger, Morris Hillquit, and Eugene V. Debs. The first two were its theoreticians and tacticians, but it was the populist, pragmatic Debs (1855-1926) who became American socialism's greatest leader until Thomas's ascendancy. Debs grounded his convictions on emotional rather than philosophic premises: He had an evangelical devotion to social justice, a generous and sensitive temperament, sincerity, warmth, and an intuitive understanding of popular opinion.

In the 1920 election, Debs received 920,000 votes, but they were largely a tribute to his courage for having chosen imprisonment (from 1918 to 1921) to dramatize his pacifism; membership in the Socialist Party was down that year, from a 1912 peak of 108,000 to 27,000. During the 1920's several conditions combined to keep the American Socialist Party's numbers and influence low: a dominant mood among the electorate of economic conservatism and intense nativism; hostility to organized labor by all three branches of government; a number of failed strikes; and the 1919-1920 Red Scare mass arrests of radicals and labor leaders by the Department of Justice under Attorney General A. Mitchell Palmer. When Senator Robert M. La Follette campaigned for the presidency in 1924, he refused to run solely as the socialist candidate, preferring to call himself a Progressive. Nevertheless, the Socialist Party energetically supported his campaign; 855,000 of La Follette's 3,800,000 votes were cast on socialist levers.

Thomas began his long career of seeking public office in 1924, running as a New York gubernatorial candidate on both the socialist and Progressive tickets. Ironically, he had risen to socialist leadership at a time when many people were leaving the party. More ironically, the income his wife inherited from her conservative father enabled him to crusade for his causes on a full-time basis. He admitted that, in this instance, "the critic of capitalism was its beneficiary."

By the mid-1920's, Thomas was the consensual choice to succeed Debs—who had never regained his health after his three-year imprisonment and who died in 1926—as the leader of American Socialism. In 1928, he was chosen the party's presidential candidate—the first of six such nominations; he received 267,000 votes. In 1932, he was to poll 885,000; in 1936, 187,000; in 1940, 100,000; in 1944, 80,000; in 1948, 140,000.

Thomas attracted the deep affection and admiration of many people, often including ideological opponents. His physical appearance was impressive: He stood over six feet two inches tall, had strongly marked patrician features, vibrant blue eyes, good manners, and an air of genteel self-confidence. Although a man of dignity, he could communicate warmth and cordiality to a wide range of people. His physical energy was phenomenal until his late seventies, when failing eyesight and disabling arthritis began to plague him. Since he had no hobbies, he focused his unflagging pace not only on campaigning but also on writing sixteen books and scores of pamphlets, maintaining an enormous correspondence, attending countless conventions and committee meetings, and delivering thousands of speeches. Perhaps his only flaw as a leader was his remoteness—in contrast to Debs—from the rough-and-tumble realities of the American political panorama. When it came to conflicting interests, he was by temperament an educator, moralist, and intellectual rather than an accommodating pragmatist. Since he had no solid prospect of winning public office, he could afford to maintain an incorruptible integrity and the noblest of principles.

Thomas's virtuosity as a public speaker was his outstanding leadership asset. He was a masterful humorist, firing quick barbs at his targets. In 1932 he asked his listeners not to fix on Herbert Hoover as the person solely responsible for their economic suffering, since "such a little man could not have made so big a Depression." As for Harry S. Truman, he "proves the old adage that any man can become President of the United States." Perhaps the best-known Thomas anecdote recounts a meeting he had with President Franklin D. Roosevelt in 1935. When Thomas complained to Roosevelt about a particular New Deal measure, the president retorted, "Norman, I'm a damn sight better politician than you." Responded Thomas, "Certainly, Mr. President, you're on that side of the desk and I'm on this."

In 1932, with the country deeply mired in the Great Depression and capitalism seriously shaken, the Socialist Party hoped for a presidential vote of more than two million. The socialist platform anticipated New Deal programs on many issues, demanding federal appropriations for public works, reforestation, and slum clearance, increased public housing, a six-hour day and five-day working week, old-age pensions, health and maternity insurance, improved workmen's compensation and accident insurance, adequate minimum-wage laws, and a compulsory system of unemployment compensation with adequate benefits derived from both government and employer contributions.

Contrary to socialist expectations, the combined popular vote for all minority party candidates in 1932 barely exceeded one million, and Roosevelt embarked on an ambitious program to save capitalism by implementing a vast amount of social welfare legislation. Thomas consistently chided the New Deal for what he regarded as its lack of any consistent underlying philosophy, for its opportunistic, helter-skelter improvisation and experimentation. This very pragmatism and daring, however, endeared Roosevelt to the majority of the electorate—much to Thomas's frustration. In his *The Politics of Upheaval* (1979), the historian Arthur Schlesinger, Jr., considers that in the 1930's Thomas's "essential contribution . . . was to keep moral issues alive at a moment when the central emphasis was on meeting economic emergencies. At his best, Thomas gave moving expression to an ethical urgency badly needed in politics. . . ."

The 1930's witnessed an increasingly dangerous world situation, with Adolf Hitler's Germany, Benito Mussolini's Italy, and, late in the decade, Francisco Franco's

Norman Thomas.
(Library of Congress)

Spain threatening the peace. Under the guise of opposing fascism, communists in both Europe and the United States wooed liberals and radicals to form a united, "popular front." Thomas temporarily flirted with the notion of such international solidarity in his 1934 book, *The Choice Before Us*. A 1937 trip he took to Europe, however, during which he witnessed communist attempts to control Spain's Loyalist government through shabby betrayals and observed Stalin's purge trials of his former comrades, reaffirmed Thomas's mistrust of totalitarian communism and his conviction of its basic incompatibility with democratic socialism. The Moscow-Berlin Pact of August, 1939, outraged him as "a piece of infamy." Thomas made certain that, from 1939 on, the United States Socialist Party would vigorously oppose communism, even when the Soviet Union was America's ally during World War II.

In the late 1930's and early 1940's, Thomas's lifelong pacifist sentiments were in agonizing conflict with his detestation of fascism and strong sympathy for the Spanish Republicans locked in civil warfare with Franco's Falangists. Thomas tried to solve this dilemma by backing aid for the Spanish government while opposing direct United States intervention on behalf of Great Britain and France after World War II had erupted in September, 1939. By late 1941, the Socialist Party's noninterventionist foreign policy, combined with Thomas's often acerbic criticism of the New Deal's socioeconomic program, had alienated many former members and well-wishers. Even though the party fielded presidential tickets through 1956, it was never to recover its health from these losses. By the 1944 presidential campaign, Thomas's insistence on maintaining the fullest measure of civil liberties even amid a world war, and his opposition to the Allied demand on Germany and Japan for unconditional surrender had cost him much of his previous popularity: His vote total proved the lowest of his six national appeals.

In the 1948 presidential election, Thomas's main target was former vice president Henry Wallace, who had left the Democratic Party to run as an antimilitarist, radical candidate for president on the Progressive ticket. Thomas became convinced that the Progressive Party was controlled by communists, with Wallace serving as a naïve front man capable of such self-damning errors as describing the Soviet Union as a "directed democracy." When Thomas received less than 100,000 votes despite a spirited campaign, he became convinced of the futility of socialist attempts to attract nationwide electoral support and renounced further office seeking. In 1952 and 1956, the party ran a Pennsylvania state legislator, Darlington Hoopes, for the presidency. He received 20,000 votes in 1952, 2,000 in 1956; no socialist has since sought the presidency.

With his buoyant energy and sparkling mind, Thomas remained dynamically active through the 1950's and early 1960's. He resigned from various official posts in the Socialist Party in 1955, at the age of seventy-one, but remained its most magnetic advocate. The major party candidate to whom Thomas was most sympathetic during this period was Adlai E. Stevenson, with whom he shared a Princeton background and eloquent speech making. The American statesman with whom he disagreed most vehemently was John Foster Dulles, Dwight D. Eisenhower's secretary of state, also a fellow Princetonian as well as fellow Presbyterian. Thomas scorned Dulles's appeasement of demagogic Senator Joseph McCarthy; the bellicosity of his opposition to mainland China; his dismissal of Eleanor Roosevelt from the United States delegation to the United Nations; and his discharge of liberals and socialists, no matter how talented, from foreign service posts.

Thomas remained a morally consistent critic-commentator on American politics to the end of his life. He voted for John F. Kennedy in 1960 and Lyndon B. Johnson in 1964, but with little enthusiasm for either candidate. In the former year, his favorite was an old friend, Hubert H. Humphrey, who lost the Democratic nomination to Kennedy. The Bay of Pigs fiasco shocked Thomas into an outraged telegram of protest, and thereafter he remained lukewarm through Kennedy's one thousand White House days, favoring the president's graceful style and careful separation of state from church, but worried about the moderate, cautious nature of Kennedy's liberalism. He voted for Johnson mainly to vote against the right-wing Barry Goldwater.

Though plagued by arthritic legs and a minor heart ailment, Thomas maintained a strenuous lecturing, debating, and writing schedule in the early 1960's, keeping in the fast lane of what his friends called the "Thomas Track Meet." The only debating opponent who succeeded in spoiling his usually good temper was William Buckley, Jr., whom he regarded as a cold-blooded imperialist and self-righteous reactionary. Thomas's preferred activity during his last years was spending several consecutive days as guest-in-residence on a college or university campus, not only lecturing but also making himself available as casual participant in bull sessions with students and faculty. On lecture platforms he would sometimes limp slowly to the podium, leaning on his cane, then address his audience with the opening line, "Creeping Socialism!"

By his eightieth birthday in late 1964 he was cast in the role of Grand Old Man, admired and loved for his integrity, dignity, intelligence, and wit, given standing ovations at his appearances. When he returned to his birthplace for a birthday tribute, the local paper printed one letter critical of Thomas's opposition to American military involvement in Vietnam. He was relieved, saying, "I feel better not to be too respectable." In 1966, he shocked his oldest grandson, a pastor, by permitting *Playboy* to interview him at considerable length. Thomas expressed a frequent regret of his old age: that he had seen the American working class becoming increasingly middle-class in its materialism; this "dilution of labor's down-the-line militancy has been one of the greatest disappointments in my life." In 1965, ophthalmologists diagnosed his retinal arteriosclerosis; by 1966 he was legally blind, bent by his arthritis, and in pain much of the time. He never complained, however, and his voice retained its booming roar. He finished dictating his twenty-first book, *The Choices*, four weeks before his death in a nursing home a month after his eighty-fourth birthday.

Significance

Thomas devoted a long, honorable life to urging a largely uninterested American public to share his vision of Democratic Socialism as a solution to social inequities and injustices. He served as a goad and gadfly in the Socratic tradition of appealing to his country's good sense and conscience. Some of the social welfare and civil rights legislation he sought was enacted into law during the administrations of Roosevelt and Johnson—with Thomas given no or scant credit for having championed it. His great hope of building a strong socialist movement in the United States was never realized, and he left his party, under circumstances beyond his control, weaker at his death than when he had joined it in young adulthood.

However, Norman Thomas's life can justly be called an extraordinary success story. He was a patrician moralist who maintained an unswerving passion for social justice; devotion to civil liberties; sympathy for the poor, deprived, and disabled; hatred of war's wasteful slaughter; and faith in the ultimate wisdom of a free people. Profoundly reasonable and fair in temperament, he found expression for his evolving views first in humanitarian Christianity, then in a muted, non-Marxist Socialism. The personal esteem he gained was extraordinary: Thomas became not simply an adornment to hundreds of liberal and left-democratic causes but also an admirable member of the pantheon of great American dissenters that includes Henry Clay, Daniel Webster, Debs, La Follette, and Martin Luther King, Jr.

—*Gerhard Brand*

FURTHER READING

Bell, Daniel. *Socialism and American Life*. 2 vols. Princeton, N.J.: Princeton University Press, 1952. An incisive, lucidly written historical and sociological analysis, particularly useful for describing the background and development of Marxist socialism in the United States.

Duram, James C. *Norman Thomas*. Boston: Twayne, 1974. A concise study of Thomas's books and pamphlets, with comprehensive notes and references.

_____. "Norman Thomas as Presidential Conscience." *Presidential Studies Quarterly* 20, no. 3 (Summer, 1990): 581-590. Duram offers another look at Thomas's significance in the realm of American politics, specifically the presidency.

Harrington, Michael. Review of two Thomas biographies in *The Reporter* 25 (November 9, 1961): 64-66. A leading young socialist whom Thomas befriended portrays him as a representative of the American Protestant drive for social justice and moral improvement.

Kutulas, Judy. *The American Civil Liberties Union and the Making of Modern Liberalism, 1930-1960*. Chapel Hill: University of North Carolina Press, 2006. This history of the formative years of the American Civil Liberties Union also discusses Thomas's work with the organization.

Rosenberg, Bernard. "The Example of Norman Thomas." *Dissent* 11 (Fall, 1964): 415-422. A review of two Thomas biographies. Rosenberg cogently analyzes Thomas's place in contemporary American society and urges fulfillment of Thomas's vision of a better world.

Seidler, Murray B. *Norman Thomas: Respectable Rebel*. Syracuse, N.Y.: Syracuse University Press, 1967. A scholarly biographical-critical study that focuses on Thomas's successes and failures as leader of the Socialist Party.

Swanberg, W. A. *Norman Thomas: The Last Idealist*. New York: Charles Scribner's Sons, 1976. A vivid, well-written biography that emphasizes the warmth and courage of Thomas's character. Includes many illustrative photographs but often gets so immersed in details that it loses sight of the larger ideological terrain.

Thomas, Norman. "When Cruelty Becomes Pleasurable." In *Hiroshima's Shadow*, edited by Kai Bird and Lawrence Lifschultz. Stony Creek, Conn.: Pamphleteer's

Press, 1998. Thomas's essay is included in this anthology of literature critical of the atomic bombings of Hiroshima and Nagasaki by the United States.

Walker, Samuel. *In Defense of American Liberties: A History of the ACLU.* 2d ed. Carbondale: Southern Illinois University Press, 1999. This history of the American Civil Liberties Union explores Thomas's role in the organization's development and mission.

JIM THORPE

> *Track and field, because it was something I could do by myself, one-on-one, me against everybody else.*

Olympic athlete

In 1950, the Associated Press voted Thorpe the best athlete of the first half of the twentieth century, a judgment based on his two gold medals won at the 1912 Olympic Games and on his athletic achievements as a football, track, and baseball star.

Born: May 22, 1888; Indian Territory (now near Prague, Oklahoma)
Died: March 28, 1953; Lomita, California
Also known as: James Francis Thorpe (full name); Wa-Tho-Huk (Bright Path)
Area of achievement: Sports

EARLY LIFE

Jim Thorpe (thorp) and his twin brother Charlie were born to Hiram Thorpe and Charlotte Thorpe, in a small cabin on the banks of the North Canadian River near what is now Prague, Oklahoma. Intermarriage among whites and American Indians had become prevalent, and both Hiram and Charlotte were of mixed race. Hiram's father, a blacksmith, was Irish; his mother was an American Indian of Sac and Fox ancestry. Hiram eventually had nineteen children from five different women. Charlotte was his third wife; her great-grandfather had been Jacques Vieux, a French fur trader who had founded Milwaukee, Wisconsin. Charlotte was also the granddaughter of the Potawatomi chief Louis Vieux. As a descendant of this multinational family tree of what might be considered the upper-class Indians of the Midwest, Thorpe was of Irish, French, and Indian stock. His rugged looks were overwhelmingly Indian, and this fact would always be emphasized in his athletic life story.

Because of the government's desire for land, American Indians were moved about like so many checkers on a board. They were compensated with both financial allotments and new land farther west. Hiram and Charlotte lived under these conditions and received land and a stipend each month based on the number of children they had.

Thorpe's early childhood was filled with endless swimming, fishing, and hunting. At the age of six, however, he and his twin brother were sent to the mission boarding school. The white instructors there imposed strict discipline to indoctrinate the Indian

Jim Thorpe. (Library of Congress)

children into the white culture. Students wore uniforms, Indian languages were forbidden, and the children's lives were regimented and time marked off by the ringing of bells. Thorpe eventually ran away, but his father forced him to return. Thorpe would never be a strong student, but he did benefit from the difficult experience: Without the basics he received in school, a college career would have been virtually impossible.

In 1897, Thorpe's schooling was sidetracked when his brother Charlie was stricken with pneumonia and smallpox and died in March. Thorpe returned to school, but, overcome with grief, he then ran away for the second time. The tragedy of the loss of his twin brother would remain with Thorpe throughout his life.

Hiram decided that his son had run away from school for the last time. At ten Thorpe was sent by train to Haskell Indian Junior College in Lawrence, Kansas, hundreds of miles from home. There, he would board with about six hundred other children of Indian parentage and receive much the same education he had received at the agency school, with one important addition: organized football.

Tragedy again struck in Thorpe's life when, on November 17, 1901, his mother died from complications while giving birth to her eleventh child. Again the smooth flow of events in Thorpe's life had been disrupted. Hiram remarried, and young Thorpe's relationship with his father became strained. In January, 1900, the Carlisle

Indian School football team had visited the students at Haskell. Thorpe dreamed of playing for Carlisle, and in February, 1904, he took the train to Carlisle, Pennsylvania.

LIFE'S WORK

The administration at the Carlisle Indian School desired to increase its national recognition through a first-rate sports program. Public support was vital to Carlisle's future, and football was the sport with which to reach a vast number of people. The administration at Carlisle hired Glenn Scobey "Pop" Warner to be their head football coach. Almost as if the Fates had planned it, one of America's most skilled and, later, most famous coaches would have as his pupil one of the best athletes of the century.

Once again, however, the flow of life was interrupted for Thorpe as he received the news that his father had died of blood poisoning. Thorpe, too far from home to attend the funeral, was sixteen and had lost both his parents and his twin brother.

Soon Thorpe got a chance to demonstrate his track-and-field abilities. Competing against students in the upper class, Thorpe easily won the 120-yard hurdles and the high jump. He placed second in the 220-yard dash. From that point on, Thorpe was assured a place on the varsity squad. Word quickly reached Warner, and soon Thorpe received special coaching and an open summer schedule to work on athletics. Thorpe became a member of the varsity football team, having already lettered as a member of the varsity track team. In 1907, Thorpe proved to be an adept runner, but, since he was still raw in terms of game skills, he was made a reserve.

During the 1908 football season, Thorpe, who now weighed 175 pounds, developed his famous placekick accuracy. His ability to kick field goals contributed to Carlisle's 10-2-1 season. That year, because of his kicking prowess, he was named a third-team All-American. During the summer of 1909, Thorpe made a decision that would prove very costly to him for the rest of his life. He loved baseball and decided to play for Rocky Mount in the East Carolina League for the princely sum of fifteen dollars a week, barely enough to cover living expenses. He enjoyed playing so much that he decided, in 1910, not to return to Carlisle and to play semiprofessional baseball instead.

In the summer of 1911, by sheer chance, Thorpe ran into a football teammate, Albert Exendine. Thorpe was now twenty-four, stood six feet tall, and weighed almost two hundred pounds. Exendine explained to Thorpe that the football team had fared poorly and that Thorpe was sorely missed. Thorpe cabled Carlisle, and with Warner's influence he was readmitted. Coach Warner wanted Thorpe to return for two reasons: to play football and to be placed in training as a candidate for the 1912 Olympics.

Thorpe returned to football with almost no effort. In the first big game with the University of Pittsburgh, he kicked and ran with extraordinary results, and the final score was Carlisle 17, Pittsburgh 0. Thirty thousand fans turned out for the Harvard game at Cambridge. The coaches at Harvard decided they could win with their reserves. Nursing a leg injury, Thorpe still managed to score a touchdown and kick field goals, and Carlisle led 15 to 9 as the Harvard varsity finally came onto the field in the fourth quarter, but it was too late. Thorpe, with his ankle bandaged, kicked his fourth field goal (from a distance of forty-eight yards), Carlisle held Harvard to one touchdown, and the final score was Carlisle 18, Harvard 15. That afternoon, Thorpe had given one

Thorpe, Jim

of his greatest game efforts, and historically it had been one of the greatest displays of football for all time.

Later that season, Thorpe punted against Brown for eighty-three yards, a new collegiate record. After that game, he was elected team captain. That same year Thorpe met Iva Miller, a Scotch-Irish Cherokee whom he would marry in October, 1913.

In the winter of 1912, Warner began training Thorpe and Louis Tewanima, a Hopi Indian, for the Olympic tryouts. In the tryouts, Thorpe won eleven gold, four silver, and three bronze medals while Tewanima won most of the long-distance races in which he competed.

Both men qualified for the Olympics that spring. The team trained rigorously as it crossed the Atlantic aboard the specially outfitted SS *Finland*, and Thorpe, who was twenty-five, found the trip to Sweden to be one of the most exhilarating parts of the whole experience.

Thorpe's first event was the pentathlon. He won the broad jump with a distance of 23 feet, 2.7 inches. In the javelin he placed third, but that loss may have propelled him to win the discus, the two-hundred-meter dash, and the fifteen-hundred-meter race, where he stunned spectators with a time of 4 minutes, 44.8 seconds. Sweden's King Gustav V presented Thorpe with the gold medal for the pentathlon.

Thorpe's next event, the decathlon, was only a few days away. Competition would be spread over three days, and during the interval Thorpe returned to the *Finland* to train. While Thorpe trained and watched his teammates dominate the Games, Louis Tewanima won a silver medal in the ten-thousand-meter race. On a rainy afternoon, the decathlon's first three events were held. Thorpe finished third in the one-hundred-meter dash and second in the running broad jump. He won first place in the shot put, heaving it 42 feet, 5.5 inches and was in a slight lead after the first day. On the second day, the weather was ideal. Thorpe easily took a first in the running high jump with a height of 6 feet, 1.6 inches. He also finished first in the 110-meter hurdles with a record time of 15.6 seconds but finished fourth in the four-hundred-meter race. Nevertheless, his lead was maintained.

Only one day was left for both the decathlon and the Games. Jumping and running came naturally to Thorpe, but he lacked the experience and training that one would assume he needed for the discus, the javelin, and the pole vault on the final day. However, he took second place in the discus, third in the javelin, and third in the pole vault. It was the final event, the fifteen-hundred-meter race, in which Thorpe displayed the qualities of the famed athlete that he had become. Despite fatigue, Thorpe proceeded to run the fifteen-hundred-meter in 4 minutes, 40.1 seconds—an impressive finish in which Thorpe had bettered his own record.

Thorpe finished the decathlon with an incredible 8,412.96 points out of a possible 10,000. This point record would not be beaten until 1926. For the second time, Thorpe stood before King Gustav V. The king placed a laurel wreath atop his head, hung the gold medal around his neck, shook hands with him, and proclaimed Thorpe to be the greatest athlete in the world.

In January, 1913, a newspaper reporter revealed that Thorpe had played semi-professional baseball prior to the 1912 Olympics, thus placing in question his status as an amateur athlete. After thorough investigations and extended testimony, the Ama-

Thorpe, Jim

teur Athletic Union, despite a worldwide outcry, decided that Thorpe must return all medals won and have his name withdrawn from the record books for all athletic events in which he had taken part after his involvement in baseball. His two gold medals were returned to the International Olympic Committee, and Gustav V awarded them to the runners-up in the pentathlon and decathlon.

To earn his living, Thorpe became a year-round professional athlete, playing baseball for the New York Giants and football for the Canton Bulldogs and later with other teams during the off-season. Thorpe and the Giants manager John McGraw never got along well, and one afternoon after an argument between the two, McGraw demoted Thorpe to the Giants Triple-A system. Thorpe would spend the rest of his baseball career being shuttled from team to team. He eventually returned to the major leagues and played with the Cincinnati Reds and the Boston Braves until 1919, but he never fulfilled his potential.

Throughout his life, Thorpe fought to regain reinstatement as an amateur, to no avail. Still, his fame did not fade, and he made a modest living lecturing and giving football exhibitions, one of which included a drop-kicking demonstration at New York's Polo Grounds when he was sixty-one.

In 1945, Thorpe married Patricia Askew. She helped him organize his life and took up his cause after his death. In that same year, Thorpe supported the war effort by becoming a carpenter in the Merchant Marine. In 1952, he suffered his second heart attack. Seven months later, on March 28, 1953, the famed athlete's heart gave out.

Significance

In January, 1950, a poll of Associated Press reporters and broadcasters named Thorpe the greatest football player of the first half of the twentieth century. The next month, the Associated Press selected Thorpe as the best male athlete of the half century. In 1963, he was elected a charter member of the Professional Football Hall of Fame. Thorpe's legendary abilities in sports had once again received recognition, and indeed he will always be remembered as one of America's greatest sports heroes. What other American athlete could make such a diversified claim on the American sporting record? The honors continued throughout his life and after it. One honor of which he would have been particularly proud was his election in 1958 to the National Indian Hall of Fame.

Alongside his monumental sports career, however, Thorpe suffered more tragedies than the average person. His wife, his children, and his supporters fought for the reinstatement of his medals after his death. The fight was a long one, filled with ugly political bickering. Finally, justice was served and the International Olympic Committee restored Thorpe's honors at an official ceremony in 1983. Thorpe was named a cowinner for the two events that he won at the 1912 Olympics, and his descendants were given replicas of his gold medals.

—*John Harty*

Further Reading

Crawford, Bill. *All American: The Rise and Fall of Jim Thorpe*. Hoboken, N.J.: John Wiley & Sons, 2004. Comprehensive biography presenting new information about

Truman, Harry S.

Thorpe's relationship with Pop Warner and the revocation of Thorpe's Olympic medals.
"Greatest Athlete." *Time* 61 (April 6, 1953): 58. This obituary pays a tribute to Thorpe as the world's greatest athlete.
Hahn, James, and Lynn Hahn. *Thorpe! The Sports Career of James Thorpe.* Edited by Howard Schroeder. Mankato, Minn.: Crestwood House, 1981. A short paperback that covers the highlights of Thorpe's life.
Jim Thorpe, All American. Directed by Michael Urtiz. Hollywood, Calif.: Warner Bros., 1951. This film is worth viewing, but it glosses over the tragedies of Thorpe's life.
Masin, H. L. "Meet Jim Thorpe, Greatest Athlete of Them All." *Scholastic* 60 (May 7, 1952): 6. Discusses Thorpe's feats as an athlete. Includes a photograph.
"Obituary." *Newsweek* 41 (April 6, 1953): 60. Thorpe's greatest moments as an athlete and a brief sketch of his life.
Richards, Gregory B. *Jim Thorpe: World's Greatest Athlete.* Chicago: Children's Press, 1984. Updated with the story of Thorpe's medal reinstatement. Detailed and well written. Includes a foreword by Grace F. Thorpe, one of Thorpe's daughters. Contains photographs, a chronology, and an index.
Wheeler, Robert W. *Pathway to Glory.* Norman: University of Oklahoma Press, 1975. Rev. ed. *Jim Thorpe: World's Greatest Athlete.* University of Oklahoma Press, 1979. Recounts Thorpe's athletic accomplishments. Includes index and bibliography.

HARRY S. TRUMAN

" *If you can't stand the heat, get out of the kitchen.* **"**

President of the United States (1945-1953)

Truman defended and institutionalized the New Deal reform program of Franklin D. Roosevelt and established the doctrine of containment that guided American policymakers in the Cold War era. Part of his legacy includes sanctioning the dropping of atomic bombs on the Japanese cities of Nagasaki and Hiroshima in August, 1945, which ended World War II in the Pacific and placed the Soviet Union in a position of accommodation to U.S. demands.

Born: May 8, 1884; Lamar, Missouri
Died: December 26, 1972; Kansas City, Missouri
Areas of achievement: Government and politics; diplomacy

EARLY LIFE

Harry S. Truman, whose career enhanced Missouri's reputation for producing tough and stubborn individuals, was born in the southwestern part of that state on May 8, 1884, but grew up in rural Jackson County, in and around Independence. His parents,

Truman, Harry S.

John Anderson and Martha Ellen Truman, were prominent, well-connected citizens of the area, and Harry looked back on his childhood years as happy, secure ones. He was captivated by the world of books, however, which revealed to him that there was a bigger, more rewarding realm within his reach. Success in that realm could be attained, he believed, by strictly adhering to the work ethic taught by his parents and by developing his ability to manipulate people by learning what motivated and pleased them. His parents also taught him a Victorian set of moral absolutes, a tendency to see the world in black-and-white terms, that later influenced his decision making.

When he was graduated from high school in 1901, his father's "entangled" finances prevented young Truman from going to college. He held several unsatisfying jobs in the next few years and then farmed until 1917, when he served in the Army during World War I. After a small business firm he had opened in Kansas City failed in 1922, Truman, whose restless ambition had always left him with an edge of frustration, finally found the career that brought him fulfillment. He entered county politics with the backing of Thomas J. Pendergast, the "boss" of the Kansas City Democratic Party machine.

In 1934, after great success in local politics, Truman, with Pendergast's support, won election to the United States Senate. He strongly supported Franklin D. Roosevelt's New Deal program and then gained national recognition during World War II as head of a committee investigating defense contracts and mobilization bottlenecks.

In 1944, a number of Democratic Party leaders plotted to remove liberal Henry A. Wallace as vice president. Truman surfaced as one of the few prominent individuals acceptable to these bosses and to all the wings of the party. Roosevelt and the convention concurred, and the ticket won the 1944 election.

LIFE'S WORK

President Roosevelt's death on April 12, 1945, gave Truman an opportunity to join the heroes who had enlivened his bookish world. The public initially responded favorably to the plainspoken Missourian, and the honeymoon continued as World War II ended, with Germany surrendering on May 7, 1945, and Japan on August 14. The end of the war brought reconversion problems, however, that would have challenged a political magician such as Roosevelt. They overwhelmed Truman. While searching for a chimerical formula that would allow him to please business, labor, consumers, and citizens hungry for scarce meat, Truman stumbled from policy to policy, convincing people that he was a bewildered throttlebottom.

Amid this turmoil, the beleaguered president formulated his domestic program. Operating within the reform legacy of the New Deal, he revealed to Congress on September 6, 1945, what later became the Fair Deal. His legislative requests included legislation requiring the government to maintain full employment, improved unemployment compensation benefits and minimum wages, major housing reforms, assistance to small business, and continued farm price supports. Later additions to the Fair Deal slate included national compulsory health insurance, federal ownership of atomic energy resources and development, aid to education, and civil rights legislation for blacks. Congressional response was disappointing. It gave Truman the watered-down Employment Act and created the Atomic Energy Commission under civilian control.

Truman, Harry S.

Through executive orders, Truman forbade discrimination against African Americans in the civil service and began to desegregate the armed forces. In his second term, Congress passed a housing act.

Perhaps his greatest reform contribution came when the Republicans won both houses of Congress in 1946 and set out to destroy much of the New Deal reform legacy. This allowed Truman to assume his most effective role: defender of the common man from the forces of reaction. He continued this role in the 1948 election and further protected the New Deal by his upset victory over Republican New York Governor Thomas E. Dewey. No major New Deal program fell before the conservative onslaught, although the Taft-Hartley Act placed some restrictions on labor.

In foreign policy, Truman left a more perilous legacy. By 1947, the Cold War had started. Soviet leaders believed that since the birth of the communist government in 1917, Western capitalist nations had been intent on destroying it. Soviet Premier Joseph Stalin intended to use his nation's great military strength, which had destroyed German dictator Adolf Hitler's armies, to build a buffer zone against these hostile Western powers. He hoped to work cooperatively with the West and cautiously refrained from meddling in areas the Western powers considered vital, but caution also compelled him to establish his nation's own sphere of dominance in Eastern Europe.

Truman was poorly suited to deal with the complexities of this situation. He had never been much interested in foreign affairs, and he held a black-and-white view of the world. He quickly came to two conclusions on which he based policy toward the Soviet Union: that Soviet leaders were breaking all of their wartime agreements, making future negotiations senseless, and that the only thing the Russians understood was force. Once committed to these propositions, he ignored all evidence to the contrary. He believed that he could use American military and economic power to coerce the Soviets into compliance with Washington's demands. The test explosion of the first atomic bomb in July, 1945, and use of the weapon against a collapsing Japan on August 6 and August 9 added to his confidence. He later claimed that his actions saved lives by eliminating the necessity of invading the Japanese mainland. The highest American military leaders believed that the bombing was unnecessary, however, especially since the Soviet Union's declaration of war on Japan, which took place on August 8, would, they believed, shock Japan into surrender. Truman dropped the bombs to force Japan to surrender and to intimidate the Soviet Union into accommodation with the United States.

By acting on the assumption that Russians only understood force, Truman convinced Stalin that the West was still intent on the Soviet Union's destruction. When Moscow countered what it viewed as a threat by, for example, tightening its control over Poland and other Eastern European nations, it confirmed Washington's belief that the Soviet Union intended world conquest. The cycle of suspicion and fear spiraled toward the Cold War, with each side taking defensive actions that appeared to be offensive threats to the other.

In 1947, Truman initialed the containment policy that became the fundamental American Cold War strategy. Abandoning serious negotiation, the United States moved to encircle the Soviet bloc, hoping such pressure would cause it to change, to mellow, internally. Over the next few years, one containment action followed another:

the Truman Doctrine that promised support for free people facing totalitarian pressures, the Marshall Plan, the Berlin Airlift, and the North Atlantic Treaty Organization (NATO). Truman's decisions to fight the Korean War, to finance the French war in Vietnam, to rearm the United States and its Western European allies, and to incorporate West Germany and Japan into the anti-Soviet bloc further raised the containment barrier.

Domestic and foreign problems increasingly merged during Truman's second term, and together they unraveled the popularity he had gained during his 1948 election campaign. China had long been torn by civil war, and in 1949 it "fell" to Mao Zedong's Communists. Republican fury made Truman vulnerable to the bizarre charge of being soft on communism and indifferent to the growing fear of internal subversion. In 1946, Truman himself had initiated a loyalty program designed to eliminate communists from government and had fed fear of subversion by using extreme anticommunist rhetoric crafted to build public support for containment. Red hysteria, led by demagogues such as Senator Joseph McCarthy of Wisconsin, surged in 1950. Although Truman had been partly responsible for McCarthyism, it turned on his administration and undermined his ability to govern.

Truman confronted what he regarded as the greatest challenge of his presidency on June 24, 1950, when the army of North Korea swept across the thirty-eighth parallel into South Korea, an American ally. Truman interpreted this as a Soviet-directed attack on the West, a test of Western resolve. He ordered General Douglas MacArthur, commander of American forces in the Far East, to dispatch American troops to Korea. In September, 1950, MacArthur's forces, operating under the authority of the United Nations, first halted and then pushed the North Koreans back in disarray.

As the North Koreans retreated, Truman faced another major decision. Should he push them back across the thirty-eighth parallel and then halt, content with achieving the original war aim, or should the forces of the United Nations cross the parallel, destroy the North Korean army, and unify Korea? He chose the latter course, and MacArthur drove north toward the Chinese border. In November, 1950, after American leaders ignored China's clear warnings, 300,000 Chinese "volunteers" intervened, shattering the offensive and forcing the longest retreat in United States history. In 1951, the battlefront stabilized near the thirty-eighth parallel, but peace did not come until 1953, during Dwight D. Eisenhower's presidency.

By early 1951, public support for the war had eroded. Then, on April 11, 1951, after a number of public disagreements with MacArthur, Truman recalled the general, who was perhaps the American people's most admired military hero. This action, during an increasingly unpopular war, coupled with the growing force of McCarthyite attacks on the administration, almost destroyed Truman's ability to govern. He had already decided not to run for reelection in 1952 and supported Adlai E. Stevenson for the nomination. Republican candidate Eisenhower, promising to clean up the "mess in Washington," easily defeated Stevenson.

Significance

On January 20, 1953, Truman returned to Independence, Missouri, where he lived until his death on December 26, 1972. In retirement, Truman had the satisfaction of seeing many of his Fair Deal proposals take effect, including Social Security and housing expansion, government health care programs, and civil rights legislation. Truman also watched his popularity rise to folk-hero status among the general public. Scholars concurred with this evaluation. In 1981, American historians ranked him as the nation's eighth greatest president, and one prominent Truman biographer predicted that he would take his place behind Abraham Lincoln as America's second most beloved president.

These admiring historians believed Truman's greatness rested on his foreign policy. Under his leadership, the United States committed itself to playing a continuing role in international affairs. His administration devised the containment strategy, which served as the foreign policy foundation for his successors in office, and established barriers, such as NATO, against the inundation of the "Free World" by aggressive communism.

Other historians, however, questioned the wisdom of his policy. The Vietnam War compelled many scholars to reexamine the American past generally, and they often focused on the Cold War period specifically. These revisionists believed that either through an arrogant attempt to impose the American system on the world or through ignorance of Soviet desires and needs and overreaction to Stalin's cautious policy, the United States provoked the Cold War and initiated the dangerous tension that imperiled civilization. Many revisionists concluded that under Truman the United States began to build a national security state that led it to meddle in the affairs of other nations, while civil liberties eroded at home. This globalism diverted resources to military adventures, while American cities decayed and social problems mounted.

Thus, while many of the tumultuous conflicts that dominated the newspaper front pages during the Truman years later seemed petty and were largely forgotten, the man from Independence remained even after his death the center of controversy revolving around issues central to modern history.

—*William Pemberton*

FURTHER READING

Beschloss, Michael. *The Conquerors: Roosevelt, Truman, and the Destruction of Hitler's Germany, 1941-1945*. New York: Simon & Schuster, 2002. Chronicles how the United States and its Allies met before and after World War II to negotiate a vision of a postwar Germany and Europe.

Ferrell, Robert H. *Harry S. Truman: A Life*. Columbia: University of Missouri Press, 1994. Ferrell, the author of numerous books on Truman, provides a comprehensive and exhaustively researched biography. He portrays Truman not only as an honest man of the people but also a shrewd and ambitious politician.

Hamby, Alonzo L. *Beyond the New Deal: Harry S. Truman and American Liberalism*. New York: Columbia University Press, 1973. Traces the tumultuous relationship between Truman and the liberals in the confusing years following Roosevelt's death.

Karabell, Zachary. *The Last Campaign: How Harry Truman Won the 1948 Election*. New York: Knopf, 2000. Chronicles Truman's surprising win in the presidential election, debunking many myths surrounding the victory. Karabell maintains that the victory was the result of negative campaigning and demagoguery before live audiences.

McCullough, David G. *Truman*. New York: Simon & Schuster, 1992. An enjoyable and complete biography that provides information about Truman's character and personality, as well as details of his life and career. Among its numerous virtues, the book contains a complete account of the 1948 presidential election and information about Truman's family.

Miller, Richard L. *Truman: The Rise to Power*. New York: McGraw-Hill, 1986. The best available study on Truman's prepresidential years. This is the starting place for an understanding of Truman.

Paterson, Thomas G. *On Every Front: The Making of the Cold War*. New York: W. W. Norton, 1979. A short analytical survey of relations between the United States and the Soviet Union.

Sherwin, Martin J. *A World Destroyed: The Atomic Bomb and the Grand Alliance*. New York: Alfred A. Knopf, 1975. Sherwin does not believe that the atomic bombs were dropped on Japan merely to frighten the Soviet Union, as some charge, but argues that possession of the bomb influenced United States policy toward Moscow. He also believes use of the bomb was probably unnecessary to bring peace.

Spalding, Elizabeth Edwards. *The First Cold Warrior: Harry Truman, Containment, and the Remaking of Liberal Internationalism*. Lexington: University Press of Kentucky, 2006. A revisionist explanation of how Truman developed a foreign policy that aimed to contain communism.

Truman, Harry S. *Years of Trial and Hope*. Garden City, N.Y.: Doubleday, 1956. Truman's memoirs, including *Year of Decisions* (1955), detail his actions and policies, often quoting extensively from key documents. While an excellent source, they should be supplemented by additional reading.

Sojourner Truth

> ❝ *If the first woman God ever made was strong enough to turn the world upside down all alone, these women together ought to be able to turn it back and get it right-side up again.* ❞

Social reformer

A featured speaker at abolitionist meetings before the Civil War, Truth worked initially to expose the immorality of the practice of slavery and later to ensure to welfare of emancipated African Americans.

Born: c. 1797; Hurley, Ulster County, New York
Died: November 26, 1883; Battle Creek, Michigan
Also known as: Isabella Baumfree (birth name); Isabella Van Wagener
Areas of achievement: Social reform; civil rights; oratory

Early Life

Sojourner Truth (SOH-johr-nur trewth) was born into slavery in New York as Isabella Baumfree. Her parents were slaves owned by Colonel Johannes Hardenbergh, a prosperous farmer of Dutch descent. Her father, James, a tall man said to be "straight as a tree" (for which he received the Dutch surname of "Baumfree"), was of African and possibly American Indian descent. Her mother, Betsey, also known as "Mau Mau Bett," was of African lineage; through family and biblical stories, she instilled in Isabella and her ten siblings the value of family and spirituality. She assured Isabella she could always talk to God when there was no one else to turn to. Formal education was not available, but Isabella developed a self-reliance and strength in her young years that would preserve her through severe testing and make her work in social reform possible. Her childhood also provided the background from which the vivid and memorable anecdotes used in her lectures would later spring.

Isabella herself was sold at the age of nine. Although she was a diligent worker, she was beaten for her inability to communicate with her owners, the Neelys (Isabella spoke a Dutch dialect). Next, she was sold to the Schryvers, who owned a tavern. During her time with the Schryvers, her mother died, and her father soon followed. Eventually, Isabella was sold to the Dumonts, where she worked part-time as a field hand and helped in the kitchen. At this time, Isabella's greatest wish was to please; sometimes, she would stay up half the night working to gain favor with her master.

When grown, Isabella fell in love with Robert, a slave from a neighboring farm, but they were forbidden to marry because Robert's master disapproved of the match. After the couple continued to meet secretly, Robert was severely beaten and made to marry another woman. Isabella, in turn, was given in marriage to another Dumont slave named Tom. She still had the youngest two of their five children with her as the date for her emancipation approached in 1827 (New York legislators had decreed that all slaves above the age of twenty-eight in that year would be emancipated; previous laws had freed slaves born after 1799).

The year 1827 marked a turning point in the life of Isabella Baumfree. Dumont had promised Isabella and her husband their freedom in 1826 and a log cabin in which to live in exchange for her hard work and faithfulness as a slave. Despite sustaining an injury to her hand, Isabella worked harder than ever for that year in order to fulfill her part of the bargain. When the time came for Dumont to deliver, however, he refused, knowing that he needed her labor in order to overcome losses from crop failure. Furthermore, he illegally sold Isabella's son Peter out of state after she escaped his farm.

Isabella sought help after her escape. Quaker friends sent her to live with Isaac and Maria Van Wagener. It was during this period that Isabella took her first successful political action, suing for the recovery of her son by entering a plea before the Grand Jury of Kingston, and winning; Quakers helped Isabella raise money to retrieve Peter and they were reunited. The fact that the Van Wageners insisted on being called by their names, rather than by "master," impressed Isabella, because she had always perceived slave holders as being innately better than slaves.

Isabella's religious conversion followed, as did the beginning of her life as Sojourner Truth. Truth recounts her conversion as suddenly being overcome by the feeling she was loved, and feeling love for everyone else—even people who had abused her. She also sensed the presence of someone between her and God (Jesus) and realized her mission in life was to preach the injustice of slavery until it had disappeared for good.

Truth moved to New York City in 1829 and worked there as a maid until 1843, when she left to begin her career as a lecturer for the abolition of slavery and human rights. Truth, who said she conversed with God as with another person, claimed that God himself had now given her the name of "Sojourner" because she was to be a traveler and "Truth" because that was what she was to spread throughout the land. This name change signaled Truth's break with her former identity as a laborer, a slave bearing her master's name, and marked the beginning of her lifelong dedication to the fight to recognize the rights of all human beings.

Life's Work

During the twenty-five years that followed, Sojourner Truth traveled thousands of miles, lecturing in twenty-one states and in the District of Columbia. She would routinely set up the white sash given to her by abolitionist women with texts written across it "proclaiming liberty throughout the land," begin singing, then preach about the injustice of slavery as people gathered around her. By the 1840's, Truth had become a popular figure and known to be an impressive speaker, six feet tall, clad in gray dress with a turbanlike scarf covering her head, and armed with a mind quick and courageous enough to adapt to, disarm, and delight audiences that were especially hostile to African Americans and women who supported abolition or women's rights.

Many lecturers left the United States at this time, rather than face proslavery mobs who frequently threatened lives and broke up meetings. Truth also inspired a famous work of art by the American sculptor, William Wetmore Story, entitled "The Libyan Sibyl"; the statue, of marble, resulted in part from the description given to the sculptor by Harriet Beecher Stowe and was known for its majesty and mysterious quality.

Truth lived for many years in Northampton, Massachusetts, where she had happened onto the Garrisonian abolitionists during her travels. The Garrisonians held the brotherhood and sisterhood of all people sacred; thus, slavery was a violation against God, and the fight against it became a holy war. The group was resolved to overthrow the system of slavery through education and persuasion, and Truth demonstrated this after Frederick Douglass's declaration in a public meeting that the only way for African Americans to gain their freedom was by force, when she asked, "Frederick, is God dead?"

The Garrisonians believed that women were men's equals and in this way were allied with the women's movement. In 1850, Truth attended the Worcester, Massachusetts, Woman's Rights Convention and participated in the Woman's Rights Convention in Ohio in May of 1851. In the refrain (also the title) of her famous speech, "Ain't I a Woman?" Truth addressed the white women present who wanted rights for women but at the same time believed African American women to be inferior because of their race. Truth also related her own lifelong history of back-breaking labor, refuting the conventional ideal of women as being unaccustomed to labor or confrontation. Most notably, she addressed biblically based claims of the natural intellectual inferiority of women, countering them with biblical facts. For example, she noted that while men based their claims of superiority upon the fact that Christ was a man, Christ himself was the product of God and a woman, leaving men out of the picture altogether.

Truth's narrative was first written down in 1850 by Olive Gilbert, a white abolitionist. Gilbert's rendering offers vivid stories of Truth's early life and transformation into revivalist and abolitionist, including humorous anecdotes and instances of Truth's effective handling of audiences, but also masks much of her renowned enthusiasm and directness—especially where this directness clashes with the ideal of womanhood during her time. An example of Truth's direct approach that is not included in Gilbert's text is Truth's response to male hecklers who asked if she were a man or a woman; she bared her breasts in proof—not to her own embarrassment, but rather to their collective shame.

A second edition of Truth's narrative, published in 1878, included news articles and correspondence regarding Truth, as well as samples from her "Book of Life"—a book she carried with her, filled with signatures of authors, senators, politicians, and friends—including President Abraham Lincoln, whom she visited in Washington, D.C., in 1864. During the Civil War, Truth nursed soldiers, bringing them food and gifts, funding her work by lecturing, singing, and selling her own photograph on which was written: "I sell the shadow to support the substance." She also became a freedom rider on the streetcars that she rode to take care of the soldiers. On one occasion after successfully fighting to remove the Jim Crow cars (cars reserved for African Americans, but often used by whites), Truth drew a crowd while voicing her desire for a ride, which was at last granted, and rode farther than she needed to make her point definite.

After the Emancipation Proclamation was signed, in 1863, Truth stayed in Washington, D.C., to work with newly freed slaves whose children were being kidnapped and taken to Maryland—still a slave state—organizing posses and persuading mothers to swear out warrants, as she once had done, finding homes and jobs in the northern states for many others. Truth also produced fifty petitions at her own expense in 1870 (when she was nearly eighty years old) asking Congress for land in the western United

States that could be used to resettle freed people who were elderly, homeless, or unemployed.

Truth believed strongly that unemployment robbed people of dignity and humanity; crime was becoming a problem among the homeless and unemployed. Truth endorsed a general plan to Christianize, educate, and provide land for freedmen, as well as prohibit the drinking of rum, another source of demoralization. Truth attempted to convince politicians that since the future of her people was at stake, money used to imprison vagabond children could be better used to give them homes, churches, and schools. Truth also believed that children would fare better if women were allowed political rights.

Truth died in Battle Creek, Michigan, in November of 1883, after almost a century of struggle for social reform. Her funeral was attended by more than a thousand people, and a marble monument was erected there in her honor in 1947.

Significance

At a time when the cooperation between white abolitionists and African Americans was limited, as was the alliance between the woman suffrage movement and the abolitionists, Sojourner Truth was a figure that brought all factions together by her skills as a public speaker and by her common sense. She worked with acumen to claim and actively gain rights for all human beings, starting with those who were enslaved, but not excluding women, the poor, the homeless, and the unemployed. Truth believed that all people could be enlightened about their actions and choose to behave better if they were educated by others, and persistently acted upon these beliefs.

Truth's written narrative is one of many narratives presented to the public by abolitionists as proof against proslavery advocates' claims that African Americans were content with slavery and incapable of caring for themselves. Her speeches were also an effective weapon against slavery and were especially successful in drawing crowds to antislavery meetings and opening eyes to the injustice and irrationality of slavery. Like other freed slaves, Truth was a primary witness who could testify to the real suffering of slaves as well as demonstrate to proslavery crowds that, contrary to popular belief, African Americans were thinking, feeling human beings. Sojourner Truth is considered, along with Harriet Tubman, to be one of the two most influential African American women of the nineteenth century. W. E. B. Du Bois conveyed the importance of her contribution best when he described Truth as "one of the seven who made American slavery impossible."

—*Jennifer McLeod*

Further Reading

Campbell, Karlyn Kohrs. "Style and Content in the Rhetoric of Early Afro-American Feminists." *Quarterly Journal of Speech* 72 (November, 1986): 434-445. Campbell discusses the difficulties African American women abolitionists faced as public speakers, which Truth was successful in combating through the power of metaphor and personal experience in speaking.

Dick, Robert C. *Black Protest: Issues and Tactics*. Westport, Conn.: Greenwood Press, 1974. Dick describes Truth's work as an African American antislavery lecturer, demonstrating her charisma, humor, and strength, as well as discussing the significance of slave narratives, both written and oral, in the antislavery movement.

Fauset, Arthur Huff. *Sojourner Truth: God's Faithful Pilgrim*. New York: Russell & Russell, 1971. This is yet another rendition of the narrative of Sojourner Truth as told to Olive Gilbert (see below), made into factual fiction by Fauset. The narrator focuses on Truth's religious devotion and strength, as does Gilbert.

Fitch, Suzanne Pullon, and Roseann M. Mandziuk. *Sojourner Truth as Orator: Wit, Story, and Song*. Westport, Conn.: Greenwood Press, 1997. An analysis of Truth's oratory, placing it within a historical context and describing its rhetorical strategies. Includes some of Truth's speeches, songs, and public letters.

Gilbert, Olive. *Narrative of Sojourner Truth*. Edited by Margaret Washington. New York: Vintage Books, 1993. In the introduction to this edition of the *Narrative of Sojourner Truth*, editor Margaret Washington explores the Dutch culture in relation to slavery, the elements of culture and community in interpreting the effects of slavery upon African Americans, and the issue of gender in relation to the authorship of the narrative.

———. *Narrative of Sojourner Truth, a Bondswoman of Olden Time: With a History of Her Labors and Correspondence Drawn from Her "Book of Life."* New York: Oxford University Press, 1991. Introduced by Jeffrey C. Stewart, the prefacing material to Olive Gilbert's rendering (originally published in 1850) outlines Truth's contribution to African American women's literature beginning with Phillis Wheatley. This book is part of a series aiming to resurrect the literature of African American women by uncovering the genre's nineteenth century roots.

McKissack, Patricia C., and Fredrick McKissack. *Sojourner Truth: Ain't I a Woman?* New York: Scholastic, 1992. This juvenile biography provides a straightforward introduction to Sojourner Truth, clarifying the details of her early life in slavery, explaining her connection with early abolitionists, and providing insights into her efforts on behalf of women's rights. Includes a bibliography of sources for further study.

Painter, Nell Irvin. *Sojourner Truth: A Life, a Symbol*. New York: W. W. Norton, 1996. Comprehensive biography that challenges the authenticity of historical sources regarding Truth's life. Painter places Truth's life in the proper social context by creating a clear picture of African American life in New York City.

HARRIET TUBMAN

❝ *I never ran my train off the track, and I never lost a passenger.* **❞**

Social reformer

Tubman was one of the towering figures in the American abolitionist movement. A fugitive slave herself, she earned the nickname of "Moses" of her people for rescuing numerous slaves from bondage and leading them to freedom through the Underground Railroad that she helped to create.

Born: c. 1820; Bucktown, Dorchester County, Maryland
Died: March 10, 1913; Auburn, New York
Also known as: Araminta Ross (birth name); Harriet Ross Tubman; Moses
Areas of achievement: Social reform; civil rights

EARLY LIFE

Harriet Tubman (TUHB-muhn) was born into slavery on the eastern shore of Maryland. She was the daughter of two slaves, Benjamin Ross and Harriet Green, one of ten or eleven of the couple's children. Her ancestors had been brought to the United States from Africa sometime during the early eighteenth century. Her master, Edward Brodas, named her Araminta, but she quickly took on her mother's name and came to be known as Harriet.

Harriet's slave status quickly became obvious to her. As a young child, she saw two of her sisters carried away in chains. She received no schooling, and by the age of five she was already at work as a baby-sitter and maid. Her mistress worked her as a maid during the day and then demanded that she remain alert to the baby's cries at night. Once when Harriet dozed off and the baby's crying awakened the mistress, the woman pummeled the young slave about her face and neck.

At the age of six, Harriet was hired out to a new master who taught her how to trap muskrats and how to weave. Once, he caught her taking a sugar cube from his table, and she had to run away to avoid punishment. When she returned, tired and hungry, after several days' absence, she was whipped. The remainder of her childhood was spent in various other occupations. She worked again as a nursemaid and later split and hauled wood, part of the time working with her father. She was also a field hand. None of her various masters seemed happy with her work, and she was frequently in trouble.

When Harriet was twelve or thirteen, she suffered an accident that was to affect her for the rest of her life. An overseer became angry at another slave for leaving his work and demanded that Harriet help in his whipping. She refused and instead tried to help the man escape. In his anger, the overseer picked up a two-pound weight and threw it at the fleeing slave. His aim proved faulty, however, and he struck Harriet on the head, knocking her unconscious. For the rest of her life, she suffered a form of sleeping sickness brought on by the blow, often falling asleep involuntarily. These spells only increased her reputation as a poor worker.

In 1844, Harriet's mother forced her to marry a free black man named John Tubman. She lived with him for five years but had no children. While discussing her husband's free status, Harriet became curious about her own background. In 1845, her inquiries turned up the fact that her mother had actually been emancipated some years previously, but a former master had hidden this fact from her. This revelation caused Tubman to look at her enslavement in an even more critical light.

The year 1849 proved to be the turning point in Harriet's life. Her master at this time was a young, sickly white man who was under the care of an adult guardian. When the young man died in 1849, the rumor spread that the guardian planned to sell all of his slaves. Tubman decided to run away. Her husband refused to join her, but two of her brothers went along. They quickly lost their nerve, however, and Tubman was forced to travel the one hundred miles or so out of Maryland, through Delaware, to Philadelphia on her own. Along the way, she found aid from sympathetic blacks and white people. When she reached free soil, she had mixed feelings. She was excited about reaching freedom but was sad that her family members were still chattel. She determined somehow to free them. Her life of slavery was over; a new career was soon to begin.

LIFE'S WORK

When Tubman reached Philadelphia, she met William Still, a black man reputed to be the chief "conductor" on what was referred to as the Underground Railroad. This collection of abolitionists, Quakers, and other sympathetic black and white people had established a series of houses, barns, caves, passageways, and the like for fugitive slaves to use as they made their way north to freedom. This so-called Underground Railroad was not nearly as well organized as myth would have it, but there is no denying that numerous individuals helped the fugitives escape. Tubman had already experienced some of this help during her own escape, and now she learned more about the system from Still and another close ally, the Quaker Thomas Garrett of Wilmington, Delaware.

Tubman first had to find work in a hotel to earn a livelihood, and thus she began the pattern she was to follow from then on. She was never a paid agent, so she had to do manual labor of various sorts to pay her own way and help finance her slave-rescuing activities. (Sometimes, abolitionists did give her some financial support for particular excursions.) In December, 1850, she made the first of some twenty trips back into slavery. She went to Baltimore and brought out her sister and two children. In 1851, she rescued a brother and his family. When she returned for her husband in the fall of that year, she found him remarried and uninterested in joining her.

Through the rest of the 1850's, Tubman engaged in her slave-stealing activities, rescuing somewhere between sixty and three hundred people. Her work was complicated by the recently enacted Fugitive Slave Law of the Compromise of 1850, which made it no longer safe for runaways to remain in the North. She began to take her fugitives into Canada, from 1851 to 1857 considering St. Catharines, Ontario, her home. From there, she made eleven trips into slave territory. Her most spectacular rescue, and the most personally satisfying one, was her success in bringing out her parents in 1857 in a specially contrived wagon. Her raids were so successful, in fact, that frightened Maryland slaveholders held a meeting in 1858 and put a price of forty thousand dollars on her head.

Tubman's success was the result of intelligence, planning, determination, a mystical faith in God, and courage. She carried drugs to anesthetize babies. She used a pistol to embolden fugitives on the verge of losing their nerve, giving them the choice of continuing or dying on the spot. She used cryptic messages to announce her arrival and sang songs with hidden messages to implement her plans. On one occasion, she and her fugitives boarded a southbound train on the supposition that no slave hunter would suspect a black person traveling in that direction. Another time, she saw a former master approaching her and loosed some chickens as a diversionary tactic to get by him unnoticed. She sometimes physically carried fugitives; she encouraged; she prayed; she bullied. As she later explained: "I never ran my train off the track, and I never lost a passenger." She was convinced that God had chosen her for her work and protected her in its execution.

During the 1850's, Tubman's fame spread among the abolitionists. She traveled to New England, where she came to know Ralph Waldo Emerson, Frederick Douglass, Gerrit Smith, and Thomas W. Higginson. William Henry Seward, though hardly an abolitionist, also befriended her and in 1857 sold her a house in his hometown, Auburn, New York, where she took up residence with her aged parents.

In 1859, when Tubman spoke to the Fourth of July meeting of the Massachusetts Anti-Slavery Society, she so mesmerized its secretary that he forgot to take notes and had to apologize to the membership for the lapse. However, others whom Tubman met during these years left descriptions of her. She was short, of dark color, medium build, with missing upper front teeth. She dressed simply, reminding one observer of her slave past and another of her Quaker acquaintances. By most standards, she was not an attractive woman, and the fact that she often fell asleep as soon as she sat down gave the impression of fragility rather than the strength that she actually possessed.

During the late 1850's, Tubman met John Brown when he was touring black communities in Canada looking for recruits to join in his attempt to capture the federal arsenal at Harpers Ferry and begin a massive slave uprising. Tubman approved of his slave-insurrection plan, and only an unknown illness at a crucial time prevented her from completing her recruiting mission. She considered him the personification of Jesus Christ because of his willingness to die for black people in slavery. Brown was similarly impressed with her, introducing her to Wendell Phillips as "General" Tubman. At another time, he offered the quintessential nineteenth century sexist praise, referring to her repeatedly as a man.

In the spring of 1860, while Tubman was on her way to an antislavery meeting in Boston, she passed through Troy, New York. She found to her dismay that federal marshals had discovered a fugitive and were preparing to take him back to slavery. Tubman helped lead the city's opposition. She grabbed hold of the fugitive and, though her clothes were nearly ripped from her, she held on. After further struggle and several near misses, she successfully gained for the fugitive his freedom. Later that year she made her last trip into Maryland, but by that time the nation was on the verge of war, and her abolitionist friends were concerned for her safety. They now escorted her into Canada, where she had led so many fugitives previously. Her slave-rescuing days were over.

Tubman remained in St. Catharines only briefly. In the spring of 1861, she returned to the United States and apparently followed General Benjamin Butler's Massachusetts troops as they marched southward to defend Washington. In May, 1862, armed with a letter from the governor of Massachusetts, she went to General David Hunter's command in South Carolina to help in the war effort. At first she served as a nurse, gaining renown for her ability to cure disease among those under her care. Later she became a spy, given authority to organize and command a black scout and spy unit. She participated in several raids, leading the successful July, 1863, Combahee River expedition. Later she watched black troops attack Fort Wagner near Charleston. In 1864, she became concerned over the health of her parents and traveled to Auburn, returning to Virginia near the end of the war to work briefly at a hospital in Fortress Monroe.

On her way home from Virginia, Tubman learned that slavery's end had not created a promised land for the newly freed people. The conductor on the railroad refused to honor her nurse's pass and called her a racist name. Despite her strenuous protests, he and three other men threw her bodily into the baggage car.

Tubman returned to Auburn, where she spent the rest of her life. She began a home for aged African Americans in her own house, married Civil War veteran Nelson Davis in 1869 (John Tubman having died several years previously), and helped Sarah Bradford write an autobiographical book entitled *Scenes in the Life of Harriet Tubman* (1869). The publication of this book allowed her to complete the purchase of her house, but she remained in difficult financial straits all of her life. Beginning during the late 1860's, with Seward's support, she requested federal payment for her Civil War service. Nothing happened until 1897, when she received a pension of twenty dollars a month.

During these post-Civil War years, Tubman was also active in the temperance and the women's rights movements, working with Susan B. Anthony and other feminists. Her fame had early spread overseas, and upon the publication of her autobiography, Queen Victoria sent her a gift and invited her to visit England.

Harriet Tubman died in Auburn, New York, on March 10, 1913. She received a full military funeral conducted by the Grand Army of the Republic. The following year, the city of Auburn dedicated a memorial to her on the county courthouse lawn. Booker T. Washington was the main speaker for the event. In 1978, when the United States Postal Service inaugurated its "Black Heritage U.S.A." stamp series, Tubman was the first person honored.

Significance

In a world that saw the slaveholder as dominant and the slave powerless, in a society that believed in white superiority and black inferiority, in a time when men were movers and women's place was in the home, Tubman was a contradiction. She showed slaveholders that they were not all-powerful; she showed slaves that enslavement might not have to be permanent. She demonstrated to a racist and sexist age the truth of black and female capability. She was a "Moses" leading people from slavery into freedom.

Though Tubman's symbolic effect was significant, her actual success was limited. She affected slaves only in a border area and no more than sixty to three hundred of them. She did not rescue any slaves in the Deep South, their chances of running away made impossible by the simple fact of distance. However, even there she had an effect. If slavery was insecure anywhere, it was threatened everywhere. Runaways in Maryland were perceived to be a threat to Mississippi slaveholders as they were to those in Maryland. The bounty for her capture demonstrated better than any words just how upsetting her activities were.

Tubman represented the ideals of freedom and the willingness to endanger one's life for others. This small woman, who never learned to read and write and thus never read the Declaration of Independence, nevertheless exemplified this document in a most profound way.

—John F. Marszalek

FURTHER READING

Bradford, Sarah E. H. *Harriet Tubman: The Moses of Her People*. Introduction by Butler A. Jones. New York: G. R. Lockwood and Son, 1886. Reprint. New York: Corinth Books, 1961. A republication of the 1886 expanded version of the 1869 original book, this is the basic source for information on Harriet Tubman's life. Bradford interviewed Tubman and also included comments about her by a number of leading nineteenth century Americans. In many ways, this is Tubman's autobiography.

Clinton, Catherine. *Harriet Tubman: The Road to Freedom*. New York: Little, Brown, 2004. One of two comprehensive, adult biographies of Tubman published in 2004 (see Larson below). Clinton's meticulously detailed book places Tubman's life within the context of the nineteenth century American south.

Conrad, Earl. *Harriet Tubman*. Washington, D.C.: Associated Publishers, 1943. This is the best biography available and is much more detailed than the Bradford book because Conrad added data not included in the earlier account. This book concentrates on the ten-year period from 1849 to 1859 and cites Tubman as a symbol of the many other nameless fugitives who fled to freedom.

Heidish, Marcy. *A Woman Called Moses*. Boston: Houghton Mifflin, 1976. A historical novel grounded firmly in historical fact. The reader receives an accurate feeling for Tubman, particularly because the book is written in the first person and emphasis is placed on the forces that shaped and directed her.

Humez, Jean M. *Harriet Tubman: The Life and the Life Stories*. Madison: University of Wisconsin Press, 2003. A collection of primary source materials, including letters, diaries, memorials, and speeches, that provides a description of Tubman's life and personality. The materials document Tubman's relationships with abolitionist John Brown, Abraham Lincoln, Frederick Douglass, Sojourner Truth, and others.

Larson, Kate Clifford. *Bound for the Promised Land: Harriet Tubman, Portrait of an American Hero*. New York: Ballantine, 2004. Comprehensive account of Tubman's life, based in part on new sources, including court records, contemporary newspapers, wills, and letters.

NAT TURNER

> ❝ *Having soon [been] discovered to be great, I must appear so, and therefore studiously avoided mixing in society, and wrapped myself in mystery, devoting my time to fasting and prayer.* ❞

Slave rebellion leader

Turner led the largest slave revolt in the history of the United States. As a slave preacher, he linked religion, liberation, and black militancy, thus providing a model for many future black liberation movements.

Born: October 2, 1800; Southampton County, Virginia
Died: November 11, 1831; Jerusalem, Virginia
Also known as: Nathaniel Turner (birth name)
Areas of achievement: Social reform; civil rights

EARLY LIFE

Nat Turner was born a slave on the Benjamin Turner plantation in Southampton, Virginia. His mother was African born, and his father escaped from slavery to the North when Turner was a young child. From the beginning, Turner was perceived as a remarkable child by both his family and his white owner. Born into a slave culture that mixed elements of African tradition with Christianity, Turner exhibited birthmarks that, according to African custom, marked him as a person with spiritual gifts and power. He was treated accordingly by his relatives and the local slave community.

Turner's owner saw his early intelligence and encouraged him to learn to read and write. Turner's paternal grandmother was extremely religious and provided religious education. Turner attended services and received religious education at Benjamin Turner's Methodist meeting house, where the slaves were encouraged to worship with their master and his family. Turner, from his childhood, read the Bible regularly and engaged in prayer and meditation, coming to believe that he had a special calling. His religious study and his visions convinced him that Christianity affirmed the equality and dignity of all people and that slavery was a sin against God and his teachings.

By the 1820's, Turner had already acquired a reputation among other slaves in terms of his intelligence and spiritual gifts. He also began to have regular religious visions. Most important was his report of an encounter with a spirit that approached him and spoke the biblical verse, "Seek ye the Kingdom of Heaven and all this shall be added unto you" (Luke 12:31). Turner interpreted this as a sign that he had a special religious mission. Later, in 1821, he escaped after a dispute with his master; however, after thirty days and another vision, he returned to his enslavement.

Turner believed that personal escape was an evasion of the greater mission to which he had been called. After this, his mystical experiences increased in number and intensity as he began to find signs in the heavens and in hieroglyphic figures that he discovered on leaves. During this time, he took on the role of a Baptist preacher. His reputation as a preacher spread, and he was allowed some freedom in traveling about, reportedly journeying as far as Hartford County, North Carolina, in 1828. His power as a preacher was so great that even some white people were impressed by his message, including a plantation overseer, Ethelred T. Brantley, who, despite disapproval from the white community, was baptized by Turner.

During this time period, Turner had a vision that was to shape future events. He saw a battle in the air between black and white spirits in which streams of blood flowed. Later, in May of 1828, he was informed by the spirit that, like Christ, he was to wage a "fight against the Serpent" and that he would receive the appropriate sign when the battle was to begin. Drawing heavily on the judgment motifs of the Old Testament prophets and the biblical apocalyptic visions of a battle that is described as the final war between good and evil, Turner came to understand himself as a messianic figure who was called to initiate an upcoming battle between good and evil that would end with the freeing of the slaves.

LIFE'S WORK

The sign that Turner was seeking and the events that gained Turner historical notoriety began with a solar eclipse in February, 1831. Turner saw this as the sign that the battle would soon begin. He began planning a slave revolt with four other slaves—Henry Porter, Hank Travis, Nelson Williams, and Sam Francis—that was to begin on July 4. The plan was to kill local slave owners, seize their weapons, rally other slaves to their cause, and then march on the county seat, Jerusalem, Virginia, and seize weapons from an armory. The hope was that by then, a well-armed slave army would be formed to engage in a final battle to end slavery. On July 4, however, Turner fell ill, and the attack was postponed.

Turner waited for another sign. It came in August, 1831. For three days—the "Three Blue Days of 1831"—the sun over North Carolina and Virginia had a strange blue cast. In response, on August 21 Turner called together his group of followers, which now numbered eight. They gathered for an evening meal, finalized their plans, and then, just after midnight on August 22, put the plan into action. They first went to the house of Turner's current owner, John Travis, and, armed with a hatchet and broadax, killed Travis, his wife, and their children—six people in all. They gathered some guns and ammunition and moved from farm to farm in the region. By Tuesday morning, August 23, the group with Turner numbered about seventy, and they had killed fifty-seven white people, over half of which were women and children, in the twenty-mile area of the Boykins district of Southampton.

As the rebels moved down the road from Cross Keys to Jerusalem, they met their first resistance in the form of a white militia under the command of Captains Alexander Peete and James Bryant. After some initial success, Turner's group was subsequently scattered. Soldiers from Fort Monroe and white militia from surrounding areas were dispatched to put down the rebellion. Many of the slave insurgents were quickly captured. White people retaliated with a terrorist campaign against black people in the area, both slave and free. As many as two hundred black people may have been murdered; many of them were lynched, and many were tortured. The massacre would have become worse had not General Eppes intervened and dismissed the militia groups.

Turner, Nat

Turner escaped and lived in the woods near Cabin Pond, eluding capture for six weeks. He was discovered by a white man, Benjamin Phipps, on Sunday, October 30, hiding in a hole he had dug under a fallen tree. He was taken to Jerusalem on November 1, convicted during a five-day trial, and hanged on November 11. During the time he was in prison, he made lengthy verbal confessions to his attorney, Thomas R. Gray, which were subsequently published and became the primary source of information about Turner and his planned revolt. When asked at his sentencing whether he had more to say, Turner showed no remorse, but only replied, "Was not Christ crucified?" Fifty-three black people, including Turner, were arrested. Twenty-one were acquitted, twelve were transported out of state, and nineteen others, in addition to Turner, were hanged.

At the time of Turner's revolt, antislavery sentiment had become strong in the North and some parts of the South. David Walker's *Appeal to the Coloured Citizens of the World*, which advocated the violent overthrow of slavery, had been published in 1829, and William Lloyd Garrison was already actively involved in advocating the abolition of slavery through political action. The Southampton rebellion intensified the debate and tended to harden positions on both sides. As a response to the revolt, legislation was passed throughout the South that set new penalties for teaching slaves to read, limited the rights of slaves to preach, and placed limits on the rights of slaves to gather for religious services. The education of free black people was also severely limited as many of the informal black schools were closed. Many free black people were pressured to move North.

The debate surrounding the rebellion emerged again during the 1960's with the publication of William Styron's fictionalized account of the life of Turner, *The Confessions of Nat Turner* (1966). According to African American critics, the book portrays Turner as a crazed fanatic and a precursor of the black militants who were gaining prominence during the 1960's and thus is a veiled criticism of black radicalism. African American scholars responded to the book with a period of intense historical research and inquiry to present a more accurate portrayal of Turner.

Significance

Nat Turner's notoriety came as a result of his leading the largest slave revolt in the history of the United States. More important, however, Turner was a black religious leader who embodied a central theme of the black religious tradition in the United States. Like those who would follow, including Martin Luther King, Jr., and Malcolm X, he proclaimed that the God of the Old Testament was a god that set slaves free and demanded social justice, a god who exacted judgment on societies that were not just and who required people to take action to rectify social injustice. Turner's actions also highlight the fact that slaves did not passively accept slavery but acted to obtain their freedom and equal rights. Turner's confessions have been an important historical source that demonstrates the continued influence of African traditions on slave culture and African American religion.

The historical debates surrounding the portrayal of Turner are significant in understanding the racial divide that exists in the United States. The focus on the brutality of Turner's revolt in the debate following the rebellion and in later portrayals by people such as Styron shows the refusal of white America to understand the context of black radicalism. Turner's revolt was a demand for freedom and rights, a response to a system that bought and sold people, separated families, and arbitrarily tortured and executed slaves. To understand the violence of some forms of black radicalism, it is necessary to understand the violence of the system to which it is a response.

—*Charles L. Kammer*

FURTHER READING
Aptheker, Herbert. *American Negro Slave Revolts*. New York: International, 1943. Aptheker places Turner's revolt in the historical context of other slave revolts during this time period.
Clarke, John Henry, ed. *William Styron's Nat Turner: Ten Black Writers Respond*. Westport, Conn.: Greenwood Press, 1968. A response to Styron's novel by a variety of black scholars who are attempting to counteract what they see as a distorted portrayal of Turner.
Duff, John B., ed. *The Nat Turner Rebellion: The Historical Event and the Modern Controversy*. New York: Harper & Row, 1971. A recounting of the ongoing debate about the interpretation of Turner and his rebellion.
Foner, Eric, ed. *Great Lives Observed: Nat Turner*. Englewood Cliffs, N.J.: Prentice-Hall, 1971. Collection of historical documents, representing reactions to, and changing interpretations of, Turner in a variety of historical time periods.
French, Scot. *The Rebellious Slave: Nat Turner in American Memory*. Boston: Houghton Mifflin, 2004. Analyzes Turner's legacy by examining how he has been depicted in popular culture. Describes how Turner's image has changed from the immediate aftermath of his rebellion to more recent debates.
Greenberg, Kenneth S., ed. *The Confessions of Nat Turner and Related Documents*. New York: St. Martin's Press, 1996. Includes the text of Turner's confessions to Thomas R. Gray and other historical documents from the time period.
———. *Nat Turner: A Slave Rebellion in History and Memory*. New York: Oxford University Press, 2003. Collection of essays about Turner, including an exploration of his relationship with the black community in Southampton County, Virginia, and the role of women in his insurrection. Includes an interview with William Styron and an essay written by Herbert Aptheker in 1937.
Oates, Stephen B. *The Fires of Jubilee: Nat Turner's Fierce Rebellion*. New York: Harper & Row, 1975. Oates provides a detailed historical account of the life of Turner, the rebellion, and the debates and legislation that ensued.
Styron, William. *The Confessions of Nat Turner: A Novel*. New York: Random House, 1966. A controversial but popular fictionalized account of Turner's life and the rebellion, written by a white southern author.
Tragle, Henry Irving, ed. *The Southampton Slave Revolt of 1831: A Compilation of Source Material*. Amherst: University of Massachusetts Press, 1971. A comprehensive collection of historical reports and accounts of the revolt and the ensuing debate.
Wilmore, Gayraud. *Black Religion and Black Radicalism: An Interpretation of the Religious History of Afro-American People*. Maryknoll, N.Y.: Orbis Books, 1983. Wilmore places Turner's life and self-understanding in the context of African American religious traditions.

EARL WARREN

❝ *In civilized life, law floats in a sea of ethics.* ❞

Chief justice of the United States (1953-1969)

The U.S. Supreme Court under Warren's leadership reached landmark decisions that struck down existing practices in the areas of racial segregation, limitations on political association, voting apportionment, the investigation of criminal suspects, and other controversial issues.

Born: March 19, 1891; Los Angeles, California
Died: July 9, 1974; Washington, D.C.
Area of achievement: Law and jurisprudence

EARLY LIFE

Earl Warren was born in Los Angeles. His father, Methias Warren, was a Norwegian immigrant who had come to the United States during his adolescence and for many years worked as a railroad car mechanic; the boy's mother, Christine Hernlund Warren, was of Swedish ancestry. Ethel Warren, Earl's sister, was four years older than he. In 1896, the family moved to Bakersfield. As a boy, Warren raised animals and worked at various jobs on the Southern Pacific Railroad; his best subjects in school were history, English, and French. His interest was aroused in 1903 when a deputy marshal killed two lawmen and was later tried in a local court; Warren saw the trial and also watched other trials. Although his father encouraged him to consider a career in engineering, Warren was intrigued by the examples of courtroom advocacy he had seen. By the time he completed high school, he had saved some eight hundred dollars, which he used to meet his expenses when he entered the University of California, Berkeley.

Warren's academic record was acceptable, if not outstanding; after his third year, he was allowed to take courses at the university's law school. He received a bachelor's degree in 1912, and two years later he was awarded his law degree. He was graduated at about the middle of his class and was not selected to serve on the school's *Law Review*. For some time thereafter, he practiced in a local law office; on the United States' entry into World War I, he joined the Army, serving as a bayonet instructor. After a period of service that took him to Fort Lee, Virginia, he was discharged in 1918 with the rank of first lieutenant in the infantry. He then began work for the city attorney in Oakland. In 1925, he became the district attorney for Alameda County, an area just east of San Francisco.

Slightly taller than six feet, Warren weighed more than two hundred pounds; he had a strong build, though in later years he had to struggle somewhat to control his girth. His features were often described as typically Scandinavian: He had a long face with a straight nose and clear blue eyes, his complexion was fair, and he had blond hair that eventually became gray. Throughout his adult life he wore glasses, in time favoring those with rounded, dark-rimmed frames.

Although hitherto he had not seriously concerned himself with women, Warren became deeply attached in 1921 to Nina Palmquist Meyers, whom he met at a morning swimming party. An attractive young widow whose husband had died shortly after their son was born, she returned Warren's affection; after a lengthy courtship, they were married in 1925. Over a period of seven years, two sons and three daughters were born to them, and Warren, as a proud father, became an archetypal family man, constantly concerned with his children's education and well-being.

LIFE'S WORK

Warren became widely known for his relentless pursuit of lawbreakers, notably bootleggers, and he took vigorous action against gambling and vice. In 1931, Raymond Moley, an important political observer and later adviser to President Franklin D. Roosevelt, called Warren "the most intelligent and politically independent district attorney in the United States." On some cases Warren went to great lengths to obtain convictions; controversy arose in 1936, during his investigation of a shipboard homicide on the SS *Point Lobos*. Four defendants, who allegedly were Communist sympathizers, were brought to trial on evidence obtained partly through electronic eavesdropping and prolonged interrogation in the absence of defense counsel. Ultimately they were found guilty of second-degree murder. Violent crime affected Warren's life directly, as well: In 1938, his father was beaten to death at his home in Bakersfield. The assailant was never found.

Later that year, Warren was elected attorney general for the state of California; his tenure in that office was characterized by the same zeal he had displayed in local law enforcement. In 1939, drawing on an extended legal definition of the state's coastal waters, he directed a major raid on the *Rex*, an offshore gambling ship. He also became involved in politics: He opposed the nomination of a noted legal scholar to the California Supreme Court, partly because of the latter's purported relations with the Communist Party. Claims of national security were invoked in 1942, when Warren supervised the forcible relocation of about 110,000 Japanese Americans; he depicted them as potential saboteurs and collaborationists. Although somewhat later many others denounced this measure, until the last years of his life Warren contended that it was necessary in view of the military situation at that time.

Warren's politics were Republican, but his positions on social issues had a wide appeal to voters at large. He campaigned for governor in 1942 and was elected overwhelmingly; four years later, under California's cross-filing system, he won the primaries of both major parties. In 1950, he became the only person to be elected to a third term as governor of that state. He supported measures to expand the state's educational system; he also advocated prison reform and improved mental health care. He was acutely conscious of the financial hardships imposed by medical expenses, which he and his family had incurred during periods of hospitalization; in 1945 he urged, unsuccessfully, that the state enact a form of health care insurance. In 1949, he signed a bill requiring that women receive equal pay for work performed on an equal basis with men.

Because of his demonstrated political appeal and the growing importance of California and the Western states in national politics, there were Republican political strategists who looked to Warren as one of the party's possible standard-bearers. In 1948, the Republican nominee for president, Governor Thomas E. Dewey of New York, chose Warren as his vice presidential running mate. He campaigned with some vigor, and even after Dewey's unexpected defeat, some of the California governor's supporters held out hopes for the next election. At that time, however, Dwight D. Eisenhower announced his candidacy and in short order obtained the Republican nomination; he was then elected president by a convincing margin. In 1953, after the sudden death of Chief Justice Frederick M. Vinson created a vacancy on the U.S. Supreme Court, Eisenhower offered the position to Warren.

A major issue that Warren, and his colleagues, had to confront was the troubled question of racial segregation; in a landmark decision that he wrote for a unanimous Court, Warren found that public facilities described as "separate but equal" were inherently unequal and therefore were in violation of the Constitution. The case of *Brown v. Board of Education of Topeka* (1954) overturned rulings ultimately based on a decision of 1896; once judicial decisions had eliminated distinctions on this level, a new era in racial relations was opened.

Political concerns also came before the Supreme Court, notably in connection with the government's efforts strictly to limit Communist and other left-wing activities. On constitutional grounds, Warren and his colleagues resisted such measures. On one Monday in June, 1957, the Court handed down four separate decisions restricting powers to investigate individuals' political backgrounds or to cite political affiliations as grounds for the termination of employment.

Warren believed that the most important case to come before him was *Baker v. Carr* (1962), which challenged Tennessee's system of electoral apportionment as unduly favoring lightly populated rural districts. The Court's decision, written by Justice William J. Brennan, effectively established that federal judicial power could be exercised to ensure equal representation for voters participating in state elections. In another case, *Reynolds v. Sims* (1964), Warren wrote the opinion of a majority of justices in holding that both houses of the Alabama legislature had to be elected on an equal and proportional basis.

Rather different, and unsettling, questions arose when Warren became chair of the commission that investigated the assassination of President John F. Kennedy. Although originally he had been reluctant to take this position, Warren conscientiously supervised the collection of evidence; after the commission's report was issued in 1964, he stoutly defended its conclusion that Lee Harvey Oswald had acted alone in killing the president.

Chief Justice Warren had often come under attack for the Court's decisions; desegregation and reapportionment had been denounced as intrusions on states' rights, in areas not hitherto subject to the Court's rulings. Several U.S. senators contended that decisions upholding individual liberties actually were concessions to the communists. Opposition arose in many quarters: In 1957, Warren resigned his membership in the American Bar Association in protest against lack of support from that organization. The militantly anticommunist John Birch Society mounted a widespread campaign calling for Warren's impeachment. During his later years on the Court, Warren became associated with controversial decisions affecting the rights of criminal suspects, for which he was castigated by many.

Cases such as *Mallory v. United States* (1957) and *Mapp v. Ohio* (1961) had over-

Earl Warren.
(Library of Congress)

turned convictions obtained through improper interrogation or search and seizure without a warrant. *Gideon v. Wainwright* (1963) established the right of the indigent to obtain counsel for their defense during criminal trials. In *Escobedo v. Illinois* (1964), the Court found that the accused has a right to counsel during initial questioning by the police; limitations on the direct investigation of suspects were stated specifically in *Miranda v. Arizona* (1966), a landmark decision that Warren wrote for a majority on the Court. The requirement that, prior to any questioning, the police must inform suspects of their rights under the Constitution established explicit guidelines for the treatment of accused persons but was bitterly attacked by many law-enforcement officers and political figures.

Warren sometimes parted company with his fellow justices; thus, he sided with a majority on decisions involving the use of sit-ins to demonstrate for civil rights but dissented in cases in which claims of obscenity were contravened by those of free speech. Weary with advancing age, and in anticipation of his retirement from the bench, in 1968 he offered to resign on the condition that a successor be found beforehand. Although his associate, Abe Fortas, was not confirmed by the Senate and ultimately resigned from the Supreme Court in the wake of a financial scandal, Warren renewed his

Warren, Earl

offer and left the Court when Warren E. Burger was confirmed as chief justice in 1969. The last years of his life were spent writing, traveling, and lecturing; Warren continued to manifest a lively interest in political controversies where they affected judicial concerns. He suffered from angina pectoris and coronary occlusion, for which he was hospitalized several times. On July 9, 1974, he died of cardiac arrest at the Georgetown University Hospital in Washington, D.C.

Significance

To friends, associates, and opponents alike, Warren's career in public service posed contrasts and questions that were not readily resolved. During his work in law enforcement, Warren had shown some deference for the rights of the accused, but in exceptional cases he disregarded them; his active role in combating crime, in Alameda County and for the state of California, did not seem to foreshadow his efforts on behalf of individual rights after his appointment to the Supreme Court. In his native state he had denounced communism, and he had carried out sweeping measures against Japanese Americans; as chief justice, he openly championed interpretations of the Constitution that ensured political liberties and promoted racial equality before the law. Although his views had been well within the political mainstream, the transition that later took place could not easily be ascribed to underlying features of continuity in his outlook or indeed to the changed historical circumstances surrounding cases that arose during his tenure on the Supreme Court.

It was sometimes contended that Warren followed the lead of other justices, such as Hugo L. Black and William Douglas, in reaching major decisions, notably those that upheld individual rights. Warren had essentially a practical, rather than an abstract or academic, philosophy of the law; he reached decisions promptly and held fast once he had made them. Other justices, moreover, have readily attested the determined leadership he exercised, even in cases in which he assigned the Court's opinions to others of like mind. While occasionally, as in cases involving pornography, a majority voted against his positions, most major decisions reflected his colleagues' views as well as his own, and often he was able to win over those who wavered.

A final issue concerns the Supreme Court's role in American politics and society. More than any other institution, the Supreme Court brought about racial desegregation; it prescribed the forms by which criminal suspects are advised of their constitutional rights. Such decisions have tangibly affected the lives of millions. Supporters and critics have described this process as a form of judicial activism, by which the Court's interpretation of the Constitution was applied directly to state and local, as well as federal, concerns. Although opposition often centers on the tenor and content of particular decisions, questions remain as to the nature and scope of the Court's powers within the framework of the Constitution. It is Warren's legacy to have demonstrated the means and range by which the Court might intervene in major questions of American public life.

—*J. R. Broadus*

Further Reading

Kurland, Philip B. *Politics, the Constitution, and the Warren Court.* Chicago: University of Chicago Press, 1970. In a series of lectures that are astringently critical of the

Court's actions, Kurland, an important scholar specializing in the Supreme Court, contends that Warren and his colleagues found new and potentially hazardous interpretations of the Constitution.

Levy, Leonard W., ed. *The Supreme Court Under Earl Warren.* New York: Quadrangle Books, 1972. The divergent standpoints of defenders and responsible critics of the Court are presented in this collection of articles by various legal specialists.

Newton, Jim. *Justice for All: Earl Warren and the Nation He Made.* New York: Riverhead Books, 2006. A definitive biography, comprehensively chronicling Warren's life and career and describing the complexities and contradictions of his personality.

Pollack, Jack Harrison. *Earl Warren: The Judge Who Changed America.* Englewood Cliffs, N.J.: Prentice-Hall, 1979. A brisk, favorable account of Warren's life that at each stage evokes the political atmosphere surrounding his work in law and government. The author emphasizes the social and political consequences of decisions handed down by the Warren Court.

Schwartz, Bernard. *Super Chief: Earl Warren and His Supreme Court, a Judicial Biography.* New York: New York University Press, 1983. Warren's sixteen terms on the high court are studied in this massive work by a noted legal scholar. The author reveals the extent to which differing positions and judicial infighting affected the court's deliberations; in the process, Warren's marked capacity for leadership is demonstrated. The unpublished papers of seven justices and a broad range of personal interviews were used in the composition of this work.

Urofsky, Melvin I. *The Warren Court: Justices, Rulings, and Legacy.* Santa Barbara, Calif.: ABC-CLIO, 2001. An examination of the court, including profiles of the justices, discussions of its decisions, and an appraisal of its influence.

Warren, Earl. *The Memoirs of Earl Warren.* Garden City, N.Y.: Doubleday, 1977. This work, which Warren composed during the last four years of his life, published posthumously, depicts Warren's work against crime, his actions as governor of California, and the concerns that guided him in reaching controversial decisions on the Supreme Court. Although not free from special pleading, some portions are lively, and there are also useful statements of his positions on racial issues, criminal investigation, and other important matters.

———. *The Public Papers of Chief Justice Earl Warren.* Edited by Henry M. Christman. New York: Simon & Schuster, 1959. Eleven of Warren's major opinions, from his first five terms on the Supreme Court, are published here, along with other addresses and statements on public issues.

———. *A Republic, If You Can Keep It.* New York: Quadrangle Books, 1972. This brief treatise sets forth, on a rather basic level, Warren's views on the constitution and its place in American history; from time to time he refers to major decisions in which he was involved.

White, G. Edward. *Earl Warren: A Public Life.* New York: Oxford University Press, 1982. This important scholarly examination of Warren's political career and judicial work points to the aspects of continuity and change in his outlook on major issues; the author provides, on a topical basis, a critical assessment of his opinions as chief justice.

BOOKER T. WASHINGTON

> " *At the bottom of education, at the bottom of politics, even at the bottom of religion, there must be for our race economic independence.* "

Educator

One of the best-known and most widely respected African Americans of his time, Washington combined an optimistic outlook with a spirit of accommodation in race relations to provide leadership and a program to black Americans during an era of segregation.

Born: April 5, 1856; near Hale's Ford, Virginia
Died: November 14, 1915; Tuskegee, Alabama
Also known as: Booker Taliaferro Washington (full name)
Areas of achievement: Education; social reform; civil rights; philanthropy; journalism

EARLY LIFE

Booker Taliaferro Washington was born into slavery on a Virginia farm. His mother, Jane Ferguson, was a slave and a cook for James Burroughs; his father was a white man whose identity is unknown. Washington had a brother John, four years his senior, also a mulatto, and a sister who died in infancy. When the family was emancipated, it settled in Malden, West Virginia, five miles from Charleston.

From 1865 to 1871, Booker worked in the local coal and salt mines, attending school between early morning and later afternoon stints of labor. For one and one-half years, he was a houseboy for the wife of the mine owner; in this capacity, he learned demanding standards of performance, attention to detail, and the virtues of hard work, cleanliness, and thrift.

Having heard of a new school in eastern Virginia where African Americans received vocational training, Washington entered Hampton Normal and Agricultural Institute in the fall of 1872. Founded by an idealistic Civil War general, Samuel C. Armstrong, the school reinforced the influences of his houseboy experience and pointed him toward his future. He later said,

> At Hampton, I found the opportunities . . . to learn thrift, economy and push. I was surrounded by an atmosphere of business, Christian influences, and the spirit of self-help, that seemed to have awakened every faculty in me.

With his emphasis on industrial education for African Americans and the virtues of hard work and self-discipline, Armstrong was perhaps the major influence in molding young Washington.

During the four years after his graduation in 1875, Washington taught school at Malden, West Virginia, and briefly attended Wayland Seminary in Washington, D.C. In 1879, he was called to Hampton Normal and Agricultural Institute to supervise instruction of Indian students whom Armstrong had recruited in the West. During his second year, he taught night classes for youths who worked for the institute during the day.

In 1881, Washington eagerly grasped the opportunity to start his own school at Tuskegee, Alabama. His model was Hampton, and he established in the Deep South an institution that expressed his by then mature social values. The Civil War and Reconstruction had brought freedom, citizenship, and suffrage to blacks, yet little had been done to prepare African Americans to live as citizens, voters, and independent workers. What was needed, Washington believed, was to give black people industrial education and moral training by which they could become economically self-sufficient and able to partake of the blessings of liberty and citizenship. The exercise of political rights and entrance into the professions could be deferred. "Let us give the black man so much skill and brains that he can cut oats like the white man; then he can compete with him," he affirmed. The liberal arts were not to be neglected, but they were not foremost.

Life's Work

At twenty-five years of age, Washington was in good health. A persuasive speaker, he stood tall, an energetic figure with striking features—gray eyes, full lips, broad nose, reddish hair, and brown skin. Throwing himself vigorously into his challenging responsibilities, he recruited students from the countryside and secured an abandoned plantation for a campus. In 1882, he married a childhood friend, Fannie N. Smith, who bore him a daughter and died in 1884. When the number of pupils grew to fifty, he employed another black teacher, Olivia A. Davidson, who became his second wife and gave birth to two sons. She died in 1889; a third marriage was to Margaret James Murray, "lady principal" at Tuskegee, who survived him.

Meager legislative appropriations and growing enrollments impelled Washington to solicit funds in the North and Midwest. Beginning in 1883, he secured assistance from the Slater and Peabody funds, the money from the first being used to build a carpenter shop and make other improvements. Fund-raising became a fixed part of his activities; in the course of time he was garnering $100,000 a year, gaining support from John D. Rockefeller, Andrew Carnegie, Julius Rosenwald, and others. By the end of his career, Tuskegee Institute owned an endowment of nearly two million dollars.

Washington quickly emerged as a national spokesperson for his race. In the summer of 1884, he was invited to address the annual meeting of the National Education Association in Madison, Wisconsin. He spoke on "the broad question of the relations of the races," foretelling the views for which he became famous eleven years later. Meanwhile, the address won for him recognition among educators and helped his fund-raising efforts.

It was the address he delivered in 1895 at the Cotton States and International Exposition in Atlanta that made Washington a national figure and the leading spokesperson for black Americans. In this address, Washington rejected ideas of return to Africa or migration to the North. "Cast down your bucket where you are," he exhorted. Black people must begin at the bottom of life and not at the top, as Reconstruction policy had attempted; the leap from slavery to freedom had been too quick. Life at the bottom meant labor in agriculture, mechanics, commerce, and domestic service. Black people must "learn to dignify and glorify common labour and put brains and skill into the common occupations of life." Seeking to allay southern white apprehensions about the potential advance of African Americans within the region, Washington gave an assurance, "In all things that are purely social we can be as separate as the fingers, yet one as the hand in all things essential to mutual progress." Progress, he went on, is inevitable, and nearly eight million blacks—one third of the South—would help in marching forward.

Black and white people listened while Washington warned against agitation on questions of social equality. Not artificial forces but production for the world's markets would bring black Americans the full privileges of the law. "The opportunity to earn a dollar in a factory just now is worth infinitely more than the opportunity to spend a dollar in an opera-house." Pledging the patient, sympathetic help of blacks, he looked forward to a time of material benefits to the South, followed by "a blotting out of sectional differences and racial animosities . . . and a willing obedience among all classes to the mandates of law."

Washington's Atlanta address came at a time of increasing discrimination against black people. The U.S. Supreme Court in the civil rights cases had opened the door to segregation; a year after the Atlanta address, the Court gave positive sanction to separate-but-equal facilities for black Americans. A movement to strip black people of the right of suffrage had begun in Mississippi in 1890, and emboldened by Washington's subordination of political privileges to economic opportunity, southern white leaders pushed forward with segregation and disenfranchisement. Lynching of black men in

Booker T. Washington.
(Library of Congress)

the South, especially on the allegation of raping white women, was on the rise.

Pushing his idea of equal economic opportunity that he thought in time would blot out racial animosities, Washington advocated a policy of black accommodation to the oppressive climate. His policy won immediate favor with southern whites, who welcomed the renunciation of political privilege and equality as well as the prospect of a harmonious section prospering through the labor of skilled, contented blacks. Northern whites, who had turned away from notions of intervention in the South, applauded Washington's giant step down the road toward reunion and his vision of a southern economy where northern capital might profitably be invested.

African Americans, in the main, were proud of the recognition Washington won and looked to the Tuskegee educator as their principal leader for the next score of years. Washington's national influence grew quickly after the "Atlanta compromise." He had already made friends with powerful figures in the North, philanthropists who were contributing to Tuskegee; he came to exert control over giving to black colleges, and his favor was necessary to secure aid.

With the accession of Theodore Roosevelt to the presidency, Washington gained control of black appointments to federal office. His influence continued under William H. Taft, and Washington's secretary claimed that "during the administrations of both President Roosevelt and Taft hardly an office of consequence was conferred upon a Negro without first consulting Mr. Washington." He lost his influence in politics when Woodrow Wilson, a southern-born leader of a party with its base in the South, became president and ordered segregated facilities for black citizens in federal service.

Besides philanthropy and politics, Washington exerted influence in the black press. Backed by most of the black press in the nation, Washington dispatched reams of releases publicizing Tuskegee and his ideas. He fed unsigned editorials to receptive editors and on occasion made financial contributions to black editors. He secretly purchased the *New York Age*, which he believed to be "the strongest and most widely circulated Negro paper in the country" and, after he sold it, continued to advise its editor.

It must not be supposed that Washington fully acquiesced in segregation and disfranchisement. His Atlanta speech was ambiguous, and if, for example, he declared that "the agitation of questions of social quality is the extremest folly," he did not intend racial inequality to be permanent. He believed in gradual evolutionary progress under which African Americans, enjoying material prosperity, would gain complete equality in the South. To this end and without fanfare, he exerted his influence to stem the tide of disenfranchisement. He wrote a public letter in 1895, urging the South Carolina convention to allow African Americans to qualify for the vote by education, and he made similar attempts to allow a degree of black voting and strengthen black education in other southern states.

Washington was less open and vocal in his opposition to segregation. Behind the scenes, he worked against the passage of laws segregating Pullman cars, though he himself was rarely accorded separate facilities. He also fought laws to segregate housing, usually in private letters and through other persons. Lynching, however, impelled him to be active; the burning alive of a Georgia black for alleged rape and murder elicited from him a letter appealing to both black and white people to maintain law and order. In later years, he continued to speak out against lynching and periodically compiled lists of lynchings in the United States that he cited in speeches and correspondence.

Washington's public stance of accommodation incurred criticism and opposition. The challenge sprang in part from a contrasting figure: a northern-born scholar who was the first black person to receive a doctoral degree from Harvard University. He was W. E. B. Du Bois, historian and sociologist, who at first supported Washington's work and toyed with the notion of teaching at Tuskegee.

Du Bois held a set of ideas that stood in contrast to those of Washington. He believed that Washington's emphasis on industrial training was too narrow, his accommodation to segregation and disenfranchisement an acceptance of injustice, his protests too moderate, his faith in the white South's cooperation with black progress misplaced. Black people should acquire a broad education; the best minds, whom he called the Talented Tenth, should be prepared for leadership of the black race; caste distinctions found in segregation and disenfranchisement should be ended; black people should not allow their faith to repose in southern whites but feel free to migrate northward; and they should not rely heavily on self-help but seek external support. In keeping with this last idea, Du Bois helped organize a movement that in 1910 produced the National Association for the Advancement of Colored People (NAACP). A biracial movement, heavily dependent upon northern white support and leadership, the NAACP took up the fight for full legal and political rights for blacks, employing litigation as a principal weapon.

The NAACP presented a challenge that Washington met by stressing two alternatives. One was the National Negro Business League that Washington had founded in 1900, drawing together black business leaders from three hundred cities; the other was the Urban League, organized in 1911 to foster economic opportunities for African Americans in cities. These activities strengthened and complemented his strategy for achieving equality for blacks.

Significance

Though he remained the preeminent leader of his race until his death on November 14, 1915, Washington saw his influence decline with the election of Wilson and the emergence of the NAACP. By 1915, his philosophy was becoming obsolete as the nation was rapidly urbanizing and industrializing and as black people were migrating to northern cities.

In many ways, Washington had caught the spirit of his age, with its stress on material advancement, faith in progress, self-help, and individualism. Living and working in the South, he probably necessarily accepted white-imposed restraints on black rights and favored white and black cooperation. Tuskegee Institute could not have existed under the administration of a militant black leader. For a generation of black Americans, Washington did much to inspire pride in race, point to a means of progress, and urge sharecroppers and tenants to become owners of farms and skilled workers.

—*James A. Rawley*

Further Reading

Baker, Houston A., Jr. *Turning South Again: Re-thinking Modernism/Re-reading Booker T. Washington*. Durham, N.C.: Duke University Press, 2001. A savage reassessment of Washington's ideas, in which the author criticizes Washington for his fear of offending whites, for founding Tuskegee Institute on the site of an abandoned plantation, and for training black people to work in servile occupations.

Brundage, Fitzhugh, ed. *Booker T. Washington and Black Progress: "Up from Slavery" One Hundred Years Later*. Gainesville: University Press of Florida, 2003. Collection of essays examining Washington's autobiography. Some of the essays discuss the book as biography, history, and legend; place Washington's thought in economic context; and explore the relevance of his autobiography to modern South Africans.

Du Bois, W. E. B. *The Souls of Black Folk: Essays and Sketches*. Chicago: A. C. McClurg, 1903. Written by Washington's leading critic, this book contains an early critique of the Tuskegee educator and his philosophy. It offers a useful contemporary perspective.

Harlan, Louis R. *Booker T. Washington: The Making of a Black Leader, 1856-1901*. New York: Oxford University Press, 1972. The first volume of the best biography, based on profound scholarship, this work is written in a clear style and with good judgment.

――――. *Booker T. Washington: The Wizard of Tuskegee, 1901-1915*. New York: Oxford University Press, 1983. The second and final volume of the prizewinning definitive life, this work fulfills the promise of the first volume.

Harlan, Louis R., et al., eds. *The Booker T. Washington Papers*. 13 vols. Urbana: University of Illinois Press, 1972-1984. These volumes bring together the voluminous papers of Washington, encompassing his speeches, telegrams, letters, and miscellany. Edited with scholarly notes, the papers are invaluable for an understanding of the man and his activities.

Scott, Emmett, and Lyman Beecher Stowe. *Booker T. Washington: Builder of a Civilization*. Garden City, N.Y.: Doubleday, Page, 1916. Written by Washington's secretary and a descendant of abolitionists, this book is valuable for its inside vantage point. Sympathetic in tone, it is nevertheless frank and revealing.

Spencer, Samuel R., Jr. *Booker T. Washington and the Negro's Place in American Life*. Boston: Little, Brown, 1955. A short, reliable, and readable biography, with ample interpretation and balanced judgment.

Verney, Kevern. *The Art of the Possible: Booker T. Washington and Black Leadership in the United States, 1881-1925*. New York: Routledge, 2001. Examines Washington's ideas and achievements, explaining his responses to segregation and his opposition to black urban migration. Compares Washington to Frederick Douglass, W. E. B. Du Bois, and Marcus Garvey.

Washington, Booker T. *Up from Slavery: An Autobiography*. Garden City, N.Y.: Doubleday, Page, 1901. The author's account of his early years, this work also contains a straightforward description of Tuskegee Institute. It has enjoyed a wide readership and stands as a classic.

GEORGE WASHINGTON

" I hold the maxim no less applicable to public than to private affairs, that honesty is always the best policy. "

President of the United States (1789-1797)

As commander in chief of the Continental army during the American Revolution, president of the Constitutional Convention of 1787, and first president of the United States, Washington was the principal architect of the nation's independence and its federal political system.

Born: February 22, 1732; Bridges Creek (now Wakefield), Westmoreland County, Virginia
Died: December 14, 1799; Mount Vernon, Virginia
Areas of achievement: Government and politics; military

EARLY LIFE

Born into a family of middling standing among Virginia's planter elite, George Washington was the eldest son of his father's second marriage. A favorite of his half brother Lawrence Washington of Mount Vernon, young George capitalized on this brother's marriage into the prominent Fairfax family and the inheritance of Lawrence Washington's estate. Thus, despite his losing his father at age eleven and his being a low-priority heir to his father's lands, he was by his mid-twenties able to achieve greater prominence both in estate and position than his ancestors.

His connections allowed him to succeed Lawrence Washington as a major and adjutant of militia in 1752, and the following year he carried a message from Virginia's governor to the French forces encroaching on Virginia-claimed lands in the upper Ohio valley. In 1754, Lieutenant Colonel Washington surrendered a small Virginia detachment under his command to French forces in southwestern Pennsylvania. Thus began the French and Indian War (1754-1763), known in Europe as the Seven Years' War (1756-1763).

Washington's war record was solid but undistinguished, except for his well-recognized bravery during General Edward Braddock's defeat on the Monongahela River in 1756. Failing to receive the royal military commission he sought, he returned to Mount Vernon, engaged in modern farming techniques, expanded his land holdings, and, in 1759, married a wealthy widow, Martha Dandridge Custis. Their marriage was childless, but Washington adopted her two children.

LIFE'S WORK

Elected to the Virginia House of Burgesses, George Washington never achieved a reputation of outspokenness comparable to that of, say, Patrick Henry. A delegate to the First and Second Continental Congresses, Washington impressed his colleagues with his mastery of military affairs and was selected by them to serve as commander in chief of the newly formed Continental army in 1775. He took command of the mostly New England force shortly after its defeat at Breed's (Bunker) Hill and immediately sought to reform it into an effective fighting force. Containing the British forces inside Boston during the winter of 1775-1776, he forced them to evacuate the city the following spring. Action then moved to New York City, where he suffered defeats on Long Island and Manhattan Island and was eventually driven across the Hudson River into and across New Jersey. His counterattacks at Trenton and Princeton during the winter of 1776-1777 revived American hopes and allowed his forces to winter in northern New Jersey.

The following year, he countered the two-pronged British invasion from Canada down the Lake Champlain-Hudson Valley route and from New York via sea against Philadelphia by sending General Horatio Gates with some of his regulars to join local units in combating the northern invasion and by leading the Pennsylvania campaign himself. In the latter area, Washington was soundly defeated by General William Howe's forces but escaped to rebuild his army during the bitter winter at Valley Forge. General Gates won a remarkable victory at Saratoga that encouraged the French government to recognize the United States. The subsequent alliance with France allowed the Americans to continue their efforts and forced the British to concentrate their naval and military forces against an ever-widening war that eventually saw combat from the Indian Ocean to the Caribbean Sea.

The new international conflict caused the British to withdraw from Philadelphia to New York in 1778. When Washington sought to destroy their forces at Monmouth, New Jersey, the result was an indecisive battle that could have turned into a route had not the American commander personally rallied his troops. For the next three years, Washington headquartered his forces near West Point, New York, while combating some British raids and pinning the British forces in the New York City-Long Island vicinity. When the British developed a southern strategy to return Georgia and the Carolinas to their empire, Washington countered by sending Generals Benjamin Lincoln and Horatio Gates to the region. The result was defeat for both officers at Charleston and Camden. In early 1781, Washington sent Nathanael Greene southward, and Greene was able to conduct an effective area defense that thwarted General Charles Cornwallis's attempts to conquer the Carolinas. Exasperated, Cornwallis sought to cut off Greene's supply line and to draw him northward by invading Virginia. At this point, Washington coordinated with the French general, the comte de Rochambeau, commander of a French expeditionary force in Rhode Island, and through him Admiral Count François de Grasse, commander of the French West Indian fleet, to unite their forces against Cornwallis in Virginia. The resultant surrender of Cornwallis at Yorktown in October, 1781, effectively ended British attempts to reintegrate the United States into the British Empire even though the treaty of peace would not be signed until 1783.

After Washington resigned his commission in 1783 (a remarkable event in itself, since most observers expected him to become another Oliver Cromwell), he maintained a high public profile during the next several years but did not seek major positions until 1787, when he became a delegate to the Constitutional Convention and presiding officer of that body. Although his position precluded his taking an active part in the deliberations, he played a significant behind-the-scenes role in the convention and, by lending his name to the final document, helped to ensure its eventual ratification.

During the convention and the ratification process, it was assumed that Washington would become the first chief executive of the new government. Elected president in 1789, he established precedents for the new office that are still followed. Unlike modern presidents, who receive the privileges and prestige of the office, Washington lent his public reputation to the presidency and thereby enhanced its repute.

His government faced difficult tasks in the fields of administrative organization, foreign relations, and economic policy. Influencing each of these areas would be both the clash of personalities and the clash of political interests. Washington sought to resolve the issues without involving himself in the controversy. For the most part, except in the area of foreign policy, he was successful.

One of the most critical areas was the creation of an independent executive system, which was not fully developed in the Constitution. Here Washington prevailed over those desiring to use the Senate as sort of a privy council under the "advise and consent" clause, and those, such as Alexander Hamilton, desiring a parliamentary cabinet system with the major executive officers responsible to the Congress. Among Washington's other achievements were the creation of federal administrative agencies separate from those of the states; the introduction of orderly and stable relationships between officials based on law, instructions, and precedents; the maintenance of high standards of integrity, honesty, and competence; the recognition of claims of locality upon political appointments (often called "senatorial courtesy"); and the dominance of federal authority over individuals, demonstrated decisively in the suppression of the Whiskey Rebellion of 1794. Some of Washington's administrative policies, such as the use of the veto only in relation to constitutional questions, did not long survive his presidency. In the same vein, his use of the cabinet as a consultative body had a short life.

Other developments during his tenure can be attributed less to Washington's personal efforts than to the circumstances of the time or to the role of others. The creation of the judicial system was largely the responsibility of Roger Sherman, the Bill of Rights that of James Madison. The latter also formulated the first national revenue system. Hamilton created a financial system that funded government debts, instituted a national central bank, and established a national mint and stable currency. Washington either actively endorsed or did not oppose (in itself an act of endorsement) these efforts.

In military affairs, Washington often used his secretary of war as a cipher and conduit in a field where he had considerable expertise. His greatest disappointment in this field was Congress's rejection of his proposals for a national military system; instead, it passed the Militia Act of 1792, which left the nation without any effective defense posture.

In foreign affairs he closely worked with Thomas Jefferson in his first administration and followed the often-misguided instincts of Hamilton in the second. Jay's Treaty of 1794 was the most divisive event of his tenure and did far more to encourage partisan politics than did any other policy matter. Despite the political consequences of Washington's diplomacy, he is generally given appreciative accolades for his maintenance of neutrality in the Anglo-French struggle that drew most of the Western world into its vortex.

Washington undoubtedly believed that the greatest weakness of his administration was the development of partisan politics. Both the president's supporters and his opponents favored a consensual political environment that saw partisan activities as divisive of national solidarity and indicative of corruption and personal ambition. The main intent of Washington's farewell address was to warn against political parties.

His final legacy to the presidency was the decision not to run for reelection in 1796 and the consequent two-term tradition that continued until 1940. He established a precedent of turning the office over to a duly elected successor instead of waiting for either death or revolt to remove him from office. Washington did not believe that his presence in the office was indispensable, and he instinctively knew that the peaceful transfer of power to a duly elected successor constituted an important building block in erecting a stable nation.

His retirement from the presidency in 1797 did not remove him entirely from public service. When the Quasi War with France broke out in 1798 (and ended in 1800), President John Adams called Washington back to command the army with the rank of lieutenant general. In this capacity he normally remained at Mount Vernon and delegated much of the running of the army to Major General Hamilton. Washington died after a short illness in late 1799.

Significance

No American figure has for so long dominated the national scene as has George Washington. For nearly twenty-five years, Washington remained the symbol of American nationhood, commanding its armies in a war for national independence, presiding over the convention that drafted its fundamental political charter, and transforming that charter's vague articles into political reality as the first chief magistrate of the republic.

As both general and president, he shaped the American military tradition with its subordination to civilian authority. As president, he established the contours of the American federal system and, even though he opposed its development, the party system. Although a far better statesman than general, he is probably better remembered for his military than for his political contributions to American history.

—*David Curtis Skaggs*

Further Reading

Alden, John R. *George Washington: A Biography*. Baton Rouge: Louisiana State University Press, 1984. A high-quality, one-volume study of Washington's life and a useful introduction to his career.

Burns, James MacGregor, and Susan Dunn. *George Washington*. New York: Times Books, 2004. A concise biography, one in a series of books on the American presidents. Much of the work describes how Washington carefully created a public image emphasizing self-sacrifice and dignity. The authors also praise his presidency, lauding his ability to establish a strong executive branch and develop the most effective style of collective leadership of any American president.

DeConde, Alexander. *Entangling Alliance: Politics and Diplomacy Under George Washington*. Durham, N.C.: Duke University Press, 1958. A good introduction to Washington's foreign policy, which the book strongly endorses.

Ellis, Joseph J. *His Excellency: George Washington*. New York: Alfred A. Knopf,

2004. A best-selling and highly acclaimed biography, based in large part on Washington's cataloged letters and papers at the University of Virginia. Ellis provides a complete account of Washington's life and career, placing both within historical context. The author discusses how Washington, who skillfully crafted his public personality, was equally adept at crafting a political system for the newly created United States.

Flexner, James Thomas. *George Washington*. 4 vols. Boston: Little, Brown, 1965-1972. Perhaps the best of the multivolume biographies, with an especially good treatment of Washington's military career in the second volume.

Freeman, Douglas Southall. *George Washington*. 7 vols. New York: Charles Scribner's Sons, 1948-1957. John A. Carroll and Mary Wells Ashworth completed the final volume of this detailed, nonanalytical study by a Pulitzer Prize-winning biographer.

Hofstadter, Richard. *The Idea of a Party System: The Rise of Legitimate Opposition in the United States*. Berkeley: University of California Press, 1969. A comprehensive analysis of the antiparty tradition of the early republic and of Washington's ambiguous place in early partisan politics.

Kammen, Michael. *A Season of Youth: The American Revolution in Historical Imagination*. New York: Oxford University Press, 1978. A thorough and imaginative reappraisal of the revolutionary theme and Washington's place in it.

Langston, Thomas S., and Michael G. Sherman. *George Washington*. Washington, D.C.: CQ Press, 2003. One in a series of books about the American presidents published by the Congressional Quarterly. The authors examine Washington's life, election campaigns, his presidential policies, and the political crises that occurred during his administration. Each of the book's six chapters includes a brief bibliographic essay.

McCullough, David. *1776*. New York: Simon & Schuster, 2005. McCullough focuses on one year in the American Revolution, 1776, describing the battles between America's ragtag troops and British forces. Using letters, journals, diaries, and other primary sources, he describes the leadership of Washington, Nathanael Greene, and General William Howe, as well as the heroic struggles of American soldiers.

Weems, Mason Locke. *The Life of Washington*. Edited by Marcus Cunliffe. Cambridge, Mass.: Harvard University Press, 1962. This reprinting of the 1809 edition of the book that did much to create the Washington myth contains an excellent introduction by Cunliffe.

Weigley, Russell F. *The American Way of War*. New York: Macmillan, 1973. Contains an excellent chapter on Washington's contributions to the American military tradition.

Wills, Garry. *Cincinnatus: George Washington and the Enlightenment*. Garden City, N.Y.: Doubleday, 1984. A scholar-journalist's often deft insights into Washington's self-image and his popular image in the eighteenth and nineteenth centuries.

John Wayne

> *" Courage is being scared to death—but saddling up anyway. "*

Actor

Wayne, one of the most popular film actors of all time, achieved his greatest work in Westerns, many of which are among the finest such films made. He also came to embody what many people saw as basic American, especially masculine, values, such as strength, courage, patriotism, and willingness to accept personal responsibility.

Born: May 26, 1907; Winterset, Iowa
Died: June 11, 1979; Los Angeles, California
Also known as: Marion Michael Morrison (birth name); The Duke
Areas of achievement: Theater and entertainment; film

Early Life

John Wayne was born Marion Michael Morrison to Clyde and Mary (Molly) Morrison, of Winterset, Iowa. Five years later, the Morrisons had a second son, Robert. Clyde moved to California in 1913 after a Rexall drugstore he had purchased failed. He was joined by his wife and sons the following year, and the family settled in the Antelope Valley north of Los Angeles, where Clyde attempted farming. They moved to Glendale, close to downtown Los Angeles, in 1916, as young Marion's father returned to what he knew best, working in a drugstore. During these childhood years, Marion gained the nickname The Duke after his dog, Little Duke.

At Glendale High School, Morrison excelled. He earned high grades, was a member of the Glendale High Dramatic Society, represented his school in a William Shakespeare competition, and was elected president of his senior class. He also starred at guard on the football team, earning an athletic scholarship to the University of Southern California (USC). During his Glendale years, two of his closest friends were the brothers Bob and Bill Bradbury, who were appearing in their father Robert's short films, *The Adventures of Bob and Bill*. Wayne would later act in about one dozen low-budget B-Westerns directed by the elder Bradbury.

Morrison entered USC in 1925, but his football success was limited; after his freshman year, he was cut from the team by the famous football coach Homer Jones. Morrison had begun working at Fox Film Corporation while attending college, and he continued after leaving USC in 1927, moving crates and furniture and appearing as an occasional extra in films. Six feet four inches tall, handsome, slim, and graceful in movement, Morrison drew the attention of John Ford, the legendary director who would earn six Academy Awards. Ford gave the young actor brief speaking roles in the films *Salute* (1929) and *Men Without Women* (1930). In *Salute*, the soon-to-be John Wayne began his association with Ward Bond, a USC football player who became one of Wayne's closest friends and who regularly appeared in Wayne's films.

1005

Wayne, John

LIFE'S WORK

Although Ford is the director most associated with Wayne, it was Raoul Walsh who transformed Marion Michael Morrison into John Wayne, renaming the aspiring actor and teaching him how to ride a horse. Walsh made Wayne into a star by giving him the lead role in *The Big Trail* (1930), but the star would be clouded by a sky of B-Westerns for the next decade.

The Big Trail was an artistically successful film, and Wayne performed convincingly in his role as the noble hero scouting for a wagon train heading west. In his first major role, Wayne already demonstrated a professionalism that would permanently characterize his work. *The Big Trail* ultimately failed, primarily because of the onset of the Great Depression in 1929. Walsh filmed the story in both traditional 35 millimeter and the new 75 millimeter that permitted a wider camera range. Many theaters could not afford the new technology and were forced to show *The Big Trail* in the standard 35-millimeter version, which deprived the film of its sense of grandeur. Fox studios went into receivership, and although the studio continued to turn out motion pictures, it did not have the money to promote its new stars.

During the 1930's Wayne moved from studio to studio, spending most of his time making B-Westerns but at the same time learning and growing as an actor. He managed to stay employed throughout the Depression. Wayne's roles for Mascot, Warner Bros., and Monogram brought him into daily contact with Yakima Canutt, the legendary stuntman with whom he began a lasting friendship. From Canutt, Wayne learned to perfect his horsemanship and master the art of staging fistfights (a continuing staple of Wayne films). Throughout his career, even when age and declining health robbed him of his agility, Wayne insisted on performing many of his own stunts.

During the 1930's Wayne married Josephine Saenz, the first of his three wives, with whom he had four children: Michael, Toni, Patrick, and Melinda. Subsequent marriages were to Esperanza "Chata" Bauer and Pilar Palette. Wayne had three children with Palette: Aissa, John Ethan, and Marissa. Several of Wayne's children appeared in his films, most notably Patrick in *The Searchers* (1956) and *The Comancheros* (1961).

Wayne's breakthrough film was a John Ford Western, *Stagecoach* (1939), which ended Wayne's long apprenticeship, reunited him with the director for whom he would make some of his greatest films, and introduced film fans to Monument Valley in Utah, soon to become a classic setting for Westerns. In *Stagecoach*, Wayne played the Ringo Kid, who was falsely accused of murder and who broke out of jail to return home and avenge his father's murder.

The Shepherd of the Hills (1941) starred Wayne with one of his personal heroes, the cowboy star of silent films, Harry Carey, Sr. The film was directed by Henry Hathaway, who later directed Wayne in his only Oscar-winning performance, as Rooster Cogburn in *True Grit* (1969). Wayne acted with Carey three more times, in *The Spoilers* (1942), *Angel and the Badman* (1947), and *Red River* (1948). In one of the most famous scenes in all of Wayne's films, Wayne stood in the doorway of a cabin at the end of *The Searchers* (1956) holding his right forearm in his left hand in a typical Carey pose eight years after the older man's death. Wayne's friendship with Carey extended to his son, Harry Carey, Jr., who performed with Wayne in such films as *Red*

River, *Three Godfathers* (1949), *She Wore a Yellow Ribbon* (1949), *Rio Grande* (1950), and *The Searchers*.

The year 1948 was a turning point for Wayne as two of the films released that year—*Fort Apache* and *Red River*—established their protagonist as one of Hollywood's leading stars. *Fort Apache*, with Henry Fonda, was the first of three Seventh Cavalry films in which John Ford directed Wayne (the others were *She Wore a Yellow Ribbon* and *Rio Grande*). Although Wayne played a cavalry officer in all three, his character changed with each film in an early indication of the versatility as an actor that Wayne possessed and for which he has often been given insufficient credit. *Rio Grande* introduced Wayne's successful acting partnership with the Irish actor Maureen O'Hara, whose flaming red hair, quick wit, and sharp tongue enabled her to hold her own in scenes with Wayne. They usually played spouses in initially antagonistic but ultimately loving relationships.

Red River offered Wayne the opportunity to work with the director Howard Hawks and play a character well removed from his usual roles. Tom Dunson, a middle-aged cattleman faced with financial reverses, set out to drive his herd to market accompanied by his adopted son, played by Montgomery Clift. The Wayne character became a tyrannical, obsessed trail boss who alienated his son, threatened to kill him, and beat him. The following year, Wayne made *Sands of Iwo Jima* (1949), where, as Sergeant Stryker, he established another Wayne persona, that of the powerful and courageous soldier whose tough love led his men at times to despise him but finally to respect his leadership and intentions.

Except for *The Quiet Man* (1952), directed by Ford and set in Ireland (and also starring Maureen O'Hara), most of Wayne's best films during the 1950's, 1960's, and 1970's were Westerns: *The Searchers*, in which Wayne, in perhaps one of his greatest performances, played Ethan Edwards, a man obsessed with his ten-year pursuit of revenge against the American Indians who kidnapped his nieces; *The Man Who Shot Liberty Valance* (1962), directed by Ford and costarring James Stewart; *True Grit* (1969); *Big Jake* (1971), with Maureen O'Hara; *Rooster Cogburn* (1975), costarring Katharine Hepburn; and Wayne's final film, *The Shootist* (1976), with James Stewart.

Wayne, who had undergone surgery for cancer in 1964 and lost part of a lung, was again diagnosed with cancer in January, 1979. After stomach surgery on January 10, he regained enough strength to attend the Academy Awards on April 9, where he gave a moving speech to a rousing ovation. Wayne was hospitalized again early in May and remained at the medical center of the University of California, Los Angeles, until his death on June 11, 1979.

SIGNIFICANCE

Wayne's films (he made more than 150) encompass many subjects and genres, but he remains best known for his war and Western films. In Westerns, Wayne became an American symbol, rugged, self-reliant, tough, but one with a heart of gold that millions of viewers imagined reflected their own behavior.

Wayne is also remembered for his conservative political views and ideological films. Both *The Alamo* (1960) and *The Green Berets* (1969), the latter released a few months after the Tet Offensive during the Vietnam War, were self-consciously patriotic and have often been viewed more as propaganda than as entertainment. Even as large numbers of intellectuals and the young turned against Wayne in the 1960's, his popularity with the general public remained high.

In his final films, Wayne continued to demonstrate his versatility as an actor. Deliberately using his age and growing waistline, he cemented his association with the American West as a way of life receding into the sunset. As the seriocomic and flawed Rooster Cogburn in *True Grit* and *Rooster Cogburn*, he portrayed an anachronism summoned to right a wrong that only he could correct; by doing so, he demonstrated the essential dignity and honor beneath his outdated veneer. In *The Man Who Shot Liberty Valance*, Wayne explicitly represented the past, in contrast to James Stewart, who learned to adjust and move into the future. Finally, in *The Shootist*, Wayne played the aging gunfighter J. B. Books, who was dying of cancer. Rather than wait for the cancer to kill him, Books ended his life by deliberately making himself a target for his enemies. The film was an eerily fitting conclusion to Wayne's career. *The Shootist* also emphasized the end of the Old West, although that West continues to live, and will continue to live, in Wayne's films.

—*Edward J. Rielly*

FURTHER READING

Davis, Ronald L. *Duke: The Life and Image of John Wayne*. Norman: University of Oklahoma Press, 1998. Davis examines many aspects of Wayne's life and career, including his impact on American culture. Includes a filmography that lists Wayne films by year with principal participants.

Kazanjian, Howard, and Chris Enss. *Young Duke: The Early Life of John Wayne*. Guilford, Conn.: TwoDot, 2007. Focuses on Wayne's life from his birth through the 1940's, describing his earliest experiences, his influences, and his film roles.

Munn, Michael. *John Wayne: The Man Behind the Myth*. London: Robson Books, 2003. Admiring chronicle of Wayne's life and career.

Roberts, Randy, and James Stuart Olson. *John Wayne: American*. New York: Free Press, 1995. This exhaustive and substantive biography written by experienced and accomplished historians is essential for an in-depth knowledge of Wayne's life and career.

Wayne, Aissa, with Steve Delsohn. *John Wayne, My Father*. New York: Random House, 1991. This intimate inside portrait of Wayne by one of his daughters gives a balanced account of the father's strengths and weaknesses as a parent. At times unclear regarding facts and dates, it nonetheless offers many insights into the character of Wayne.

Wayne, Pilar, with Alex Thorleifson. *John Wayne: My Life with the Duke*. New York: McGraw-Hill, 1987. Written by Wayne's third wife, this book is perhaps the most valuable primary source of knowledge about the actor because it includes much information known only by the author.

Wills, Garry. *John Wayne's America: The Politics of Celebrity*. New York: Simon & Schuster, 1997. Wills explores Wayne's accomplishments and friendships, including detailed accounts of his relationships with John Ford and Harry Carey. The author also examines the relationship between Wayne and his country, including his ideological films and his status as an American icon.

Zolotow, Maurice. *Shooting Star: A Biography of John Wayne.* New York: Simon & Schuster, 1974. This was the most important biography of Wayne until the 1990's. Zolotow was the ghostwriter of Wayne's unfinished autobiography, which gave Zolotow access to a rich trove of personal information.

IDA B. WELLS-BARNETT

❝ *One had better die fighting against injustice than die like a dog or a rat in a trap.* **❞**

Civil rights activist

An organizer of the antilynching movement, Wells-Barnett was an indefatigable crusader for equal rights for African Americans in the violent decades around the turn of the twentieth century. She also worked on issues of education, social services, woman suffrage, and racial violence.

Born: July 16, 1862; Holly Springs, Mississippi
Died: March 25, 1931; Chicago, Illinois
Also known as: Ida Bell Wells (birth name); Iola (pseudonym)
Areas of achievement: Civil rights; social reform; women's rights; journalism

EARLY LIFE

Ida B. Wells-Barnett was the eldest of eight children born in slavery to slave parents who were both of mixed racial parentage. (Her paternal grandfather was her grandmother's white owner, and her mother's father was an American Indian.) Both had learned trades during slavery—carpentry and cooking—which they were able to continue after the Civil War. In the yellow fever epidemic of 1878, both parents and their youngest child died, leaving Ida as the sole support of the younger children. Refusing offers from relatives and friends to parcel out the children, sixteen-year-old Ida decided to get a job as a schoolteacher. She had been educated at the Freedmen's School in Holly Springs (later Rust College). She successfully took the teacher's exam for the rural county schools and was able to "pass" for eighteen, teaching all week and riding a mule six miles home for the weekend. (A family friend stayed with the siblings during the week.) Later, she secured a better-paying position in Memphis. In 1886—after traveling to Fresno, California, with her aunt and siblings—she actually taught school in three different states: California, Missouri, and Tennessee.

Wells-Barnett's activist career began in 1884, when she was forcibly ejected from the ladies' car on the Chesapeake and Ohio Railroad for refusing to sit in the segregated smoking car. (Jim Crow segregation of transportation facilities was just beginning then.) She sued the railroad and won $500 in damages; an appeal by the railroad to the Tennessee Supreme Court reversed the decision, however, and she had to pay court costs.

1009

Wells-Barnett, Ida B.

Wells-Barnett's interest in journalism began in Memphis, where she participated in a weekly lyceum with other black schoolteachers, reading and discussing the weekly black newspaper *The Evening Star*, among other things. When she saw how much influence the newspapers had, she began writing a weekly column, which became popular and was printed in many newspapers across the country. She signed her articles "Iola." The name of the protagonist of fellow African American Frances Ellen Watkins Harper's popular novel *Iola Leroy* (1892) may have alluded to Wells-Barnett. In 1889, she purchased a one-third interest in the *Memphis Free Speech and Headlight*, resigned her teaching job, and began organizing, writing, and selling subscriptions for the newspaper in black communities and churches throughout the South.

LIFE'S WORK

In 1892, three black men who owned a successful grocery store that competed with a white-owned store in a black neighborhood were lynched in Memphis, Tennessee. Wells-Barnett not only editorialized against the lynching in her newspaper but also counseled black citizens to leave Memphis and move west to Arkansas and the newly opened Oklahoma Territory. Thousands took her advice. Those who remained heeded her call to boycott the streetcar system. In 1892, therefore, Wells-Barnett organized a successful public transportation boycott, sixty years before Rosa Parks began the Montgomery bus boycott after she refused to vacate her seat in the back of the bus to let a white person take it. Thus began Wells-Barnett's life work—her crusade for justice.

When Wells-Barnett left Memphis for a speaking and writing trip to Philadelphia and New York, angry whites destroyed her offices and press and published notices that if she returned she herself would be lynched. She was hired by the important black paper the *New York Age* to gather lynching statistics and expose as a fallacy that black men raped white women. Only one-fourth of all those who were lynched were even accused of sexually accosting or insulting a white woman. Women and children as well as white men were victims of lynch mobs. Most lynchings, she found, were economically motivated, designed to intimidate the black community if it attempted to become financially independent. She used white newspaper accounts to gather her evidence, publishing in 1892 her first feature story (later a pamphlet): "Southern Horrors: Lynch Law in All Its Phases." She listed all lynchings by name, state, alleged crime, method of killing, and month, and continued this practice in the following years.

Even in the North, Wells-Barnett's speeches and writings exposing lynch law were not well covered by a frightened white press, and she despaired of making any changes. She knew that international pressure could aid the cause, so she took her antilynching crusade worldwide, traveling to England to 1893 and again in 1894. She was warmly received by former abolitionists, and she published her stories in the mainstream press, lectured daily, and founded the first antilynching organizations. Her strategy worked—the American press picked up the stories from England, and the antilynching story was disseminated to a wider audience. When she attacked well-known white Americans Frances Willard (the president of the Women's Christian Temperance Union) and evangelist Dwight L. Moody for addressing segregated white audiences in the South and not speaking out against mob violence, Wells-Barnett became the center of an international controversy but gained much publicity for her cause.

Wells-Barnett, Ida B.

In 1893, Wells-Barnett returned from England and, along with the venerable former slave Frederick Douglass and Ferdinand Barnett (a Chicago attorney to whom she was later married), organized the protest of excluded African Americans at the Chicago World Columbian Exposition. The three activists wrote and distributed twenty thousand copies of their pamphlet, *The Reason Why the Colored American Is Not in the Columbian Exposition*, to people from all over the world. Douglass, the ambassador to Haiti at that time, was the only African American who was officially a part of the exposition. The pamphlet pointed out that without blacks there would be neither American civilization nor the industrial miracle so celebrated at the fair.

Remaining in Chicago after her second trip to England, Wells-Barnett was married to Barnett and eventually gave birth to four children, but she continued her political organizing and journalism in Chicago's black newspaper *The Conservator* (which she purchased from Barnett). Although she was criticized by other women activists such as Susan B. Anthony for marrying and thus having "divided duty," Wells-Barnett managed to be both a mother and an organizer, often traveling to lectures with one or another child, nursing between meetings. In Chicago, she founded the first black woman's club (later named the Ida B. Wells Club), the Alpha Suffrage Club (the first black woman's suffrage organization), and the Negro Fellowship League (which set up a reading room, job referrals, and a rooming house for black men newly arrived in Chicago). She helped to found a black kindergarten and a black orchestra, and she worked as a probation officer.

Wells-Barnett's political position was very much opposed to that of accommodationists such as Booker T. Washington. She espoused a radical view akin to that of W. E. B. Du Bois and later the pan-Africanism of Marcus Garvey. She believed that African Americans should use both the law and agitation to gain equal rights in all areas and that nothing was impossible. Along with Du Bois, she was one of the founding members of the National Association for the Advancement of Colored People (NAACP) in 1909, but she later broke with the organization because of its timid stance on racial issues.

As an Illinois delegate to the national woman suffrage parade in Washington in 1913, Wells-Barnett refused to march with the black delegates at the back of the procession; she quietly integrated the ranks of the Illinois delegates as the parade moved down Pennsylvania Avenue. She helped Chicago elect its first black alderman in 1915 and continued to work within the political structure, running herself unsuccessfully for the state senate in 1930.

Wells-Barnett continued her investigative work in the South with a campaign to give justice to the black soldiers involved in the 1917 24th Infantry rebellion in Texas during World War I. She personally investigated the causes of the East St. Louis and Chicago riots of 1919 (which she predicted in print two weeks before they occurred). In 1922, she visited and wrote an exposé of the prison conditions of the Arkansas black farmers who had formed a cooperative and were attacked by whites—and then were arrested for starting a riot. For this journalistic work, she was hounded by the Federal Bureau of Investigation as a dangerous subversive during the Red Scare of the early 1920's.

Wells-Barnett labored to the end of her life, leaving her autobiography unfinished in midsentence when she succumbed to her final illness. She died of uremic poisoning at the age of sixty-eight.

Wells-Barnett, Ida B.

Significance

Wells-Barnett was radical, disputatious, angry, hard to get along with, and had arguments with nearly everyone with whom she worked. She said that she did not want publicity, but her autobiography makes it clear that she craved personal publicity. Still, she was a genius of an organizer: She had political savvy and a photographic memory. She was a powerful woman who played by the men's rules. She organized and carried out a successful economic boycott of public transportation facilities in the 1890's, she integrated the American woman suffrage movement, she single-handedly brought international attention to bear on the lynching scandal in the United States, and she kept the Chicago school system from being segregated by enlisting the help of social worker Jane Addams.

Wells-Barnett knew everyone and alienated everyone, and she took her issues personally to two presidents—William McKinley and Woodrow Wilson. She worked with, at various times, African Americans Washington, Du Bois, Garvey, Madam C. J. Walker, Douglass, Anna Gaily Cooper, Fannie Barrier Williams, Mary Church Terrell, Mary McLeod Bethune, and many others. Although Wells-Barnett worked with whites when it was politically expedient to do so, she believed that a unified black community should band together for its own betterment. Her radical position and her refusal to compromise resulted in her near-erasure from American history, but Wells-Barnett has begun to garner more attention as the result of scholarly efforts in the fields of women's history and African American history.

—*Margaret McFadden*

Further Reading

Bedermank, Gail. "'Civilization,' the Decline of Middle-Class Manliness, and Ida B. Wells's Antilynching Campaign (1892-94)." *Radical History Review* 52 (1992): 5-30. An analysis of the racist evolutionary rhetoric of the end of the century, with special reference to Wells-Barnett's work in England and at the Chicago World Columbian Exposition of 1893.

Giddings, Paula. *When and Where I Enter: The Impact of Black Women on Race and Sex in America*. New York: William Morrow, 1984. A history of black women in the United States, with large interpretive sections on Wells-Barnett's activist career, especially the antilynching campaign in England, the founding of the NAACP, and her activist work in Chicago. A good index and a bibliography are included.

Hendricks, Wanda. "Ida Bell Wells-Barnett." In *Black Women in America: An Historical Encyclopedia*, edited by Darlene Clark Hine. Brooklyn, N.Y.: Carlson, 1993. An important reference work that includes photographs and primary and secondary bibliographies.

Loewenberg, Bert James, and Ruth Bogin, eds. *Black Women in Nineteenth Century American Life*. University Park: Pennsylvania State University Press, 1976. Includes the introduction and a selection from Wells-Barnett's antilynching writings published in London in 1892.

McMurry, Linda. *To Keep the Waters Troubled: The Life of Ida B. Wells*. New York: Oxford University Press, 1998. Biography portraying Wells as a fierce social advocate.

Schechter, Patricia A. *Ida B. Wells-Barnett and American Reform, 1880-1930*. Chapel Hill: University of North Carolina Press, 2001. Chronicles Wells-Barnett's role in early efforts toward civil rights, women's suffrage, and Progressivism.

Sterling, Dorothy. "Ida B. Wells: Voice of a People." In *Black Foremothers: Three Lives*. Old Westburg, N.Y.: Feminist Press, 1979. A well-written and accessible narrative about all aspects of Wells's life. Contains a useful list of sources.

Wells, Ida B. *Crusade for Justice: The Autobiography of Ida B. Wells*. Edited by Alfreda M. Duster. Chicago: University of Chicago Press, 1970. This is Wells-Barnett's unfinished autobiography, which was edited and published by her daughter. It is the best source for biographical detail about Wells-Barnett's organizing and political work and is an important source for newspaper clippings and articles, many of which are printed verbatim.

ELIE WIESEL

" *Because I remember, I despair. Because I remember, I have the duty to reject despair.* **"**

Holocaust survivor and peace activist

Wiesel, a prize-winning novelist, dramatist, and religious philosopher, wrote about the Holocaust and its remembrance, the nature of God, and God's terrible silence, all on behalf of the world's victims. He became the conscience of modern times and was awarded the Nobel Peace Prize in 1986.

Born: September 30, 1928; Sighet, Transylvania, Romania
Also known as: Eliezer Wiesel (full name)
Areas of achievement: Literature; social reform; religion and theology

EARLY LIFE

Elie Wiesel (EHL-ee vee-ZEHL) was born in Sighet, a small town in the Carpathian Mountains, in an area that belonged to Hungary during World War II but that was Romanian territory before and after the war. Wiesel's father, Shlomo Wiesel, though a practicing member of the Jewish religious community, questioned traditional Judaism; a tolerant humanist, he emphasized the modern world at large and the need to be a part of it. Wiesel's mother, Sarah Wiesel, had a lasting and, probably, deeper influence. A devout woman steeped in Hasidism, she hoped that her only son would become a rabbi. To that end, Wiesel studied the Torah and the Talmud in a local yeshiva known for its ascetic mysticism and Kabbalist teachers. This sheltered, bookish existence was irrevocably shattered in the spring of 1944, when the Nazis invaded Hungary and rounded up all its Jews, including Wiesel, his parents, and three sisters.

The fifteen-year-old Wiesel, along with his father, was sent first to Auschwitz and then to Buchenwald, from which he was liberated by American troops on April 11, 1945. (His two elder sisters survived as well.) The horrors he witnessed there, the despair he felt, and the anger he directed at God were all to be incorporated in his literary and philosophical writings. Shortly after the war, the young adolescent went to a refugee home in France, where in two years he learned French by carefully reading the classics, especially Jean Racine, whose style he was later to adopt; indeed, French remained Wiesel's preferred written language. In addition, he was developing a lifelong passion for philosophy (starting with Immanuel Kant and Karl Marx) and for philosophical fiction.

From 1948 to 1951, Wiesel studied philosophy, psychology, and literature at the Sorbonne, but, forced to work, he never finished his thesis on comparative asceticism. Instead, he began a career as a journalist, which allowed him to travel extensively; after immigrating to the United States in 1956, he became the United Nations correspondent for an Israeli newspaper, *Yediot Aharonot*.

At the urging of the French Roman Catholic novelist François Mauriac, Wiesel agreed to bear witness to the six million Jews murdered in Europe's concentration camps. From a massive work he wrote in Yiddish, *Un di Velt hot geshvign* (1956, and the world remained silent), Wiesel distilled a very brief but exceedingly powerful memoir of the Holocaust, published in French as *La Nuit* (1958; *Night*, 1960). Both a wrenching account of the presence of evil and a terrifying indictment of God's injustice, this book received international acclaim. Wiesel had found his voice and his themes.

In 1955, Wiesel traveled to New York City. Following a traffic accident there in 1956, unable to travel, he was forced to stay past the expiration of his visa. The U.S. government granted him citizenship to legalize his status.

Life's Work

Following the success of *Night*, Wiesel wrote in rapid succession two short novels presenting the guilty anguish of those who survived the mass slaughter: *L'Aube* (1960; *Dawn*, 1961) and *Le Jour* (1961; *The Accident*, 1962). That every act is ambiguous and implies a loss of innocence and that "God commit[s] the most unforgivable crime; to kill without a reason" are central to the protagonists' conduct and outlook. Little by little, however, Wiesel's characters come to realize that friendship can help them live in the post-Holocaust world. This is especially true in *La Ville de la chance* (1962; *The Town Beyond the Wall*, 1964), where, despite society's indifference to persecution and cruelty, loving and being a friend allow people to attain a kind of equilibrium. Questions about God, evil, and suffering, while they cannot be satisfactorily answered, must nevertheless be asked, since from the beginning such a dialogue has been established between God and His creation. By rejoining his religious community, Wiesel seems to suggest further, in *Les Portes de la forêt* (1964; *The Gates of the Forest*, 1966), that the survivor may finally create joy from despair.

At the same time that he was publishing his novels, Wiesel began writing eyewitness accounts and autobiographical pieces and stories of his life during the Hitler years. After a 1965 trip to the Soviet Union, he described in a series of articles originally published in Hebrew in *Yediot Aharonot* (collected and translated as *The Jews of Silence*, 1966) the plight of Soviet Jewry, as they tried to maintain their ethnic and religious identity in the face of often implacable anti-Semitism. His yeshiva and Sorbonne

Elie Wiesel.
(© The Nobel Foundation)

studies, along with more mature and in-depth readings of biblical texts and exegeses, were to form the basis of other nonfiction works, including several studies of Hasidism and Hasidic masters.

The prize-winning novel *Le Mendiant de Jérusalem* (1968; *A Beggar in Jerusalem*, 1970) marked a turning point for Wiesel. The novel shows how, through Israel's victory in the Six-Day War, a tormented people came of age; while celebrating this moment, the novel is both a memorial to the dead and an appeal on behalf of the world's "beggars." Although still haunted by the Holocaust, Wiesel could thereafter write about other human issues and problems faced by the next generation. For example, is madness, he asked in the first of several plays, an acceptable option for dealing with persecution (*Zalmen: Ou, La Folie de Dieu*, 1968; *Zalmen: Or, The Madness of God*, 1975)? Is silence a method for overcoming horror (*Le Serment de Kolvillàg*, 1973; *The Oath*, 1973)?

In 1969, Wiesel married Marion Erster Rose, who was to become his principal translator and with whom he would have one son. In the fall of 1972, he began his tenure at the City College of New York as Distinguished Professor of Judaic Studies. This endowed chair gave him the opportunity to teach young students (he considered himself an educator first) the celebrations and paradoxes of Jewish theology and the meaning of modern Jewishness and to continue writing in diverse genres. He left this position in 1976 to become the Andrew Mellon Professor of Humanities at Boston University. In 1982 he was the first Henry Luce Visiting Scholar in Humanities and Social Thought at Yale University, and from 1997 to 1999 he held the Ingeborg Rennert Visiting Professorship of Judaic Studies at Barnard College.

During this period Wiesel also was involved in various social and political activities, from fighting against racism, war, fanaticism, apartheid, and violence to commemorating the Holocaust. In fact, some historians credit him with introducing "Holocaust" as the primary name for the Nazis' death camps policy. (He was a member of the U.S. Holocaust Memorial Council until 1986, when he resigned in protest over U.S. president Ronald Reagan's controversial visit to the military cemetery in Bitburg, West Germany.) For his humanitarian work and his concern for the oppressed everywhere, as well as for his literary achievements, he received numerous honorary degrees, prizes, and awards, including the Congressional Gold Medal, the rank of Commandeur in the French Legion d'honneur, and, in 1986, the Nobel Peace Prize. It was bestowed both for his practical work in the cause of peace and for his message of "peace, atonement, and human dignity." He used the money from the prize to establish the Elie Wiesel Foundation, which is dedicated to combat indifference and misinformation about the Holocaust through international dialogue and educational programs. Moreover, in 1992 he received the Ellis Island Medal of Honor, was elected to the American Academy of Arts and Letters in 1996, and in 2006 was awarded an honorary knighthood from the United Kingdom for his efforts in Holocaust education there.

Meanwhile, Wiesel continued to publish plays, novels, and nonfiction at a prolific pace, producing more than forty books; in these he again wove post-Holocaust despair and divine cruelty, but above all he denounced the world's forgetfulness of and indifference to humankind's inhumanity to humans. In 1995 he published the first volume of his memoirs, *All Rivers Run to the Sea*, which describes his childhood in Romania, internment in concentration camps, life in France following World War II, and life in the United States until 1969 and his marriage to Marion. The second volume, *And the Sea Is Never Full*, appeared in 1999 and takes up the story of his writing and activism into the late 1990's. In 1999 he also added children's literature to his accomplishments with the publication of *King Solomon and the Magic Ring*.

Among Wiesel's late novels is *Les Juges* (1999; *The Judges*, 2002), a moral fable set in Connecticut. Five travelers are stranded in the home of a man who is deluded with the belief that he is a judge and will sentence one of them to death during their brief stay. He terrorizes them with insinuating questions, and their responses reveal their essential character—a brutal process that summons up the dangers of unbridled state-sponsored interrogation. *Le Temps des déracinés* (2003; *The Time of the Uprooted*, 2005) concerns a Czech refugee from World War II who was raised in Hungary and moved to New York, working as a ghostwriter. In a complex plot he weaves his own memories with those of other displaced Jews among his friends to plumb the lasting effects of the Holocaust on their morality, ability to love, and faith.

Wiesel continued his efforts at peace and reconciliation. He became a member of the Human Rights Foundation, and in 2004 the Romanian government invited him to head what came to be known as the Wiesel Commission to study the history of the Holocaust in Romania. In 2006, with American actor George Clooney, he testified before the United Nations Security Council, urging it to confront the humanitarian disaster wrought by Sudan's civil war.

Wiesel also was a popular lecturer, often to the consternation of his critics. In 2007 he was attacked and nearly kidnapped by a Holocaust denier while staying in a hotel in San Francisco, California.

Significance

The Holocaust and its remembrance, the nature of God and the terrible silence of God: These themes recur throughout Wiesel's novels, plays, personal recollections, and nonfiction. In trying to understand the mystery of theodicy, this modern humanist encompassed much of Jewish lore, tradition, and memory. In addition, by asking—but without answering—the hard questions that have always plagued humans and by relating the Jews' unique experience to the universal legacy of humanity, he succeeded in creating the quintessential Everyman: "What I try to do is to speak for man, but as a Jew. I make no distinction and I certainly make no restriction."

Wiesel wrote with contempt against revisionist historians who deny the very existence of the Nazi extermination camps. He passionately defended the conduct of the murdered and the survivors to his fellow Jews—those who are ashamed of the submissiveness of the victims and those who are skeptical of the survivors' integrity. He no less passionately criticized novelists and playwrights, television and film directors for trivializing the tragedy of six million martyrs, for whom he became the greatest memorialist.

—*Pierre L. Horn*

Further Reading

Berenbaum, Michael. *The Vision of the Void: Theological Reflections on the Works of Elie Wiesel*. Middletown, Conn.: Wesleyan University Press, 1979. Although discussing works published before 1979, this is an excellent study of the Jewish tradition as evident in Wiesel's religious writings and sociocultural position. The bibliography on theological philosophy is quite useful.

Cargas, Harry James. *Harry James Cargas in Conversation with Elie Wiesel*. New York: Paulist Press, 1976. In a series of fascinating and varied interviews, Wiesel speaks not only about the Holocaust but also about his audience, his craft, and his mission as a writer and witness.

_____, ed. *Responses to Elie Wiesel*. New York: Persea Books, 1978. A stimulating collection of articles, interviews, and book chapters (a few are new, most are reprinted), which presents specific aspects of Wiesel's thought. Maurice Friedman's essay on "the Job of Auschwitz" is particularly perceptive; letters, written by Christian philosophers and theologians, show Wiesel's influence outside the Jewish world as well.

Estess, Ted L. *Elie Wiesel*. New York: Ungar, 1980. In spite of its brevity, this general introduction of Wiesel's life and career is well argued and often insightful.

Horowitz, Rosemary, ed. *Elie Wiesel and the Art of Story Telling*. Jefferson, N.C.:

McFarland, 2006. The eleven essays in this book examine Wiesel's use of Jewish traditions, folklore, and religion in his fiction, as well as the influence of his Yiddish and Hebrew education, Holocaust experience, and moral imperative.

Rosenfeld, Alvin H., and Irving Greenberg, eds. *Confronting the Holocaust: The Impact of Elie Wiesel*. Bloomington: Indiana University Press, 1978. A balanced collection of provocative essays, written by scholars from different disciplines. Also interesting is Wiesel's own short statement, "Why I Write." Includes a highly selective and partly annotated bibliography of his writings.

Roth, John K. *A Consuming Fire: Encounters with Elie Wiesel and the Holocaust*. Atlanta, Ga.: John Knox Press, 1979. This examination by a philosopher of ethics and religion, to which Wiesel contributed an informative prologue, is both thorough and intelligent.

Wiesel, Elie. *All Rivers Run to the Sea: Memoirs, Vol. 1, 1928-1969*. New York: Knopf, 1995. A moving account of Wiesel's early life and struggle to regain belief in hope for humanity following his time in Nazi concentration camps and the loss of family members.

_____. *And the Sea Is Never Full: Memoirs, Vol. II, 1969-Present*. New York: Knopf, 1999. Wiesel recounts his career as a journalist, novelist, and political activist, during which he met many world leaders and chaired the effort to build a memorial to the Holocaust.

Wiesel, Elie, and Richard D. Heffner. *Conversations with Elie Wiesel*. New York: Schocken Books, 2003. Drawn from the Public Broadcasting Service's program *The Open Road*, hosted by Heffner, the conversations range over topics such as nationalism, philosophy, religion and politics, capital punishment, and euthanasia. They afford insights into Wiesel's manner of thinking, moral principles, and humility.

HAZEL WIGHTMAN

> **“** *My brothers, who had played a little tennis . . . took me to San Rafael to see a match . . . and we all decided then and there that this would be an excellent game for me.* **”**

Tennis player

Labeled the Queen Mother of American tennis, Wightman was a four-time national singles champion of the United States Lawn Tennis Association who paved the way for the acceptance of women's tennis as a reputable sport in the United States.

Born: December 20, 1886; Healdsburg, California
Died: December 5, 1974; Chestnut Hill, Massachusetts
Also known as: Hazel Virginia Hotchkiss (birth name); Hazel Hotchkiss Wightman (full name)
Area of achievement: Sports

EARLY LIFE

Hazel Wightman (HAY-zuhl WIT-man) was born Hazel Virginia Hotchkiss in the Northern California town of Healdsburg. On her mother's side, she was the descendent of Virginia expatriates who had moved west following the Civil War. Her father's parents had moved from Kentucky and settled in California shortly after it was admitted to the Union in 1850.

Wightman's father, William Joseph Hotchkiss, a respected and successful Sonoma Valley rancher and owner of a cannery, encouraged her to play aggressive sports (perhaps as an antidote for her poor health as a child) with her three older brothers and her younger brother. Although frail and petite, Wightman played baseball and football with her four brothers and more than held her own. She would later recall that her mother, Emma Groves Hotchkiss, worried that Wightman might become too much of a tomboy and admonished her never to forget to act like a lady. She was encouraged by her mother to give up the rough sports she played with her four brothers and concentrate instead on playing tennis.

Shortly after her family moved to Berkeley, California, in 1900 when she was fourteen, Wightman began playing tennis. Her style of play was established early. Most of her practice was on the makeshift gravel court at her home, since girls were not permitted on the single asphalt court at Berkeley after eight in the morning. Because of the challenges of playing on a gravel surface, she developed a game that depended on hitting the ball before it had an opportunity to bounce, and she soon became accomplished at this technique of volleying.

LIFE'S WORK

After six months of intensive preparation, Wightman entered her first tournament. She and her partner, Mary Radcliffe, won the women's doubles championship in the Bay Counties tournament held in San Francisco. In the next seven years she not only helped change the prevailing belief that women should play a baseline rather than a volleying game, but also helped to popularize changes in tennis attire by wearing loose-fitting

Hazel Wightman. (Library of Congress)

dresses when she played. She even popularized sleeveless dresses to provide greater freedom of movement for the arms. Combining tennis and academics while she attended the University of California, Berkeley, Wightman won the United States singles, doubles, and mixed doubles championships three consecutive years (1909-1911), an accomplishment equaled only by two other women (Alice Marble, 1938-1940; Margaret Osborne du Pont, 1948-1950). Her performance in the 1911 championships is even more remarkable because she won the singles, doubles, and mixed doubles championships on the same day. Her rivalry with May Sutton in the tournaments in California at this time was perhaps the first publicly recognized rivalry for women in tennis. Although she brought a strong spirit of competition to this intense rivalry, Wightman quickly developed a reputation for authentic sportsmanship and was mentioned by subsequent women tennis players as a model they used in their careers.

Following her graduation from college in 1911, Wightman married George W. Wightman, a former Harvard tennis player and member of a prominent Boston family. The births of three children between 1912 and 1919 did not stop Hazel's activities as a competitive player on the national level. She resumed playing competitively after the birth of her first child, George, Jr., and added another United States Doubles Championship to her list of accomplishments in 1915. She also won the United States mixed doubles titles in 1918 and 1920, and in 1919, at the age of thirty-three, Wightman captured her fourth and final U.S. National Championship singles title. She went on to win two more United States Doubles Championships in the 1920's, the last one coming in

1928 when at the remarkable age of forty-two she paired with twenty-three-year-old Helen Wills. Meanwhile, although she had become the mother of five children, Wightman captained the women's team in the 1924 Olympics, winning gold medals in the doubles and mixed doubles competition. She also demonstrated her skills in other racquet sports, winning the National Squash Singles and finishing as a finalist in the National Badminton Mixed Doubles championships in 1927.

Wightman's contributions to tennis were not restricted, however, to her performances as an individual player. In 1919, she donated a silver vase to the United States Lawn Tennis Association (USLTA), attempting to create an international cup for women comparable to the international cup for men inaugurated by Dwight F. Davis in 1900. She met implacable resistance to her proposal to the International Lawn Tennis Federation and temporarily was forced to withdraw her offer. The creation of the West Side Tennis Club in Forest Hills, New York, however, provided an opportunity for a renewal of her dreams, and the first Wightman Cup match was played at that facility in 1923. The U.S. team, captained by Wightman herself, defeated the British team 7-0. The following year, the Wightman Cup was played at the newly created Center Court at Wimbledon in England, and the British team won 6-1. The evenness of the competition in the next six years assured the success of the Wightman Cup. Even though the American teams dominated the British teams between 1931 and 1958, the Wightman Cup became a respected part of tennis competition and helped to improve the image of women's tennis in the world. The decision to move the competition indoors in 1974 coincided with the tennis boom of that decade and increased the appeal of the Wightman Cup competition; it was not uncommon for the matches to draw between ten and fifteen thousand spectators, figures that were comparable to Davis Cup matches.

Meanwhile, Wightman continued to remain involved with the promotion and development of tennis in the United States. She played on five Wightman Cup teams between 1923 and 1931, and she captained thirteen Wightman Cup teams in all, making her final appearance as captain in 1948. She continued to compete in national tournaments, playing in her last national championship when she was seventy-three years old.

Had these been her only accomplishments in tennis, Wightman might still have earned her title as the Queen Mother of Tennis, but she also contributed to tennis in several other ways. After her divorce from George Wightman in 1940, she graciously opened her home near the Longwood Cricket Club in Chestnut Hill, Massachusetts, as a home away from home for aspiring women players who went east to prepare for the summer tournaments that culminated in the United States Nationals at Forest Hills. Wightman developed a reputation for a quick recognition of talent, and she aided several prominent tennis players, including Sarah Palfrey, Helen Wills, and Helen Jacobs. She became a respected tennis teacher and promoter, giving free clinics at the Longwood Cricket Club, running tournaments for players of all skill levels, and writing a manual that became a guide for many players.

As a tennis instructor, Wightman had a particular fondness for ordinary players. The awkward and shy players, she claimed, gained "confidence and poise" by being able to do "something well that other people admire." Her approach to the teaching of tennis emphasized the mental as well as the physical and technical sides of the game.

She encouraged her students to "cultivate a buoyant spirit" as well as develop good footwork. She emphasized the fact that tennis was a sport that helped in the development of personal as well as physical grace. She always noted that she believed that ordinary players could gain as much from perfecting their skills as could the more accomplished players. Moreover, she argued long before the tennis boom of the 1970's that tennis should be a sport open to the entire public, not simply the wealthy members of elite private clubs. *Better Tennis* (1933), an instruction book that Wightman composed during the hours she waited in the car to pick up her children from school, became a standard teaching book during the 1930's.

Wightman's contributions to tennis were recognized in 1957, when she was inducted into the Tennis Hall of Fame at Newport, Rhode Island. She also was recognized on the fiftieth anniversary of the Wightman Cup in 1973, when Queen Elizabeth II made Wightman an honorary Commander of the British Empire. Wightman died in 1974 at the age of eighty-seven in Chestnut Hill, Massachusetts.

Significance

Wightman's life mirrors in several ways the development of women's tennis in the United States. Her performance on the court as a national champion came at a time when few sports other than tennis were open to women. She excelled during an era in which women's tennis was dominated primarily by women whose wealth permitted them to have the travel and leisure time necessary for capturing championships. She changed the style of play for women by emphasizing a more aggressive game that combined volleying with the traditional ground-stroke elements, and she was an active participant in the dress reform movement in women's tennis. She introduced the Wightman Cup during the Golden Age of Sports in the 1920's, supported and encouraged the development of international competition in tennis for women, advocated the acceptance of tennis as an Olympic sport, and helped nurse women's tennis through the Depression and World War II years. Although she at first was opposed to the professionalization of women's tennis, Wightman became one of its strongest supporters. It was therefore appropriate that she was chosen to present the first monetary award for women that was equal to the men's prize—an award Wightman presented to Margaret Court at the United States Tennis Association championship in 1973.

—*Robert L. Patterson*

Further Reading

Carter, Tom. *First Lady of Tennis: Hazel Hotchkiss Wightman*. Berkeley, Calif.: Creative Arts, 2000. Short biography chronicling Wightman's career, the honors she received, contributions to tennis, and her lifelong dedication to teaching others how to play the game.

Jacobs, Helen Hull. *Gallery of Champions*. Reprint. Freeport, N.Y.: Books for Libraries Press, 1979. Originally published in 1949, this collection of essays about many of the champion women's tennis players was written by Jacobs, a leading player who competed directly against many of the women she profiled. Includes a discussion of Hazel Hotchkiss Wightman's career during the years between World War I and World War II.

Klaw, Barbara. "Queen Mother of Tennis: An Interview with Hazel Hotchkiss Wightman." *American Heritage* 26 (August, 1975): 16-24, 82-86. Conducted only a few weeks before her death, Klaw's interview with Hazel Wightman reveals an individual who was capable of change but who remained true to the values that she had learned in the first quarter of the twentieth century.

Wightman, Hazel Hotchkiss. *Better Tennis.* Boston: Houghton Mifflin, 1933. Written in longhand while she juggled her roles as social director and chauffeur for her school-age children, Hazel Wightman used this popular manual of the 1930's to promote the mental as well as the technical aspects of the game.

Wind, Herbert W. "From Wimbledon to Forest Hills: A Summer to Remember." *The New Yorker* 51 (October 13, 1975): 116-120. Although quite brief, this article was used by Wind as a means to reminisce about women's tennis in general and Wightman in particular.

Woolum, Janet. *Outstanding Women Athletes: Who They Are and How They Influenced American Sports.* Phoenix, Ariz.: Oryx Press, 1992. A thoroughly researched collection of sports biographies that includes a sketch on Wightman. Provides a thorough assessment of Wightman's career as a player and explains her role in popularizing a more aggressive style of play for women, in advocating dress reform for women in the sport, and in promoting greater opportunities and equality for women in the world of tennis.

OPRAH WINFREY

" What I know for sure is that what you give comes back to you. "

Media celebrity, businesswoman, and philanthropist

Winfrey became a widely popular talk-show host and actor, as well one of the richest women in the world, after forming a successful media career that started with jobs as a television new reporter-anchor and morning-show host. Her film and television production company, Harpo, is the first such company owned by an African American.

Born: January 29, 1954; Kosciusko, Mississippi
Also known as: Oprah Gail Winfrey (full name)
Areas of achievement: Theater and entertainment; film; journalism; social reform; philanthropy

EARLY LIFE
Oprah Winfrey (OH-pruh WIHN-free) was born to Vernita Lee and Vernon Winfrey, a young unmarried couple barely out of their teens. Vernon was in the armed forces when a postcard from Vernita notified him that he had become a father. Winfrey's first

Winfrey, Oprah

name was to have been Orpah, but a misspelling on her birth certificate renamed the child Oprah.

Vernita decided to move to the North to find work. Intent on settling in Milwaukee, she left Winfrey in the care of the child's paternal grandmother. According to Winfrey, the influence of her elderly caretaker was an important element in her life. She described her grandmother as disciplined, strong, and religious, and she was raised to be a churchgoer. As a child, she proved to be intelligent, articulate, and animated. She learned to read early and became a voracious reader. Her quick mind was never idle, and she craved mental challenges. Her school environment soon proved to be restrictive, and she found the lack of adequate mental stimuli stifling and confining.

At home, Oprah was under the strict care of her grandmother, whose care-taking techniques included living by the adage that children were "to be seen and not heard." The rod was not to be spared, if the occasion warranted its use. The strong-willed child resented her restrictive environment and ultimately proved to be too difficult and recalcitrant for her grandmother to handle. Her grandmother decided that Oprah would have to move to Milwaukee to live with her mother.

Life in Milwaukee was very different from the kind of life Oprah had known in rural Mississippi. Vernita, who had little money, lived in a single room. Living without enough money and the comforts of her grandmother's home made Oprah more rebellious. Vernita soon decided that because both she and Oprah's paternal grandmother had been unable to handle what they deemed a recalcitrant child, it would be best for everyone for Oprah to live with her father; she moved yet again.

Life in Tennessee with her father and stepmother proved to be good for Oprah. They encouraged her in her academic work and provided a loving yet firm environment. She thrived in her new surroundings, excelling academically and socially. After a year, she went to visit her mother for summer vacation. When it was time for Oprah to return to Tennessee, Vernita refused to let her return to her father. She wanted Oprah back. Reluctantly, Vernon gave in.

Life immediately turned sour for Oprah. Her self-esteem suffered badly. She felt unwanted and believed that her lighter-skinned sister was treated better than she was. She took refuge in reading books. The quality of Oprah's academic work never decreased, although she suffered from many years of sexual abuse by male relatives and acquaintances. She suffered in silence. She manifested her inner suffering and rage by lying and destroying property. Her mother's confusion and exasperation with Oprah increased, and soon it was decided that alternate living arrangements would have to be made. The move back to Tennessee to live with her father in 1968, however, did not work out as well as the move in 1962. Oprah had difficulty readjusting to her new environment.

In her senior year at Nashville's East High School, Oprah decided that she wanted her future to be in entertainment. Her aspirations were well on the way to being realized. She excelled academically and won several titles, including that of Miss Black Tennessee. She read the news for the local radio station while she was still in her teens. Despite her decision to attend college outside Tennessee, her father insisted that she enroll in Tennessee State University in Nashville. With an oratorical scholarship in hand, Oprah entered Tennessee State as an English major.

Oprah Winfrey.
(AP/Wide World Photos)

LIFE'S WORK

During her college years, Winfrey worked for several media organizations. She was employed in Nashville by radio stations WVOL and WLAC and later worked as a television reporter-anchor for WLAC-TV. Only a few months before she was to graduate from Tennessee State, she accepted a position with WJ2-TV in Baltimore. Her enthusiasm and personality attracted many admirers within the journalistic community, and she quickly became a favorite with the public. She became the cohost of a local morning show, *People Are Talking*.

Winfrey's popularity soon extended outside Baltimore. After having sent demo tapes to media markets throughout the country, she was asked to host *A.M. Chicago*. She now was in the national arena, competing with television talk-show hosts such as Phil Donahue. She quickly won the ratings war against Donahue, who left Chicago in 1985 to relocate in New York.

It was at this time that Winfrey began to gain weight. She became concerned about her health and her appearance, and she tried many diets but failed to lose the weight.

Winfrey, Oprah

Winfrey underwent extensive psychoanalysis and concluded that her weight gain came from her lacking a positive self-image, which itself was the result of her childhood experiences. Despite her success as a media personality, she continued to gain weight.

Winfrey decided that she wanted to work as an actor. In 1985, she requested a leave of absence from her show to costar in Steven Spielberg's film *The Color Purple*, which went on to garner extensive critical acclaim. The film, based on Alice Walker's novel, portrayed strong African American females but depicted, to some controversy, many of its African American male characters as abusive and weak. Winfrey was nominated for an Academy Award for her role in the film.

Winfrey returned to television, where her popularity led to *A.M. Chicago* being renamed *The Oprah Winfrey Show*. In 1986, the show became nationally syndicated, and by 1988, Winfrey was the most highly paid entertainer in show business. The show continued as a hit into the first decade of the twenty-first century.

In 1988, Winfrey revealed that she had lost sixty-seven pounds, appearing on her show in tight blue jeans and wheeling a wagon loaded with fat. Only a few months later, however, she had regained all of her former weight, and more. The public became obsessed with how much she weighed, and it became a frequent subject of tabloid journalism. In 1992, her weight peaked at 237 pounds, and she checked into a Telluride, Colorado, spa. Bob Greene became her personal trainer, and he helped her see the connection between her emotions and her overeating. A few months later, Winfrey had completed a half-marathon in San Diego, California, and by 1993, she had lost ninety pounds. She shared her success in becoming fit with her talk-show audience and in *Make the Connection: Ten Steps to a Better Body and a Better Life* (1996), which she coauthored with Greene.

In 1996, Winfrey created Oprah's Book Club, a monthly reading group that began with discussion of Jacquelyn Mitchard's *The Deep End of the Ocean* (1996). The book club's popularity dramatically increased Winfrey's television audience and made best sellers of many of the club's selections. The club also inspired many people to form reading groups of their own. In 1999, Winfrey received the National Book Foundation's Fiftieth Anniversary Gold Medal for encouraging reading. In 2002, the book club went on hiatus and resumed in 2003, featuring a new format of three or four books per year. The club was the center of controversy in 2001, when author Jonathan Franzen expressed dismay that his novel had been chosen by the club, which he considered not literary enough and, therefore, too popular. In 2005, James Frey's memoir *A Million Little Pieces* (2003), a book club selection, was determined to be largely fabricated, causing somewhat of a furor not only because Frey lied about his life experiences (or duped his readers into believing so) but also because of the general glut of memoirs on the market.

Winfrey's talk show, however, was not free from controversy. In 1996, Winfrey made a remark regarding her new repulsion to "hamburgers" on a show examining mad cow disease. Along with that show's guest, Howard Lyman, she was sued by Texas cattlemen for causing sales of cattle to dip precipitously. However, Winfrey and Lyman were found not liable in the case.

Winfrey made many firsts as an African American woman in business. In addition to owning and producing *The Oprah Winfrey Show*, she formed her own company, Harpo Productions, in 1998. She ventured into film and television production, producing and costarring in the hit television film *The Women of Brewster Place*, based on the novel by African American author Gloria Naylor. In 1998, Winfrey produced and starred in the acclaimed film version of Toni Morrison's Pulitzer Prize-winning novel *Beloved* (1987). She also appeared in *There Are No Children Here* (1993), based on a book by Alex Kotlowitz, and *Before Women Had Wings* (1997), based on the novel by Connie May Fowler. In 1997, Harpo launched *Oprah Winfrey Presents*, a series of made-for-television films that included *Tuesdays with Morrie* (1999), based on a best-selling book by Mitch Albom, and *Their Eyes Were Watching God* (2005), from the classic novel by Zora Neale Hurston. In 2002, Harpo branched out into creating a television series with *Dr. Phil*, a syndicated daytime talk show featuring Phil McGraw, a psychologist who had been a frequent guest on Winfrey's talk show.

In February, 2000, Winfrey founded Oxygen, a women's cable network. Beginning in 2002, the network aired *Oprah After the Show*, which showed Winfrey and guests in informal after-show talks. Oxygen was purchased in 2007 by NBC Universal. Also in 2000, Winfrey created Oprah.com, a Web site covering her talk show, magazines, charities, book club, and other activities.

Winfrey also ventured into magazine publishing, onto Broadway, and onto satellite radio. In April, 2000, in a joint venture with Hearst magazines, she launched *O: The Oprah Magazine*, which focused on self-improvement. The magazine presented issues similar to those discussed on her talk show, and many of the experts who appeared as guests on her show also had columns in the magazine. Financial adviser Suze Orman and physician Mehmet Oz, for example, both helped Winfrey as guest experts on her show and received a career boost from their associations with her. In 2004, *O at Home*, a spin-off magazine featuring home living, began publication.

In December, 2005, a musical version of *The Color Purple*, produced by Winfrey, opened on Broadway. In April, 2007, singer Fantasia Barrino, a winner of the hit reality show and competition American Idol, assumed the role of Celie in the Broadway production, and the musical toured nationally, beginning in Chicago. In September, 2006, Winfrey established Oprah and Friends, a channel on XM Satellite Radio that presented a short weekly show by Winfrey and programs by many of the experts and consultants featured on her television show and in her magazines.

In 2007, *Forbes* magazine estimated that Winfrey had become the eighty-second richest American and had been earning her income at the rate of about $2,000 per minute. In addition to this commercial success, Winfrey received numerous awards acknowledging her achievements in broadcasting and business, and for her humanitarian efforts. Along with *The Oprah Winfrey Show*, she has won more than forty Daytime Emmy Awards, including seven for Best Talk Show Host and nine for Best Talk Show. After receiving the Lifetime Achievement Award from the National Academy of Television Arts and Sciences in 1998, she asked not to be considered for future Emmys, and show producers requested the same in 2000. Winfrey was named one of *Time* magazine's one hundred most influential people in the twentieth century in 1998 and one of its one hundred most influential people in the world in 2004, 2005, 2006, and 2007. She received a Global Humanitarian Action Award from the United Nations As-

Winfrey, Oprah

sociation of the United States of America in 2004 and a Humanitarian Award from the Elie Wiesel Foundation for Humanity in 2007.

Winfrey made multimillion-dollar donations to multiple causes. She supported the United Negro College Fund and formed a Tennessee State University scholarship fund for ten students annually who are deemed economically disadvantaged as well as academically talented. In 1997 she established Oprah's Angel Network, which set up a college scholarship fund, helped build houses through Habitat for Humanity, helped people displaced by Hurricane Katrina, provided school uniforms for children in Africa, and helped build rural schools in ten different countries, including the Seven Fountains School, a new primary school for boys and girls in Kwa-Zulu Natal, South Africa. The Oprah Winfrey Foundation (OWF) funded ChristmasKindness South Africa 2002, an initiative that took Winfrey to South Africa, where she visited orphanages and schools and donated clothing and other supplies to children. In 2007 she opened the Oprah Winfrey Leadership Academy for Girls, a boarding school for disadvantaged girls in grades seven through twelve, near Johannesburg, South Africa. The academy, funded by OWF, enrolled more than 150 girls in its first year.

Winfrey also served as a spokesperson against child abuse. A victim of sexual and mental abuse as a child, she dedicated herself to helping those in similar situations. She testified on the subject of child abuse in front of a congressional committee in support of the National Child Protection Act, which was signed into law in December, 1993. She continued to help educate the public about the many problems that children face in the United States, such as abuse, homelessness, and illness.

Significance

Winfrey's rise to stardom may seem to many to have been quick and easy. However, her achievements came through effort and tenacity. She demonstrated that one's dreams and aspirations can be realized if they are supported by diligence and persistence, making her quite a popular and well-admired person not only in the United States but also around the world.

Winfrey had an impact on millions of individuals through her television show. Her personal revelations and her emotional openness created a sense of intimacy and understanding between her and her audience. Her programs informed, enlightened, influenced, and inspired her predominantly female audience. Her talk show, like most of the talk shows that began airing in the 1980's, first concentrated on social issues such as racism, sexism, spousal abuse, acquired immune deficiency syndrome (AIDS), violence in schools, drunk driving, political corruption, and child abuse. *The Oprah Winfrey Show* later grew to emphasize spiritually uplifting topics, positive experiences, and issue of self-improvement.

Winfrey, who started life as a poor black girl from Mississippi, rose to become an award-winning talk-show host and the first black woman billionaire (according to *Forbes* magazine). Even as she climbed the ladder of success, she remained accessible to the public and remained one of the most famous and likable people in the world.

—*Annette Marks-Ellis, updated by Rowena Wildin Dehanke*

Further Reading

Garson, Helen S. *Oprah Winfrey: A Biography*. Westport, Conn.: Greenwood Press, 2004. A wealth of materials was used in the production of this book aimed at students. Presents a well-researched biography that avoids speculation and undocumented rumors.

Harris, Jennifer, and Elwood Watson, eds. *The Oprah Phenomenon*. Lexington: University Press of Kentucky, 2007. A collection of essays that examine various aspects of Winfrey's life and achievements, including her appeal to white women, her book club, her spirituality, and her problems with weight.

Illouz, Ella. *Oprah Winfrey and the Glamour of Misery: An Essay on Popular Culture*. New York: Columbia University Press, 2003. Illouz presents a cultural analysis of Winfrey's role as a moral and therapeutic guide.

Paprocki, Sherry Beck. *Oprah Winfrey: Talk Show Host and Media Magnate*. New York: Chelsea House, 2006. A biography of Winfrey that looks at her business ventures and philanthropic works. Contains a chronology and index.

Rooney, Kathleen. *Reading with Oprah: The Book Club That Changed America*. Fayetteville: University of Arkansas Press, 2005. Discusses Oprah's Book Club, including its "end" and second start, and the Franzen incident.

Tiger Woods

> *" It's the child's desire to play that matters, not the parent's desire to have the child play. Fun. Keep it fun. "*

Golfer

Woods helped transform the sport of golf, serving as an example of perseverance, especially for young people of color. He broke and set records with superb shooting skills and was the youngest Masters Tournament champion at age twenty-one.

Born: December 30, 1975; Cypress, California
Also known as: Eldrick Woods (birth name)
Areas of achievement: Sports; philanthropy

Early Life

Tiger Woods was born in Cypress, California, to Earl and Kultida Woods. Earl was from Manhattan, Kansas, while Kultida was from Bangkok, Thailand. They were married in 1969 and dreamed of having a child. After six years, the baby boy that Earl thought would never arrive was born. He nicknamed his healthy son Tiger in honor of his South Vietnamese army combat partner and friend Nguyen Phong during the Vietnam War. Earl had given Phong the nickname Tiger for his unrelenting prowess and bravery on the battlefield. In fact, Phong had saved Earl from sniper fire. It was also during his years in the service that Earl became hooked on golf.

As a toddler, Woods quickly picked up golfing, and his father knew from the begin-

Woods, Tiger

ning that his son had talent and potential. He was driven by the game and by the age of six sunk his first hole in one. By the age of eleven, Woods had entered more than thirty junior golf tournaments and won them all. One of the reasons Woods succeeded in the sport was his discipline and the mental concentration his father instilled in him by purposely creating distractions (jingling pocket change) as the young golfer practiced. Earl never forced Woods to play; it was always the youngster's choice. His father taught him to take the initiative in the sport and helped him develop the skills and techniques he needed to win in the game. Earl, a great teacher and motivator, had some impressive qualifications. For instance, Earl's love of baseball enabled him to become the first African American baseball player in the Big Eight Conference, playing for Kansas State University. Later, he began to work on a career as an educator and was a U.S. Army Green Beret in Vietnam. He retired from the Army in 1974.

Woods had two significant coaches during his childhood years. One, of course, was his father, and the other was Rudy Duran, who was an exceptional golf instructor. Duran coached Woods from the ages of four to ten. Woods's wizardry on the links during his childhood and early teens enabled him to appear on such national television

Tiger Woods.
(AP/Wide World Photos)

shows as *The Mike Douglas Show*, *That's Incredible*, *The Today Show*, and *Good Morning America*. After gaining the attention of the media at an early age, Woods began gaining the interest of universities by the age of thirteen. Stanford University's golf coach wrote Woods a letter suggesting that he might someday consider playing golf for the university. Woods wrote back and reported that he was thankful for the letter and that he would seriously consider the offer in the future. In the meantime, Woods was preparing for Western High School in Anaheim, California.

LIFE'S WORK

By the early 1990's, Woods was a junior golf phenomenon who had won several junior titles. When he was only sixteen and still in high school, Woods was invited to play in the Los Angeles Open. It was his first Professional Golfers' Association (PGA) tournament, and he had met a goal—to become the youngest player to compete in a PGA tournament and play against the pros. Though he did not win, he rightfully acknowledged that the event was a significant learning tool for him. His experiences in professional golf tournaments as an amateur were, for the most part, uneventful. He did make the cut in some tournaments but usually finished well behind the leaders. The important thing was that he gained knowledge of how the pro game was played, and it gave him the opportunity to learn what he had to work on to take his game to another level.

By the time Woods enrolled at Stanford, he was already a celebrity. One of the major stepping-stones to greatness for Woods was becoming not only the first African American but also, at age eighteen, the youngest player to win the United States Amateur Championship. He went on to win the championship for three consecutive years. In 1995, Woods made his Masters Tournament debut, in which he finished in forty-first place with a score of five over par. He competed in other tour events as an amateur: the U.S. Open (where he had to withdraw in the second round because of a wrist injury), the Scottish Open, and the British Open. Again, there is no doubt that he came out of these PGA Tour events a much better golfer.

Woods, however, seemed to be disassociating himself from Stanford golf. He did not appear to care about the weekly competition in college, just how he could make his game better. After two years, in August of 1996, Woods left Stanford and turned professional at the age of twenty. He was by far the best National Collegiate Athletic Association (NCAA) golfer that the sport had ever seen. He vowed to his parents that he would return to college someday and get his degree.

A little more than one month after Woods joined the ranks of professional golfers, he won his first professional tournament: the Las Vegas Invitational. Only a couple of weeks later, he won again at the Disney Classic in Orlando, Florida. Nobody other than Jack Nicklaus had such a quick impact on the sport. Indeed, his first year as a professional was extraordinary. Beginning in August, he competed in only eight tournaments in 1996 and won two of them. His winnings for all of those tournaments was $790,594, which put him in twenty-fifth place on the PGA Tour money list for 1996. In addition to more calls for autographs and interviews, Woods was soon signing endorsement contracts that were worth millions of dollars.

Unfortunately, one theme that hounded Woods was racism. The media labeled him the "great black hope" for African Americans in the sport of golf. African Americans felt that Woods offered a chance to finally end discrimination in the golf world, especially in the American South. Woods was quick to point out that his heritage included not only African American but also Chinese, American Indian, Thai, and Caucasian. The media, however, continued to portray Woods as black, and black only. Woods, though, wanted to be known as the best golfer in the history of the sport, not just the best black golfer. Still, some of his fan mail was littered with racial slurs and racist remarks. Like a true champion, Woods let his golf game do the talking for him.

The highlight of Woods's young professional career was his victory at the Masters in Augusta, Georgia, on April 13, 1997. On the way to victory, he broke numerous records: He won by a phenomenal twelve strokes, came in with the lowest score ever (270), and finished eighteen under par. At the age of twenty-one, he was also the youngest player ever to win the event. He had dreamed of winning the Masters since he was a child, and he celebrated the victory with his parents. By winning this prestigious event, Woods perhaps did more for the game of golf than any other player before him. African Americans and other minority groups soon began playing the game en masse, and Woods became an idol to millions of children who also began playing the sport. He was overwhelmed by the publicity he received, but he had the support and guidance of his parents, his managers, and other star athletes such as basketball player Michael Jordan, who reached out to give him much-needed advice on how to handle the publicity and his celebrity status.

In 1997, Woods also won the GTE Byron Nelson Classic and the Mercedes Championships and signed a whopping $30 million advertising contract with American Express. Woods also set the record for achieving $1 million in winnings faster than any other PGA player by doing so in just nine events (the previous record of twenty-seven had been held by Ernie Els).

Despite early success, Woods's golf career has seen its share of ups and downs. Shortly after his impressive start as a golf phenomenon, his growing impatience, distance, and control issues affected his game. He hired a new coach, Butch Harmon, who helped him change his swing—and his image. Though he experienced a winning streak in 2000, including the Grand Slam (winning four majors consecutively), his game faltered yet again. Some blamed burnout, some distraction, others a knee injury, and even love. Another new coach, Hank Hanley, helped him develop yet a new swing. By 2005, Woods was making a comeback, finishing second at the Mercedes Championship. He went on to win six major tournaments in 2005, including the British Open and the Masters. In 2006, for the eighth time in ten years, he was also named PGA Player of the Year, a point-based award.

In 2004, Woods married former Swedish model Elen Nordegren, and in 2007 they celebrated the birth of their daughter, Sam Alexis Woods. In 2006, he opened a 35,000-square-foot children's learning center in Anaheim, featuring community outreach, online learning programs, and a golf training area.

SIGNIFICANCE

Woods's evolving legacy includes more professional victories—by age twenty-three—than any other pro golfer. He surpassed the record of Horton Smith, who had fifteen career victories by age twenty-three in 1931. Woods also tied with Nicklaus in five major championship victories, two professional and three U.S. amateur titles. (Nicklaus had three professional and two amateur victories by age twenty-three.) However, Woods's popularity and his impact on the sport were more far-reaching than any player before him, including Nicklaus.

Woods refined the way golf was played and viewed by the general public. A frenzy of interest in the sport, from players and fans, followed his rise to the top. Most significant, perhaps, was that his success increased the interest in golf both of people of color and youngsters of all backgrounds, making him an ambassador for the game. This, perhaps, is his major legacy.

—*David Trevino, updated by Lisa A. Wroble*

Further Reading

Edwards, Nicolas. *Tiger Woods: An American Master.* New York: Scholastic, 1997. Edwards provides a solid account of Woods's life from childhood through his Masters victory. Includes photographs and lists of Woods's career highlights, general achievements, and scores of all his tournaments. Also includes a glossary of golf terms and a list of golf-related Web sites.

Rosaforte, Tim. *Raising the Bar: The Championship Years of Tiger Woods.* New York: Thomas Dunne Books, 2001. Acclaimed golf writer and commentator Rosaforte focuses on post-1997 tournaments and the work Woods put into changing his image, his swing, and improving his discipline to achieve his winning streak of 2000.

Ross, Charles K., ed. *Race and Sport: The Struggle for Equality On and Off the Field.* Jackson: University Press of Mississippi, 2004. A history of race, racism, segregation, and equality issues in sports in the United States.

Sampson, Curt. *Chasing Tiger.* New York: Atria Books, 2004. Provides a glimpse not only of Woods as a player but also his impact on the game of golf. Sampson casts a wide net in learning about Woods through the eyes of his opponents, tournament directors, family, and coaches, and of golf professionals of the past.

Strege, John. *A Biography of Tiger Woods.* New York: Broadway Books, 1997. This behind-the-scenes look at Woods's rise to the top of the sports world was written by a golf writer and friend of the Woods family. Includes photographs and personal anecdotes from Woods, his parents, and others.

Teague, Allison L. *Prince of the Fairway: The Tiger Woods Story.* Greensboro, N.C.: Avisson, 1997. Teague's engaging biography contains a good opening chapter on Woods and the background of his parents. Includes photographs, a chronology of his life, a bibliography, and a glossary of golf terms.

Tiger Woods: The Making of a Champion. New York: Simon & Schuster, 1996. A compilation of articles excerpted from the pages of *Sports Illustrated* over the years that cover Woods's rise to golfing stardom. Includes an introduction, photographs, rich commentary, and an epilogue.

Woods, Earl, with Pete McDaniel. *Training a Tiger: A Father's Guide to Raising a Winner in Both Golf and Life.* New York: HarperCollins, 1997. This interesting work takes an in-depth and personal view at the training and mental philosophy that went into raising Woods to become a golf champion. Equally important, it shows how parents can teach their kids to play the game correctly and love it at the same time. Includes a foreword by Tiger Woods, photographs, and diagrams.

Woods, Tiger. *How I Play Golf.* New York: Little Brown Book Group, 2004. Primarily a golf guide packed with tips on the sports side-by-side with stunning photographs of Woods's memorable shots. Goes beyond being a mere golf guide, however, as Woods expresses his passion and respect for the game while imparting both his experiences and his attitudes toward golf and life.

ORVILLE AND WILBUR WRIGHT

> *If we all worked on the assumption that what is accepted as true is really true, there would be little hope of advance.* (Orville Wright)

Aviation pioneers

The Wright brothers invented the first practical piloted powered aircraft, thereby initiating the age of aviation.

ORVILLE WRIGHT

Born: August 19, 1871; Dayton, Ohio
Died: January 30, 1948; Dayton, Ohio

WILBUR WRIGHT

Born: April 16, 1867; near Millville, Indiana
Died: May 30, 1912; Dayton, Ohio

Areas of achievement: Aviation; engineering

EARLY LIVES

The Wright brothers belonged to a midwestern family of five children. Wilbur (WIHL-bur) and Orville (OHR-vihl) were the third and fourth boys, respectively; their younger sister, Katherine, was the only girl. Their father, the Reverend Milton Wright of the Evangelical United Brethren Church in Christ, had a large personal library, particularly of scientific and mechanical books. Their mother, née Susan Catherine Koerner, had been college educated and, with her husband, had invented several practical household items. As children, Wilbur, Orville, and Katherine established a closeness that became lifelong, especially after 1889, when Katherine took over running the home on their mother's death. The Wright brothers initially fashioned and sold toys; later they made tools, including a lathe, a newspaper-folding device, and a printing press. Between 1889 and 1894, they used the latter to produce a small local journal; Wilbur did the writing. Since their father's calling required the family to move often, the boys attended public schools in Iowa, Indiana, and Dayton, Ohio. Wilbur and

Orville were the only Wright children not to attend college.

The two brothers shared a remarkable genius for mechanics and complemented each other so closely as to give the appearance of being practically of one mind. Both had serious, no-nonsense, and reserved personalities. Wilbur was more pragmatic, had a steadier business sense, read much, and wrote for his father's church bulletin. Orville was more meticulous, temperamental, and full of ideas; he became a fairly successful bicycle racer. Late in 1892, the two young men opened a shop for the sale and repair of bicycles, utilizing their own mechanical skills to ensure quality workmanship. They were so successful that within three years they had sold their printing press, had expanded their bicycle business, and had begun to assemble their own cycles, using improved designs and tools of their own making. Orville even devised a crude calculating machine. An early gift from their father of a toy helicopter stimulated a gradual interest in the rudiments of flight.

Lives' Work

By the mid-1890's, the Wright brothers were closely following the successful experiments of the German Otto Lilienthal with gliders, only to be stunned by news of his death in a gliding mishap in 1896. The tragedy, however, served as a catalyst for both men, who thereupon embarked on a common quest to solve the problem of piloted flight. At first they read the scanty scientific literature on aerodynamics. From 1899, they experimented with kites and gliders in their spare time, usually to the derision of witnesses. The task came to dominate both their lives, and neither one ever married. From 1900, Wilbur corresponded extensively with the French expert in gliders, Octave Chanute, who was endeavoring to discover where Lilienthal had erred. Chanute greatly encouraged the Wright brothers and promoted their work.

The approach of the Wrights toward mastering the air was novel. They differed from the experimenters in Europe, who, ever since the adoption of the internal combustion engine to the automobile in the 1880's, had concentrated on developing power plants. Instead, the two brothers—after observing birds in flight in 1899—believed that pilot control of the vehicle under wind power had to be established before mechanical power could be applied. Orville theorized that lateral balance held the key. (Lateral balance is the ability of the pilot to adjust air pressure against the wing tips to his right and left at different angles to the wind to bank to either side.) Wilbur provided the means: a twisting or "warping" of the wings at correspondingly opposing angles. They built and tested a small kite-like glider in 1899 that proved their thinking correct. They discovered that a piloted "aeroplane" not only had to be controlled simultaneously along the horizontal axis to bank right or left but also had to be steered vertically to climb or descend. The plane also had to be directed to turn right or left.

Concurrent control of flight along these three axes thus dominated the Wrights' subsequent experiments before a motor could ever be mounted. Solution of the three-axis control problem was their greatest contribution to the science of aerodynamics. Between 1899 and 1903, they constructed and tested a succession of biplane gliders, incorporating the horizontal wing-warping mechanism, a forward elevator for vertical control, and a movable rear rudder tail for turning. The latter became standard for all subsequent aircraft. Because existing tables of air pressure and drift proved inaccurate,

Wright, Orville and Wilbur

*Wilbur (left) and
Orville Wright.*
(Library of Congress)

Orville devised two small wind tunnels to make his own innumerable correct measurements of wing surfaces. Wilbur revealed these figures to the world of aeronautics in 1901. Though the Wrights' scientific work was undertaken at Dayton, their glider flights were made in the ideal breezes over the sand dunes on the beach at Kitty Hawk and nearby Kill Devil Hill, North Carolina.

By 1903 the brothers not only had solved the three-axis challenge but also had calculated the amount of engine power required to lift their most advanced biplane glider. Their talents as mechanics enabled them that year to build a superb, lightweight four-cylinder engine with approximately four horsepower. They also constructed an unprecedentedly efficient airscrew propeller for the engine to drive. They then joined these two inventions with bicycle chains, which drove two propellers mounted aft of the wings as pushers. Skids rather than wheels ensured stable landings. The entire flying machine was to be launched by a weight-dropping catapult. With Orville at the controls, the completed aircraft, the *Flyer I*, made its first flight at Kill Devil Hill on December 17, 1903. It flew 120 feet in twelve seconds, but by the end of the day Wilbur had achieved a flight of 852 feet. Only five other people, all local citizens, witnessed the epic event.

The world took no notice of the Wright brothers' monumental achievement, especially since the Wrights discouraged publicity until after their pending patents had been granted in 1906. Returning to Dayton, they devoted all of their time to creating and testing the first practical airplane. They were frustrated in their attempts to sell it to the United States or foreign governments; only in 1908 did their success become known. That summer, Orville dazzled U.S. Army observers at Fort Myer, Virginia, while Wilbur did the same in France for European observers. The effect was electric, and aviation enthusiasts now adopted the Wright method of aerodynamical control. Although a U.S. Army officer was killed and Orville seriously injured in a crash at Fort Myer, the Army accepted a Wright plane. European governments made similar purchases. In 1909, the Wright Company was incorporated, with Wilbur as president. Orville was content to be vice president and leave the business to his brother while he taught flying and improved aircraft designs.

Their fame assured, the Wrights now prospered, yet the adoption of their wing-warping techniques by competitors led them to institute legal action against many manufacturers. In the United States, their chief rival was Glenn H. Curtiss, who, like many other manufacturers, had adopted the European-invented aileron in preference to the full warped wing for lateral control. The Wrights protested that any wing-warping device owed ultimate credit to themselves. The bitter lawsuits did not endear them to the world's aviation community, and they absorbed much of their energies. Furthermore, after 1909, they were quickly bypassed by advancing technology in Europe, and several of their army planes suffered fatal crashes. Then, in May, 1912, Wilbur succumbed to typhoid fever, and this blow sapped much of Orville's enthusiasm.

Succeeding to the presidency of the company, Orville carried on. He continued to test every improvement to his planes, even though whenever a plane vibrated in flight he suffered pains stemming from his 1908 injuries. Because his interest was in research and not business, he sold out his interest in the company late in 1915 and gave his final flying lesson. Orville remained thereafter a consulting engineer with the company. The lawsuits, and countersuits, were not resolved until the United States entered World War I in 1917, at which time all the aircraft manufacturers agreed to a cross-licensing system whereby their patents were pooled to enable the United States to produce unlimited numbers of warplanes. Orville served as a major in the Army Air Service, primarily as a technological adviser at Dayton. He gave up flying in 1918 and spent the rest of his life devising aeronautical equipment, mechanical toys, and other ingenious gadgets. He also for many years lent his expertise as a member of the National Advisory Committee on Aeronautics (NACA).

Rival claims and ensuing controversies did not abate until the early 1940's. However, Wilbur and Orville Wright are firmly recognized as the undisputed inventors of the airplane.

Significance

The Wright brothers exemplified the great era of individual invention that preceded the massive team research efforts funded by large corporations, foundations, governments, and universities. Their discovery of the key to piloted, powered flight—pilot control over the free-flying aircraft—stemmed largely from the mechanical "Yankee know-how" passed on to them by their parents and honed in their bicycle business. Their practical experiments, therefore, succeeded whereas those of the theoretical scientist Samuel Pierpont Langley (1834-1906) of the Smithsonian Institution did not. Similarly, the bicycle and motorcycle racing and manufacturing of their major American competitor, Curtiss, yielded the same results as those of the Wrights—after Curtiss profited from their basic discovery. Also, the Wrights did not succumb to the European fascination with engines until the fundamental aerodynamical problems had been solved; nor were they air sportsmen, like many enthusiasts of the day.

The historical timing was right. Technology and science were merging in all aspects of the rapidly industrializing Western world, enabling the Wrights to apply existing knowledge in the creation of the first airplane. In addition, the conquest of the air had become but one aspect of the last phase of public preoccupation with terrestrial exploration—of the polar regions, remote jungles, and "lost" civilizations—a preoccupation that the Wrights shared. They also exploited the public's craving for adventure with an exhibition team of stunt-flyers, though they did this only in response to competitors; by nature, neither man enjoyed popular hoopla of any kind. Finally, the drift of the European powers toward world war brought the Wrights the contracts they needed to continue their work with formal companies at home and in Europe.

The American military had no such sense of urgency and adopted early Wright flying machines only slowly, turning to the brothers to teach several officers to fly. The U.S. Army relied most heavily on Wright planes in the early years, 1908-1912, but several crashes led the Army to turn increasingly to other manufacturers. By contrast, the U.S. Navy initially preferred "hydroaeroplanes" that took off from and landed on the water, machines Curtiss provided since the Wrights opted for "landplanes." To compete in seaplanes, however, the Wright brothers subcontracted with the only other airplane manufacturer of the early days, W. Starling Burgess (1878-1947), who used Wright blueprints but designed his own pontoon floats. Still, the Wright control mechanism of levers proved too cumbersome and was eventually overshadowed by the Deperdussin method, another example of the brothers' failure to innovate beyond their basic design. Ironically, the Wright Company merged with the Curtiss firm in 1929 to become Curtiss-Wright.

The tragic aspect of the Wright brothers was their attempt, through litigation, virtually to patent powered flight itself with their claims over the wing-warping concept. Whatever the legal merits of their case, the airplane was one of those inventions that belonged to humanity as a whole and could not be controlled through patents. They did not object to others imitating their design, but they steadfastly opposed any who used it for profit without recompense to them. The ensuing lawsuits inhibited much aeronautical progress in Europe and the United States in the early years. The principal focus of their anger was Curtiss, a man of almost identical character, integrity, and mechanical genius whose seaplanes and flying boats provided the bulk of Allied naval aviation during World War I. Orville's resentment only deepened after Wilbur's untimely death, which he attributed partly to his brother's exhaustion from the dispute. Another source of irritation was the insistence of the Smithsonian Institution that its pioneer scientist, Langley, really deserved the credit for the key initial discoveries in aeronautics—a claim not abandoned until World War II.

The Wrights conquered the problems of piloted flight and by so doing initiated the air age, that essential historic bridge between the final conquest of the planet's surface and the ultimate leap into outer space.

—*Clark G. Reynolds*

FURTHER READING

Adams, Noah. *The Flyers: In Search of Wilbur and Orville Wright*. New York: Crown, 2003. Adams, one of the hosts of the radio program *All Things Considered*, tells the story of the Wright brothers through their letters, diaries, and visits to the significant sites associated with their lives and work.

Crouch, Tom D., and Peter L. Jakab. *The Wright Brothers and the Invention of the Aerial Age*. Washington, D.C.: National Geographic and Smithsonian Air and Space Museum, 2003. The authors, curators at the Smithsonian Air and Space Museum, published this book to commemorate the one-hundredth anniversary of the Kitty Hawk flight. It includes biographical information, extensive descriptions of how the Wright brothers devised the airplane they flew at Kitty Hawk, and one hundred archival photographs.

Freudenthal, Elsbeth Estelle. *Flight into History: The Wright Brothers and the Air Age*. Norman: University of Oklahoma Press, 1949. An adequate popular biography of the two men.

Gibbs-Smith, Charles H. *Aviation*. London: Her Majesty's Stationery Office, 1970. A historical survey of flight from its origins in antiquity to the end of World War II, this work is the best single volume on the subject, giving a balanced treatment of the Wrights' key role. It is dedicated to them, their entry in the *Encyclopaedia Britannica* also being written by Gibbs-Smith.

_____. *The Wright Brothers: A Brief Account of Their Work, 1899-1911*. London: Science Museum, 1963. A well-illustrated booklet on the crucial years.

Heppenheimer, T. A. *First Flight: The Wright Brothers and the Invention of the Airplane*. Hoboken, N.J.: Wiley, 2003. Heppenheimer, an aviation writer, provides a comprehensive look at the brothers' lives, the design and construction of the airplane flown at Kitty Hawk, the Kitty Hawk flight, and the brothers' subsequent business and technological ventures.

Kelly, Fred C. *The Wright Brothers*. New York: Harcourt Brace, 1943. The closest volume to an autobiography, this work was authorized by Orville Wright, who contributed heavily to it. It remains the standard work on their lives, though it is weak on the technological aspects and on the rivalry with Glenn Curtiss.

McFarland, Marvin W., ed. *The Papers of Wilbur and Orville Wright*. 2 vols. New York: McGraw-Hill, 1953. An exhaustive, meticulously annotated compendium of all papers relating not only to the Wrights' careers but also to that of Octave Chanute.

Renstrum, Arthur G., comp. *Wilbur and Orville Wright: A Bibliography Commemorating the Hundredth Anniversary of the Birth of Wilbur Wright*. Washington, D.C.: Library of Congress, 1968. An essential listing of books and articles.

Yeager, Chuck

Wright, Orville, and Wilbur Wright. *Miracle at Kitty Hawk: The Letters of Wilbur and Orville Wright.* Edited by Fred C. Kelly. New York: Farrar, Straus and Young, 1951. A very complete collection of the personal and technical correspondence of the brothers.

CHUCK YEAGER

" *Never wait for trouble.* "

Test pilot

Yeager, one of the best-known American pilots of all time, was an accomplished wartime aviator during World War II and the first pilot to break the sound barrier in level flight.

Born: February 13, 1923; Myra, West Virginia
Also known as: Charles Elwood Yeager (full name)
Area of achievement: Aviation

EARLY LIFE

Born into a rural family, Chuck Yeager (YAY-gur) spent his early years working with his father in the family gas-drilling business near Hamlin, West Virginia. Like his father, Yeager was mechanically inclined, and he developed the skill to repair and maintain complex machinery, an advantage that later served him well. Yeager lived a normal Depression-era existence, graduating from high school in Hamlin just as the United States entered World War II in December, 1941.

Yeager's first experience with aviation was rather inauspicious. As a teenager, he had observed a damaged airplane make an emergency landing near his home, leaving the future pilot unimpressed with the prospects of flight. With the United States now at war, he enlisted in the U.S. Army Air Force (AAF) and became an airplane mechanic at a base in California. In 1942 he enrolled in the Flying Sergeant Program, a course designed to attract skilled enlisted men into the pilot's ranks. Bored with repair work and attracted by the higher rank and monthly pay, Yeager entered the program, graduating in early 1943.

Initially, the AAF trained Yeager and the other pilots of his first unit, the 357th Fighter Squadron, to fly the P-39 Airacobra fighter. The P-39 proved an unsuccessful aircraft, however, and Yeager was reassigned to the 363d Fighter Squadron equipped with the more successful P-51 Mustang fighter. In November, 1943, Yeager arrived at his first combat base, a British Royal Air Force facility at Leiston, England.

LIFE'S WORK

Yeager flew his first combat mission in early 1944 in his P-51 that he nicknamed the Glamorous Glenn for his girlfriend back home, Glennis Dickhouse. On March 4, on his seventh combat mission, Yeager downed his first enemy aircraft, a German Messerschmitt Me 109 fighter. The next day, however, Yeager tangled with three German fighters in combat over Bordeaux, France, and was shot down. Evading capture by the Germans, Yeager made contact with the Maquis, an underground group resisting the German occupation of France. The Maquis hid Yeager from the Germans for nearly three weeks until late-winter snows melted and the group could move Yeager across the Pyrenees Mountains into neutral Spain. Yeager repaid the Maquis by instructing them how to fuse plastic explosives, one of the many mechanical skills Yeager had acquired as a youngster.

Once returned to England, Yeager found himself in a dilemma. Army rules forbade pilots rescued by the Maquis or other resistance groups from again flying combat missions. The Army feared that if a pilot was shot down a second time, the Germans might be able to extract information about the Maquis. Faced with losing his flight status, Yeager and another escaped pilot, Frederick Glover, pled their case to General Dwight D. Eisenhower, supreme commander of Allied forces in Europe. While Eisenhower pondered Yeager's fate, Yeager downed his second aircraft, a German Junkers Ju 88 bomber, over the English Channel. Eisenhower eventually returned both Yeager and Glover to duty, and Yeager returned to his squadron, now with the rank of lieutenant.

Once back in the war, Yeager added to his total of destroyed German planes. On October 12, 1944, he shot down five German fighters in a single day. A month later, he became one of the few Allied pilots to shoot down a fearsome German Me 262 fighter. The first jet fighter to enter combat, the Me 262 could fly 150 mph faster than Yeager's P-51, but Yeager caught the German fighter in its final airfield approach and shot the vulnerable German aircraft out of the sky.

With the air war starting to wind down, Yeager flew his final combat mission on

Chuck Yeager. (NARA)

January 14, 1945, and returned to the United States to report for duty at Wright Field, Ohio. Yeager, now a captain, married Glennis on February 26.

Uncertain about his future, Yeager assumed his duties at Wright Field. His primary task was to test-fly repaired aircraft, and he had the opportunity to demonstrate his flying skills in a number of different aircraft. His versatility and mechanical skills caught the attention of Colonel Albert Boyd, head of the Aeronautical Systems Flight Test Division at Wright Field, who invited Yeager to become a test pilot. Yeager accepted the invitation and transferred to Muroc Airfield (now Edwards Air Force Base) in California.

Among Yeager's early projects was the X-1, an experimental aircraft built by Bell Aircraft Corporation to study high-speed flight. The goal of the X-1 project was to break the sound barrier and fly beyond the speed of sound (supersonic speed). Bell Aircraft and its test pilot, Chalmers Goodlin, were initially in charge of the project, but the Air Force (the Army Air Force became the Air Force in 1947) believed the project was moving too slowly. When Goodlin demanded hazard pay for the risky flights, the Air Force took over the project and made Yeager the main test pilot.

The Air Force planned a flight to break the sound barrier on October 14, 1947. Two days before the flight, however, Yeager broke two of his ribs in a horseback-riding accident. Afraid the Air Force would find another pilot, Yeager told only his wife, and project engineer-pilot Jack Ridley, about the injury. On the day of the flight above the Mojave Desert in Southern California, Ridley helped Yeager into the X-1 and provided part of a broom handle for Yeager to use as a lever to close the inside aircraft hatch. Yeager was able to secure himself into the aircraft and complete the flight, reaching a top speed of Mach 1.07 (700 mph). Due to national security concerns, the facts of Yeager's history-making flight did not become public for several months. Once the flight became public, Yeager became a national celebrity and was awarded both the MacKay and Collier Trophies for his achievement.

Although less newsworthy than breaking the sound barrier, Yeager had many other achievements during his Air Force career. During the Korean War, Yeager was one of a handful of pilots to test fly a Soviet-built MiG 15 fighter that had been flown to South Korea by a defecting North Korean pilot. In 1953, Yeager participated in a number of research flights that continuously set new speed records, culminating with a flight that reached Mach 2.44 in October. For the rest of the 1950's, Yeager commanded U.S. fighter squadrons based in Germany, France, and Spain.

Significance

With the U.S.-Soviet space race just beginning during the 1950's, Yeager was primed to become the leading adviser to the National Aeronautics and Space Administration (NASA) and the space program itself. Although he was not an astronaut, he did serve as the first commanding officer of the Air Force Aerospace Research Pilot School, which provided trained pilots for NASA and the Air Force.

Yeager's test-flight days would end in 1963, when he was badly burned in an accident while flying an NF-104 aircraft, but he recovered enough from his injuries to fly once again during the Vietnam War. He command the 405th Fighter Wing in 1966, flying 127 combat missions over Vietnam with the rank of brigadier general. He then served in several administrative posts until his retirement from the Air Force in 1975. In 1986, U.S. president Ronald Reagan appointed Yeager to the investigative team looking into the explosion of the space shuttle *Challenger*.

Yeager, whose very name has become synonymous with risky, but necessary, flight, excelled at meeting challenges and accomplishing great feats. Moreover, he achieved notoriety by repeatedly risking his life in incredibly dangerous situations. Even when given the option of taking the safe path, such as the option of going home after being shot down in World War II, Yeager saw challenges as jobs to be done. By accomplishing his great tasks, Yeager furthered the causes of aviation and space travel in the late twentieth century, becoming a legend in the process.

—*Steven J. Ramold*

FURTHER READING

Caygill, Peter. *Sound Barrier: The Rocky Road to Mach 1.0 +*. Barnsley, England: Pen & Sword Aviation, 2006. A detailed history of the projects to break the sound barrier, centering on Yeager's participation in the X-1 project after World War II.

Courtwright, David. *Sky as Frontier: Adventure, Aviation, and Empire*. College Station: Texas A&M Press, 2005. A complete history of aviation from the first pioneers through the space shuttle. Details the significance of air and space in American history.

Hallion, Richard P. "The Air Force and the Supersonic Breakthrough." In *Technology and the Air Force: A Retrospective Assessment*, edited by J. Neufeld, G. M. Watson, and D. Chenoweth. Washington, D.C.: Air Force History and Museums Program, 1997. A concise history of the events leading up to and immediately after Yeager's first supersonic flight.

Hallion, Richard P., and Michael H. Gorn. *On the Frontier: Experimental Flight at NASA Dryden*. Washington, D.C.: Smithsonian Institution Press, 2003. A 554-page history of U.S. government research aircraft. Contains detailed accounts of record-setting aircraft and flights, from those of Yeager and the X-1 through the X-15 and Mach 2 flight.

Yeager, Chuck. *The Quest for Mach One: A First-Person Account of Breaking the Sound Barrier*. New York: Penguin Studio Books, 1997. Emphasizes the engineering and technology necessary to make the supersonic flight possible. Less of a life story than that of Yeager's autobiography.

Yeager, Chuck, with Leo Janos. *Yeager: An Autobiography*. New York: Bantam Books, 1985. A firsthand account of Yeager's accomplishments as told by Yeager himself. The book provides many personal accounts of Yeager and his contemporaries.

Babe Didrikson Zaharias

" *The formula for success is simple: practice and concentration, then more practice and more concentration.* "

Athlete

Participating in numerous sports in which she excelled and set several records, Zaharias is recognized as the greatest woman athlete of the first half of the twentieth century.

Born: June 26, 1914; Port Arthur, Texas
Died: September 27, 1956; Galveston, Texas
Also known as: Mildred Ella Didriksen (birth name); Babe Didrikson; Mildred Ella Zaharias
Area of achievement: Sports

Early Life

Babe Didrikson Zaharias (bayb DEE-drihk-sehn zeh-HAR-ee-ehs) was born Mildred Ella Didriksen in Port Arthur, Texas. Her mother, née Hannah Olson, was born in Norway and immigrated to the United States in 1908; her father, Ole Didriksen, also born in Norway, came to Port Arthur in 1905 and worked as a sailor and carpenter. Throughout her adult life she was known as Babe Didrikson, taking the name Babe from the sports hero Babe Ruth and the spelling of her surname, Didrikson, to emphasize that she was of Norwegian rather than Swedish ancestry.

After the 1915 hurricane that devastated Port Arthur, the family, which included her sister and two brothers, moved to nearby Beaumont. Growing up in the rugged south end of the city, Didrikson was a tomboy who shunned feminine qualities and excelled at a variety of athletic endeavors. She was slim and of average height but had a muscular body and was exceptionally well coordinated. Her hair was cut short, and she usually wore masculine clothing. As a youth, Didrikson had a belligerent personality and was constantly involved in fights and scrapes.

At Beaumont High School, Didrikson was outstanding at a number of sports, including volleyball, tennis, baseball, basketball, and swimming, but she was not popular with her classmates. Didrikson was a poor student, usually passing only enough courses to remain eligible for athletic competition. All of her energy was directed toward accomplishment on the athletic field, where she had no equal. Didrikson's best sport was basketball, which was the most popular women's sport of the era. During her years in Beaumont, her high school team never lost a game—largely because of her aggressive, coordinated play.

Life's Work

In February, 1930, Colonel Melvin J. McCombs of the Casualty Insurance Company recruited Didrikson to play for the company's Golden Cyclone basketball team in Dallas. She dropped out of high school in her junior year and took a job as a stenographer with the company with the understanding that she would have time to train and compete in athletics. During the next three years, 1930-1932, Didrikson was selected as an All-American women's basketball player and led the Golden Cyclones to the national championship in 1931. She often scored thirty or more points in an era when a team score of twenty for a game was considered respectable. While in Dallas, she competed in other athletic events, including softball. Didrikson was an excellent pitcher and batted over .400 in the Dallas city league. Increasingly, however, her interest was drawn to track and field and she became a member of the Golden Cyclone track team in 1930. Profiting from coaching provided by the Dallas insurance company and relying on her innate athletic ability, Didrikson soon became the premier women's track-and-field performer in the nation.

Between 1930 and 1932, Didrikson held American, Olympic, or world records in five different track-and-field events. She stunned the athletic world on July 16, 1932, with her performance at the national amateur track meet for women in Evanston, Illinois. Didrikson entered the meet as the sole member of the Golden Cyclone team and by herself won the national women's team championship by scoring thirty points. The Illinois Women's Athletic Club, which had more that twenty members, scored a total of twenty-two points to place second. In all, Didrikson won six gold medals and broke four world records in a single afternoon. Her performance was the most amazing feat by any individual, male or female, in the annals of track-and-field history. The outstanding performance at Evanston put Didrikson in the headlines of every sports page in the nation and made her one of the most prominent members of the United States Olympic team of 1932.

Although Didrikson had gained wide recognition in her chosen field of athletics, many of her fellow athletes resented her. They complained that she was an aggressive, overbearing braggart who would stop at nothing to win. During the trip to Los Angeles for the Olympic Games, many of her teammates came to detest her, but her performance during the Olympiad made her a favorite among sportswriters and with the public. At Los Angeles, Didrikson won two gold medals and a silver medal, set a world's record, and was the coholder of two others. She won the javelin event and the eighty-meter hurdles and came in second in the high-jump event amid a controversy that saw two rulings of the judges go against her. Didrikson came very close to winning three Olympic gold medals, which had never been accomplished before by a woman. She became the darling of the press, and her performance in Los Angeles created a springboard for Didrikson's lasting fame as an athlete.

After the 1932 Olympic Games, Didrikson returned to Dallas for a hero's welcome. At the end of 1932, she was voted Woman Athlete of the Year by the Associated Press, an award that she won five additional times, in 1945, 1946, 1947, 1950, and 1954. After a controversy with the Amateur Athletic Union concerning her amateur status, Didrikson turned professional in late 1932. She did some promotional advertising and briefly appeared in a vaudeville act in Chicago, where she performed athletic feats and played her harmonica, a talent she had developed as a youth. Struggling to make a living as a professional athlete, Didrikson played in an exhibition basketball game in Brooklyn, participated in a series of billiard matches, and talked about becoming a long-distance swimmer. In 1933, she decided to barnstorm the rural areas of the country with a professional basketball team called Babe Didrikson's All-Americans. The tour was very successful for several years, as the team traveled the backroads of America playing against local men's teams. In 1934, Didrikson went to Florida and appeared in major-league exhibition baseball games during spring training and then played on the famous House of David—all the men on the team sported long beards—baseball team on a nationwide tour. As a result of her many activities, Didrikson was able to earn several thousand dollars each month, a princely sum during the depths of the Depression.

During the mid-1930's, Didrikson's athletic interests increasingly shifted to golf. Receiving encouragement from sportswriter Grantland Rice, she began intensive lessons in 1933, often hitting balls until her hands bled. She played in her first tournament in Texas in 1934 and a year later won the Texas Women's Amateur Championship. That same year, Didrikson was bitterly disappointed when the United States Golf Association (USGA) declared her a professional and banned her from amateur golf. Unable to make a living from the few tournaments open to professionals, Didrikson toured the country with professional golfer Gene Sarazen, participating mainly in exhibition matches.

On December 23, 1938, Didrikson married George Zaharias, a professional wrestler; they had no children. Her marriage helped put to rest rumors that she was in fact a male and other attacks on her femininity. Zaharias became her manager, and under his direction she won the 1940 Texas and Western Open golf tournaments. During World War II, Babe Zaharias gave golf exhibitions to raise money for war bonds and agreed to abstain from professional athletics for three years to regain her amateur status. In 1943, the USGA restored her amateur standing.

After the war, Babe Zaharias emerged as one of the most successful and popular women golfers in history. In 1945, she played flawless golf on the amateur tour and was named Woman Athlete of the Year for the second time. The following year, she began a string of consecutive tournament victories, a record that has never been equaled by man or woman. During the 1946-1947 seasons, Zaharias won seventeen straight tournaments, including the British Women's Amateur. She became the first American to win the prestigious British championship. In the summer of 1947, Zaharias turned professional once again, with Fred Corcoran as her manager. She earned an estimated $100,000 in 1948 through various promotions and exhibitions but only $3,400 in prize money on the professional tour, despite a successful season. In 1948, Corcoran organized the Ladies Professional Golfer's Association (LPGA) to help popularize women's golf and increase tournament prize money. During the next several years, the LPGA grew in stature, and Zaharias became the leading money winner on the women's professional circuit.

In the spring of 1953, doctors discovered that Zaharias had cancer, and she underwent radical surgery in April, 1953. Although many feared that her athletic career was over, Zaharias played in a golf tournament only fourteen weeks after the surgery. She played well enough the remainder of the year to win the Ben Hogan Comeback of the Year Award. In 1954, Zaharias won five tournaments, including the United States Women's Open, and earned her sixth Woman Athlete of the Year Award. During 1955, doctors diagnosed that the cancer had returned, and she suffered excruciating pain during her final illness. Despite the pain, Zaharias continued to play an occasional round of golf and through her courage served as an inspiration for many Americans. She died in Galveston, Texas, on September 27, 1956.

Significance

Zaharias was a remarkable woman in many respects. Her place in American sports history is secure in her athletic accomplishments alone: In addition to her six Woman Athlete of the Year Awards, she was named the Woman Athlete of the Half Century by the Associated Press in 1950. No other woman has performed in so many different sports so well. She is arguably one of the greatest athletes, female or male, of all time.

Beyond this, however, Zaharias was a pioneer who struggled to break down social customs that barred women from various segments of American life. During an era when society dictated that women conform to a particular stereotype, Zaharias persisted in challenging the public's view of women's place in society. She not only insisted on pursuing a career in sports but also participated in sports considered in the male domain. In her dress, speech, and manner, Zaharias refused to conform to the ladylike image expected of female athletes. She did it successfully because she was such an outstanding athlete. It nevertheless took courage, because she was subjected to the most insidious rumors and innuendos concerning her gender and femininity, attacks that she endured without outward complaint.

During her final illness, Zaharias displayed the kind of strength and courage that was a trademark of her career. She was a great athlete, but beyond that she was a courageous pioneer blazing a trail in women's sports that others have followed.

—*John M. Carroll*

Further Reading

Gallico, Paul. *The Golden People*. Garden City, N.Y.: Doubleday, 1965. A moving tribute to Didrikson is part of this anthology by a sportswriter who covered her career.

Hutchison, Kay Bailey. *American Heroines: The Spirited Women Who Shaped Our Country*. New York: William Morrow, 2004. Hutchison, a U.S. senator, provides profiles of women who made history, including Zaharias.

Johnson, William O., and Nancy P. Williamson. *Whatta-Gal: The Babe Didrikson Story*. Boston: Little, Brown, 1975. This popular biography offers the fullest account of Didrikson's life but tends to be uncritical.

Miller, Helen Markley. *Babe Didrikson Zaharias: Striving to Be Champion*. Chicago: Britannica Books, 1961. A juvenile book aimed at high school students; glorifies Didrikson's life.

Rader, Benjamin G. *American Sports: From the Age of Folk Games to the Age of Spectators*. Englewood Cliffs, N.J.: Prentice Hall, 1983. Gives an overview of American sports history, in the context of which Didrikson's career can be best understood. Rader attempts an assessment of Didrikson's place in history.

Schoor, Gene. *Babe Didrikson: The World's Greatest Woman Athlete*. Garden City, N.Y.: Doubleday, 1978. Strictly a popular account that adds a few details and stories omitted by Johnson and Williamson.

Warren, Patricia Nell. *The Lavender Locker Room: Three Thousand Years of Athletes*

Zaharias, Babe Didrikson

Whose Sexual Orientation Was Different. Beverly Hills, Calif.: Wildcat Press, 2000. This book about lesbian and gay athletes includes the chapter "Babe Didrickson Zaharias: Golfing Amazon of the Newsreels."

Wimmer, Dick, ed. *The Women's Game: Great Champions in Women's Sports.* Short Hills, N.J.: Burford Books, 2000. A compilation of magazine articles, interviews, and book excerpts about great women athletes, including a chapter about Zaharias.

Zaharias, Babe Didrikson, with Harry Paxton. *This Life I've Led: My Autobiography.* New York: A. S. Barnes, 1955. Avoids the rough spots in Didrikson's life but is good on her family and personality. Useful when read in conjunction with other sources.

INDEXES

Subjects by Category

Agriculture	1051	Labor Movement	1053
Astronomy	1051	Law and Jurisprudence	1054
Aviation and Space Exploration	1051	Literature	1054
		Mathematics	1054
Biology	1051	Medicine	1054
Botany	1051	Mental Health	1054
Business	1051	Military	1054
Civil Rights	1051	Native American Affairs	1054
Computer Science	1052	Nursing	1054
Consumer Rights	1052	Oratory	1054
Diplomacy	1052	Philanthropy	1055
Education	1052	Philosophy	1055
Engineering	1052	Physics	1055
Environmentalism	1052	Public Health	1055
Evangelism	1052	Religion and Theology	1055
Exploration	1052	Social Reform	1055
Film	1053	Sports	1056
Government and Politics	1053	Telecommunications	1056
Invention and Technology	1053	Theater and Entertainment	1056
Journalism	1053	Women's Rights	1056

AGRICULTURE
George Washington Carver, 144

ASTRONOMY
Benjamin Banneker, 60

AVIATION AND SPACE EXPLORATION
Neil Armstrong, 48
Richard Byrd, 124
Bessie Coleman, 179
Jimmy Doolittle, 243
Amelia Earhart, 265
John Glenn, 356
Charles A. Lindbergh, 600
Shannon W. Lucid, 632
Sally Ride, 819
Alan Shepard, 902
Orville and Wilbur Wright, 1034
Chuck Yeager, 1040

BIOLOGY
Rachel Carson, 133
Jonas Salk, 885

BOTANY
George Washington Carver, 144

BUSINESS
Neil Armstrong, 48
Walt Disney, 231
Bill Gates, 337
Steve Jobs, 503
John D. Rockefeller, 838

CIVIL RIGHTS
Ralph Abernathy, 4
Maya Angelou, 38
Mary Mcleod Bethune, 75
John Brown, 109
Carrie Chapman Catt, 152

Subjects by Category

César Chávez, 161
Shirley Chisholm, 164
Frederick Douglass, 254
W. E. B. Du Bois, 259
William Lloyd Garrison, 327
Marcus Garvey, 333
Fannie Lou Hamer, 398
Jesse Jackson, 488
Robert F. Kennedy, 551
Martin Luther King, Jr., 562
Abraham Lincoln, 594
Malcolm X, 650
Thurgood Marshall, 675
Rosa Parks, 752
Alice Paul, 763
A. Philip Randolph, 785
Paul Robeson, 824
Sojourner Truth, 974
Harriet Tubman, 979
Nat Turner, 984
Booker T. Washington, 994
Ida B. Wells-Barnett, 1009

COMPUTER SCIENCE
Bill Gates, 337
Grace Murray Hopper, 450
Steve Jobs, 503

CONSUMER RIGHTS
Ralph Nader, 705

DIPLOMACY
John Adams, 14
Ralph Bunche, 119
Jimmy Carter, 138
Benjamin Franklin, 309
Cordell Hull, 478
John F. Kennedy, 546
George C. Marshall, 664
Colin Powell, 779
Ronald Reagan, 798
Paul Robeson, 824
Eleanor Roosevelt, 847
Franklin D. Roosevelt, 852
Adlai E. Stevenson, 928
Harry S. Truman, 968

EDUCATION
Abigail Adams, 9
Maya Angelou, 38
Mary Mcleod Bethune, 75
Olympia Brown, 115
Frances Xavier Cabrini, 129
George Washington Carver, 144
Mary Ann Shadd Cary, 149
Bill Cosby, 183
W. E. B. Du Bois, 259
Marian Wright Edelman, 277
Samuel Gridley Howe, 460
Helen Keller, 542
Juliette Gordon Low, 627
Anne Sullivan, 938
Booker T. Washington, 994

ENGINEERING
Orville and Wilbur Wright, 1034

ENVIRONMENTALISM
Rachel Carson, 133
Al Gore, 367
John Muir, 696
Ralph Nader, 705
Theodore Roosevelt, 859

EVANGELISM
Frances Xavier Cabrini, 129
William Lloyd Garrison, 327
Billy Graham, 376

EXPLORATION
Robert D. Ballard, 55
Daniel Boone, 84
Richard Byrd, 124
David Crockett, 194
John C. Frémont, 315
Meriwether Lewis and William Clark, 584
John Muir, 696
Robert Edwin Peary, 768
Sacagawea, 880
Junípero Serra, 898

Subjects by Category

FILM
- Walt Disney, 231
- Katharine Hepburn, 426
- Bob Hope, 446
- Ronald Reagan, 798
- Paul Robeson, 824
- James Stewart, 934
- John Wayne, 1005
- Oprah Winfrey, 1023

GOVERNMENT AND POLITICS
- John Adams, 14
- Samuel Adams, 19
- Jimmy Carter, 138
- Shirley Chisholm, 164
- Hillary Rodham Clinton, 171
- David Crockett, 194
- Eugene V. Debs, 212
- Helen Gahagan Douglas, 247
- Dwight D. Eisenhower, 292
- Benjamin Franklin, 309
- Emma Goldman, 361
- Al Gore, 367
- Alexander Hamilton, 402
- Patrick Henry, 422
- Oveta Culp Hobby, 441
- Sam Houston, 455
- Cordell Hull, 478
- Andrew Jackson, 483
- Jesse Jackson, 488
- Thomas Jefferson, 498
- Barbara Jordan, 524
- Kamehameha I, 538
- John F. Kennedy, 546
- Robert F. Kennedy, 551
- Robert M. La Follette, 569
- Liliuokalani, 589
- Abraham Lincoln, 594
- Henry Cabot Lodge, 610
- Huey Long, 616
- Dolley Madison, 642
- James Madison, 646
- Golda Meir, 680
- Ralph Nader, 705
- Barack Obama, 728
- Thomas Paine, 747
- Colin Powell, 779
- Jeannette Rankin, 793
- Ronald Reagan, 798
- Paul Revere, 814
- Eleanor Roosevelt, 847
- Franklin D. Roosevelt, 852
- Theodore Roosevelt, 859
- Margaret Chase Smith, 917
- Adlai E. Stevenson, 928
- Zachary Taylor, 947
- Norman Thomas, 956
- Harry S. Truman, 968
- George Washington, 1000

INVENTION AND TECHNOLOGY
- Alexander Graham Bell, 70
- Thomas Alva Edison, 281
- Benjamin Franklin, 309
- Bill Gates, 337
- Thomas Jefferson, 498
- Steve Jobs, 503

JOURNALISM
- Mary Ann Shadd Cary, 149
- Walter Cronkite, 198
- Dorothy Day, 207
- Frederick Douglass, 254
- Mary Baker Eddy, 270
- William Lloyd Garrison, 327
- Marcus Garvey, 333
- Oveta Culp Hobby, 441
- Edward R. Murrow, 700
- Ida Tarbell, 942
- Booker T. Washington, 994
- Ida B. Wells-Barnett, 1009
- Oprah Winfrey, 1023

LABOR MOVEMENT
- César Chávez, 161
- Eugene V. Debs, 212
- Aileen Clarke Hernandez, 432
- Dolores Huerta, 465
- Mother Jones, 519
- John L. Lewis, 579
- A. Philip Randolph, 785

Subjects by Category

LAW AND JURISPRUDENCE
   Louis D. Brandeis, 94
   William J. Brennan, 105
   Clarence Darrow, 201
   William O. Douglas, 251
   Learned Hand, 408
   Patrick Henry, 422
   Wild Bill Hickok, 437
   Charles Evans Hughes, 471
   Robert F. Kennedy, 551
   Belva A. Lockwood, 606
   John Marshall, 669
   Thurgood Marshall, 675
   Sandra Day O'Connor, 733
   Earl Warren, 988

LITERATURE
   Abigail Adams, 9
   Maya Angelou, 38
   Benjamin Franklin, 309
   Ernest Hemingway, 417
   Elie Wiesel, 1013

MATHEMATICS
   Benjamin Banneker, 60
   Albert Einstein, 287
   Grace Murray Hopper, 450

MEDICINE
   William Crawford Gorgas, 371
   Walter Reed, 809
   Jonas Salk, 885

MENTAL HEALTH
   Dorothea Dix, 238
   Betty Ford, 305

MILITARY
   Omar Nelson Bradley, 89
   David Crockett, 194
   Stephen Decatur, 217
   Jimmy Doolittle, 243
   Dwight D. Eisenhower, 292
   John C. Frémont, 315
   Nathanael Greene, 380
   Mary A. Hallaren, 390
   William F. Halsey, 393
   Alexander Hamilton, 402
   Oveta Culp Hobby, 441
   Grace Murray Hopper, 450
   Sam Houston, 455
   Andrew Jackson, 483
   Stonewall Jackson, 494
   John Paul Jones, 513
   Robert E. Lee, 574
   Charles A. Lindbergh, 600
   Douglas MacArthur, 635
   George C. Marshall, 664
   Chester W. Nimitz, 723
   George S. Patton, 758
   John J. Pershing, 774
   Colin Powell, 779
   Theodore Roosevelt, 859
   William Tecumseh Sherman, 907
   Zachary Taylor, 947
   George Washington, 1000

NATIVE AMERICAN AFFAIRS
   Black Hawk, 80
   Joseph Brant, 100
   Crazy Horse, 187
   Geronimo, 346
   Chief Joseph, 533
   Kamehameha I, 538
   Liliuokalani, 589
   Wilma Mankiller, 655
   Osceola, 739
   Red Cloud, 805
   John Ross, 864
   Sitting Bull, 913
   Tecumseh, 952

NURSING
   Clara Barton, 64

ORATORY
   Ralph Abernathy, 4
   Frederick Douglass, 254
   Marcus Garvey, 333
   Billy Graham, 376
   Patrick Henry, 422
   Jesse Jackson, 488
   Mother Jones, 519
   Barbara Jordan, 524
   Abraham Lincoln, 594

Malcolm X, 650
Paul Robeson, 824
Sojourner Truth, 974

PHILANTHROPY
Jimmy Carter, 138
Bill Gates, 337
Billy Graham, 376
Bob Hope, 446
Samuel Gridley Howe, 460
Helen Keller, 542
John D. Rockefeller, 838
Booker T. Washington, 994
Oprah Winfrey, 1023
Tiger Woods, 1029

PHILOSOPHY
Thomas Merton, 686
Thomas Paine, 747

PHYSICS
Albert Einstein, 287
Grace Murray Hopper, 450
Sally Ride, 819

PUBLIC HEALTH
Clara Barton, 64
Betty Ford, 305
William Crawford Gorgas, 371
Oveta Culp Hobby, 441
Walter Reed, 809
Jonas Salk, 885
Margaret Sanger, 893

RELIGION AND THEOLOGY
Ralph Abernathy, 4
Frances Xavier Cabrini, 129
Dorothy Day, 207
Mary Baker Eddy, 270
Louis Farrakhan, 302
Billy Graham, 376
Barbara Harris, 413
Malcolm X, 650
Thomas Merton, 686
John R. Mott, 690
Junípero Serra, 898
Elie Wiesel, 1013

SOCIAL REFORM
Ralph Abernathy, 4
Abigail Adams, 9
Jane Addams, 26
Benjamin Banneker, 60
Mary Mcleod Bethune, 75
Louis D. Brandeis, 94
John Brown, 109
Olympia Brown, 115
Frances Xavier Cabrini, 129
George Washington Carver, 144
Mary Ann Shadd Cary, 149
Carrie Chapman Catt, 152
César Chávez, 161
Shirley Chisholm, 164
Bill Cosby, 183
Dorothy Day, 207
Eugene V. Debs, 212
Dorothea Dix, 238
Frederick Douglass, 254
W. E. B. Du Bois, 259
Marian Wright Edelman, 277
Albert Einstein, 287
Louis Farrakhan, 302
William Lloyd Garrison, 327
Marcus Garvey, 333
Emma Goldman, 361
Billy Graham, 376
Fannie Lou Hamer, 398
Barbara Harris, 413
Aileen Clarke Hernandez, 432
Samuel Gridley Howe, 460
Jesse Jackson, 488
Mother Jones, 519
Helen Keller, 542
Martin Luther King, Jr., 562
Carry Nation, 709
Paul Robeson, 824
Margaret Sanger, 893
Elizabeth Cady Stanton, 922
Ida Tarbell, 942
Norman Thomas, 956
Sojourner Truth, 974
Harriet Tubman, 979
Nat Turner, 984
Booker T. Washington, 994
Ida B. Wells-Barnett, 1009
Elie Wiesel, 1013
Oprah Winfrey, 1023

Subjects by Category

SPORTS
Hank Aaron, 1
Muhammad Ali, 31
Wilt Chamberlain, 158
Ty Cobb, 175
Jack Dempsey, 221
Joe DiMaggio, 227
Chris Evert, 297
Lou Gehrig, 341
Althea Gibson, 351
Wayne Gretzky, 387
Bobby Jones, 507
Michael Jordan, 529
Billie Jean King, 557
Joe Louis, 621
Rocky Marciano, 660
Martina Navratilova, 714
Jack Nicklaus, 719
Jesse Owens, 742
Sally Ride, 819
Paul Robeson, 824
Jackie Robinson, 832
Knute Rockne, 844
Bill Russell, 868
Babe Ruth, 874
Pete Sampras, 889
Jim Thorpe, 963
Hazel Wightman, 1019
Tiger Woods, 1029
Babe Didrikson Zaharias, 1044

TELECOMMUNICATIONS
Alexander Graham Bell, 70
Thomas Alva Edison, 281
Bill Gates, 337
Steve Jobs, 503

THEATER AND ENTERTAINMENT
Bill Cosby, 183
Walt Disney, 231
Katharine Hepburn, 426
Bob Hope, 446
Ronald Reagan, 798
Paul Robeson, 824
James Stewart, 934
John Wayne, 1005
Oprah Winfrey, 1023

WOMEN'S RIGHTS
Abigail Adams, 9
Maya Angelou, 38
Susan B. Anthony, 43
Olympia Brown, 115
Mary Ann Shadd Cary, 149
Carrie Chapman Catt, 152
Amelia Earhart, 265
Betty Ford, 305
Betty Friedan, 322
Emma Goldman, 361
Mary A. Hallaren, 390
Barbara Harris, 413
Katharine Hepburn, 426
Aileen Clarke Hernandez, 432
Oveta Culp Hobby, 441
Belva A. Lockwood, 606
Wilma Mankiller, 655
Alice Paul, 763
Eleanor Roosevelt, 847
Margaret Sanger, 893
Elizabeth Cady Stanton, 922
Ida B. Wells-Barnett, 1009

Ethnicity Index

AFRICAN AMERICANS
  Hank Aaron, 1
  Ralph Abernathy, 4
  Muhammad Ali, 31
  Maya Angelou, 38
  Benjamin Banneker, 60
  Mary Mcleod Bethune, 75
  Ralph Bunche, 119
  George Washington Carver, 144
  Mary Ann Shadd Cary, 149
  Wilt Chamberlain, 158
  Shirley Chisholm, 164
  Bessie Coleman, 179
  Bill Cosby, 183
  Frederick Douglass, 254
  W. E. B. Du Bois, 259
  Marian Wright Edelman, 277
  Louis Farrakhan, 302
  Marcus Garvey, 333
  Althea Gibson, 351
  Fannie Lou Hamer, 398
  Jesse Jackson, 488
  Barbara Jordan, 524
  Michael Jordan, 529
  Martin Luther King, Jr., 562
  Joe Louis, 621
  Malcolm X, 650
  Thurgood Marshall, 675
  Barack Obama, 728
  Jesse Owens, 742
  Rosa Parks, 752
  Colin Powell, 779
  A. Philip Randolph, 785
  Paul Robeson, 824
  Jackie Robinson, 832
  Bill Russell, 868
  Sojourner Truth, 974
  Harriet Tubman, 979
  Nat Turner, 984
  Booker T. Washington, 994
  Ida B. Wells-Barnett, 1009
  Oprah Winfrey, 1023
  Tiger Woods, 1029

EURO-AMERICANS
  Abigail Adams, 9
  John Adams, 14
  Samuel Adams, 19
  Jane Addams, 26
  Susan B. Anthony, 43
  Neil Armstrong, 48
  Robert D. Ballard, 55
  Clara Barton, 64
  Alexander Graham Bell, 70
  Daniel Boone, 84
  Omar Nelson Bradley, 89
  Louis D. Brandeis, 94
  William J. Brennan, 105
  John Brown, 109
  Olympia Brown, 115
  Richard Byrd, 124
  Frances Xavier Cabrini, 129
  Rachel Carson, 133
  Jimmy Carter, 138
  Carrie Chapman Catt, 152
  William Clark, 584
  Hillary Rodham Clinton, 171
  Ty Cobb, 175
  David Crockett, 194
  Walter Cronkite, 198
  Clarence Darrow, 201
  Dorothy Day, 207
  Eugene V. Debs, 212
  Stephen Decatur, 217
  Jack Dempsey, 221
  Joe DiMaggio, 227
  Walt Disney, 231
  Dorothea Dix, 238
  Jimmy Doolittle, 243
  Helen Gahagan Douglas, 247
  William O. Douglas, 251
  Amelia Earhart, 265
  Mary Baker Eddy, 270
  Thomas Alva Edison, 281
  Albert Einstein, 287
  Dwight D. Eisenhower, 292
  Chris Evert, 297

1057

Ethnicity Index

Betty Ford, 305
Benjamin Franklin, 309
John C. Frémont, 315
Betty Friedan, 322
William Lloyd Garrison, 327
Bill Gates, 337
Lou Gehrig, 341
John Glenn, 356
Emma Goldman, 361
Al Gore, 367
William Crawford Gorgas, 371
Billy Graham, 376
Nathanael Greene, 380
Wayne Gretzky, 387
Mary A. Hallaren, 390
William F. Halsey, 393
Alexander Hamilton, 402
Learned Hand, 408
Barbara Harris, 413
Ernest Hemingway, 417
Patrick Henry, 422
Katharine Hepburn, 426
Wild Bill Hickok, 437
Oveta Culp Hobby, 441
Bob Hope, 446
Grace Murray Hopper, 450
Sam Houston, 455
Samuel Gridley Howe, 460
Charles Evans Hughes, 471
Cordell Hull, 478
Andrew Jackson, 483
Stonewall Jackson, 494
Thomas Jefferson, 498
Steve Jobs, 503
Bobby Jones, 507
John Paul Jones, 513
Mother Jones, 519
Helen Keller, 542
John F. Kennedy, 546
Robert F. Kennedy, 551
Billie Jean King, 557
Robert M. La Follette, 569
Robert E. Lee, 574
John L. Lewis, 579
Meriwether Lewis, 584
Abraham Lincoln, 594

Charles A. Lindbergh, 600
Belva A. Lockwood, 606
Henry Cabot Lodge, 610
Huey Long, 616
Juliette Gordon Low, 627
Shannon W. Lucid, 632
Douglas MacArthur, 635
Dolley Madison, 642
James Madison, 646
Rocky Marciano, 660
George C. Marshall, 664
John Marshall, 669
Golda Meir, 680
Thomas Merton, 686
John R. Mott, 690
John Muir, 696
Edward R. Murrow, 700
Ralph Nader, 705
Carry Nation, 709
Martina Navratilova, 714
Jack Nicklaus, 719
Chester W. Nimitz, 723
Sandra Day O'Connor, 733
Thomas Paine, 747
George S. Patton, 758
Alice Paul, 763
Robert Edwin Peary, 768
John J. Pershing, 774
Jeannette Rankin, 793
Ronald Reagan, 798
Walter Reed, 809
Paul Revere, 814
Sally Ride, 819
John D. Rockefeller, 838
Knute Rockne, 844
Eleanor Roosevelt, 847
Franklin D. Roosevelt, 852
Theodore Roosevelt, 859
Babe Ruth, 874
Jonas Salk, 885
Pete Sampras, 889
Margaret Sanger, 893
Junípero Serra, 898
Alan Shepard, 902
William Tecumseh Sherman, 907
Margaret Chase Smith, 917

Ethnicity Index

Elizabeth Cady Stanton, 922
Adlai E. Stevenson, 928
James Stewart, 934
Anne Sullivan, 938
Ida Tarbell, 942
Zachary Taylor, 947
Norman Thomas, 956
Jim Thorpe, 963
Harry S. Truman, 968
Earl Warren, 988
George Washington, 1000
John Wayne, 1005
Elie Wiesel, 1013
Hazel Wightman, 1019
Orville Wright, 1034
Wilbur Wright, 1034
Chuck Yeager, 1040
Babe Didrikson Zaharias, 1044

JEWISH AMERICANS
Louis D. Brandeis, 94
Betty Friedan, 322
Emma Goldman, 361
Golda Meir, 680
Jonas Salk, 885
Elie Wiesel, 1013

LATINO AMERICANS
César Chávez, 161
Aileen Clarke Hernandez, 432
Dolores Huerta, 465

NATIVE AMERICANS
Black Hawk, 80
Joseph Brant, 100
Crazy Horse, 187
Geronimo, 346
Chief Joseph, 533
Kamehameha I, 538
Liliuokalani, 589
Wilma Mankiller, 655
Osceola, 739
Red Cloud, 805
John Ross, 864
Sacagawea, 880

Sitting Bull, 913
Tecumseh, 952
Jim Thorpe, 963

PACIFIC ISLANDER AMERICANS
Kamehameha I, 538
Liliuokalani, 589

WOMEN
Abigail Adams, 9
Jane Addams, 26
Maya Angelou, 38
Susan B. Anthony, 43
Clara Barton, 64
Mary Mcleod Bethune, 75
Olympia Brown, 115
Frances Xavier Cabrini, 129
Rachel Carson, 133
Mary Ann Shadd Cary, 149
Carrie Chapman Catt, 152
Shirley Chisholm, 164
Hillary Rodham Clinton, 171
Bessie Coleman, 179
Dorothy Day, 207
Dorothea Dix, 238
Helen Gahagan Douglas, 247
Amelia Earhart, 265
Mary Baker Eddy, 270
Marian Wright Edelman, 277
Chris Evert, 297
Betty Ford, 305
Betty Friedan, 322
Althea Gibson, 351
Emma Goldman, 361
Mary A. Hallaren, 390
Fannie Lou Hamer, 398
Barbara Harris, 413
Katharine Hepburn, 426
Aileen Clarke Hernandez, 432
Oveta Culp Hobby, 441
Grace Murray Hopper, 450
Dolores Huerta, 465
Mother Jones, 519
Barbara Jordan, 524
Helen Keller, 542
Billie Jean King, 557

1059

Ethnicity Index

Liliuokalani, 589
Belva A. Lockwood, 606
Juliette Gordon Low, 627
Shannon W. Lucid, 632
Dolley Madison, 642
Wilma Mankiller, 655
Golda Meir, 680
Carry Nation, 709
Martina Navratilova, 714
Sandra Day O'Connor, 733
Rosa Parks, 752
Alice Paul, 763
Jeannette Rankin, 793
Sally Ride, 819

Eleanor Roosevelt, 847
Sacagawea, 880
Margaret Sanger, 893
Margaret Chase Smith, 917
Elizabeth Cady Stanton, 922
Anne Sullivan, 938
Ida Tarbell, 942
Sojourner Truth, 974
Harriet Tubman, 979
Ida B. Wells-Barnett, 1009
Hazel Wightman, 1019
Oprah Winfrey, 1023
Babe Didrikson Zaharias, 1044

Subject and Personages Index

Aaron, Hank, 4
Abbey of Our Lady of Gethsemani, 687
Abernathy, Ralph, 4-8, 490, 565
Abolition movement, 63, 110, 150, 256, 313, 328, 462, 923, 976, 980
Abortion, 107, 736
Accommodationism, 262
Account of Colonel Crockett's Tour to the North and Down East, An (Crockett), 196
ACLU. *See* American Civil Liberties Union
Across the River and into the Trees (Hemingway), 419
Activism, 107, 156, 210, 289, 363, 543, 794, 849, 957
Adams, Abigail, 9-14
Adams, John, 9, 14-19
Adams, John Quincy, 484
Adams, Samuel, 19-25
Addams, Jane, 26-31
Adoula, Cyrille, 122
Aerodynamics, 1035
Affirmative action, 736
Afghanistan War (beg. 2001), 783
AFL. *See* American Federation of Labor
African Americans. *See* Ethnicity Index
African Queen (film), 429
Agassi, Andre, 890
Age of Reason, The (Paine), 749
Aging, 324, 359
Agramonte, Aristides, 811
Agricultural Workers Association, 467
Agriculture, 145. *See also* Category Index
AIDS; Ronald Reagan, 801
Aileen C. Hernandez Associates, 433
Air shows, 181
Air traffic controllers strike, 801
Airplanes, 244, 1035, 1042
Alamo, 196
Albany Congress (1754), 312
Alcott, Bronson, 328
Aldrin, Edwin E., Jr., 52
Aleiya, 534

Ali, Muhammad, 31-37, 663
Alien and Sedition Acts (1798), 17, 501, 648
Alito, Samuel, 738
All God's Chillun Got Wings (O'Neill), 825
All in the Day's Work (Tarbell), 946
All Rivers Run to the Sea (Wiesel), 1016
Allen, Paul, 338
Almanacs, 61, 196, 311
Alone (Byrd), 127
Altair 8800, 339
American Anti-Slavery Society, 45, 329, 923
American Association to Promote Teaching of Speech to the Deaf, 72
American-British conflicts, 1000
American-British diplomacy, 16, 312, 514
American Civil Liberties Union, 957
American Colonization Society, 328, 672
American Dilemma, An (Myrdal), 121
American Federation of Labor, 581
American-French diplomacy, 312
American frontier. *See* Frontier settlement
American Indians. *See* Category Index under "Native American Affairs"
American Magazine, The (journal), 944
American Missionary Association, 150
American Railway Union, 214
American Red Cross, 66
American Revolution, 11, 15, 22, 24, 86, 101, 217, 260, 312, 381, 424, 514, 748, 815, 1000
American Socialist Party. *See* Socialist Party of America
American Woman Suffrage Association, 46, 925
Amundsen, Roald, 126
Anarchism, 363
Anatomy of a Murder (film), 937
And the Sea Is Never Full (Wiesel), 1016
And the Walls Came Tumbling Down (Abernathy), 7
Angelou, Maya, 38-42
Anglican Church, 101, 647

Subject and Personages Index

Annapolis Convention (1786), 647; Alexander Hamilton, 403
Anne Sullivan Macy (Henney), 941
Antarctica, 126
Anthony, Susan B., 43-48, 153, 212, 608, 925
Anti-Semitism, 95, 248, 303, 490, 1014
Antislavery. *See* Abolition movement
Antitrust legislation, 841, 861, 946
Antitrust suits, 340
Apaches, 346
Apollo 11, 52
Apollo 14, 904
Apollo program, 51-52, 904
Appeal to the Coloured Citizens of the World (Walker), 986
Apple Computer, 505
Arab-Israeli War (1948), 122
Arctic, 125, 768
Arizona, 320, 348
Armstrong, Neil, 48-54
Army, U.S., 381
Articles of Confederation (1781), 647
Assad, Hafez al-, 490
Assassination attempts; Ronald Reagan, 801
Assassinations, 363-364, 489, 550, 555, 653, 990
Assault on Reason, The (Gore), 369
Astronauts, 51, 358, 633, 819, 902
Astronomical tables, 61
Astronomy. *See* Category Index
Astrophysical Observatory of the Smithsonian Institution, 74
Astrup, Eivind, 770
Augusta National Golf Club, 510
Autobiography of Benjamin Franklin (Franklin), 313
Autobiography of Malcolm X, The (Malcolm X), 650
Autobiography of Values (Lindbergh), 604
Aviation, 51, 125, 179, 243, 267, 357, 394, 601, 632, 819, 902, 1040. *See also* Category Index
Avodah, Achdut Ha, 683

Bacteriology, 810
Bad Axe, Battle of (1832), 948
Bad Faces, 805
Baker, Frank, 177
Baker v. Carr (1962), 990
Ballard, Robert D., 55-59
Ballmer, Steve, 338
Bambi (animated feature film), 235
Bank of the United States; founding, 405
Banks, Nathaniel, 496
Banneker, Benjamin, 60-64
Barbary Wars (1801-1815), 219
Barron, James, 218
Bartlett, Bob, 772
Barton, Clara, 64-69
Baseball, 175, 227, 342, 834, 875
BASIC (computer language), 339
Basketball, 158, 530, 869
Bataan, Battle of (1941-1942), 638
Batteries, storage, 284
Bay of Pigs invasion (1961), 549, 932
Bear Flag revolt (1846), 317
Beggar in Jerusalem, A (Wiesel), 1015
Bell, Alexander Graham, 70-75
Bell Telephone Company, 71
Ben-Gurion, David, 683
Benjamin Banneker's Pennsylvania, Delaware, Maryland and Virginia Almanack and Ephemeris for the Year of Our Lord, 1792 (Banneker), 62
Benton, Thomas Hart, 316
Berger, Victor, 957
Berkman, Alexander, 363
Bernadotte, Count Folke, 121
Bethune, Mary McLeod, 75-80
Bethune-Cookman College, 77
Betty Ford Center, 308
Bevin, Ernst, 681
Bibb, Henry, 150
Big Broadcast of 1938, The (film), 447
Big Trail, The (film), 1006
Bill & Melinda Gates Foundation, 340
Billy Graham Evangelistic Association, 377
Biology. *See* Category Index
Birmingham march (1963), 565
Birth control, 895
Black Folk (Du Bois), 262
Black Hawk, 80-84
Black Hawk War (1832), 82, 948

Black Reconstruction (Du Bois), 262
Black Star Line, 335
Blair Mountain, Battle of (1921), 522
Blue Ridge Broadcasting Corporation, 378
Bogart, Humphrey, 429
Bonus Army, 637
Book of Common Prayer (Mohawk version), 103
Boone, Daniel, 84-88
Boone's Station, Kentucky, 86
Boonesborough, Kentucky, 85
Booth, John Wilkes, 598
Boston Celtics, 159, 871
Boston Massacre (1770), 22
Boston Port Act (1774), 23, 381
Boston Red Sox, 875
Boston Tea Party (1773), 14, 23, 424, 815
Botany. *See* Category Index
Boudinot, Elias, 865
Boxing, 33, 222, 622, 661
Boycotts, 5, 24, 162, 213, 468, 565, 755, 788, 1010
Boyhood on the Upper Mississippi (Lindbergh), 604
Bozeman Trail, 188, 806
Braddock, James, 623
Bradford, Sarah, 982
Bradley, Omar Nelson, 89-93, 760
Brady, Ed, 363
Brandeis, Louis D., 94-100
Brant, Joseph, 100-105
Brant, Molly, 100
Breckinridge, John C., 597
Brennan, William J., 105-109
Bridgman, Laura, 461
Bringing up Baby (film), 428
British-American conflicts, 1000
British-American diplomacy, 16, 312, 514
British-American Indian alliance, 86, 101
British East India Company, 23
Brotherhood of Sleeping Car Porters, 789
Brown, John, 109-115, 257, 462, 981
Brown, Olympia, 115-118
Brown v. Board of Education of Topeka (1954), 677, 990
Brownian motion, 288
Bryan, William Jennings, 204

Buchanan, James, 319
Buena Vista, Battle of (1847), 949
Buffalo Bill's Wild West Show, 915
Bull Bear, 805
Bull Run, Battles of. *See* Manassas
Bunche, Ralph, 119-123
Bunker Hill, Battle of (1775), 1000
Burgess, W. Starling, 1038
Burnside, Ambrose, 496
Burr, Aaron, 501, 672; duel with Alexander Hamilton, 406
Bus boycott (Montgomery, Alabama), 5, 565, 755
Bush, George H. W., 782
Bush, George W., 368, 492, 737, 783
Bush v. Gore (2000), 737
Business. *See* Category Index
Butler, Benjamin, 67
Butte, Battle of (1877), 191
Buxton, Angela, 353
Byrd, Richard, 124-128

Cabinet government, 1002
Cabrini, Frances Xavier, 129-133
California, 317, 911
Calling Youth to Christ (Graham), 377
Cameras, motion picture, 284
Canada, 102, 150, 190, 534, 914, 980
Canonization, 900
Canutt, Yakima, 1006
Capital punishment, 107, 204
Carey, Harry, Jr., 1006
Carey, Harry, Sr., 1006
Carnegie Corporation Survey of the Negro in America, 121
Carpentier, Georges, 224
Carrel, Alexis, 604
Carrington, Henry B., 188
Carroll, James, 811
Carson, Kit, 316, 438
Carson, Rachel, 133-137
Carter, Henry Rose, 812
Carter, Jimmy, 138-144
Carver, George Washington, 144-149
Cary, Mary Ann Shadd, 149-152
Catholic Worker, The (tabloid), 209
Catholic Worker movement, 209
Catholicism, 208, 415, 552, 686, 900
Catt, Carrie Chapman, 29, 152-157

1063

Subject and Personages Index

CBS Evening News with Walter Cronkite (TV news show), 199
CCC. *See* Civilian Conservation Corps
Central Intelligence Agency, 293, 549
Challenger, 53
Chamberlain, Wilt, 158-160
Chancellorsville, Battle of (1863), 496, 576
Chanute, Octave, 1035
Charbonneau, Toussaint, 880
Charleston, South Carolina, 382
Chávez, César, 161-164, 467
Cherokees, 85, 316, 456, 607, 656, 672, 864
Cheyennes, 189
Chicago Bulls, 530
Children's Defense Fund, 279
Chilton, Thomas, 195
Chippewas, 80
Chiricahuas, 347
Chisholm, Shirley, 164-170
Choice Before Us, The (Thomas), 960
Christian Science Monitor, The, 275
Christian Science Publishing Society, 274
Christian Science Sentinel, The, 274
Church of Christ, Scientist, 272
Cinderella (animated feature film), 235
CIO. *See* Congress of Industrial Organizations
Civil liberties, 475
Civil rights, 98, 252, 549, 749, 991, 1011. *See also* Category Index
Civil Rights Act of 1875, 257
Civil Rights Act of 1957, 295
Civil Rights Act of 1960, 295
Civil Rights Act of 1964, 566
Civil Rights movement, 6, 278, 400, 489, 565, 653, 753
Civil War (1861-1865), 65, 331, 439, 496, 576, 598, 909
Civilian Conservation Corps, 637
Clark, George Rogers, 102
Clark, William, 584-589, 880
Clarke Institution, 462
Clay, Cassius. *See* Ali, Muhammad
Cleveland, Grover, 698
Clinton, Bill, 171, 491
Clinton, Hillary Rodham, 171-174, 731

Coal miners' strike of 1919, 580
Coal miners' strike of 1943, 582
Cobb, Ty, 175-178
COBOL (computer language), 453
Cochise, 347
Cochise War (1861-1872), 347
Cody, William, 915
Coercive Acts (1774), 15
Coins and currency, 311, 1002
Cold War, 549, 970
Coleman, Bessie, 179-183
Collins, Michael, 52
Col. Crockett's Exploits and Adventures in Texas, Written by Himself, 196
Colonialism, 828, 899
Color and Democracy (Du Bois), 263
Color Purple, The (film), 1026
Colorado Iron and Fuel Company, 522
Colored Women's Progressive Franchise Association, 151
Columbus Hospital, 131
Colville Indian Reservation, 536
Comedy, 183, 447
Committee of Correspondence (American Revolution), 22
Committee of Correspondence (United States), 815
Common Sense (Paine), 748
Communications. *See* Category Index under "Telecommunications"
Communism, 474
Community Service Organization, 466
Compromise of 1850, 111, 950
Computers, 339, 452, 504. *See also* Category Index under "Computer Science"
Comstock, Anthony, 895
Congo Crisis (1960-1965), 122
Congress of Industrial Organizations, 581
Conjectures of a Guilty Bystander (Merton), 688
Conn, Billy, 624
Connor, Patrick E., 188
Connors, Jimmy, 300
Conquering Bear, 187
Conscription, 35
Conservation, 603, 698, 862
Conservatism, 16

1064

Subject and Personages Index

Constitution, Cherokee, 865
Constitution, U.S., 16, 424; analysis in *The Federalist*, 405; Alexander Hamilton, 403
Constitution of 1887 (Hawaii), 592
Constitutional Convention (1787), 670, 1001
Consumer movement, 706. *See also* Category Index under "Consumer Rights"
Containment policy, U.S., 970
Continental army, 1000
Continental Congresses, 15, 312, 403, 424, 499, 647, 1000
Cook, Frederick, 769
Cook, James, 538
Copeland, John, 112
Coppoc, Edwin, 112
Coral Sea, Battle of (1942), 394
Cornwallis, First Marquess, 383
Corrigan, Michael, 130
Cosby, Bill, 183-186
Cosby Show, The (TV show), 184
Craig v. Boren (1976), 107
Crazy Horse, 187-193
Creek War (1813-1814), 739
Creeks, 484, 739, 952
Crisis papers (Paine), 748
Crockett, David, 194-198
Cronkite, Walter, 198-201
Crook, George, 189, 348
Crosby, Bing, 447
Cross Keys, Battle of (1862), 319
Cruickshank, Bobby, 509
Crusade in Europe (Eisenhower), 293
Cuban Missile Crisis (1962), 549, 554
Culture of Organs, The (Lindbergh and Carrel), 603
Currency. *See* Coins and currency
Curtiss, Glenn H., 73, 1037
Custer, George A., 189, 914

Darrow, Clarence, 201-206
Davis, Jefferson, 82
Davis v. Monroe County Board of Education (1999), 737
Day, Dorothy, 207-211
Death in the Afternoon (Hemingway), 419
Death penalty, 107, 204

Death Valley Days (TV show), 800
Debs, Eugene V., 202, 212-217, 520, 957
Decatur, Stephen, 217-221
Declaration of Conscience speech (1950), 919
Declaration of Independence, 15, 499
"Declaration of Rights" (Adams, J.), 15
Declaration of Sentiments, 924
Declaration of Women's Rights, 44
Defense of the Constitutions of the United States of America, A (Adams, J.), 16
Delano grape strike (1965-1970), 161, 467
Democracy, 15, 498, 648
Democracy and Social Ethics (Addams), 29
Dempsey, Jack, 221-226
Dennis v. United States (1951), 252
Desegregation, 107, 476, 790
Destry Rides Again (film), 935
Dewey, Thomas E., 989
Dichloro-diphenyl-trichloroethane, 135
Dickinson, Charles, 483
Didriksen, Babe. *See* Zaharias, Babe Didrikson
Dietrich, Marlene, 935
DiMaggio, Joe, 227-231, 343
Diplomacy, 312, 500. *See also* Category Index
Discovery, Settlement, and Present State of Kentucke (Filson), 87
Discrimination, 2, 77, 107, 122, 159, 180, 257, 260, 333, 432, 563, 790, 828, 832, 872, 996, 1010
Disney, Walt, 231-238
Disney cartoonist strike (1941), 234
Disneyland, 235
Dissertations on Government, the Affairs of the Bank, and Paper Money (Paine), 748
District of Columbia survey, 62
Dix, Dorothea, 238-242, 461
Dixon, Robert, 81
Doolittle, Jimmy, 243-246, 394
Douglas, Helen Gahagan, 247-251
Douglas, Stephen A., 596
Douglas, William O., 251-254
Douglass, Frederick, 114, 254-259
Dreams for Sale (Davis), 247

1065

Subject and Personages Index

Du Bois, W. E. B., 259-265, 335, 998
Dumbo (animated feature film), 235
Dunn, Jacob P., Jr., 534
Dusk of Dawn (Du Bois), 263

Earhart, Amelia, 265-270
Earth in the Balance (Gore), 368
Economy; United States, 801
Eddy, Asa Gilbert, 272
Eddy, Mary Baker, 270-276
Edelman, Marian Wright, 277-281
Edge of the Sea, The (Carson), 135
Edison, Thomas Alva, 281-286
Edmonton Oilers, 388
Education, 9, 28, 77, 101, 239, 461, 995. *See also* Category Index
1812, War of. *See* War of 1812
Einstein, Albert, 287-291
Eisenhower, Dwight D., 292-297, 931
Electricity, 311
Eleventh Virgin, The (Day), 208
Elie Wiesel Foundation, 1016
Ellsworth, Lincoln, 126
Emancipation Proclamation (1863), 331, 598, 976
Emathla, Charley, 740
Emerson, George, 239
Emperor Jones, The (O'Neill), 825
Engineering. *See* Category Index
Engraving, 815
Enlightenment, 502
Entertainment. *See* Category Index under "Theater and Entertainment"
Entrepreneurship, 71, 282, 839
Environmental Protection Agency, 136
Environmentalism. *See* Category Index
EPCOT (Experimental Prototype Community of Tomorrow), 235
Episcopal Church, 414
Equal Employment Opportunity Commission, 433
Equal Rights Amendment, 307, 765
Equal Rights Association, 45
Escobedo v. Illinois (1964), 991
Espionage Act of 1917, 215
Euro-Americans. *See* Ethnicity Index
Eutaw Springs, Battle of (1781), 383
Evangelism, 377, 692. *See also* Category Index

Everett, Edward, 330
Evert, Chris, 297-302, 559, 715
Every Man a King (Long), 619
Evolution, 204
Executive Order 8802, 790
Experimental Prototype Community of Tomorrow. *See* EPCOT
Exploration, 438, 586, 881. *See also* Category Index

Factories, 817
Fair Deal, 969
Fair Employment Practices Commission, 790
Fallen Timbers, Battle of (1794), 953
Family Limitation (Sanger), 895
Fantasia (animated feature film), 234
Farewell to Arms, A (Hemingway), 418
Farmington (Darrow), 202
Farmworkers' movement, 161
Farrakhan, Louis, 302-305
Fat Albert and the Cosby Kids (TV show), 184
Federal Aid Highway Act of 1956, 293
Federal Mine Safety Law of 1952, 582
Federalism, 16, 425, 501, 647, 737; Alexander Hamilton, 404
Federalist, The (Hamilton, Madison, and Jay), 404, 647
Federalist Party, 17; founding, 406
Feminine Mystique, The (Friedan), 323
Fetterman, William J., 189, 806
Fetterman Massacre, 189, 806
Fighting Irish, 844
Fillmore, Millard, 319
Film. *See* Category Index
Financial reform; Alexander Hamilton, 405
Finlay, Carlos Juan, 811
Firpo, Luis Angel, 225
First Amendment, 107, 252
First Continental Congress, 15, 24
FLOW-MATIC, 453
Football, 845
For Whom the Bell Tolls (Hemingway), 419
Ford, Betty, 305-309
Ford, Gerald R., 306; Ronald Reagan, 800

Subject and Personages Index

Ford, John, 1005
Foreman, George, 35
Fort Apache (film), 1007
Fort Gibson, Treaty of (1833), 740
Fort Wayne, Treaty of (1809), 954
Fountain of Age, The (Friedan), 324
Franciscans in the New World, 899
Franklin, Benjamin, 15, 309-315
Frazier, Joe, 35
Fredericksburg, Battle of (1862), 496
Free love, 364
Freedmen's Bureau, 462
Freedom, 17, 647
Freedom Farm Cooperative, 400
Frémont, John C., 315-321
French-American diplomacy, 312
French-American Treaties (1778), 15, 313
French Revolution (1789), 748
Frick, Henry Clay, 363
Friedan, Betty, 322-326
Friendly, Fred, 703
Friends. *See* Quakers
Frontier settlement, 85, 899
Fugitive Slave Law (1850), 111, 331
Fun of It, The (Earhart), 268
Fundamentalism, 204

Gage, Thomas, 21
Gallopin' Gaucho (animated feature film), 234
Gandhi, Mahatma, 563
Garrett, Thomas, 980
Garrison, William Lloyd, 256, 327-332, 986
Garvey, Marcus, 165, 262, 333-337, 788
Gates, Bill, 337-341
Gather Together in My Name (Angelou), 39
Gehrig, Lou, 341-345
Gemini program, 51
General Electric Company, 284
Geneva, Treaty of (1864), 66
Genius of Universal Emancipation, 328
George III (king of Great Britain and Ireland), 24
Geronimo, 346-350
Gettysburg Address (Lincoln), 598
Ghost Dance, 807, 915
Gibbon, John, 190

Gibbons v. Ogden, 672
Gibson, Althea, 351-355
Gibson, William, 939
Gideon v. Wainwright (1963), 991
Gipp, George, 845
Girl Guides, 628
Girl Scouts of the United States of America, 630
Girondins, 749
"Give me liberty, or give me death!" (Henry), 424
Glenn, John, 356-361
Gloyd, Charles, 709
Goethals, George Washington, 374
Gold rushes, 189, 318, 440, 533, 807, 911, 914
Goldberg v. Kelly (1970), 107
Goldman, Emma, 361-366
Golf, 509, 719, 1031, 1046
Gompers, Samuel, 580
Good Neighbor Policy, 474, 481
Gore, Al, 367-370, 737
Gorgas, William Crawford, 371-376
Government and politics. *See* Category Index
Graham, Billy, 376-380
Grant, Cary, 428
Grant, Ulysses S., 534, 576, 598, 909
Grape strike (1965), 161
Great Depression, 161
Great Salt Lake, 317
Green, Shields, 112
Green Hills of Africa (Hemingway), 419
Green Party, 707
Greene, Bob, 1026
Greene, Nathanael, 380-386
Greenville, Treaty of (1795), 953
Gregg v. Georgia (1976), 107
Gretzky, Wayne, 387-390
Grimké, Angelina, 330
Grimké, Sarah, 330
Griswold v. Connecticut (1965), 252
Grutter v. Bollinger (2003), 737
Guadalcanal, Battle of (1942-1943), 395, 725
Guess Who's Coming to Dinner (film), 429
Guffey Act (1935), 581
Guilford Courthouse, Battle of (1781), 383

Subject and Personages Index

Habitat for Humanity International, 142
Hallaren, Mary A., 390-393
Halsey, William F., 393-398, 638, 724
Hamer, Fannie Lou, 398-402
Hamilton, Alexander, 17, 402-408, 500; duel with Aaron Burr, 406
Hammarskjöld, Dag, 122
Hand, Learned, 408-413
Hard, Darlene, 353
Harding, Chester, 87
Harding, Warren G., 473
Harlem Globetrotters, 159
Harney, W. S., 188
Harpers Ferry raid, 111, 257, 462, 575
Harpo Productions, 1027
Harris, Barbara, 413-416
Harris v. Forklift Systems (1993), 737
Harrison, Benjamin, 698
Harrison, William Henry, 954
Harvey (film), 936
Hauptmann, Bruno Richard, 601
Hawaii, 538, 589, 856
Hawaii's Story by Hawaii's Queen (Liliuokalani), 592
Hayer, Talmadge, 653
Haywood, William D., 202
Health, Education, and Welfare, Department of, 444
Hearst, William Randolph, 377, 472
Hemingway, Ernest, 417-422
Henney, Nella Braddy, 941
Henry, Patrick, 422-426
Henson, Matthew A., 770
Hepburn, Katharine, 426-431
Hepburn Act (1906), 862
Hernandez, Aileen Clarke, 432-437
Hickok, Wild Bill, 437-441
Hidatsas, 880
Hillquit, Morris, 957
Hints to the Colored People of the North (Cary), 150
Hiroshima; atomic bomb, 970
History of Massachusetts Bay (Hutchinson), 23
History of the Standard Oil Company, The (Tarbell), 841, 944
History of Woman Suffrage (Stanton et al.), 925
Hitchcock, Alfred, 937

Hobby, Oveta Culp, 441-446
Hockey, 387
Hoffa, Jimmy, 553
Holocaust, 96, 1013
Holtzman v. Schlesinger (1973), 253
Homans, Eugene V., 510
Homestead strike of 1892, 95
Homosexuality, 303, 716
Hood, John Bell, 910
Hooker, Joseph, 496
Hoover, Herbert, 854
Hope, Bob, 446-449
Hopper, Grace Murray, 450-455
Hour of Decision, The (radio and TV show), 378
House Committee on Un-American Activities; Ronald Reagan, 799
Houston, Charles H., 676
Houston, Sam, 455-459
Howard, Oliver Otis, 347, 534
Howe, Julia Ward, 461
Howe, Samuel Gridley, 239, 460-464
Huerta, Dolores, 161, 465-471
Hughes, Charles Evans, 471-477
Hull, Cordell, 478-482
Hull House, 27-28
Humphrey, Hubert H., 168
Hussein, Saddam, 782
Hutchinson, Thomas, 22

I Know Why the Caged Bird Sings (Angelou), 39
IBM, 339
iMac computer, 506
Immigration, 130, 612
Impeachment, 526; Bill Clinton, 173
In Our Time (Hemingway), 418
Incandescent lighting, 283
Inconvenient Truth, An (Gore), 369
Indian Removal Bill (1830), 195, 865
Infectious diseases, 372, 886
International Ladies' Garment Workers Union, 433
Internet Explorer, 340
Interstate Commerce Act (1887), 841
Invention, 71, 282, 311, 461, 1035. *See also* Category Index
iPod, 506
Iran-Contra affair, 802

1068

Subject and Personages Index

Iran hostage crisis, 141
Iraq War (beg. 2003), 784
Iroquois Country, 100
Israel, 681, 1015
It Changed My Life (Friedan), 324
It's a Wonderful Life (film), 936
Iwerks, Ub, 233

Jackson, Andrew, 195, 456, 483-488, 672, 865
Jackson, Jesse, 488-494
Jackson, Stonewall, 319, 494-498
Jacobins, 749
Jacobs, Mike, 623
Japan, 639
JASON Project, 57
Jay, John, 16
Jay's Treaty (1794), 1002
Jefferson, Thomas, 63, 498-503, 643
Jesup, Thomas S., 740, 949
Jewish Americans. *See* Ethnicity Index
Jobs, Steve, 503-507
John McClellan Committee, 553
Johnson, Hinton, 652
Johnson, Jack, 622
Johnson, Lyndon B., 549, 677
Johnson v. Transportation Agency of Santa Clara County (1987), 736
Johnston, Joseph E., 576, 910
Johnstown flood (1889), 67
Jones, Bobby, 507-512
Jones, John Paul, 513-519
Jones, Mother, 519-523
Jordan, Barbara, 524-528
Jordan, Michael, 529-532
Joseph, Chief, 533-537
Journal of Christian Science, The, 273
Journalism, 256, 274, 328, 701, 944, 997. *See also* Category Index
Judges, The (Wiesel), 1016
Jurisprudence. *See* Category Index under "Law and Jurisprudence"

Kahekili, 539
Kalanikupule, 539
Kalanimoku, 539
Kamehameha I, 538-541
Kansas Jayhawks, 158
Kansas-Nebraska Act (1854), 111, 458

Kansas territory, 438
Kaskaskia, 80
Kaumualii, 539
Kearns, Jack, 222
Kearny, Stephen Watts, 318
Keller, Helen, 72, 542-546, 939
Kennedy, John F., 58, 546-552, 932, 990
Kennedy, Robert F., 162, 548, 551-557
Kentucky, 85
Kentucky Resolutions (1798-1799), 501, 648
Keokuk, 81
Khrushchev, Nikita S., 294
Kidd, Thomas I., 202
Kimmel, Husband E., 724
King, Billie Jean, 298, 557-562
King, Ernest J., 724
King, Martin Luther, Jr., 5, 122, 489, 562-568, 755
King's Row (film), 799
Kiwalao, 539
Knute Rockne, All American (film), 799, 846
Korean War (1950-1953), 293, 639, 971
Koya, 805

La Causa, 161
Labor movement, 202, 213, 467, 520, 580, 787. *See also* Category Index
Lafayette, Marquis de, 500
La Follette, Robert M., 569-573, 957
Lakota, 187, 805, 913
Langley, Samuel Pierpont, 1038
Larkin, Thomas O., 317
Latino Americans. *See* Ethnicity Index
Law, 607. *See also* Category Index
Lazear, Jesse, 811
League of Women Voters, 765
Lee, Robert E., 496, 574-579, 598
Leo XIII, 130
Leopold, Nathan F., Jr., 204
Letter from Birmingham City Jail (King), 566
Lewinsky, Monica, 173
Lewis, John L., 579-584
Lewis, Meriwether, 584-589, 880
Lexington and Concord, Battle of (1775), 15
Leyte Gulf, Battle of (1944), 396, 726

1069

Subject and Personages Index

Liberator, The, 256
Liberty incident (1768), 24
Life and Times of Frederick Douglass, 1881 (Douglass), 256
Life of Ma-ka-tai-me-she-kia-kiak (Black Hawk), 80
Life of Martin Van Buren, The, 196
Life So Far (Friedan), 325
Lighting, incandescent, 283
Liliuokalani, 589-594
Lincoln, Abraham, 319, 594-599
Lindbergh, Charles A., 600-605
Liston, Sonny, 34
Literature. *See* Category Index
Little Bighorn, Battle of the (1876), 190, 914
Little Steel Strike (1937), 581
Lloyd, John, 300
Lockwood Bill, 607
Lockwood, Belva A., 606-610
Lodge, Henry Cabot, 610-615
Loeb, Richard, 204
Long, Huey, 616-621
Long Day's Journey into Night (film), 429
Longstreet, James, 496
Looking Glass, 534
Lord Dunmore's War (1774), 85
Los Angeles Kings, 388
Los Angeles Lakers, 160
Lost generation, 418
Louis, Joe, 621-627, 662
Louisiana Territory, 587
Lovejoy, Elijah, 330
Low, Juliette Gordon, 627-631
Loyalists, British, 16
Lucid, Shannon W., 632-634
Ludlow Massacre (1914), 522
Lundy, Benjamin, 328
Lynchings, 1010
Lyon, Nathaniel, 319

MacArthur, Douglas, 92, 292, 395, 635-641, 667, 724, 971
McCarthy, Eugene, 555
McCarthy, Joseph, 295, 553, 703, 919, 971
McClellan, George B., 496, 576, 598
McClellan Committee, 553

McDowell, Irvin, 496
McGovern, George, 168
Macintosh computer, 505
McKinley, William, 861
McLaughlin, James, 915
McNamara, James B., 203
McNamara, John J., 203
Madison, Dolley, 642-646
Madison, James, 500, 642, 646-650
Make the Connection (Winfrey and Greene), 1026
Malaria, 811
Malcolm X, 650-654
Man Who Knew Too Much, The (film), 937
Man Who Shot Liberty Valance, The (film), 1008
Manassas, First Battle of (1861), 496
Manassas, Second Battle of (1862), 496
Manila, Battle for the Liberation of (1945), 639
Mankiller, Wilma, 655-659
Mann, Horace, 240, 461
Manual of the Mother Church (Eddy), 274
Manufacturing, 816; United States, 406
Marbury v. Madison, 671
March to the Sea, Sherman's, 910
Marciano, Rocky, 625, 660-664
Mark I, 452
Marshall, George C., 91, 293, 664-668, 777
Marshall, John, 669-674
Marshall, Thurgood, 675-679
Marshall Plan, 667
Mary Poppins (film), 236
Massachusetts, 9, 14, 19, 22
Massachusetts Anti-Slavery Society, 330
Massachusetts State Kansas Committee, 111
Massacres in the Mountains (Dunn), 534
Massie, Thomas, 204
Mathematics. *See* Category Index
Maurin, Peter, 209
May, Samuel Joseph, 328
Meade, George G., 576
Medicine. *See* Category Index
Meir, Golda, 680-685

1070

"Memorial and Remonstrance Against Religious Assessments" (Madison), 647
Mental health. *See* Category Index
Mental illness, 239
Mercury program, 357
Merton, Thomas, 686-689
Messenger (magazine), 788
Metro-Goldwyn-Mayer, 935
Mexican War (1846-1848), 949
Mickey Mouse, 234
Mickey Mouse Club (TV series), 235
Microsoft Corporation, 339
Midway, Battle of (1942), 57, 394, 724
Miles, Nelson, 190, 348, 536
Military. *See* Category Index
Military desegregation, 790
Militia Act (1792), 1002
Miller v. California (1973), 252
Million Man March (1995), 304
Milwaukee Braves, 2
Mining, 284
Minneconjous, 191
Minute Men of Louisiana, 619
Mir space station, 634
Miracle Worker, The (Gibson), 939
Miranda v. Arizona (1966), 991
Missionaries, 691
Missionary Sisters of the Sacred Heart, 131
Missions, 899
Mississippi Freedom Democratic Party, 400
Missouri, 587
Mr. Smith Goes to Washington (film), 935
Mohawks, 101-102
Mondale, Walter, 801
Monopolies, 840
Monroe, Marilyn, 230
Montgomery, Bernard Law, 91
Montgomery bus boycott, 5, 565, 755
Moody, Dwight L., 691
Moonwalk, 905
Morelli, Felice, 131
Morgenthau, Henry, Jr., 479
Morgenthau Plan (1944), 479
Morning Glory (film), 428
Moscow-Berlin Pact of 1939, 960
Most, Johann, 363

Mother Earth (journal), 364
Motion pictures, 284
Mott, John R., 690-695
Mountains of California, The (Muir), 699
Moveable Feast, A (Hemingway), 420
MS-DOS, 339
Muhammad, Elijah, 303, 651
Muir, John, 696-700
Mulberry Grove, 384
Muller v. Oregon (1908), 96
Murderer's Row, 343
Murrow, Edward R., 700-705
My American Journey (Powell), 783
My Bondage and My Freedom (Douglass), 256
My First Summer in the Sierra (Muir), 699
My Religion (Keller), 544
Myrdal, Gunnar, 121

NAACP. *See* National Association for the Advancement of Colored People
Nader, Ralph, 705-709
NARAL Pro-Choice America, 323
Narrative of the Life of David Crockett of the State of Tennessee (Crockett), 195
Narrative of the Life of Frederick Douglass (Douglass), 256
NASA. *See* National Aeronautics and Space Administration
Nation, Carry, 709-713
Nation, David, 710
Nation of Islam, 35, 303, 651
National Aeronautics and Space Administration, 51, 295
National American Woman Suffrage Association, 46, 153
National Association for the Advancement of Colored People, 262, 676, 998, 1011
National Defense Education Act, 295
National Equal Rights Party, 608
National Geographic Society, 73
National Labor Relations Act (1935), 581
National Negro Business League, 998
National Organization for Women, 323, 433
National Recovery Act (1933), 475

1071

Subject and Personages Index

National Republicans, 16, 500, 817
National Woman Suffrage Association, 45, 925
National Woman's Party, 155
National Woman's Rights Convention (1850), 976
Nationalism, 647, 1003; United States, 403
Native Americans, 86, 101, 189, 484, 534, 587, 807, 866, 900, 915, 952. *See also* Category Index under "Native American Affairs"; Ethnicity Index under "Native Americans"
Navratilova, Martina, 298, 714-718
Navy, Russian, 516
Navy, U.S., 514
Nazism, 1013
Negro Factories Corporation, 334
Negro World (newspaper), 334
New Deal, 854
New Echota, Treaty of (1835), 866
New England Anti-Slavery Society, 329
New England Courant, The, 310
New England Nonresistance Society, 330
New Orleans, Battle of (1815), 484
New Seeds of Contemplation (Merton), 688
New York City, 500, 1001
New York Times v. Sullivan (1964), 107
New York Yankees, 227, 343, 877
NeXT, 506
Nextstep, 506
Nez Perce, 533
Nez Perce War (1877), 534
Niagara Movement, 262
Nicklaus, Jack, 719-722
Nicollet, Joseph Nicolas, 316
Night (Wiesel), 1014
Nimitz, Chester W., 394, 639, 723-727
Nineteenth Amendment, 155, 764
Nixon, Edward, 6
Nixon, Richard M., 250, 307, 526, 549
Nonviolent resistance, 566
Noonan, Fred, 268
Noriega, Manuel, 782
North Pole, 126, 772
North Star, The (newspaper), 256
Northern Confederate Indians (Canada), 102

Northern Pacific Railroad, 189
Notes of Canada West (Cary), 150
Notre Dame University, 844
Nursing, 68. *See also* Category Index

Obama, Barack, 728-733
Occidental Literary Club, 212
O'Connor, Daniel Basil, 885
O'Connor, Sandra Day, 733-739
Of Flight and Life (Lindbergh), 603
Oglala, 188
O'Hara, Maureen, 1007
Ohio Country, 102
Old Man and the Sea, The (Hemingway), 420
Old Northwest, 953
Old Smoke, 805
Ollokot, 534
Olmstead v. United States (1928), 98
Olympic Games of 1912, 966
Olympic Games of 1932, 1045
Olympic Games of 1936, 743
Olympic Games of 1960, 32
Olympic Games of 1992, 531
Onassis, Jacqueline Kennedy, 547
Operation Breadbasket, 489
Operation Desert Storm, 782
Operation People United to Save Humanity, 490
Oprah Winfrey Show, The (TV talk show), 1026
Oratory. *See* Category Index
Oregon, 316
Osage, 80
Osceola, 739-741, 949
Other People's Money and How the Bankers Use It (Brandeis), 95
Our National Parks (Muir), 699
Out of the Dark (Keller), 543
Owens, Jesse, 742-746
Oxygen, 1027
Ozawa, Jisaburō, 396

Pacific Islander Americans. *See* Ethnicity Index
Paine, Thomas, 747-751
Paiutes, 915
Palestine, 121
Palmer, Arnold, 720

1072

Subject and Personages Index

Panama Canal, 373, 862; end of U.S. control, 140
Pankhurst, Emmeline, 763
Paris, Treaty of (1783), 17
Parks, Rosa, 565, 752-758
Parson's Cause (1763), 423
Partisan politics (United States), 1003
Patterson, Floyd, 34
Patton, George S., 91, 758-762
Paul, Alice, 155, 763-767
"Paul Revere's Ride" (Longfellow), 815
Payne's Landing, Treaty of (1832), 740
Peace activism, 156, 210, 289
Peale, Charles Willson, 516
Peanut crops, 146
Pearl Harbor, bombing of, 856
Peary, Robert Edwin, 768-774
Pennsylvania Gazette, The (Franklin), 310
Pensacolas, 484
Pepsodent Radio Show Starring Bob Hope, The (radio show), 447
Perkins, Francis, 444
Perkins Institute for the Blind, 461
Pershing, John J., 665, 759, 774-779
Persian Gulf War (1990-1991), 782
Person to Person (TV show), 703
Pesticides, 163
Philadelphia Convention, 313, 403, 647
Philadelphia Negro, The (Du Bois), 261
Philadelphia 76ers, 159
Philadelphia Story, The (film), 428, 935
Philanthropy, 841. *See also* Category Index
Philippines, 637
Philosophy. *See* Category Index
Phoenix Coyotes, 388
Phonograph, 282
Phrenology, 463
Physics. *See* Category Index
Pickett's charge (1863), 576
Pixar, 506
Plane Crazy (animated feature film), 234
Planned Parenthood of Southeastern Pennsylvania v. Casey (1992), 736
Plate tectonics theory, 56
Poinsett, Joel, 316
Polio, 886
Political parties, 648

Politics. *See* Category Index under "Government and Politics"
Pollution, 136
Poor People's Campaign, 7
Poor Richard's Almanack (Franklin), 311
Pope, John, 496
Portolá, Gaspar de, 899
Powell, Colin, 779-785
Prayer Book of the Anglican Church (Mohawk version), 103
Presidency, U.S., 1002-1003
Presidential elections, 46, 484, 707
Printing, 311
Prison reform, 208
Privacy, right to, 94, 252
Profiles in Courage (Kennedy), 548
Progressive Party, 571
Prohibition, 156
Project Apollo, 51
Project Gemini, 51
Project Mercury, 357
Propaganda, 748, 815
Provincial Freeman, 150
Public Advertiser (newspaper), 21
Public Citizen, 707
Public Good, The (Paine), 748
Public health. *See* Category Index
Pullman Company, 789
Pullman workers' strike, 202, 214
Punitive Expedition, 776
Pure Food and Drug Act (1906), 862

Quakers, 62
Quantum mechanics, 288
Quasi War (1798-1800), 1003
Quimby, Phineas P., 271

Racial discrimination, 351
Racism, 492. *See also* Discrimination; Segregation
Radio, 701
Randolph, A. Philip, 785-792
Rankin, Jeannette, 793-797
Rauschenbusch, Walter, 957
Ray, James Earl, 566
Reagan, Ronald, 798-804; Jimmy Carter, 141
Reaganomics, 801
Rear Window (film), 937

1073

Subject and Personages Index

Reciprocal Trade Agreements Act (1934), 480
Red Cloud, 188, 805-809
Red Cloud's War (1866-1868), 188, 806
Red River (film), 1007
Red Scare (1919-1920), 660, 957
Reed, Walter, 372, 809-813
Reflections on the Revolution in France (Burke), 749
Rehnquist, William H., 734
Reitman, Ben, 364
Relativity, 288
Religion and theology. *See* Category Index
Religious conversion, 101, 898
Religious Liberty, Statute of (1786), 647
"Remember the Ladies" (Adams, A.), 11
"Report on Manufactures" (Hamilton), 406
Report Relative to a Provision for the Support of Public Credit (Hamilton), 405
"Republican motherhood," 12
Reservations (Native American), 190, 536, 807, 914
Revere, Paul, 814-818
Revolutionary War. *See* American Revolution
Reynolds v. Sims (1964), 990
Rickard, George L. "Tex," 222
Rickey, Branch, 833
Ride, Sally, 819-824
Ridge, John, 865
Riggs, Bobby, 560
Right Stuff, The (Wolfe), 359
Rights of Man, The (Paine), 749
Rio Grande (film), 1007
Road to Singapore (film), 447
Robeson, Paul, 824-831
Robinson, Jackie, 832-837
Rockefeller, John D., 838-843
Rockefeller Foundation, 842
Rockne, Knute, 844-846
Roman Catholic Church, 129, 208, 415, 552, 686, 900
Roosevelt, Eleanor, 847-852
Roosevelt, Franklin D., 98, 479, 581, 848, 852-859

Roosevelt, Theodore, 859-864
Rooster Cogburn (film), 1008
Rosebud, Battle of (1876), 190
Ross, John, 864-868
Roth v. U.S. (1957), 107
Rough Riders, 861
Russell, Bill, 159, 868-874
Russell-Einstein Manifesto, 290
Ruth, Babe, 342, 874-879

Sabin, Albert, 887
Sacagawea, 880-884
Sacred Heart Orphan Asylum, 131
Salk, Jonas, 885-889
Salk Institute for Biological Studies, 888
Sampras, Pete, 889-892
San Carlos Agency, 347
San Jacinto, Battle of (1836), 457
Sands of Iwo Jima (film), 1007
Sanger, Margaret, 893-898
Sanitary Commission, U.S., 462
Santa Anna, Antonio López de, 196, 457
Sauks and Foxes, 80
Scalabrini, Giovanni Battista, 130
Scenes in the Life of Harriet Tubman (Bradford), 982
Schäffer, Anton, 540
Schmeling, Max, 623
Schwarzkopf, H. Norman, 783
Science and Health (Eddy), 272
Science magazine, 73
Scopes, John T., 204
Scott, David R., 51
Sculley, John, 505
Sea Around Us, The (Carson), 135
Searchers, The (film), 1006
Seattle SuperSonics, 872
Secession, 458
Second Stage, The (Friedan), 324
See It Now (TV show), 703
Segregation, 5, 997. *See also* Discrimination; Racism
Selma marches, 122, 566
Seminole War, First (1817-1818), 740
Seminole War, Second (1835-1842), 740, 949
Seminoles, 740

Subject and Personages Index

September 11, 2001, attacks on U.S., 783
Serra, Junípero, 898-901
Seven Storey Mountain, The (Merton), 687
Sewall, Samuel E., 328
Shawnees, 952
Shenandoah (film), 937
Shepard, Alan, 902-906
Sheridan, Philip, 189
Sherman, William Tecumseh, 907-912
Sherman Antitrust Act of 1890, 841, 861, 946
Sherman's March to the Sea, 910
Shiloh, Battle of (1862), 909
Shootist, The (film), 1008
Shoshones, 880
Sierra Club, 698
Sign of Jonas, The (Merton), 688
Silent Spring (Carson), 135
Silversmiths, 814
Singin' and Swingin' and Gettin' Merry Like Christmas (Angelou), 40
Sioux War (1876-1877), 807
Sitting Bull, 913-916
Six-Day War (1967), 683, 1015
Sixteenth Street Baptist Church bombing (1963), 566
Sketches and Eccentricities of Colonel David Crockett of West Tennessee, 196
Skinner v. Oklahoma (Douglas), 252
Slave rebellion of 1831, 329
Slavery, 45, 255, 319, 597, 672, 975, 980, 985
Small, Albion, 28
Smith, Clyde H., 917
Smith, Gerrit, 110, 923
Smith, Margaret Chase, 917-922
Snow White and the Seven Dwarfs (animated feature film), 234
Social reform. *See* Category Index
Social Security Administration, 855
Socialist Party of America, 215, 957
Society of Friends. *See* Quakers
"Solemn League and Covenant" boycotts, 24
Song of the South (film), 235
Song of the Stone Wall, The (Keller), 543
Sons of Liberty, 815
Soul of a Butterfly, The (Ali), 36
Souls of Black Folk, The (Du Bois), 261

Sound barrier, 920
South Pole, 126
Southern Christian Leadership Conference, 6, 565
Soviet Union, 474; U.S. relations with, 140
Space exploration, 358. *See also* Category Index under "Aviation and Space Exploration"
Space shuttle program, 820
Spanish-American War (1898), 68, 613
Spanish Civil War (1936-1939), 960
Speaker, Tris, 177
Spirit of Liberty, The (Hand), 411
Spirit of St. Louis, The (Lindbergh), 604
Spirit of Youth and the City Streets, The (Addams), 29
Sports. *See* Category Index
Spotted Tail, 191
Square Deal, 861
Stagecoach (film), 1006
Stalin, Joseph; Harry S. Truman, 970
Stamp Act crisis (1765-1766), 14, 22, 423
Standard Oil Company, 840
Stanton, Elizabeth Cady, 45, 922-927
Stanton, Henry, 923
States' rights (United States), 648
Steamboat Willie (animated feature film), 234
Stenberg v. Carhart (2000), 736
Stevens, Aaron, 112
Stevenson, Adlai E., 294, 928-934
Stewart, James, 934-938
Stickeen (Muir), 699
Stockton, Robert F., 318
Story of My Boyhood and Youth, The (Muir), 699
Story of My Life, The (Keller), 543, 940
Strategic Defense Initiative, 802
Stride Toward Freedom (King), 565
Strikes, 95, 161, 214, 234, 467, 521, 580
Studd, J. E. K, 691
Student Nonviolent Coordinating Committee, 565
Student Volunteer Movement for Foreign Missions, 691
Suffrage, 29, 45, 117, 121, 150, 153, 399, 566, 608, 672, 763, 794, 924, 1011
Sullivan, Anne, 542, 938-942

1075

Subject and Personages Index

Sumner, Charles, 239
Sun Also Rises, The (Hemingway), 418
Supreme Council of the United Orders of Railroad Employees, 214
Supreme Court, U.S., 96, 106, 252, 472, 671, 677, 735, 990
Sweet, Ossian, 204

Talented Tenth, 260
Tarbell, Ida, 841, 942-947
Taxation, 22, 424, 748
Taxation without representation, 22
Taylor, Zachary, 947-951
Tea Act (1773), 23
Tea trade, 23
Teacher, Anne Sullivan Macy (Keller), 545, 941
Technology. *See* Category Index under "Invention and Technology"
Tecumseh, 952-956
Telecommunications. *See* Category Index
Telephone, 71, 282
Television, 199
Temperance movement, 710, 925
Tennis, 298, 351, 558, 715, 890, 1020
Tenskwatawa, 953
Terrorism, 114, 783, 985
Terry, Alfred, 190, 914
Terry v. Ohio (1968), 252
Test pilots, 51, 357, 902, 1042
Texas, 457, 949
Texas Revolution, 196, 457
Thames, Battle of the (1813), 954
Theater and entertainment. *See* Category Index
Theology. *See* Category Index under "Religion and Theology"
Thirteenth Amendment (U.S. Constitution), 331
Thomas, Norman, 956-963; John Foster Dulles, 960
Thompson, Wiley, 740
Thorpe, Jim, 963-968
Thoughts on African Colonization (Garrison), 329
Three Little Pigs (animated feature film), 234
Tigers, Detroit, 176

Time of the Uprooted, The (Wiesel), 1016
Tippecanoe, Battle of (1811), 954
Titanic, 56
Tobacco, 423
Tokyo, 245
Tonight or Never (Hatvany), 248
Toohoolhoolzote, 534
Town Beyond the Wall, The (Wiesel), 1014
Townshend Acts (1767), 23
Toy Story (animated feature film), 506
Track and field, 742, 1045
Tracy, Spencer, 429
Traffic Safety Act of 1966, 706
Trail of Tears, 866
Train, George Francis, 46
Transatlantic flight, 125, 601
Trappists, 687
Treaty, Sauk and Foxes, 81
Treaty of 1868, 190, 914
Trials, 46, 112, 672, 986
True Grit (film), 1006
Truman, Harry S., 968-973
Truth, Sojourner, 974-978
Tshombe, Moise, 122
Tubman, Harriet, 979-983
Tunney, Gene, 225
Turner, Nat, 329, 984-987
Turtle Creek strike (1897), 521
Tuskegee Institute, 995
Twenty Hours Forty Minutes (Earhart), 267
Twenty Years at Hull House (Addams), 28

U-2 incident, 295
Under the Sea-Wind (Carson), 135
Underground Railroad, 980
Union, Act of (1839, Oklahoma), 866
United Farm Workers, 161, 467
United Mine Workers, 202, 520, 579
United Service Organizations. *See* USO
UNIVAC I, 452
Universal manhood suffrage, 672
Universal Negro Improvement Association, 333
Universal Peace Union, 608
Universalism, 116

Subject and Personages Index

Unsafe at Any Speed (Nader), 706
Urban League, 998
Use and Need of the Life of Carry A. Nation, The (Nation), 712
USO, 447

Valley Forge, 1001
Vancouver, George, 539
Vertigo (film), 937
Vietnam War (1959-1975), 555
Villa, Pancho, 520, 776
Virginia Resolutions (1798-1799), 648
Virginia Statute of Religious Liberty (1786), 500
Volta Laboratory, 71
Voting rights, 29, 45, 117, 121, 150, 153, 399, 608, 672, 763, 794, 924, 1011
Voting Rights Act of 1965, 566

WAACs. *See* Women's Army Auxiliary Corps
WACs. *See* Women's Army Corps
Wagner, Honus, 176
Wagner Labor Relations Act, 475
Wahlitits, 534
Wakarusa War (1855), 111
Walcott, Jersey Joe, 625
Walker, David, 986
Wallace, Henry, 960
Walt Disney World, 235
War of 1812 (1812-1814), 219, 484, 644, 948, 954
War on Drugs, 801
Warren, Earl, 295, 988-993
Wartime Journals (Lindbergh), 604
Washington, Booker T., 261, 994-999
Washington, George, 1000-1004
Washington, March on (1963), 566, 790
Washington Conference on Naval Disarmament (1921), 473
Watson, Thomas A., 71
Wayne, Anthony, 953
Wayne, John, 1005-1009
We (Lindbergh), 603
Weill, Al, 662
Weiss, Carl Austin, 619
Welles, Sumner, 474, 479
Wells-Barnett, Ida B., 1009-1013
Western American settlement, 85, 899

Wethered, Roger, 510
Whiskey Rebellion (1794), 406, 501, 1002
White Bird, 534
Whitney v. California (1927), 98
Whittier, John Greenleaf, 328
Wiesel, Elie, 1013-1018
Wiesel Foundation, 1016
Wightman, Hazel, 1019-1023
Wilderness, Battle of the (1864), 576
Wilderness concept, 87
Wilderness Road, 85
Willard, Jess, 223
Williams, Sunita, 633
Wilson, Woodrow, 96, 613
Windows operating system, 340
Winfrey, Oprah, 1023-1029
Withlacoochee, First Battle of the (1835), 740
Wolfe, Tom, 359
Woman of the Year (film), 429
Woman suffrage, 29, 45, 117, 150, 153, 608, 763, 794, 924, 1011
Woman's Bible, The (Stanton and Gage), 926
Woman's Christian Temperance Union, 710
Woman's Rights Convention (1848), 44, 257, 924
Woman's State Temperance Society of New York, 45
Women. *See* Ethnicity Index
Women's Armed Services Integration Act of 1948, 391, 918
Women's Army Auxiliary Corps, 391, 442
Women's Army Corps, 391, 443
Women's Christian Temperance Union, 153
Women's health movement, 307
Women's International League for Peace and Freedom, 29
Women's Loyalty League, 45
Women's movement, 257, 330, 608, 976
Women's rights, 9, 11, 117, 167, 267, 323, 364, 415, 434, 737, 766, 924. *See also* Category Index
Women's Social and Political Union, 763
Women's State Temperance Society, 924
Woodhull, Victoria, 608

Subject and Personages Index

Woods, Tiger, 1029-1034
Working Woman's Association, 46
Works Progress Administration, 855
World I Live In, The (Keller), 543
World War I, 637, 777
World War II, 245, 293, 602, 666, 723, 761, 856, 1041; Harry S. Truman, 969
World Wide Pictures, 378
World Zionist Congress, 96
Wounded Knee Massacre (1890), 915
Wovoka, 915
Wozniak, Steve, 504
Wright, Henry C., 330
Wright, Orville, 1034-1040
Wright, Wilbur, 1034-1040
Wright Company, 1037

X, Malcolm. *See* Malcolm X
XYZ affair (1797-1800), 16, 648

Yamamoto, Isoroku, 394
Yeager, Chuck, 1040-1043
Yellow fever, 372, 811
Yom Kippur War (1973), 684
Yorktown, Siege of (1781), 1001
Yosemite, The (Muir), 699
Yosemite National Park, 698
You Can't Take It with You (film), 935
Young, Brigham, 317

Zaharias, Babe Didrikson, 1044-1048
Zionism, 96, 289

LRC - Batavia HS
Batavia, IL 60510